STRANGERS
AT HOME

STRANGERS AT HOME

VIETNAM VETERANS SINCE THE WAR

Edited by

CHARLES R. FIGLEY
SEYMOUR LEVENTMAN

PRAEGER

PRAEGER SPECIAL STUDIES • PRAEGER SCIENTIFIC

Library of Congress Cataloging in Publication Data

Main entry under title:

Strangers at home.

   Includes bibliographical references and index.
   1. Veterans--United States. 2. Vietnamese
Conflict, 1961-1975--United States. I. Figley,
Charles R., 1944-   II. Leventman, Seymour.
III. Title: Vietnam veterans since the war.
UB357.S84   355.1'15'0973   79-24398
ISBN 0-03-049771-X
ISBN 0-03-049776-0 pbk.

Published in 1980 by Praeger Publishers
CBS Educational and Professional Publishing
A Division of CBS, Inc.
521 Fifth Avenue, New York, New York 10017 U.S.A.

© 1980 by Charles R. Figley

0123456789   038   987654321

Printed in the United States of America

to Geni Figley
and the millions of other mothers
of Vietnam veterans

ERRATA

FOREWORD

Frank Freidel

The tragedy of the Vietnam War continues years after the signing of the truce, long after the final American withdrawal. Among those still suffering are numerous veterans who have felt forgotten, unappreciated, and even discriminated against. For some of them, the trauma of their battle experiences or their physical disabilities have shattered their lives. For even more, adjustment to civilian life has not been easy; they have been truly "strangers at home."

Much of the travail of the Vietnam veterans is in keeping with the lot of veterans since Homeric times or earlier. For Americans returning from earlier wars, psychological and economic adjustments were painful, even for Revolutionary War heroes. Captain Daniel Shays, who several years after the war led the abortive Massachusetts rebellion bearing his name, was so poverty-stricken that he had to sell the sword that had been awarded to him for his exploits. Many an aspirant for membership in the DAR has been pained to discover in tracing back her lineage that one of her ancestors was a deserter. The hardships and perils facing the Continental Army were so acute, and the needs of families back on the farms were so imperative, that large numbers of soldiers quietly slipped home. During the Civil War the numbers of deserters from both the Union and Confederate armies were in the hundreds of thousands. In World Wars I and II, discipline was so much tighter that desertion was kept to a minimum, but the vicissitudes of army life and the horrors of fighting were the lot of millions of combat troops. Many veterans never fully recovered either physically or psychologically.

For all these veterans there were certain compensations. Those who fought in the Revolution received land. Civil War veterans formed powerful lobbies, dominated politics, and ultimately obtained federal pensions (for the blue) or state pensions (for the grey). Veterans of the two World Wars received disability compensation and other benefits—for those of World War II there was the unprecedented GI Bill of Rights to help train them and establish them in the postwar economy.

Above all, those who fought in these major wars from the Revolution on could have the satisfaction of feeling that they had struggled to attain great and just ends (even, as in the case of the Confederate soldiers, they had failed). They could identify themselves as being among the heroes extolled on every patriotic occasion, and, indeed, garbed in their old uniforms, made their presence felt upon these holidays. Thus, as late as the 1930s every parade contained a few aged but conspicuous representatives of the Union Army or those who had risked their lives for the "Lost Cause." Their appearance brought cheers along the parade route, and the years that elapsed had transformed their experience from one of frightfulness to a romantic adventure on behalf of one's country that gave meaning to one's youth. For the Civil War veterans the realities of blood and dysentery gave way after their passage into middle age to nostalgia for swords and roses and for belles in crinolines.

Quite possibly in years to come, as perceptions of the Vietnam War alter, a larger proportion of the veterans of this war will, like those of earlier wars, come to enjoy the roles of heroes. Already by 1979, the Vietnam government's invasion of Cambodia and its cruel treatment of the Chinese minority, the forced exodus of the "boat people," were making a difference. In time the Vietnam War, too, might generally be perceived as a "just war."

What has distinguished the Vietnam veterans from most of their predecessors is precisely that point—that a considerable part of the articulate abhorrence of the war seemed to spill onto them. They returned not as heroes, but as men suspected of complicity in atrocities or feared to be drug addicts. Not only the underprivileged but even the most prestigious were under a cloud. A West Pointer who had been a special assistant to the commanding general in Vietnam was asked when he was interviewed for a position with a Washington law firm if he had committed any war crimes. "It blew my mind," he says.

The grievances of the Vietnam veterans are a combination of those of most veterans of the past and their own relatively unusual problems. They have ranged from feeling ignored to being regarded as unrepentant villains. These veterans have received less benefits than their immediate predecessors, and have felt poorly treated by the Veterans Administration, although in 1977 a triple amputee from among them became its head. In their quest for employment they have found their legal advantages in "veterans' preference" coming into conflict with the movement for equal rights for women. Some of them, disturbed over the lack of honors paid to the 57,000 dead, have been seeking funds to erect a monument to them in Washington.

By calling attention to themselves the Vietnam veterans have gradually become a focal point of public attention, much of it sympathetic. This collection of scholarly papers consequently appears at a time when it will help erase some of the misconceptions and give a factual basis for understanding the veterans' problems.

The findings are so well summed up in the editors' introduction that it would be redundant to state them in any detail here, except to place them in some historical perspective.

A large part of the Vietnam soldiers were very young and quite underprivileged. Wars are usually fought by the underprivileged, but these troops differed from their predecessors both in being younger and being better educated; 83 percent were high school graduates. The disadvantaged did less well in the service and have fared poorly since leaving it. Army technical training was of relatively little help; a 1969 study indicated that only 12 percent of the veterans were using skills gained in military service. Unemployment was indeed high among all veterans, running an overall 15 percent, which broke down into 9.5 percent of the whites and 30 percent of the blacks. Minorities may well have suffered especially from discrimination, although much may have come from lack of previous education. Among blacks and those with Spanish surnames there were disproportionately high casualties. On the other hand, it was not disproportionately a black man's army. Between 1964 and 1971 it contained 29 percent of the total pool of white eligibles and 26 percent of the blacks.

Overall most of the veterans adjusted well both to military service and to their return to civilian life. However, less than half were stationed in Vietnam, and only part of these were combat veterans. It is upon those who served in Vietnam, and especially those who were in combat, that this study, and public attention, rightfully focuses.

In the perceptive analysis and the excerpts from excellent oral history interviews one finds all of the varied responses to combat service that earlier soldiers have experienced, from becoming "war lovers" to suffering shocked revulsion against killing, and especially feeling guilt over not somehow preventing the death or wounding of a buddy.

What is of transcendent importance in understanding the plight of the combat veterans is the fact that in the late 1960s the Vietnam War slowly changed into a guerrilla conflict. In a guerrilla war everyone— guerrillas, the populace, and the troops trying to put down the guerrillas—becomes a victim.

The American troops were victims in the massive guerrilla war in Vietnam. They found it almost impossible to distinguish between civilian and foe. At times young women and even children tried to kill them, and upon occasion the soldiers did indeed turn their guns upon everyone in sight regardless of age and sex. Sympathy among television watchers back home was with the villagers, but consider the anguish of one soldier on patrol who encountered a beautiful young woman. She touched him on the chest, then seconds later fired an automatic rifle, its bullet passing close to his ear: "And I turned in reflex, in the space of a single breath . . . and fired half a magazine into this girl. . . . She had no face left."

That was the especial horror Vietnam combat troops went through. There have been almost forgotten counterparts in American history. The hardships of the troops struggling to put down the Philippine Insurrection in the early 1900s were quite comparable, and at home indignant antiimperialist reformers decried the inhuman treatment of the Filipinos. Too, there were veterans of Indian wars, and of the expedition into Mexico in 1916, and those who served with the Marine Corps in Haiti and Nicaragua, all frustrated in seeking elusive guerrilla opponents.

For the Vietnam veterans the experience was worse for several reasons. They were placed in and out of units so quickly that they seldom had time to form cohesive, thoroughly seasoned units sustaining each other. In the air age they could be shuttled from home where everything went on as usual into the battlefront literally almost overnight. Their awareness of vociferous protest at home was much greater in an age of video communication, even though public opinion polls indicated a substantial majority supporting them. Their return, not to cheering throngs but often to vituperative protestors, added to their pain.

Another new difficulty was because some prospective employers feared they were drug addicts. Their drug use had been highly publicized. The fact was that only a small proportion became addicted to either alcohol or drugs; the larger part of those who used drugs smoked a rather potent marijuana. For many in the back areas, use of drugs served as a form of self-therapy, as has alcohol through the ages. After leaving the service most users of drugs dropped the habit, but the bad reputation dogged the veterans.

A final irony is that the superior medical techniques in this unfortunate war greatly lowered the death rate among those who had lost a limb or limbs or suffered spinal injuries. In consequence there was a far higher proportion of disabled veterans and paraplegics with their especially acute problems than there had been in earlier wars.

The anguish of Vietnam veterans, although not in most respects different from that resulting from previous wars, is not easy to alleviate. The fact that public opinion is more sympathetic and that the government may be of more help is encouraging. Most Vietnam veterans have successfully become civilians; life may become more tolerable for the remainder. It is difficult to visualize any number ever living to look with nostalgia upon their experiences, as did Civil War veterans, but the future should bring them a sense of dignity and pride.

PREFACE

Charles R. Figley

Seventeen authors from law, political science, rhetoric, sociology, economics, psychiatry, and psychology have contributed manuscripts to this collection focusing on the war, its wake, and its impact on those who fought it. Most of these authors are Vietnam veterans themselves and saw the war first hand.

The discouraging and tragic story of Vietnam is told from the perspective of not only the men who fought it, but also the scientists who studied the troops there and at home, and the policy makers who must decide which veterans will be granted assistance and which will not.

Among the legacies of Vietnam is mystery. It was a crazy war with invisible battle lines, constantly rotating combat troops, and television coverage of futile battles. Also, it was the blood bath millions of draft-age men ran from; not because they loved their country less than those who entered the military, but because they felt that the things we were fighting for in South Vietnam did not warrant sacrificing their lives. Most Vietnam vets would agree that it certainly was not worth the lives of their buddies or for that matter the lives of any of the 57,000 who died there.

Like the survivors of a natural disaster, all of us are beginning to come out of the shock of it all, six years after its termination. We are now ready as a people to try to unravel the mystery of Vietnam and to consider once more those political, philosophical, and moral questions that were on everyone's minds during the late 1960s and early 1970s. Questions like: What is patriotism? What right does the citizenry have to decide what is or is not an appropriate American war? Do we trust government to decide what public protest shall be ignored and what shall be heeded?

No one knew back in 1965 that our "intervention" into Southeast Asia would lead to catastrophy, but as that outcome became more obvious, an entire nation would be forced to take sides for or against the war. Those on either side watched the evening news reports, films, and videotapes of the battles: the seemingly undisciplined troops, drug abuse, mistreatment of prisoners on both sides; the destruction of the civilian population through bombing, spraying, burning, and shooting. Everyone had advice for the troops, of course. As one Vietnam veteran put it, "The Doves wanted us to kill less and the Hawks wanted us to kill more." When it was finally over the men who fought in this mixed-up war returned to find themselves in the middle of the debate. They felt hated by the defenders of the war as "those spoiled kids from inferior stock." At the same time they also were hated by the war's opponents as compliant mercenaries in an immoral war. For the nearly 9 million in uniform during the war, and especially the nearly 3 million who served in Vietnam, the postwar years were bitter, frustrating times. One 26-year-old Marine described it this way:

> I never cussed much until I got *Out* of the crotch (Marine Corps): the way the people, your own people—Americans—treated you. F------ G - - D - - - P - - - - -! I say "hey, I didn't run away from going into the service." All these people telling me how wrong the war is. Like Jane Fonda. Well, when I get over there it sucks all right, but for different reasons. The "people of South Vietnam look the same as the people of North Vietnam" and we are fighting both of them. We saw a lot of bad scenes: atrocities on both sides. The people back in Berkeley saw everything as black and white. It wasn't, and I felt like blowing some of those long-haired jerks away hearing them talk about how we were all baby killers and we're all immoral by fighting over there. I couldn't figure out why in the f - - - they didn't tell that to Johnson and Nixon and all those old f - - - ers who put us over there in the first place. I swear, the next bastard who comes up to me and says ANYTHING about 'Nam, I'm going to waste him with my bare hands.

Rage and bitterness are two combat-related stress reactions exhibited by a large majority of Vietnam veterans. More and more Vietnam veterans are standing up today and saying they are proud of serving their country and not so happy about being used in international politics and the whipping boys for the Hawks and the Doves. Today Vietnam veterans are not tolerating any more negative stereotypes and mistreatment in the press, but the press is treating the Vietnam vet differently, too. Many things are different.

Over the last five years the Consortium on Veteran Studies at Purdue University has tried to bring some degree of objective analysis to the readjustment problems of Vietnam veterans. With a multidisciplinary membership and no financial support, the Consortium was able to mobilize colleagues throughout the country to turn their attention to the special circumstances of the "forgotten warriors" of Vietnam.

During five years of existence the Consortium sponsored six

scholarly symposia, consulted with hundreds of individuals and several dozen organizations and agencies, wrote numerous scientific articles, and two books (*Stress Disorders Among Vietnam Veterans: Theory, Research and Treatment* [New York: Brunner/Mazel, 1978], and the present volume). The Consortium received hundreds of letters from individual Vietnam veterans and their families seeking help. There are many accomplishments to be proud of, yet much remains to be done by those who will continue to work in this important area of veteran studies. As the Consortium was formed back in 1975 the attitude of the country was considerably more hostile toward the Vietnam veteran in contrast to today. Myths about the violent, drugged, inferior, shiftless, and disturbed characteristics of Vietnam veterans are waning. Vietnam veterans and their advocates have risen to positions of importance in government and the private sector. The special problems and circumstances of the Vietnam warrior are finally receiving attention. Some solutions are on the way at last. We hope this volume will provide informative reading to all those beginning to reconsider the Vietnam war and its warriors. As one Consortium contributor commented upon completion of his chapter, "Welcome to our war America!"

ACKNOWLEDGMENTS

The editors gratefully acknowledge grants to establish a research group (composed of John Helmer, Jack Ladynski, Charles Moskos and the editors) on the sociology of Vietnam veterans received from the Committee on Special Problems of the Discipline of the American Sociological Association. The grants encouraged professional recognition of this as an important area of human concern as well as research. We are indebted to the excellent editorial assistance of Vickie Figley and Vicki Hogan Camp.

CONTENTS

LIST OF TABLES

LIST OF FIGURES

INTRODUCTION: ESTRANGEMENT AND VICTIMIZATION

Charles R. Figley and Seymour Leventman

This work examines a tragic by-product of one of the most disastrous episodes in American history. The discussions to follow focus on the processes by which American society made strangers of the men who returned home after fighting in Vietnam during the decade 1964–74.

Glorious wars produce heroic veterans. Inglorious wars produce antiheroes, even villains and deviants. The Vietnam War was long and inconclusively fought in such a firestorm of political and moral controversy that it produced as much tension and ambiguity upon its conclusion as throughout its duration. One result of this tension and ambiguity was American society's shifting the blame for the war from its own structure to the men who fought it. In so doing, America estranged its youngest patriots, the very men who went against their peers and entered the military, and were sent to risk their lives in a dubious struggle in Southeast Asia. In this drama of classic Greek proportions, Vietnam is not just a matter of war and peace. The issues go to the very core of American society and the structural conflicts it experienced, which culminated in the events of that fateful period.

WHO SERVED

War veterans have always played an ambiguous role in American society. While treating returning veterans as heroes worthy of special recognition, American society has also viewed them as potential threats to postwar domestic tranquility. Also, since American society guarantees civilian over military rule, warriors perform vital wartime functions but have no clear-cut role in peacetime and are expected to abandon their military mentality immediately. While offering veterans some compensation for their sacrifices as earned benefits, Americans remained committed to the norms of a competitive and open society stressing a heritage of individual merit and achievement. Some consider VA benefits and employment preferences for veterans to be a boondoggle. At closer inspection, however, these compensations are hardly extraordinary and, in fact, are shamefully inadequate. Programs for Vietnam veterans were promoted and supported by few. Their cause was doomed from the start.

Inheriting a situation from the defeated French, the United States in the early 1960s still seemed guided by the Cold War impulse to save the world from the threat of international communism. The tenuousness of this goal and the dubiousness of the entire Vietnam operation was nowhere more apparent than when the American president drank champagne toasts with communist leaders in 1972 while American men continued to fight and die to contain this presumed enemy—a déja vu of the toast at the 38th parallel in Korea 20 years earlier.

Indeed, the deployment of American troops to Vietnam was determined not by a constitutional mandate declared by the U.S. Congress but by presidential order under emergency powers preempted by the president in 1964. Under pretense of (dubious) intelligence reports concerning an enemy threat to American security, President Lyndon B. Johnson sought and received the Tonkin Gulf resolution by the Congress in August of that year, authorizing his sending American troops to Vietnam. Until the truce of 1973 approximately 3 million men served there, almost 60 percent of whom were drafted. Since this was an undeclared war, American society was never totally mobilized for it and the burden of the draft fell unequally on the population. Specifically, because of superior financial and educational resources, young men of middle class backgrounds were better able to avoid being drafted than the poor, nonwhites. The result was a military force heavily represented by working class and minority men. The men who served were not necessarily moved ideologically or committed to official national policy; for most it was a matter of being unable or unwilling to avoid the draft and of increasing personal options within the military by enlisting. Furthermore, as the war progressed, the most risky front-line positions in Vietnam were filled by men from the poorest economic backgrounds. So the question of who was to do the fighting and dying in Vietnam was determined not by chance but by the structure of social inequality operative in American society during that era. Recruiting combat personnel for Vietnam was another instance of "good people" of the "respectable classes" debating the merits of the war over cocktails while lower class men did society's dirty work.

THE WAR

The Vietnam War was a projection of American society: the selection of its army, the manner of fighting, and the manner of "winning." Believing in its own invincibility through technology, America fought in Vietnam, as the sociologist Paul Starr (1973) put it, in a "technological blizzard [and] moral vacuum." The United States deployed a vast array of sophisticated military hardware there but often with indeterminate results. Firing devices would break down prematurely or not function at all due to unavailability of critical parts sidetracked in improper supplying procedures. Such hardware was ineffective anyway in a guerilla-type conflict complete with booby-trapped children. Moreover, since the political and military goals of the war were rarely apparent or articulated, technological deployment was often counterproductive. Saturation bombing only hardened opposition and fortified the morale of the North Vietnamese.

When in 1968 Senator George Aiken (R. Vermont) advised President Johnson to "withdraw from Vietnam and say we won," he acutely perceived the symbolic significance yet concrete futility of the war. This alienation of meaning and activity was also reflected in the first-hand experiences of men fighting in Vietnam. Winning the hearts and minds of the Vietnamese was the goal. Hamlets were destroyed only to increase the number of Vietcong recruits. Containment policies and confusing restrictions often resulted in GIs taking and retaking the same hill or hamlet five or six times a year. With such meaningless risk and loss of life, it is small wonder that those ordering these tactics themselves were viewed as the "enemy" and became targets of numerous fraggings by their own men. Faulty intelligence reports, fabricated body counts, an invisible enemy, high civilian involvement, an inability to measure positive military results, and awareness of divided political support at home all contributed to a sense of deep despair and anomie among combatants in Vietnam. These men were figures in a game of power imagery in which the fighting seemed more important to official American policy than any concrete results.

All wars are highly stressful. With sufficient support systems available, however, most combatants endure. The Americans fighting in Southeast Asia did not receive adequate support. Suffering seemed meaningless, and Catch-22-type mismanagement was everywhere.

In most previous wars men served for the duration, but in Vietnam the tour lasted a year. It might seem that a year rather than an indeterminate tour was dictated by humane considerations, but in Vietnam such timing also supported the illusion of a war that would soon be over, the ever-elusive "light at the end of the tunnel." What better way to prevent full witness to the bizarre war than to limit combatant stay to the shortest time feasible? Furthermore, the lack of duration tours reflected a shallow official commitment to actually winning the war. In previous wars total commitment had enabled combatants to adapt to combat conditions in the form of long-term peer group attachments that would protect them against the horror of war. Men in Vietnam, however, experienced combat via continuously attenuating peer ties. As a result, they kept to themselves in an attempt simply to survive until their tour was up and they left for home. Demoralization and cynicism set in even before homecoming.

THE PHYSICAL AND EMOTIONAL SCARS

Ironies were numerous in the Vietnam War. American technology saved lives but took more limbs. Effective helicopter operations delivered the wounded to well-equipped and –staffed hospital units so efficiently that untold lives were saved, in contrast to previous wars. As a result, many thousands went home alive, but Vietnam sent more permanently disabled veterans back into civilian society than any previous war.

In regard to mental health the reverse *seemed* to be true. Based on military psychiatry reports, Vietnam seemed to produce fewer psychological casualties than did previous wars. Officially, this was attributed to the high level of mental health expertise deployed in Vietnam, the 12-month rotation system, and the availability of rest and recuperation periods. Yet other factors also seem to have operated. High drug use in Vietnam masked reactions to stress. Also, mental health problems were underrepresented due to widespread administrative discharges the military used to rid itself of "discipline problems." These "problems" often were closely associated with stress disorders. Rather than receiving needed psychiatric treatment, the combatant was shipped home with an undesirable discharge, stigmatized for life, and, ironically, denied needed mental health services of the Veterans Administration (VA) due to his ineligibility. Thus, psychiatric casualty rates were artificially lowered by casting potential cases from the military into the civilian population where they appeared later as part of the "post-Vietnam syndrome." Only as civilians could many veterans reexperience the events and feelings they couldn't or wouldn't deal with during and immediately following the war. There would be many who would mentally re-experience those stressful events again and again. Most would permanently seal in their memories vast parts of those months there.

Actual departure from Vietnam also followed technological patterns designed to produce the most rapid estrangement possible from a familiar situation. When their tour was completed, with neither fanfare nor much official recognition, men were silently whisked home from Vietnam in a jet flight—not weeks or even months of transition as in World War II, but often no more than 48 hours from battlefield to home. Men left largely as they entered, alone. It is not surprising that few Vietnam veterans show much interest in reunions with buddies or in recalling the "good old days." As one veteran put it, "We are a morbid group."

HOMECOMING

Poets, dramatists, and writers from Homer to Erich Maria Remarque and Thomas Wolfe were not thinking of Vietnam when they wrote, "You can't go home again." But for the Vietnam veteran, his homecoming was fraught with special anxiety and trepidation beyond the disorientated homecoming of veterans of past wars. Although he may have hoped for a hero's welcome, the Vietnam vet recognized that in a "no-win war" heroism is deprived of its moral meaning and that perhaps the best thing *is* to slink home quietly and unnoticed. He may have wanted victory parades, but in a stalemated war what he got instead were peace marches.

Furthermore, estrangement is a reciprocal process and such was the apprehensiveness of veterans by civilians that even a quiet homecoming often was impossible. The experiences of one combat veteran returning home to Boston in 1968 are especially revealing. Walking across the Boston Common his first day home, his service uniform and gear fully apparent, he was greeted by peace demonstrators with shouts of "Killer! How many babies did you burn over there?" Returning home, his brother offered, "You asshole! Why did you go to Vietnam anyway?" Seeking solace and companionship that night in the American Legion Hall, he was confronted with "Hey buddy! How come you guys lost the war over there?"

The emotional numbness reported by many combat veterans was a response not only to war experiences but also to the silent war conducted against them on the home front. Many veterans came to realize that the anomie and normlessness experienced in Vietnam were forerunners of what they were to experience at home. A major practical problem was that many veterans came to feel isolated even from the most likely sources of meaningful support. Alienated from the older generation, robbed of their own generational identification with antiwar youths, veterans had only each other and then were often wary of one another's company. If, as Emile Durkheim (1951) pointed out, coherent and cohesive group support can allow an individual to withstand much social stress and tension, such support was precisely what Vietnam veterans lacked. As with black Americans and other ethnic minorities, veterans had to cope with their situation alone, left to their own devices and resources. Even their families and friends misunderstood them. Since so many veterans of Vietnam did come from minority backgrounds, their maltreatment at home also reflected their other stigmatized status.

STIGMATIZATION

Inability of Vietnam veterans to experience the "positive privilege" normally associated with the warrior's role is one thing, being forced to experience the "negative privilege" of a caste is quite another. Perhaps the most difficult problem for veterans to overcome and certainly the cruelest irony of the war's aftermath was their being blamed for the war itself. In a manner of the ancient kings' executing messengers who brought bad news, Vietnam veterans were socially killed for the very fact of *being* veterans. Rarely is it possible to find persons who did what they thought was expected of them yet became morally tainted deviants in their own society for so doing. American society could not seem to bear the realization that one of the strongest nations on earth could not defeat one of the weakest (North Vietnam). So the men who were victimized by even fighting the war were blamed for its outcome, an indecisiveness bordering on defeat for the United States.

Blaming the Victim

Psychologist William Ryan (1971) has described this process of "blaming the victim" as follows:

> First, identify a social problem. Second, study those affected by the problem and discover in what ways they are different from the rest of us as a consequence of deprivation and injustice. Third, define the *differences* as the *cause* of the social problem itself. Finally, of course, assign a government bureaucrat to invent a humanitarian action program to correct the *differences*

Adopting and applying Ryan's model to Vietnam veterans we find a very apt illustration of his syndrome. Veterans indeed were seen as a "social problem" even before the war was over. There was fear that these recently released veterans would flood the job market and dramatically increase unemployment while also swelling the welfare rolls. There was concern they would bring back all sorts of evils from the jungles of Vietnam, including heroin addiction, incurable strains of venereal disease, a propensity for violence, in addition to their own skills of destruction developed in combat. That none of these fears materialized is only part of the process itself, blaming and labeling.

According to this pattern, Vietnam veterans are then studied noting the various ways they are "different" from the normal population. It is important to specify that these differences were present even *before* they entered the service. Next these factors are identified as the "cause" of the problem itself, implying that the veteran had some control over his fate. Thus, many veterans report being told in so many words, "Look, don't tell me about how bad it was in Vietnam and now—you shouldn't have been there in the first place." Of course, blaming veterans for the war successfully inhibits discovering the root causes of the war and their plight—American society itself.

Where did these perceptions of Vietnam veterans come from and how did they persist? Clearly, Vietnam veterans were feared, even hated, not as individuals but as symbols of America's embarrassment and dishonor in Southeast Asia. Few Americans during or following the war could or would effectively separate the warrior from the war. Indeed, veterans became entangled in a web of ideological battles on the homefront. Americans opposed to the war saw veterans as a potential menace to society due to their potentially "violent nature." Those favoring the war viewed veterans as inferior stock, without guts and substance, unworthy of adult status and responsibility. Both perspectives helped reinforce the stereotype of the Vietnam veteran as a "sick" social type.

Structurally, there were at least three major sources for the development and perpetuation of popularly held negative stereotypes of Vietnam veterans that are associated with their general social estrangement: the college campuses, the mass media, and the behavioral sciences.

College Campuses

Some of the earliest opposition to the Vietnam war surfaced on America's college campuses where animosity toward those who willingly or not fought in Vietnam was inevitable. Those veterans who returned to attend college quickly learned they weren't welcome, and being rejected by the college community was a two-edged blow for many veterans. After all, many veterans had come from working-class backgrounds where chances for advanced education were not very great; it was due only to the GI Bill that they could go to college at all. Once at college however, young veterans found themselves rejected by their age peers, those who were "smart enough" to avoid the draft or were in the process of so doing.

'Responding to antagonism toward them, many veterans followed the path of upwardly mobile minorities before them: they disowned the war, disowned their veteran status, or both. They attempted as best they could to blend into college life unnoticed, hoping they could thus avoid condemnation for being part of the "bad" war as well as the usual negative stereotypes. This situation changed with the new generation of nonantagonistic college students, but generally veterans retain a low profile on most campuses.

The Media

In the homecoming period of the early 1970s, the mass media—electronic and print, entertainment and news—played roles in the negative labeling of Vietnam veterans. One label veterans resent particularly is "PVS" or "post-Vietnam syndrome." Apparently, the term surfaced following a New York *Times* story about a black Medal of Honor winner killed while involved in a Detroit robbery. The reporter accounted for the incident by suggesting that it was war-related. Indeed, the Vietnam vet was under the care of Army psychiatrists at the time, but less-informed journalists—and later several psychiatrists—generalized the incident to all Vietnam vets and PVS was born. Veterans themselves believe its use implies they "have" PVS automatically as a result of being associated with Vietnam—whether or not one served in combat, whether or not one acts strangely. News stories of violent crimes do single out, where pertinent, the factor of the perpetrator being a Vietnam veteran to account for "psychopathic" actions. On television, prime-time "cop shows" further the negative image of veterans by portraying them as major antagonists, addicts, rapists, mass killers, and particularly morally offensive criminals.

Mental Health "Experts"

A majority of Americans would prefer Vietnam veterans to either remain invisible or fit their image of the war—sick and inhumanly violent. Mental health "experts," playing upon the prevailing image of Vietnam veterans, invented terms like PVS to consciously or unconsciously reinforce the sick vet image. Many early psychiatric studies of Vietnam veterans were affected by the antiwar sentiment of their authors. Thus, veterans were portrayed as pathetic victims of the war but nevertheless personally disorganized, problem-ridden, and potentially dangerous. Publicity-minded clinicians quickly learned that portraying veterans as a largely normal group elicits an apathetic public response. Emphasizing veterans' problems, on the other hand, attracts more publicity but also supports prevailing stigma and stereotypes. This is a characteristic "no win" situation in dealing with spoiled identity both on theoretical and policy levels. In the public eye, "normal" is considered deviant for these groups while "pathology" is the normative expectation. Through this storm of speculation the Vietnam veteran continued to hide his identity and continued to endure as he did in 'Nam—in spite of the American people.

INSTITUTIONAL NEGLECT

The social vulnerability of Vietnam veterans is also revealed in patterns of institutional responses to their needs. Since American public policies are sensitive to prevailing moods, opinions, and political pressures, predictably such policies will be least sensitive to needs of stigmatized groups and those with the least ability (or willingness) to exert counterpressure to overcome negative social definitions. Thus, during and immediately following the war, the only public programs specifically designed for Vietnam veterans were those to protect the public *against* Vietnam veterans (that is, drug and venereal disease screening programs). Most Vietnam veterans were released in the early 1970s, a time of rising unemployment at home. Many went from mustering-out lines in the military to unemployment lines in civilian society. Among the unemployed were the 250,000 poor and uneducated men drafted under former Defense Secretary Robert McNamara's plan (Project 100,000) in the late 1960s to provide needed troops in Vietnam and "provide income and a set of skills for young men headed for the welfare rolls." With no effective postwar veterans' employment programs, eventually these recruits merely swelled the unemployed ranks with few skills other than using rifles and bayonets. Those who did have marketable skills scrambled for the few jobs not taken by those who avoided military service.

Furthermore, because Vietnam veterans returned home as individuals hiding their identity rather than as a coherent entity capable of collective action, they remained estranged from sources of political power. Initially, veterans had potential political impact as members of the Vietnam Veterans Against the War (VVAW), but this organization was infiltrated by agents of the Federal Bureau of Investigation and the

Central Intelligence Agency who effectively disrupted and destroyed the group.

Because of generational, political, and life-style differences between Vietnam veterans and those of previous wars, the former have remained alienated from the large conventional veterans' organizations like the American Legion and Veterans of Foreign Wars. Symbolizing and "befitting" their marginal status, the only veterans' groups in which Vietnam veterans have been represented are those by and for disabled vets. The appointment of a triple amputee veteran of Vietnam to the directorship of the Veterans Administration broke with the pattern of such directors being former commanders of the American Legion or the VFW.

Unlike veterans of "good wars," veterans of Vietnam were excluded from that traditional political cult of American war heroes, the veterans lobby. Functioning ostensibly to promote public consciousness of veterans' needs, this structure has also represented society's needs to co-opt a potentially "dangerous" group (veterans themselves) into accepting rather than opposing the existing system. Being denied access to the best resources of their homeland, Vietnam veterans came to resemble a prototypically estranged group, an ethnic minority such as American blacks who because of brutalization and alienation from their own original culture came to lack a fundamental self-pride, seeing themselves through the eyes of the dominant group, albeit hatefully.

All veterans returned from Vietnam to economic cutbacks and considerable job competition, but veterans with "less-than-honorable discharges" (estimated to be over 800,000) found it virtually impossible to obtain any jobs, let alone satisfying careers. Furthermore, veterans' tensions resulting from their job plight were not eased by realization of "affirmative action" programs designed for other groups. Such programs for veterans lacked a political base and "preference" for Vietnam veterans seemed more negative than positive; at best the public attitude was uncaring.

In the post-Vietnam era, educational institutions, especially private colleges and universities, were experiencing their own economic crises. Since GI Bill benefits for Vietnam veterans were significantly limited— especially in contrast to World War II and Korean eras—schools were neither inclined nor motivated to develop outreach programs especially sensitive to veterans' needs, desires, and aspirations as they had during previous postwar eras. Meanwhile, the Veterans Administration was involved in its own struggles with other government agencies for budgetary viability and seemed structurally too inhibited to respond to the special needs of Vietnam veterans. Influenced in its own past policies by leadership derived from the traditional veterans' lobby, the

VA seemed most oriented toward the needs of veterans of previous wars (for example, providing custodial medical care for generations of older men). Many Vietnam veterans experienced considerable frustration in dealing with the VA bureaucracy and came to realize they were also alienated from what they had hoped and believed was their last refuge in an otherwise apathetic, even hostile, society.

The generalized estrangement of Vietnam veterans from the more policy-oriented institutions of American society served to disaffect them from any notion that they could "make it" as a group. As in the case of other subordinated groups, Vietnam veterans have learned they are expected to enter the "mainstream" of American society as "proven" individuals, ordinary civilians, one at a time with no special claims based on prior service, sacrifice, or commitment. Public policy conveniently shifts to a stance of traditional American "individualism" when mobilized efforts of stigmatized groups are at hand.

Thus we have come full cycle. As we said at the outset, the Vietnam War was an American experience, and America's treatment of its new veterans reveals as much about the society and its problems as about the veterans and their problems. In a fundamental sense this is what the following chapters reveal and illuminate.

REFERENCES

Durkheim, Emile. 1951. *Suicide*. Glencoe, Illinois: Free Press.
Ryan, William. 1971. *Blaming the Victim*. New York: Random House.
Starr, Paul. 1973. *The Discarded Army: Veterans after Vietnam*. New York: Charter House.

SECTION I

THE WAR AND THE WARRIOR

THE GLORY AND THE GORE: AN
INTRODUCTION TO SECTION I

Charles R. Figley

Four of the chapters in this first section focus on the characteristics of the Vietnam War that make it unique in American history. We hear from Vietnam veterans themselves in Clark Smith's (Chapter 1) and Norma Wikler's (Chapter 5) interviews, from sociologists who studied combatants while they were in Vietnam, as did Charles Moskos (Chapter 4), and since the war as a Vietnam veteran as did Paul Camacho (and Seymour Leventman) in Chapter 3. In Chapter 2 Willard Waller links the Vietnam vet with vets of all other wars. He observes that all combat veterans' reactions are predictable and remarkably similar regardless of the circumstances of the war they fought in.

In Chapter 1 Clark Smith combines brutally blunt and graphic descriptions of Vietnam combat veterans with his insights and experiences as an "oral historian." Both are the result of hundreds of hours of personal interviews he conducted over several years during and following the Vietnam War. Smith explains that oral history is "history speaking," in which participants of historic events recount their experiences, making these events come alive for the listener. Through oral history it is possible to examine not only the historic events as they emerge from the collective impressions of those who were there but also the psychosocial, motivational, and behavioral characteristics of interview subjects themselves. This is illustrated in the case of Tim, a former Marine interrogator who relates his grisly experiences while serving in Vietnam for 13 months at the height of the war and the antiwar protests. Although many readers will be incredulous about Tim's experiences, none of the incidents he relates are unique. In fact, Norma Wikler's subjects in Chapter 5 report similar atrocities.

Clark Smith's candid subjects startle us with the brutality and endless numbers of absurdities, contradictions, and "Catch-22s" of the Vietnam War. As insane as the war seemed while they were involved in it, the veterans found that coming home from it was even less understandable and considerably more emotionally painful than leaving for war. Combatants departing from Vietnam felt panic just before boarding the "Freedom Bird," because there was always a chance of getting hit or, even worse, getting delayed at the last minute. Retiring soldiers and Marines report being shipped home and being processed out of the war and the military as efficiently and as heartlessly as they were processed into it. They felt the initial shock of confusion and disappointment upon return, the desperate attempts to "get your head straight" before facing the folks back home who wanted to know what it was like to kill somebody, and the sting of recognition that their actual homecoming was nothing like the one they had dreamed about in 'Nam. They found that apathy was everywhere. Vietnam had become a household word and, thanks to TV news coverage, the battle scenes were as familiar to most Americans as Johnny Carson's mannerisms. In the public's eye, Vietnam emerged as an American institution, like a sport with constantly changing fields, changing players, changing scores, changing rules, changing coaches, and changing home support. The only ones who really knew what the war was like were those who fought it, like those quoted by Smith and Wikler.

In Chapter 2 Willard Waller provides some important linkages between the experiences and attitudes of Smith's interviewees and veterans of previous wars. Although written 30 years before the end of the Vietnam War, Waller's observations are both timely and timeless. We find many common themes: the returning warriors' sense of bitterness and resentment toward the public's complacency (especially employers) about their sacrifices; their disappointment in finding that their wartime visions of peacetime events, home, and homecoming were far better than what they eventually found upon return; their disorientation within the transition between military and civilian worlds; their feelings of numbness caused by the isolation, brutality, and stress of war; their attempts to somehow recapture the human qualities they had prior to the war.

Waller captures the bitterness of the returning vets toward those who did not serve: the draft dodgers, those who feigned illness to escape serving, those who served in the military but never left the country, the proverbial "swivel chair heroes," and finally, those who served overseas but not in combat. The combatants were angry and resentful because they were singled out to suffer the toll of war. A considerable amount of the veterans' vehemency was reserved for what one vet referred to as "those who talk about ideals [but] do not fight for them . . . [because] those who fight for them do not talk about them." As Waller so elequently points out, "a patriot is a man who is always willing to lay down his life for his country, while an orator is willing to lay down your life for his country."

Perhaps more than any other, Waller's chapter articulates the theme of the volume: those who fight the wars return as immigrants in their own homeland: "He is like the immigrant because he has no sure and settled place in society and because he derives much, if not most, of his social satisfaction from the company of others of his own kind; partly because he prefers their society and partly because he does not fit in anywhere else." What Waller concludes from this has important implications for understanding and easing the plight of the Vietnam veteran: The best way to assist the veteran and prevent his feelings of estrangement is to encourage veteran interaction and participation in society as a group.

Chapter 3 by Seymour Leventman and Paul Camacho focuses on the internal dynamics of the struggle of military willpower as well as manpower and firepower in Vietnam. Race and racism were integral parts of the American combatant's experiences in Vietnam. Draftees who fought in Vietnam were disproportionately drawn from the least-privileged groups of Americans: the poor, the less-educated, the colored—black, yellow, or brown—and the most politically conservative, paradoxically and consistently the antonym for those who conceived the war in the first place. The authors suggest another racial element particularly prevalent later in the war: Interestingly, when the black-white differences were becoming dangerously tense, the Vietnamese became "gooks."

Leventman and Camacho observe that race consciousness is a critical factor in understanding the unique dynamics of the war and, in addition, it appears to be closely correlated with the changing social nature of the war. Being a "nigger lover" in some parts of the United States would engender less harsh treatment than being a "gook lover" did in the latter years of Vietnam. This is consistent with my own research, which found that the least respected of all Asians were soldiers of the Army of the Republic of Vietnam (ARVN, or what the American combatants called "ARFN, a real fucking nuisance").

Although it is almost impossible to explain the My Lai massacre they lend some ordered objectivity by suggesting that racially-based aggression was directed mainly against the Vietnamese farmers, the most accessible representatives of a hated race that continued to frustrate and humiliate American forces. No doubt, as Leventman and Camacho observe, that is why Lt. Calley, the only American "victim" of the My Lai could casually and matter-of-factly explain that "wasting" civilians was "no big deal."

One of the most respected authorities on military sociology, Charles Moskos was one of the first social scientists to study the Vietnam War. He spent the summers of 1965 and 1967 conducting field research with combat units in Vietnam. His numerous interviews and careful analyses resulted in the first seminal work to evolve from studies of the Vietnam War-era veteran: *The American Enlisted Man* (New York: Russell Sage, 1970). His Chapter 4 draws extensively from those data collected in Vietnam from American combatants. Viewing the war in retrospect, however, Moskos goes beyond his data to make some important observations about the war and the soldiers who fought in it. When reading the chapter it is important to first view the Southeast Asian conflict as a war, with many of the trappings of past wars in that it was fought by the young and—most often—the poor and least privileged. Moreover, only a small percentage of soldiers actually fought in the war; most were support troops who saw the war from base camps complete with many of the comforts of home. Combatants, on the other hand, had to endure the physical and emotional stresses of combat, including, as Moskos notes: "the weight of the pack, tasteless food, diarrhea, lack of drinking water, leeches, mosquitoes, rain, torrid heat, mud, and loss of sleep." Another similarity is the soldier's constant grumbling about troops and civilians who enjoyed considerably more of life's pleasures than he did. These and other factors appear to be quite consistent with the other chapters in the section; they are universal to all combatants past, present, and future. Most of Chapter 4 by Moskos, however, points out the unique features of the Vietnam war: In contrast to earlier wars, especially the world wars, Vietnam was "individualistic"; primary groups and group cohesion were not operative in Vietnam. The rotation system of limiting tours in Southeast Asia to one year (plus an extra month for marines) with occasional periods for rest and relaxation outside the war zone was at that time assumed by most to be a way to bolster military morale and thus increase effectiveness, actually may have had the opposite effect. Again, in contrast to the customary cleavage in the military between ranks (for example, enlisted men versus noncommissioned officers [NCOs] and NCOs versus officers), the cleavage in Vietnam was largely between those troops interested in a military career and those troops who were not. There was a tremendous difference in the morale of the combatants who served in Vietnam in the early years of the war (1964–67) compared with those who served after 1968. Somewhat related to all these factors, antiwar sentiment back home was, perhaps, the single most important facet that made the war unique in American history.

Moskos concludes his chapter with an interesting thought: the Vietnam veteran "might take a joyless satisfaction that events in Indochina since his departure show [their] mission there had some moral justification." Few veterans would suggest, however, that American presence in Southeast Asia did little more than delay the eventual subjugation of one Southeast Asian country by another.

Norma Wikler's chapter continues where Smith's left off by considering the words and thoughts of Vietnam combat veterans. Wikler's interviewees discuss the anguish of losing buddies, their fear of death and injury, their self-discovery as a result of the "maturing" effect of war, their adjustment to violence and one's own violent capacities, and the moral readjustment to one's own killing acts—both legal and illegal. In the final section of her chapter, Wikler, drawing upon her intimate discussions with so many combatants, discusses how the Vietnam War was different from other wars. She notes, as do Moskos and Leventman and Camacho, that the war was ill-conceived, inconsistently fought, and abruptly and unceremoniously stopped—unlike any other war in history. Even worse, notes Wikler, the economy was cooling off in the early 1970s, causing a highly competitive labor market. As Chapter 4 confirms, this accounted for an extremely high unemployment rate among returning Vietnam veterans.

Collectively, the chapters in this section suggest that the undeclared war America fought in Southeast Asia was for those who fought in it as unpredictable, convoluted, and senseless as those "patriots" whose foreign policy spawned it. As the war went on year after year and soldiers became civilians again without appreciation and assistance, many became bitter and felt used and abused. They felt, as comedian George Carlin (a Vietnam veteran himself) once quipped, "like Nixon Niggers." "Nixon Niggers" were shipped off to fight an impossible war for a year or more and then thrust back into mainstream American society to try to pick up their lives where they had left them before Vietnam and to fulfill the American dream—difficult tasks under the circumstances. Section II will describe how they fared.

1

ORAL HISTORY AS "THERAPY": COMBATANTS' ACCOUNTS OF THE VIETNAM WAR

CLARK SMITH

Coming home. Everyone looks forward to it. And finally that day comes when you can come home. My unit was off to war and a lot of guys were being killed that week. And there was one little notice on this bulletin board outside the C.O.'s hootch: "J.I., ETS, 4 days." When I heard about some of my friends being killed in the field it just blew me away. "But I'm going home." You know? I was so glad to leave. I was going to leave with two arms, two legs, two eyes, two ears—or pretty much two ears; I lost a lot of my hearing from recoilless rifle explosions. I'd been shot at, really closely, and I'd survived; I was going to make it. I was so short I could count the hours.

Who knows? It's an unproven thing that you die in the first 21 days or the last 21 days, as the old saying went. Sure, I was out in the field six days before I was going home and got shot at. In fact, the guys that were going to take me to Phu Bai to catch the airplane were going to go identify some bodies that just came in. So when we pulled out in the jeep, I sat in the back, and I just looked all over Camp Eagle and said, "Man, I'm leaving this place finally. *Finally*! I'm not safe yet, but I'm leaving."

The author is grateful to Dr. Louis Starr, Director of the Oral History Research Office, Butler Library, Columbia University, and Mrs. Elizabeth Earley for their continuing support of his Vietnam Veterans' Oral History Project.

Got to Phu Bai and I knew this guy in data processing that re-upped. Well, he was a good friend of the guy scheduling all the flights out of Phu Bai. The faster you got out of Phu Bai, the faster you got to Cam Ranh Bay; the faster you got home. So I got to Phu Bai finally about 3:00 in the afternoon, and through the power of knowing someone, I was on the plane by 3:30. I got to Cam Ranh Bay about 7:30; slept outside all night long. About 10:00 the next morning, I finally found out we were going to have a flight out at about 1:00 or 2:00 in the afternoon. When I first came to Vietnam, about two hours before I came in, 122-rockets had hit a short-timer's hootch, just about two hours before those guys were to board the airplane that flew me in. Right? It killed about 12 of them on their last day. So no one was safe till that bird left the ground.

So, I sat around in Cam Ranh until finally we got on the buses and went to the Freedom Bird. And when I got on that Freedom Bird, I was superstitious. I took one of the back seats because I knew the tail sections usually survive best in a crash. And I got back there with a bunch of blacks; we had a good time, talking. That second the bird lifted off the ground about 160 people just shouted—we were so happy when it climbed out. The stewardesses were really nice. A comfortable flight. We got to Japan and stayed there for about four hours for some odd reason. Most people just stayed around the flight pad. As I got back on the Freedom Bird, some people had decided to dispose of the pot they had before we got to Customs at Fort Lewis. They went back to the bathroom and smoked a lot of pot. But some E-7 smelled it and told the commanding officer. Well, nothing happened.

We finally came into that Air Force base near Fort Lewis. I'll never forget it. We got off the plane and it was just colder than hell. It was late in the afternoon; it had been a long flight. We just patted the ground, kissed it. There wasn't a soul around. And we went through these glass doors and up to these booths that we lined up with signs: "E-4 and below, E-5, E-6, E-7, officers." Everyone was segregated according to rank and branch of service with a line for ETS—the guys getting out of the service.

You got in your group and went by the customs officer who just looked at your stuff. He didn't care. In fact, there was a guy who had a padlock on his dufflebag; he had lost the key (so he said), and they just waved him through. Then they sent us to Fort Lewis. All of us were getting out of the service. We got this asshole sergeant, E-5. And he says, "I hope you guys don't think you're going to get out of the army tonight, because there's not a damn thing we can do. So we're just going to process you in the morning, because I don't want anything to do with you guys." He had that kind of attitude. Really weird. In the service there are patches for your division and he had never been in Vietnam.

So screw him. We can tolerate it. So we went to our barracks and then finally some guy came up and said, "OK, it's time to get your steaks." And we were just cold, I remember, so cold; our blood must have been so thin from Vietnam's heat. Even though we were in 60-degree weather we had two coats on. So he took us to this single-floor barracks with a kitchen. You walked in and got your steak and your baked potato. That's your thanks from the United States government—you get a steak, cooked just the way you want it! So you ate your steak, and went back, and smoked some more pot, because everyone had more pot. We just waited until morning. We got up at 6:00. They took us down and fitted us for Class-A uniforms, put on all our ribbons and awards and buttons and paraphernalia. Then we went off to our physical. It consisted of "Fill in line 4A, 80 over 120"—two medics are telling us what to fill in. We went to this orientation. They asked us if we had any service disabilities or problems connected with the war. Well, I couldn't hear. But I wanted out of the service so bad, I wasn't going to say anything about it. And I had to have perfect hearing to get into flight school. So I filled in the questionnaire "No." Finally, they gave us our DD 214, which is a little carry-all discharge. They gave you your uniform. And there was a funny ceremony at the end, where they had Koolaid and they wanted to know if we wanted to buy the pictures of the people coming off the Freedom Bird for two dollars. Obviously, "No."

We all climbed on the buses they had waiting and they sent us to SEATAC—Seattle-Tacoma Airport. When we got there, everybody that got off that damned bus bee-lined it for the men's room. I was in the second bus. By the time I got there, there were 40 uniforms stuffed in the urinals and toilets with Silver Stars on them, Purple Hearts; it didn't matter. Class-A uniforms stuffed in garbage cans—all dumped for civilian clothes. I don't think anyone cared that they had to pay $30 or $40 for their ticket. I wore my uniform home, but I didn't wear any ribbons. I didn't pick up my Bronze Star, plaques, or any of that stuff. I just couldn't see being proud of a Bronze Star awarded for combat or a combat infantryman's badge.

My Mom and Dad and family were in Seattle at the time. So I called them up after a period of time. I was in SEATAC for about three hours. I did a bit of drinking, trying to mellow out. I didn't want to face them yet. It was an awful burden, a pressure, to meet them right away. In fact, I'd much rather have done what a lot of guys had done—gone off to Seattle for the night, caught a show, and quietly adjusted to being home. Because you'd gone from that stench that never left you, you came home, and even though you have pollution, it was a nice smell; it was home.

So when you first got off that airplane and went to Fort Lewis and went to this building to see that sergeant, there's a sign that sets up there—and it's in Oakland, too, because I've seen it. And it says, "Welcome Back, Soldier. America is Proud of You." Huh. That's incredible, that sign. Cause that's all there is—that sign. That's all there are—those words. And they're empty. And no steak dinner, and no amount of words written in red are going to prove anything different. Once you get back, you know that no one really cares. When you see the lights of the city of Seattle, or if you come back through Oakland-San Francisco, and you're on your way home, wherever home is, you know that the world has gone on without you. That that war was some isolated thing, a bad thought, a foul-tasting thing that's over there—something that Walter Cronkite talks about for five minutes every night. You know?

PSYCHOLOGY AND POLITICS

At the core of the so-called post-Vietnam syndrome is public indifference to the experience of veterans returned from that war. Though time has brought even greater indifference, the Vietnam veteran still carries the psychosocial stain of that war. The war impinged upon the realm of the general American experience, however, in a fragmentary and marginal way, despite the ultimate rejection of war policies. The absence of an all-embracing homecoming was prefigured by the character of a rotational system that returned veterans from the war in an individual and isolated manner. Men who had shared the experience were lost from each other and prevented from sharing the homecoming. The fragment of oral narrative above suggests the frenzy of rejection of military attitudes and values at the same instant that the Vietnam experience made the returnees vulnerable to criticism to which they had no viable reply. As another veteran remarked: "We're the ones that did the shit." Compelled as youthful executioners of corrupt war policies, the veteran became the victim in an irremedial situation. In the proverbial court of public opinion, the Vietnam veteran was morally accused and condemned. His silence on the experience of the war became a psychological index of what was labled post-Vietnam syndrome. With the war experience suppressed, the emotional catharsis of homecoming was nullified.

As an oral historian who confronts the Vietnam experience directly through the interview process, I encountered the various and compelling features of post-Vietnam syndrome. Of the numerous interviews I have done—some lasting six or eight hours—the concluding responses of veterans, like the narrative fragment above, seem most resonant with a sense of bitter irony. As one Vietnam veteran noted: "I talked to friends who were in Berkeley when I was in 'Nam and they said, 'Look, we're doing this [protesting] for you. Don't you understand that?' And I thought I was doing that [service in Vietnam] for them." One feature of post-Vietnam experience for the combatant is the pervasive sense of betrayal. It is a permanent emotional scar in which the political and the psychological are not easily separated, in fact, an initial accommodation with the political attitudes accompanying identifiable feelings of despair and melancholy by combatants support this linkage. Veterans themselves have repeatedly indicated an awareness of the proximity of the political and the psychological:

> I just got home and there's the Cambodian invasion and this massive surge of people. I was in a weird position. I was ready to beat heads of the people who were protesting the war and I hated the country; I knew it was doing something wrong because I lost friends in Vietnam and I kept saying to myself, "Well, the people who should be complaining about this fucking war are the people who are there. Yet they're not saying anything." And I was one of the first ones to say that I'm going to crawl into a little hole and pretend it never happened. I made these huge pendulum swings from ultra-conservative Right hawk to a real let's-blow-up-the-establishment type, you know, fuck it. Look what it's doing to our generation. Then I made it back to the middle somehow.

Emotional and political confusion coalesced into a barely suppressed anger that seems pervasive among Vietnam veterans. Anger and isolation were the twin psychological hazards of post-Vietnam "adjustment." As another Vietnam returnee remarked to me: "The hardest thing to get used to was when someone said, 'You haven't changed.'" Dismissal of the *value* of the Vietnam experience, even in its negative dimensions, makes "adjustment" virtually impossible.

Without even the smallest acknowledgement of the profound intensity of the Vietnam experience, little can be accomplished in therapy with Vietnam veterans. That intensity was transformed to anguish after the "homecoming" when the war experience was replaced by the veteran experience. Political alienation combined with psychological despair, as the following narrative fragment suggests:

> We came home through Travis [Air Force Base], then got bussed back to Oakland. I went through the same building that I left the country from. I'll never forget it. We walked in this door—it's like a rail-car building with doors that slide—and there's this great big American flag painted on the wall right in front of you. And most of the guys are ready to spit on it, if not kick it. They had lost people who really didn't die because of any kind of belief. It wasn't like they had walked across the street and got killed. It was because somebody else had pushed them out in the street. The flag represented the people who were pushing. It was just a huge feeling of alienation. We were alienated by our peers—the people we're going to end up associating with back in the States, back in the world. As far as we were concerned, we were alienated by our country. It was like we were the last men on the

totem pole, at the end of the stick. We felt kinda lost. From '68 to '70 there was such a big transition in social consciousness in the United States. People were saying, "What the hell are we doing [in Vietnam]?" Then all of a sudden people are saying things like, "The people coming back from Vietnam ought to be put in detention camps." I can't remember whether it was in *Newsweek* where there was talk about doing psychoanalysis to make sure they could adjust Vietnam veterans so that they could fit back into society. All I wanted to do was pull a blanket over my head and go through everything incognito. For the most part, other vets would just as soon not talk to anybody about what happened. You just take your honorable discharge and stick it in the closet and if anybody asked, out of the corner of your mouth you'd say, "Yeah, I got it." But as far as waving it around, it's not something you're going to do. It was a pretty hard thing to get used to.

While an institutionally enforced silence blocked the avenues of communication, Vietnam veterans had come to a political maturity not generally shared by their stateside counterparts. They had witnessed in varying degrees the grim consequences of counterinsurgency warfare. They had seen the extension of the American system in all its preponderance *and* inadequacy. The effect was devastating; the consequences significant for a fair estimate of the nature of post-Vietnam syndrome:

I don't put anyone down for it, but for me, buying of the flesh was another degradation of the war. It was really a total degradation of the Vietnamese society. Refugees are made when people lose their livelihood. The Vietnamese did live in villages with grass roofs and earthen floors; they collected the rain water they drank off the roof in giant pots. When whole families were moved from the rice paddies to cities (grandparents, young kids, brothers and sisters) there's no damn way to make a living. They're not going to go down to a GM plant and get a job making cars. So the women would turn to whores. You've got umpteen million soldiers over there. It's amazing how the American war machine could go on at that level, not only destroying the country with bombs, but destroying the lives of families. Whores could make a lot of money compared to the regular standard of living. Some of them I heard were supporting fifty relatives. So in a very sick way, what they did was beneficial. To me the war was just a total disease, a total sickness, a total cancer.

I remember the first few times I got out of the hospital in San Francisco; my Dad would come over and drive me home. I remember looking at the cars going in the other direction on the freeway. It would be a nice sunny Sunday. American families were going by, their kids in the back seat, the parents in front. I just had this terrible feeling of animosity and disgust, this repulsiveness at what Americans were, what the American system was. I had experienced the very immediate effects of death and the war. And to most Americans, it was just another Sunday drive to the zoo, regardless of what was in the news. For umpteen years the American public went along with the war with the attitude, "no artillery shells are landing in my backyard with the kids playing in the swings; so I don't give a damn." I remember being just totally aggravated about the American system. I still am today. It's a kind of awareness that has shaken me pretty much for the rest of my life.

Underlying post-Vietnam syndrome is a nagging *aggravation* complicated by contemporary anxieties, frustrations, and persuasions. The aggravation is compounded by the manifold aspects of guilt: survivor guilt, war guilt, criminal guilt, complicity guilt. For the therapist engaged in interaction with Vietnam veterans, the emotional landscape contains a minefield of politically induced alienation and emotional upset.

Thousands of alienated and aggravated Vietnam veterans have never divulged to their families and friends the character of their Vietnam experience. At least 25 percent of the veteran participants in my oral history project have commented—usually at the conclusion of the interview, off the tape—that the interview was the first time they had recounted their Vietnam experience to anyone. In most cases I was a virtual stranger who would not see these veterans again. It was also clear during the interview that veterans were eager to share the most important experience of their lives once a small degree of trust had been established. When the pain in their experiences is shared, it is partially alleviated. When it is not shared, the consequences for some can be fatal, as this newspaper account suggests:

| The Argus | Fremont-Newark, Calif. |
| Page 8 | Tuesday, June 6, 1978 |

VIET WAR MEMORY TRIGGERED SUICIDE

San Lorenzo—A haunting war experience that kept a Hayward man from sleeping at nights apparently drove him to commit suicide Sunday, according to sheriff's deputies.

Steven L. Anderson was found dead in his parents' home by his father, who was to meet him Saturday for a weekend in Reno.

Anderson died from a bullet wound in the head, deputies said. A pistol was still in his hand, they reported.

A note was found which read in part: "I can't sleep anymore. When I was in Vietnam, we came across a North Vietnamese soldier with a man, a woman and a 3 or 4-year-old girl. We had to shoot them all. I can't get the little girl's face out of my mind. I hope that God will forgive me. I hope the people in this country who made millions of dollars off of the men, women and children that died in that war can sleep at night (I can't, and I didn't make a cent) . . ."

Anderson began his two-year stint in the army 14 years ago, according to his mother, Betty J. Anderson. She said he had never mentioned the incident to anyone in the family and had never indicated that he was disturbed by it.

What is so striking in this sad notice is the 12-year delayed response to complicity in an atrocity and the isolation of the veteran. The release from the veteran's tragic confrontation with himself was apparently lacking. If the basic elements of post-Vietnam syndrome are depression, alienation, and aggravation experienced in a situation in which no one seems willing to listen, then the Vietnam survivor succumbs to an internalized pressure that the smallest amount of release might deflect. It is a surmise well established in the canons of psychotherapy that had the suicide spoken of his "haunting war experience" he might have survived his self-aggression. But the pressures to remain silent, to put the experience "behind us"—except as the electronic media type-casts vets—helps to defeat speaking out in a therapeutic situation. It complicates tremendously the problems veterans face in resolving personal conflicts rooted in their experience of the war. From both a social and psychiatric perspective, the Vietnam veteran stands isolated and estranged from those in society who are indifferent or hostile to the war experience.

ORAL HISTORY AND STRESS

Just as it is impossible to know the full impact of stress factors on someone in therapy without taking a psychosocial history, it is *a fortiori* impossible to provide a balanced appraisal of the symptomology without a contextual understanding of the external experiences of stress. This context involves two wars: the war experience of Vietnam and the silent war most Vietnam veterans continue to fight against the homefront. The first war involves varying degrees of combat stress that are experienced by the soldiers of all wars; the second war involves the postwar condition of the veteran—his damaged self-esteem, his dehumanization in a counterinsurgency struggle, his victimization through humiliation and public scorn, his anonymity as part of a defeated and half-forgotten past, and, as a psychological consequence, his pervasive depression and suicidal self-contempt. The situational neurosis that emerges out of the Vietnam experience is primarily conditioned by the direct experience of the war and the military in the war, but it is exacerbated by attitudes and policies on the homefront. The neurosis thus defined is magnified by the preoccupation with the notion of "survival." "Survival" has become a virtual buzz word among veterans. The character of the military institution in the Vietnam War made survival a very individualized matter at the same time that a new and more advanced military technology combined with the strategy and tactics of counterinsurgency made the war particularly brutal and unpredictable. That is, the very nature of the war greatly magnified stress factors intrinsic to combat. Such characteristics compounded relative military hazards making rear-echelon troops equally susceptible to combat neurosis, though sometimes by vicarious means, and not always to the same degree. Complete safety was always relative in Vietnam and, therefore, combat paranoia was endemic. Even though the military experience for individual military personnel was quite varied in terms of duty station, military specialization, and proximity to military hazards, a uniform experience of the war is shared by all veterans and combat-related stress is common to that experience.

There is a sense in which oral history is a synthesis of the two wars that Vietnam veterans have experienced; with the advantages of hindsight of the present, the veteran recreates his past experience. Oral history is "history speaking," but it does so out of a contemporaneous situation. Unlike the use of traditional empirical methods designed to arrive at historical generalizations and explanations by conventional historians, oral history functions as *portrayal*. Though this function is distinctly historical, it is suspect among historians because of the prevailing preference for an appropriate amount of "historical distance" from which to measure the meaning of events without the hazards of unsuspecting bias. In addition, the passage of time allows for the emergence of crucial documentation considered instrumental in the truthful assessment of historical records and events. Oral history reverses the role of the time factor. Rather than historical distance, the oral method preserves "historical immediacy." As portrayal, oral historical narrative (with minimal commentary or evaluation) offers insight into historical developments to the attentive reader because its function is not so much to bring forth generalizations but rather to plunge the reader into the experience itself. Because it presents experience in a highly individualized form, it contains a psychological terrain. Much as fiction is not, in itself, self-explanatory but gives an appreciation of the psychology of the author, so oral historical narrative offers the possibility of interpretation from a psychological point of view. The personality of the narrator emerges, as if by degrees, within a particular situation or set of circumstances. Much depends upon the skill of the oral historian, his interview technique and historical knowledgeability, in transforming an interview into oral narrative. Most important within the interview situation is the trust and confidence engendered by the interviewer. This latter factor is an important functional requirement for gaining any serious degree of depth in the interplay between personality and events. In the exchange between oral historian and interviewee, a social pathology may well emerge as a by-product of the interview process. The oral history interview shares certain common features with the psychiatric interview. Though the purpose and the means of the former are historical, important latent implications of that method are clinical.

The accepted clinical view of the psychiatric interview is one in which the exchange between therapist and patient is a means to therapeutic ends. The appearance of the emotionally distraught patient before the therapist is mute evidence that there is a therapeutic goal to be achieved, however vague such a goal might be at the outset. A mutually responsive collaboration between therapist and patient is intrinsic to the establishment of emotional balance. The oral history is analogous, though hardly identical. History, not therapy, is its end and the means are formulated as personal narrative. The oral historian is a conduit through which the experience of war (or whatever) passes; his function, analogous to the psychotherapist, is carefully nonjudgmental. Like the psychiatric interviewer, the oral historian is a listener who facilitates the thread of narrative development as it is recorded for posterity. At the same time that he must know much of the experience of the war, this information is a means to push ever deeper into the narrator's involvement in the events he describes. The narrative fragments, interrupted by questions that are either directive or supportive or empathetic, contain many of the ingredients heard by the clinician. Nevertheless, for the oral historian, the person interviewed is objectified as a historical source rather than a psychoanalytic problem. In both cases the Vietnam veteran is a person in juxtaposition to events both psychosocial and historical and the evaluation of these two features of human activity are perilously intertwined. When the veteran enters into the psychiatric interview there is the tacit admission of emotional imbalance that is lacking in the oral historical interview. Because of the special nature of the Vietnam veteran's situation, chiefly post-Vietnam syndrome, his experiences at the outset militate against an accommodation with the procedures and the processes of the psychiatric interview. Given this general problem of therapy with the Vietnam veteran, oral history offers both a method and a perspective that in some cases could be helpful.

The understanding at the outset of the oral history interview is that it is informational; it lacks any overt psychotherapeutic intent. The veteran in the interview process is not considered "disturbed" or in any way "defective." Rather, what is problematic is "the war." The focus of the oral historian is on political, social, institutional features of the military experience in Vietnam, though it is also fair to say that the soldier's state of mind in the military situation is equally important. Making the situation the subject of discussion rather than the person relieves considerably the strain of the interview and shifts the focus from inner turmoil to *objective* conflict. At the same time, the veteran who tells "his story" does so with the tacit permission to unburden himself, to tell all and conceal nothing. It is also understood at the outset, through prior agreement with the oral historian, that the veteran-as-narrator can withdraw any portion of his narrative account upon subsequent reconsideration. Both tacit admissions and overt confessions may be blocked out of the tape at the veteran's discretion. The veteran knows in advance he will receive a verbatim transcript of the tape, which makes this discretionary action possible. Given such procedural safeguards that engender an ethos of fairness, the veteran feels freer to talk, though the tape recorder may initially cause some inhibition. The dynamics of the interview, whose only obvious guide-line is the historicity of the narrative, proceeds to open only those doors that time and circumstance allow. Many veterans are more ready to narrate their experiences of the war at one time than at another. Some prefer several interview sessions with the obvious relish of finally telling their story—indeed, reliving their experiences—after the passage of almost too much time. The vast majority have told their experiences to no one else, though fragments of these accounts surface among veterans themselves anecdotally as "war stories"; often enliv-ened through emphasis and repetition and shared intimacy of the experience of war, they are the true oral history of the war. But war stories, told with animation and verve among veterans themselves are distinct from oral historical narrative because of the latter's formal character. The veteran enters into the oral history interview with some apprehension and often a keen desire to set the record straight.

Oral history, therefore, offers the veteran who is suspicious of psychiatric counseling a hesitant first step in that direction. On the other hand, the oral history interview might equally offer the veteran that one-stop encounter necessary to ward off the hazards of post-Vietnam syndrome; it might be all that is really possible for some veterans, all that is really necessary for others. For many veterans the oral historical interview provides the means of memorial self-affirmation, which functions largely as a symbolic statement that they are not defeated but rather that they are contenders.

It is a vast oversimplification to assert that oral history may facilitate an alternative to the prevailing situation among alienated and isolated veterans experiencing the latent effects of combat stress. Like the Vietnam veteran support organization, the function of oral history is meant, in part, to fill the gap left when the junction between patient needs and therapy requirements becomes overly broad. An oral history that speaks positively of the Vietnam experience in spite of its unspeakable negative content bridges the gap by balancing the positive and negative elements into a therapeutically coherent whole. Oral history attempts to accomplish this task vicariously. Its methodology not only creates a portrayal of the Vietnam experience to be shared by other veterans but, in addition, it is a device designed to break through the silence imposed upon and accepted by Vietnam veterans.

The isolation of the veteran is deeply psychological in its impact upon individual veterans, but it is also part of a predetermined political policy. When political leaders urged Americans to "forget the war," they implicitly urged "forget the veteran." Antiwar sentiment crystallized against the veteran at the very moment in which the veteran turned against the war and recognized the need for strong social support. The rotational system of the military, designed to serve only the needs of manpower allocation, left the veteran isolated in both his entry into the alien Vietnam experience and his reentry into the alienating postwar experience. Military morale, which is a basic psychological support against the hazards of combat stress, collapsed during the war; this collapse of morale meant that a major means of warding off postwar combat stress and depression was lost. All of these situational factors account for depression and loss of self-esteem. Oral history breaks down the barriers erected by Americans, covertly aided by the government and the media, to that experience. Without dodging the criminality of the war, it focuses on the everyday experience of the GI in the war. Public scorn and humiliation can be overcome through exposing the public to the war experience in its human dimensions. In effect, a sympathy for the veteran in an experience that was uniquely his cuts through the silence that is a consequence of negative public attitudes, which in part are government fostered. Isolated and outnumbered by a shift in attitudes and public policy, the stage was set for situational restraints against individual psychotherapeutic problem solving. Vietnam veterans became the total recipients of the Vietnam war guilt, which was complicated by survivor's guilt and other forms of psychological attrition. In such circumstances, oral history performs the compensatory function. For some veterans it is an initial step away from an identity that is among the most meaningful despite its profoundly negative content. Oral history helps bring that identity into clearer and more positive focus. In so doing, it releases pent-up emotions; this catharsis is added to the positive assurance that if the Vietnam War was morally wrong, the experience in the war was a lesser evil.

ORAL HISTORY EXAMPLE

An oral historical case study exemplifies both a desirable procedure in the acceptance of the Vietnam experience as intrinsic to a psychotherapeutic evaluation and the manner in which the war experience shaped the evolution of combat-related stress. Psychic trauma was a direct consequence of both the experience of the war and the particular training of the veteran. Indeed, trauma is induced by the counterinsurgency character of the war. This feature of the experience exists in the narration as if by implication. The narrator is Tim, a Marine interrogator assigned in May 1969 initially to the 13th Interrogation Translation Team (ITT) of the First Marine Division stationed at An Hoa and LZ (Landing Zone) Baldy; later he was reassigned to the 19th ITT of the Third Marine Division at Quang Tri. Tim's tour of 13 months came while the military "standdown" was still in its aggressive first phase; he left Vietnam several months after the "incursion" into Cambodia in 1970. It was during exactly this time that the major shift in the public mood against the war took place; between the moratoria of the late fall of 1969 and the attack on Cambodia, the antiwar protests reached their peak. By this time, the antiwar movement was having a substantial impact on military morale. The extent of that impact is difficult to estimate and impossible to quantify. Yet Tim is one of those veterans whose experience of the war, with its conflict between humanitarian values and the military mission, exemplifies the difficulties of coping with the shift in the public mood against the war.

The phases of Tim's Vietnam experience moving him toward situational trauma are threefold: the training experience, the Vietnam experience in general, and the experience of trauma. The homefront experience, coming on the heels of psychic trauma, put Tim in a situation of potential suicide. Tim was discharged from the Marine Corps in December 1970. He returned home to Massachusetts and in April 1971 became involved with Vietnam Veterans Against the War:

> I'm back in the States and everything's coming down on me about what went on in Vietnam and I'm thinking it was only me. I went to pick up my Vietnam bonus and I started talking to this dude. He was the first dude I had talked with since I had gotten out who had been to Vietnam. It had been four months of this going ape shit, seriously considering suicide. God, everything was torturing me. You know, my head. The isolation, the loneliness; why am I going through this? So I got into VVAW very much and all these people, man, they're feeling the same things I'm feeling. I ain't alone and I ain't going out of my head anymore. We can all go bug fuck together. It was beautiful. That was in April of 1971; I went with VVAW until the following January.

Tim participated in several VVAW mock military operations including the takeover of the Statue of Liberty. "It was a really stoned out idea. The original plan was to take over the island and do a kind of Wounded Knee trip, secede from the Union, declare ourselves a sovereign state and recognize North Vietnam." Tim and another veteran participated in this bit of guerrilla theatre by displaying the American flag upside down from the top of the Statue. He also made a statement in Vietnamese recorded by a French reporter to be used in Vietnam. His obvious antagonism to American policies and provocations in Vietnam can certainly be viewed as cathartic; he himself seems to suggest that participation with fellow veterans helped turn his internalized rage against himself into an external aggression, however symbolic. Doubtless fraternal collaboration among fellow pariahs provided some small measure of "adjustment" ("We can all go bug fuck together"), but it seems likely that it saved Tim from a suicide that has become a pervasive feature of the experience of the Vietnam returnee.

It is perhaps ironic that Tim referred to his suicidal state as "self-torture." The Marine Corps provided Tim with 32 weeks of Vietnamese language training for his combat specialty as translator-interrogator. An additional part of his training involved a two-month temporary assignment to the Army intelligence school at Fort Holabird, Maryland, where he was trained in the techniques of interrogation:

> There was a heavy emphasis on Russian and Chinese military organization. A lot of bullshit that has nothing to do with what you need to know. And then you get into the basics of interrogation. Most of the good instructors were Germans; they had heavy German accents. They were good instructors; they had been in World War II. They were very much preoccupied with Europe, NATO, you know: "the Warsaw Pact crosses this river; we'll bring in the Eighth Army over here and we'll have 400,000 prisoners." What did that have to do with Vietnam? The rest of the instructors were dudes who had been to Vietnam as interrogators. The enlisted men who were instructors were short-timers with a few months left. They didn't give a flying fuck about anything. They just said, "Oh, it's a bunch of shit, man, just get by!" A typical short-time attitude; it just made me frustrated. If you have a lot of time left to do you can't stand the short-timers. You want to hit them. The basics of interrogation involve lines of questioning. You don't ask leading questions or "yes" or "no" questions. You don't say, "You have 40 men in your platoon, right?" One line of questioning is the direct questioning method. Then there's the Mutt and Jeff line, where one guy goes in and he's a real asshole. He starts slapping the prisoner and yelling at him, saying, "You're lying, we have information." After a few minutes, when the prisoner is supposedly scared shitless, another guy comes in with a higher rank,

ideally a higher insignia, and grabs the first guy off, throws him to attention, yells at him and says, "God damn it, you can't be doing this. We have rules against this. This guy is just an unfortunate victim of war," and all this crap. Then the second guy says to the prisoner, "Jesus, I'm sorry; here, have a smoke. What can I do?" Then you try to show him the futility of his obstinance. "Come on, you know you're just going to go to a prison camp for the rest of the war, so what the fuck . . ." Or, you simply try to prove to him that you know everything already. This is where your history of all the information you have on the enemy comes in. A good interrogator has to know it in his head. A lot of times you know as much about his unit as he does. They are always very careful in interrogation school not to mention anything like violence, torture, and lying. You're not supposed to go in there and say that you're a member of the Red Cross: "We have to fill out this form so that we can get in touch with your family." It's very much against the Geneva Convention, but it was a common practice in Vietnam.

The oral narrative begins to suggest the anomalous moral circumstance that the interrogator trainee experienced. Likewise he experienced the disintegration of morale. Such factors were important in shaping the emergence of psychic trauma. As luck would have it, Tim's transit to Vietnam was delayed so that he arrived in Vietnam a year later than his training led him to believe: "I was assigned to [Camp] Pendleton, to a unit of the 5th Marine Division. They had more interrogators than they needed to fill the slots in Vietnam so I sat around for about a year doing typical military bullshit—cutting hedges, standing inspections, climbing hills; it was horrible." This bad luck meant that the military was in greater decline and the impact upon Tim would, therefore, be that much greater.

It must be remembered that while Tim's account is uniquely his own, it fits into both the general military experience in Vietnam and into those areas of military specialty intrinsic to counterinsurgency intelligence operations. He had never told it before and came to oral narration with some suspicion and apprehension. Once his initial reluctance was overcome through support from another veteran friend who had been interviewed, he entered freely into his personal account whose effect, apart from the enthusiasm for memorialization, is the relief of discharging tightly contained and carefully guarded information.

I went to the 3rd Marine Division in May of '69; its headquarters was in Dong Ha near Quang Tri. I got assigned to an interrogation-translation team which is only about 15, maybe 20, people. There's a captain in charge and it's set up with a lieutenant and an enlisted man attached to each battalion. Before I joined the team, I had to go to headquarters company to get my rifle and blanket and see the first sergeant. He's got to get my ration card out of the safe. So I saw him and he says, "Jesus Lance Corporal, I'm making up the new mess duty roster." I was a real shit bird at Camp Pendleton; I'd been a lance corporal for two years. I said, "Oh fuck, just getting in and they put me on mess duty? Shit!" So I went back and told the staff sergeant, the team chief, who runs the place, and he says, "Okay, I'll give you a choice. You can either do mess duty for a month" (which sucks) "or you can go out to the bush. It's up to you." I said, "Okay, I'll go out in the bush." I had my fill of mess duty at Pendleton.

First I did a little interrogating for about three weeks at the Chu Hoi [defection] center in Quang Tri city which was run by Vietnamese. It was supposed to be an initiation [to interrogation] but Chu Hoi isn't. I had just gotten there, so I had expected to be interrogating soldiers; you know, "I'm sorry, I cannot say anything, Ho Chi Minh says that we cannot say this." But there are just old, don't-give-a-fuck people, just sliding along, inviting me for a beer across the street. Shit, they're just old people, getting by. After about three weeks, I went out in the field with First Battalion, Ninth Marines.

I was with the headquarters company at first and then, once we got up in the hills, I was with Charlie Company. We walked to the fire base and we stayed there for a while. Then we walked off the fire base and climbed around in the hills near the fire base. The bushes were really thick and the sides of the hill came down to a V. I'm with the colonel's staff. The fucking colonel said, "Walk right up through that V and go right up that hill." The lead squad stopped and that stopped the whole battalion—a thousand men walking along in line. And someone said, "Hey colonel, how about let's get some arty [artillery] or some air [force assaults] on these hillsides here. Those motherfuckers could be sitting up there with 50 cals. and if we're in the middle of the V we're fucked." And the colonel said, "No, we don't have time; we have to get to the top of that hill." It was late in the afternoon. The colonel's saying this from about 500 yards back. The Vietnamese can hear you coming 20 miles away. A whole platoon went in and they got opened up on with 50 cals. Everybody eventually scrambled up the hill, but nine people in the lead platoon got killed; I don't know how many people got wounded. I was at the top of the hill by the time the medivac chopper came sort of scooting in on the side of the hill.

I saw some OB-10 Broncos flying around spotting. Then the Phantoms came in. I figured the Vietnamese could have run away but I guess they didn't want to. The Phantoms dropped napalm; time and time and time again they came in—swoosh! We had to go in there the next morning. It was very thick jungle. Then all of a sudden there is a scorched clearing stripped of all foliage, with a shitload of bunkers all over the place.

I remember when I first walked up on one side of the hill, a half of a face was against this tree and there's a whole bunch of burnt bodies. Later on we were coming back up the other side. About five guys were in front of me and we'd stop every once in a while to rest 'cuz it was so hot. We walked two paces off the little path that the lead guy's making and found this North Vietnamese laying there all full of shrapnel. So, I got my first field interrogation. I'm supposed to be writing out this spot report to go to the regiment. And I got out this interrogation kit. All these spot reports were made on a mimeograph mechanism. There was a light rain, so I'd write and everything would run and I'd keep trying to do it over again. In the meanwhile, the colonel's standing over me: "Ask him this, ask him that." And we had Vietnamese interpreters, too. I was relying upon an interpreter. So the interpreter's trying to ask and the colonel's fucking with me and I'm trying to write and it's not writing. So I finally finished and we carried the dude up the hill. And the doc examined him and said, "He's fucked up, but he'll live in time for tonight's medivac."

Just before dusk they have a regular chopper that picks up all the routine medivacs. The doc had said, "He'll be all right until the medivac comes in." But this is in the morning. So I kept talking to him, "How old are you?" "17." "Umph." "I just got here." "What do you mean by here?" "I don't know." The interpreter didn't give a fuck about anything, he'd been doing this for years. Later the dude died; he just died. And the doc came over and said, "Shit, I don't know. He wasn't supposed to die; he should have lived." I remember, the thing about him dying got to me because time and time again from then on when a Vietnamese person would be wounded and the doc says, "He [or she] will be all right." And the doc isn't just saying that. Sometimes they are, but a real doctor, not a medic, a real doc will say, "Yeah, he will live," and then they die. I'd ask doctors, and they'd say, "God damn, I don't know. They just don't have the strength."

So I spent three weeks out in the bush that time and then me and another guy got assigned to the document translation center in Dong Ha. The E-6 staff sergeant, who had been running it all by himself, had been in [the service] 18 years and didn't give a fuck about anything except intelligence. He wasn't into shining shoes or anything like that, so he never got promoted; he always told people what he thought of them. His whole setup was just for him. We go in and try and figure out what's going on and we couldn't. You know, 4 million coffee cups laying around and papers piled this high and we had no idea what they were. If we ask him for something he can dig way down and pull it out. He knows right where it is. It's great for him. They wanted people who had an interest in the Vietnamese language, which I had. Not that I was that all-fired good, but most of the guys didn't give a fuck about the Vietnamese language, didn't give a fuck about Vietnam, they hated it. They wanted someone who would have the patience to sit down and figure out what all the captured documents said.

I worked at Dong Ha until August and then I went down to the Da Nang area. I got sent right out with Kilo Company, 326 Third Battalion, 26th Marines. Headquarters of Kilo Company sat on a hill on a big defense line outside of Da Nang. It was supposed to be in charge of this big flat area along this river. It was all paddies and there was a whole shit-load of hamlets there. And we were supposed to prevent VC [Vietcong] and North Vietnamese from coming into those hamlets and getting past them into Da Nang. So we sat out there about ten miles outside of the city. We went out on ambushes and worked with CAP [civil action patrols] units.

I tried to interrogate prisoners who were so shot up they couldn't even think or talk. A unit will go out somewhere and pick up someone and bring them in and say, "I've got a VC for you." According to the lingo, anyone who is picked up is a "detainee" first. So it was my job to classify this detainee according to the information I attained. And the classifications were "North Vietnamese prisoner of war," "VC prisoner of war," and civil defendant." "Civil defendant" is anyone who had at anytime worked for the enemy in any capacity other than carrying a weapon. If he was bearing a weapon that meant he was prisoner of war rather than a civil defendant. Civil defendants were tried, supposedly, by the military. After I turned them over to the South Vietnamese I only know what was supposed to have happened; I don't know what really happened. If they were guilty, they were either killed or went to prison.

Another classification is "innocent civilian," but they weren't just released. We had to bring them to district headquarters which is a level between village and province HQ. A district is sort of like county, I guess. According to the Geneva Convention, we were supposed to return innocent civilians to where they lived or where they were picked up. But I wasn't going to do it in a lot of cases because they were picked up in enemy territory. So I'm supposed to drive my jeep out and say, "Oh, we'll see ya"? Since it was impossible for us to drop somebody off, we brought them to district. The standard approach was to work them for a couple of weeks for no pay. A lot of times the person, after being an "innocent civilian," goes to district, works two or three weeks there, and then just walks down the road back to his village. On the way back he gets picked up again by the Americans and they bring him to me and I say, "What the fuck are you bringing him here for?" And they say, "God damn it, I've seen him before and there he is again. He's gotta be VC." So I try to explain the whole thing but it was too late, I couldn't just let him go. So he had to go through the whole thing all over again. It was one of those typical stupidities. Interrogations teams had their bitches about all the fuckups and what everyone else is doing to prisoners. They didn't follow any of the rules. That pissed us off. About 99 percent of the time they brought in "JSRs," Joe shit the ragman—you know, no one.

Up until the last quarter of my time in Vietnam I did feel that my whole justification for how I acted in interrogation, torturing and beating, and everything was justified by the fact that I could be saving lives. It was my job to get all the information possible. Also, us Americans were there to help the South Vietnamese people against these commies, these soldiers, this military that was trying to take them over. Interrogation in the broadest sense of slapping happened 90 percent of the time. The said slappee ended up slap-happy. My job is to make them very aware that I am in the position of superiority, that I hold their fate in my hand, which I did. I had to make them well aware of it. If they play along, they'll make out better than if they don't play along. And you just have to figure out where to draw that line. I never wanted to hit people; I didn't enjoy it; I found it very distasteful. But I found that it was very necessary. I didn't know if the person knew what I was looking for, but I thought that it was well worth trying every possibility to get it. Besides the physical torture, that included such things as filling out reports in a certain way. Take a Chu Hoi who had actually defected. I had the power to say in my report, "Source has not acted in the true faith of the Chu Hoi program. Therefore, I recommend that source's classification be changed to that of 'Prisoner of War.'" That's very heavy. That means a POW camp instead of freedom. I could initiate it and they would act upon these recommendations. I did this three times. I also felt in all three cases that they were not telling me all that they knew. I very much suspected that they were plants. I suspected that they were told to Chu Hoi, but weren't really Chu Hoi. It's impossible to prove. Supposedly the South Vietnamese intelligence would find out because they have informers. And they were finding some people who were plants.

The other forms that I have used, besides beating them up with my hands, was electricity. I'd attach two wires of a field telephone usually to the earlobe or the cheek or the temple, sometimes the balls or the crotch. It fucks them up. That's the next step after slapping. Doing it was usually up to the interrogator. You could make them stand at attention 24 hours a day and not let them move or with their hands out. You could put a stick behind their legs. I learned this in boot camp when they did it to us. Put your rifles behind your knees, and you had to bend back all the way with your head touching the ground. It fucks you up bad; it's just amazingly painful. It happened to me once in bootcamp. I would have done anything. If the DI said kill that man, I would have killed that man, really; it was horrible; I hated it. Well, we used that on them. Electricity, water, I never used the water. But other people did. But as I say, and I think I'm being honest with myself, I didn't feel this high moral purpose of doing these things but I felt that it was necessary. And I did not enjoy it.

The most important POW was a bona fide North Vietnamese soldier [NVA]. You could tell the difference between an NVA or VC by his haircut, by his clothes, by the sores on his body. You can tell any bush VC; he's skinnier than fuck and he looks like shit. He's out in the bush, so he gets cuts from the sharp grass and then over the cuts he gets jungle rot. GIs got these sores too, but GIs have medicine. You can tell he's North Vietnamese as soon as he opens up his mouth, by his accent.

Most POWs were wounded. And they all talked. I only saw one prisoner in the 20 months that I was there that didn't talk out of a couple thousand. They all talked their ass off. But they all lied their ass off, too, at first. I never got a North Vietnamese prisoner who wasn't wounded. What happened to a wounded prisoner was up to the interrogator. I would always have the doc work on him while I'm asking him preliminary questions for a spot report. And then I would decide whether or not I wanted him back at the hospital. If I felt that he had information that could be of use to the unit right there, if they needed tactical data I thought he had, then I would want him there, of course. But, given the circumstance of being out there in the bush, you can't do a thorough interrogation. You can ask questions but you don't have all your references, your order of battle, your information files. If you suppose he knows a fuck load of stuff, you really want him to live. So in that case, I would send him back. But I would also talk to the doctor. Nine times out of ten he'd say, "Huh, he'll live."

It was standard to use the fact he's wounded to make threats or give rewards: "That really hurts, but you can get it all fixed up if you just . . ." A lot of prisoners just resigned themselves to dying. It's pretty much impossible to deal with that. They would just tell you outright that they didn't give one flying fuck, "I'm dead, it doesn't matter. My leg is missing, there's no life for me." You are giving all these threats: "Look, you're not going to eat tonight." "I'm dying." "We won't work on you." "I'm dying." I would tell the doc not to work on him right then. I wouldn't do it if blood was gushing out all over, though. And touching wounds: You have to. I think North Vietnamese and VC expected interrogators to slap prisoners around. Innocent civilians didn't expect it. They didn't expect to get shot; they didn't expect to get picked up. So they're very surprised and scared.

Getting reliable info is called "making money." First off, you find out his unit. You know what units are in the area and have been in the area for a long time. So if he tells you 9th battalion, 36th regiment and if you know that 9th battalion, 36th regiment has been there for a fuck of a long time and it's no big deal, then you're not going to make any money. You can see you're not going to make any money after the follow up, "Why are you here?" They say, "I'm going to get some rice" rather than, "I'm leading an attack on Da Nang." You can make some money when you find out his unit is, say, the 3rd battalion, 575th regiment which, according to all your information, is 20 miles away. And you say to yourself, "What the fuck. Either he's lying or the unit's moved." That's something to sweat. So then you question him heavily about the unit's movement; you're checking this against what you already know. Your knowledge depends on other interrogations and captured documents. Some information comes from informers and from reconnaissance people—from Green Beret's and from CIA contingents. The VC and NVA have their table of organization and sectors of operation too. So you sum this up to see if it jibed with the information that you already had. That's mostly it. I worked at the NSA hospital in Da Nang, where your bona fide POWs are. That's where you get some good info. But it's all pretty historical. It's good for your files and builds up your information. You very seldom get anything like the 3rd battalion is going to attack such and such a place tonight. So you just have to keep pressing and even though you know that that person probably doesn't know about an attack. He may know something is coming up, though, and he'll admit that to you: "I don't know; we've been moving all over the place doing this and that." He could know something that fits your info. So that's the heavy part. You just have to keep hammering, going over everything again and again, trying to trip him, asking control questions. Personalities are the best control questions. You have a list of about ten names. You start a heavy interrogation. All of a sudden, without warning, you pop these names to catch him up. "Who is your platoon commander, who is the supply officer?"

If he tries to lie his way out of it and you get pissed off, you slap him around. And you tell him, "God damn it, you're not going to get out of this until you come across. What the fuck do you bother lying for? Let's have it." You do that with a straight POW. A straight POW knows that he's not going free so the only thing that you can give him is, say, "As soon as you get it over with, you can go back to the camp and lay down and eat rice." Whereas with an innocent civilian you can make promises like, "Oh, we'll bring you back to your village; we'll try and contact your long-lost brother." With a Civil Defendant you can tell him or her that you'll classify them "Innocent Civilian" and explain to them that if you classify them "Civilian Defendant" what's going to happen, probably get killed. You've got to make them aware that there is a way out. If you convince them that they're going to get killed, then they won't believe anything you say and they won't give a shit.

It is necessary to be really methodical by going over every little thing. This is the way to "make money." You find out a POW is from a particular front, which is like a whole province. Say he is from Front headquarters; he's been with the heavies and he knows "places." You're looking for where they are, so you can hit them. You concentrate on finding out where they are. So the dude is from 70-C, Front 4, which is the highest you could go in Quang Nam province. You know where he was picked up, so you try to find out why he was there, who was with him, what he was doing, where he was coming from, where his unit is, how many people, how is it set up, whether there are bunkers, how deep, how large, the exact measurements, how many rifles, how many rounds does each man have per rifle, how much they eat, what they've been discussing when they have their group discussions, what they've been doing, what the political officer's been telling them, everything. The main thing you want to know right there is where they are. To "make money" means finding out where they are and getting a hit. When you find out unit 70-C is at "X," you go up with your team commander to the colonel. Your team commander says, "They're right here," such and such six-digit coordinate, and if he believes you, then they'll do a bombing run. Usually they'll do a Phantom with Bronco spotter if it's a regular unit. If it's a listening post or something like that, they'll use helicopters. If it's a big unit, they'll use B-52s. And getting a B-52 strike is making the most money! This is where you find out how good you are and how much he lied. He could have been telling the truth and you could have just map-tracked wrong. It's a bitch. The map shows steep hills; it's all jungle and you've got to track them. It's an acquired skill.

I only had one B-52 strike. I don't know how many bodies they got. I got this info from a member of unit 70-C. He was a liaison communications officer. He had a radio and he knew that there was no way that he was going to lie his way out of it. He was a North Vietnamese in his early 30s from somewhere south of Hanoi. You could tell by his dialect. They can't lie about that. He had been in South Vietnam for about three years and in the army for a long time, a professional. He had to act as liaison with a guerrilla unit in the villages and the hamlets. He also picked out sites for rocket firings and hiding weapons, food and ammo and avenues of approach. After the air strike I went in to look. The bunkers have low roofs with logs and earth over the logs and they're only about one and a half feet deep and big enough for two people laying flat. The place was all fucked up. Maybe 20 dead people were found.

These were called Kingfisher operations. We'd scour all the sites where there had been firing. With the bodies we'd find documents. On this particular operation we were looking for this general. We used drawings of the dude from a description the prisoner provided— just like the police use. We didn't find the general's body and we assumed that he hadn't been hit. That's what we were trying for. We got a shit load of documents and a printing press putting out the VC province newspaper. There were no weapons, no radios; it was supposed to be a communications center. But to make money on a B-52 strike was unusual for me. Nine-tenths of the time I interrogated a Chu Hoi or a POW. He'd say, "such and such a unit there." Maybe "80 men are there" or "two tons of rice are hidden here." If he's a Chu Hoi, I'd go with a platoon or a company out to the spot with him leading the way. If it was a small unit we were concentrating on, we'd surround it and then hit it with arty. If it was a big unit, we'd hit it with air or arty or both, and then move in. Usually with big units we'd find a base camp and sometimes we'd get shot at.

Towards the end of my time in Vietnam a girl was brought in

who was about 16 or 17 years old. She lived in a village that was a free fire zone. Some of the people living out there wouldn't move. I started interrogating her. I was slapping her around the hooch and beating on her and she shit in her pants. She was very embarrassed. I was very conscious that she was very embarrassed. She was trying to wipe it up and hide it and it was impossible. How can she wipe it up? She didn't have anything to wipe it up with and she's trying to use the bottom of her pants. And I stopped. I said, "Where's your father?" "He's dead." "How was he dead?" "Killed by artillery." You hear this a million times. Always someone's killed by artillery. And so the next question, "Whose artillery?" And they look at you: "American," of course. I heard it a million times. Well, it just so happened that this time it just hit me, dong, *American*! Why are we killing all these people? These aren't soldiers. I'm beating on this girl and it all hit me. I'm beating up this girl, what for? Who am I? What the fuck am I doing? I just felt like shit. It was as if for the first time I was looking at myself. Here's this guy, slapping, beating on this girl, for what?

I wrote the girl up as an "Innocent Civilian." Plus she was fucked up. Her abdomen was swollen, I don't know what it is. A lot of women had the disease and they look like they're pregnant, but they're not. The corpsmen in the regimental aid stations were guys who had been out in the bush all the time with the grunts; they're a different breed. They hated gooks and they had the typical grunt attitude towards the Vietnamese people. So whenever you try to get care for any of your detainees, you weren't going to get it from them. I've seen corpsmen carry wounded Vietnamese out on a stretcher to the chopper and they'd be throwing them up. They wouldn't do it when officers were around. No one I ever knew thought about doing anything about it. I didn't like it, but I thought, those fucking corpsmen, just like those fucking grunts. Most of the doctors were different, though; they did their bit. They didn't seem to care whether they were working on a Vietnamese or on an American, though they would work on Americans first. So I tried to get treatment for this girl. And they said, "Well, she'll have to go out to Da Nang, you know." As a detainee she couldn't do that. Plus, I knew she'd have to be brought to district and I knew the district would either work her or fuck her. So I didn't really do anything. I asked if she could just be released, but that didn't mean anything. All it really meant was that for the first time I was looking at this person, a detainee, as a real human being, not as a source of information. I wasn't a very good interrogator from that time on. I lost all motivation.

The psychic trauma of individual veterans had its ultimate roots in the counterinsurgency character of the Vietnam War. Who is Tim? In oral history, the reader draws his or her own conclusions. But one thing is clear: in his capacity as translator-interrogator, Tim was what the military made him. With the sanction of the American public, his trauma was nothing less than a situational neurosis. The neurosis carried with it accompanying realizations that amounted to a resistance to the military mission. This phenomenon manifested itself throughout the military occupation of Vietnam during the middle and late war period. The realization that so many veterans have had that encouraged them to view the American military, not the Vietnamese communists, as the enemy is grounded in their particular experience of the war—in its contradictions and confusions and especially in the inhumanity that Americans as a people have been taught to abhor. Veterans like Tim were caught in a double bind: The Vietnam experience was exhilarating, awesome, dreadful, sickening. To survive it physically was elevating, but to return to "the world" from it in shame was humiliating. Shame, that special kind of guilt, made the Vietnam experience the veteran's personal problem. Tim's commitment to the military mission was thwarted by his humanness; for thousands of other veterans, whose experiences are generally analogous, their rejection of war policies was grounded in a very personal response to their presence in Vietnam. The shame that has been placed on them awaits some recompense just as they await a necessary adjustment that is ultimately political. Most of the veterans I have interviewed expressed the value of oral history as a kind of "political" therapy. They recognize that they are not only survivors of the war, but survivors of a political alienation that in some cases therapy can ameliorate but which no amount of therapy can cure. What therapy that does exist in the oral history process is contained in the cathartic response and in a rethinking of the veteran's situation. Much of that response requires the expression of anger as a desired end.

There is no escape from the experience of the war of the responsibilities for individual acts. For most veterans, the experience is indelibly etched into memories suspended in the preconscious and available for activation in given circumstances. By organizing and filtering these memories in an organized manner, oral history can allow for greater control in order that they not become explosively triggered. The viable alternative for the veteran is to gain perspective on the entire experience. Therefore, its most disastrous consequences can be mitigated. Oral history offers the veteran of the Vietnam War an important opportunity for the last word on who he is and what he was.

> I liked Vietnam. I extended six months for a number of reasons. I really dug walking or driving along and smelling all the different smells, seeing the people working in the rice field. I really dug it. I don't know why. Probably because every day was new. I loved to go someplace. There was always something new to see. I was always interested in everything that was going on. Everyday I'd learn some-

thing new about the language, about how they conceived things. Of course I realized that most Americans didn't give a fuck. I saw that this was the reason why we were doing some things that we should not have been doing. But that was the military. I had been in the military for two and a half years; it wasn't like I went to boot camp and right to Nam and didn't know. I knew the regular military was fucked up and that you were very lucky if anything got done right. I blamed it just on the inherent sloppiness and inefficiency of the military system rather than the fact that we shouldn't be there. I just accepted the supposed reason why we were there. I thought it was just the way we're doing it that was wrong. And then I switched over to: if we're doing it wrong then we shouldn't be doing it. More and more I realized how wrong we were. I was bummed out about my job. I really noticed it. This was around August of '70.

When I was stateside I was a shit bird; I didn't give a fuck about nothing. But when I got to Vietnam, all of a sudden after two and a half years I had this responsibility; people listened to me. I could save lives. If I could get this information, Jesus Christ, this could mean a lot. I had this status, it was a very heavy deal, a death deal. Couple this with the fact that I was speaking Vietnamese and having Vietnamese friends, I was really digging it. The vast majority of the Americans hate it. And all they ever talked about was buying a Corvette and being back home with Susie May. As far as I was concerned, I wanted to stay in Vietnam. My friends were mostly Arvin because that's who I came to know on a daily basis. I could identify more with them than with the VC because the VC were so alien. I never could become friends with them, but I tried. When I finished an interrogation, I wanted to shoot the shit with them to find out about them; it was interesting. And I'd say, "Okay, the interrogation's all over; have a cigarette and coke. How's things in Tun Hoa village." I realized it sounded like more interrogation and I really felt stupid, but I kept trying. A couple of times I tried it in the presence of the interpreter and the interpreter would just laugh. So I stopped. I wanted more than anything just to be a regular guy sitting there in the market, or sitting in my hooch, having a wife and kids. And not an American Marine. I just wanted to live there. This happened when I was with the First Marine Division northwest of Da Nang.

Later I was with 5th Marine Regiment southwest of Da Nang, An Hoa, the Que Song mountains, Dodge City, Indian country. I did a fuck of a lot of interrogating. That was Indian country; our base was near the town. Beyond that it was all free fire zone. In these areas the VC forces were really depleted. The First Marine Division had been there since '65. So there just weren't that many VC around. Their forces were beefed up by North Vietnamese. The North Vietnamese feel and act and seemingly are superior to the South Vietnamese in terms of organization. South Vietnamese were known to be lackadaisical and inefficient but the North Vietnamese aren't. The language of the North Vietnamese is zzzzzzz, hard, and the South Vietnamese is soft and there is less distinction between words. The North Vietnamese have bigger vocabularies and had more technical words. It seemed like communism had a lot to do with that. There was this friction between NVA and VC. They wrote reports to different units that we captured and I translated them. They'd say "North Vietnamese lieutenant so-and-so is getting double rations. We're getting a can and a half of rice a day. He's taking three cans a day and this has got to stop. It's screwing up our morale." The North Vietnamese would write reports that the guerrillas don't clean their rifles and are sloppy on patrol. I really dug translating those documents. And on the human side, the VC and the NVA all wrote poetry. Of course all Vietnamese write poetry. Every soldier has a goddamn poetry book; it's just a little notebook. And they're so goddamn mushy, sentimental, really fine. They're all writing about how far away from home they are and wishing they could see their moon rather than this strange moon and they miss the flowers of their home. I remember one, "Oh, Da Nang, I am in love with you." It was like Da Nang is a woman and they're gazing from the mountain at the lights of Da Nang and wishing they could be coupled together. It was really fine. I really dug it.

2

THE VICTORS AND THE
VANQUISHED

WILLARD WALLER

Who cared for the men who had risked their lives and bore on their bodies the scars of war? The pensions doled out to blinded soldiers would not keep them alive. The consumptives, the gassed, the paralyzed were forgotten in institutions where they lay hidden from the public eye. Before the war had been over six months "our heroes," "our brave boys in the trenches," were without preference in the struggle for existence. . . .

What knowledge had they of use in civil life? None. They scanned advertisements, answered likely invitations, were turned down by elderly men who said, "I've had two hundred applications. And none of you young gentlemen from the army are fit to be my office-boy." They were the same elderly men who had said, "We'll fight to the last ditch. If I had six sons I would sacrifice them all in the cause of liberty and justice."[1]

When they return to civil life, victors and vanquished are very much alike. Their skills are equally useless. They are equally unready for "the savage wars of peace."

This chapter has been abstracted from the author's book, *The Veteran Comes Back* (New York: Dryden, 1944), pp. 93–110; 180–82.

When the soldier returns to the home of which he has dreamed through the years of war, he finds it smaller, dingier, more sordid than he had ever imagined it to be, and his life within it is flavorless. Something has gone out of him that once gave zest to the old life, and there is nothing to take its place. The parents whom he has idealized seem strange to him; he cannot find words to talk with them, he cannot tolerate their well-meant ministrations. He is unwilling to accept his place in the economic world, not yet ready to tie himself to the drudgery of detail, not prepared at all to take up the sort of status for which his experience qualifies him.

Perhaps the soldier realizes that the lack is in himself. "The difficulty," says a young veteran recently discharged, "The difficulty, I find, is to regain those lost emotions which enable a man to take his place in civilian life. . . . I can understand now why members of the so-called 'lost' generation of the 1920's went to such extremes in their search for animation. It may sound like exaggeration, but I actually feel like a stranger in my own home, because everyday living in America requires emotional responses which I am incapable of giving."[2]

The literature of World War I contains many similar bits of introspection. A character of Jules Romains phrased it well:

I sometimes find myself wondering, in a sudden panic, whether I'm not in the way of developing great numb patches in my sensibility of which I shall never be cured—even if I do come through this war. Delicacy of feeling. What a wonderful expression! Shall I ever again know what delicacy of feeling is? I may be nervous, irritable, exasperated by trifles, but shall I ever recover that sensitiveness which is the mark of the civilized man? I sometimes see myself in the future transformed into a sort of invalid who has suffered an amputation of all his delicate sentiments, like a man who has lost all his fingers and can only feel things with a couple of stumps. And there will be millions of us like that.[3]

One of Erich Maria Remarque's characters becomes a school-teacher and has a moment of vivid awareness of his maladjustment in society, created by the disparity between what he knows and what he is supposed to teach.

Morning comes. I go to my class. There sit the little ones with folded arms. In their eyes is still all the shy astonishment of the childish years. They look up at me so trustingly. . . .
    What should I teach you then you little creatures, who alone have remained unspotted by the terrible years? What am I able to teach you then? Should I tell you how to pull the string of a hand-grenade, how

best to throw it at a human being? Should I show you how to stab a man with a bayonet, how to fell him with a club, how to slaughter him with a spade? Should I demonstrate how best to aim a rifle at such an incomprehensible miracle as a breathing breast, a living heart? Should I explain to you what tetanus is, what a broken spine is, and what a shattered skull? Should I describe to you how brains look when they scatter about? What crushed bones are like—and intestines when they pour out? Should I mimic how a man with a stomach wound will groan, how one with a lung wound gurgles and one with a head wound whistles? More I do not know. More I have not learned.

Should I take you to the brown and green map there, move my fingers across it and tell you that here love was murdered? . . .

About your brows still blows the breath of innocence. How then should I presume to teach you? Behind me, still pursuing, are the bloody years. . . . How then can I venture among you. Must I not first become a man again myself?[4]

THE SOLDIER COMES HOME ANGRY

The soldier is glad to come home, but he comes home angry.

In the early months of 1919, the writer talked with a great many other demobilized soldiers on Chicago streets. Although he had felt something of the service-man's rebellion, he was astonished as any civilian at the intensity of their fury. They were angry about something; it was not clear just what. The writer questioned many of them, but found no one who could put his grievances into understandable form. But there was never any mistaking their temper. They hated somebody for something. There were angry men on West Madison Street in 1919, and, as one learned later, there was rancor on Market Street in St. Louis and at Eighth and Race in Philadelphia, and in all the little angry knots where soldiers gathered were bitterness and disillusion and discontent.

These men, these veterans-on-the-street, the reader remarks, were hardly typical veterans. That is true; they were a sort of residue of men whom industry had not employed and family and community life had not yet reabsorbed. They were not average veterans. But we can best understand the average by studying the reactions of extreme cases; the statistically unusual man may be representative; he may stand for something, express something that is in us all; and so it seems to be with veterans.

The attitude of these men was puzzling, even to one who participated in a milder way in their feelings. Not one of them was able to explain why he felt as he did. For years the writer has been trying to puzzle it out and to understand what these inarticulate men wanted to say. In order to make sense of what they said it has been necessary to find words for them, to supply logic for their grievances, to sort out and throw away minor grievances in the attempt to penetrate to the great feelings of injustice from which these smaller complaints arose. When, some years after 1919, the war novels and autobiographies began to appear, they were helpful, especially for the verbalization of attitudes, but for the most part they merely expressed and recorded attitudes and stated the reasons for them only by inference. Still it is a contribution to express a complex state of mind clearly, and novels are very valuable in this respect, even though they have little utility as proof. Autobiographies, of course, have greater value as evidence.

Perhaps the reader, in his struggle to understand the soldier's bitterness, should start with what the returned soldiers said on West Madison in 1919. They said, specifically, "God damn the obscenity obscenity obscenity! Of all the obscenity obscenity raw deals! The obscenity obscenity obscenities!" They said, "The next war, if they want me, they'll have to burn the woods and sift the ashes." They said, with a knowing wink, "The next war, they'll be two guys don't go, me and the guy they send after me." They said, "Brother, I've had a belly full!" For 25 years the writer has been trying to decipher the meaning of their inarticulate rage.

Whom does the soldier hate? Jules Romains has an excellent answer, so far as it goes.

> If you were to ask me who it is we despise and hate the most, whom it would give us the greatest pleasure to punish, my answer would be: First of all, the war profiteers, business men of all kinds, and, with them, the professional patriots, the humbugs, the literary gents who dine each day in pajamas and red leather slippers, off a dish of Boche. . . . Next in order come the soldiers who have worked themselves into nice safe jobs, officers for the most part. They form a very special category—fellows who are lucky enough to have been posted to some back-area town, twenty or thirty miles behind the line, where they are in no greater danger than you are in your boot store, but play the brave soldier and say, "We in the trenches." Those are the men who put in a claim for decorations, and who get them—before we do. They'd be perfectly happy if the war went on for ten years. Never in their lives have they touched so many perquisites as now. And don't they love one another! Their time is as much taken up with intrigues, back-biting and plots as the most squalid of peace-time garrisons! The worst offenders are the regulars, the men who deliberately chose the army as a calling in the days before the war, but who now when we civilians are asked to spill our blood, just take to cover. Their fellow soldiers hate them as bitterly as we do. Who else shall I mention?

Certain ambitious generals, with hearts of stone, to whom the lives of thousands or tens of thousands mean nothing if, by sacrificing them they can assure their own advancement, or, moved by slightly less selfish motives, carry through pet schemes of their own. . . . Oh, but I was forgetting perhaps the most symbolic of all these back-area figures, the well-set gentleman of a certain age, in a nice warm suit, freshly bathed and pomaded who sips his chocolate and reads the communiques and says: "Damn slow progress. Trouble is the Staff's too timid. The important thing is to know when to make sacrifices."[5]

Some of these hatreds are readily understandable. Others might require further elucidation. But they are all real. American soldiers felt the same way in 1919.

Why is the soldier angry? Because he was the one singled out to fight and die and suffer and see horrors. He feels akin to everyone who has suffered as he has, even the enemy; he hates everyone who has not. There is a famous speech to this effect in *What Price Glory?*

Oh God, Dave, but they got you. God, but they got you a beauty, the dirty swine. God damn them for keeping us up in this hellish town! Why can't they send in some of the million men they've got back there and give us a chance? Men in my platoons are so hysterical every time I get a message from Flagg, they want to know if they're being relieved. What can I tell them? They look at me like whipped dogs—as if I had just beaten them—and I've had enough of them this time. I've got to get them out, I tell you. They've had enough. Every night the same way. And since six o'clock, there's been a wounded sniper in the tree by that orchard angle crying "Kamerad! Kamerad!" Just like a big crippled whip-poor-will. What price glory now? Why in God's name can't we all go home! Who gives a damn for this lousy, stinking little town but the poor French bastards who live here? God damn it! You talk about courage, and all night long you hear a man who's bleeding to death on a tree calling you "Kamerad" and asking you to save him. God damn every son of a bitch in the world who isn't here![6]

In the same play is another speech, almost as eloquent, by Flagg:

Show him, Kiper. Damn headquarters! It's some more of that world-safe-for-democracy slush! Every time they come around here I've got to ask myself is this an army or is it a stinking theosophical society for ethical culture and the Bible-backing uplift! I don't want that brand of Gideons from headquarters. Now you watch that door. Watch it! In ten minutes we're going to have another of these round-headed gentlemen of the old school here giving us a prepared lecture on what we're fighting the war for and how we're to do it—one of these bill-poster chocolate soldiers with decorations running clear around to his

backbone and a thrilling speech on army morale and the last drop of
fighting blood that puts your drive over to glorious victory!. . . The
side-whiskered butter-eaters! I'd like to rub their noses in a few of the
latrines I've slept in keeping up army morale and losing men because
some screaming fool back in the New Jersey sector thinks he's playing
with paper dolls.[7]

It is easy to understand why the soldier hates the young man of his
own age who manages somehow to escape military service. The draft
board in its wisdom decides that Tom Jones must go to war, and off goes
Tom to be a soldier. But Henry Smith, who lives next door, has had the
foresight to get entrenched in a necessary industry; he stays at home,
works for high wages, wins a promotion, gets married, and buys a little
home in the suburbs. When Tom returns, Henry is still a necessary man
in industry, still entrenched; he keeps his job and Tom goes on relief.
The soldier's animosity toward such people is deep and powerful. After
World War I they were known as slackers. When it was discovered that
Jack Dempsey had suffered through World War I as a shipyard worker,
he became so unpopular that he was jeered on the city streets. (The
fight promoters were able to turn this unpopularity to good use by
arranging a match with Carpentier, who was a glamorous veteran but
did not belong in the same ring with Dempsey.)

Not only the soldier, but all his relatives and friends take up the
burden of such feelings of hostility. There is no resentment deeper than
that of the mother whose son has been taken when some other
mother's son has been left behind. And if her son dies, she carries that
hatred to her grave. There is no way of avoiding such injustices except
by taking every member of an age group, say from 18 to 25, exempting
only those with such obvious physical defects as a missing leg or arm,
and allowing no one to stay home because he is a medical or engineering
student or a shipyard worker or the sole support of eleven children. We
are apparently moving toward such an arrangement, and after a few
more wars we may attain it. Our current draft arrangements are
infinitely fairer than those of the Civil War. During that conflict, the
reader will remember, a conscripted man could hire a substitute to fight
for him, or he could buy himself off for only $300. (This was a survival
of the medieval custom of scutage.) The Civil War was truly a rich
man's war and a poor man's fight. These arrangements provoked deadly
riots, probably the worst in American history, in that great European
city on the banks of the Hudson—never a center of martial spirit except
in time of peace. Troops were rushed to the city, their ears still roaring
from the Battle of Gettysburg, to quell the riots. Apparently the riots
were successful: the draft thereafter received only nominal enforce-

ment in New York.[8] We have had nothing of quite that sort in subsequent wars.

Scarcely less violent is the soldier's hatred for that other soldier who manages to wangle for himself a safe position behind the lines. The soldiers particularly resent officers in this category, those swivel-chair heroes who distinguish themselves in the Battle of Washington, which, we are to understand, is a fierce and sanguinary engagement. There are young men who have secured commissions in the Navy although "the only ship they have ever seen is a junior partnership," who have never missed a meal or a night of sleeping with their wives, who yet have become very nautical, even salty, in their language and are accustomed to welcome their guests of the evening by saying, "I'm very glad you are on board tonight." In World War I there were other dashing and intrepid gentlemen who wore spurs the better to control their plunging swivel-chairs, or side-arms to protect themselves against the hazards of Washington streets. For such men, determined never to risk their necks during the war and equally determined to play the hero afterwards, the soldier has an abiding contempt. But there is nothing he can do about it; the swivel-chair heroes will be heroes just the same. These embusques will always win; they will have their safety and their glory too.

The soldier is angry because he knows the war is bitter hard for him, and at the same time realizes that for many of the people back home it is a distinctly pleasant experience. While soldiers die, speculators and profiteers get rich, and politicians make capital of campaigns that cost the lives of many men. Workers at home draw fabulous wages and still go on strike, as many of the soldiers believe, for frivolous reasons. The soldier resents the striker more than he does the profiteer, because what the striker does is readily visible, and besides, the striker is a man from his own world, a man with whom he can compare himself, while the profiteer remains a rather shadowy figure. The soldier resents the dancing and the gaiety of the people at home, and remarks bitterly that he can hold out, he can stand anything, but he does hope that the civilians at home manage to keep up their morale.

> Miners were striking for more wages, factory hands were downing tools for fewer hours at higher pay, the government was paying any price for any labor—while Tommy Atkins drew his one-and-twopence and made a little go a long way in a wayside estaminet before jogging up the Menin road to have his head blown off. . . .
>
> In all classes of people there was an epidemic of dancing, jazzing, card-playing, theatre-going. They were keeping their spirits up wonderfully. Too well for men slouching about the streets of London on leave, and wondering at all this gaiety, and thinking back to the things

they had seen and forward to the things they would have to do. People at home, it seemed, were not much interested in the life of the trenches; anyhow, they could not understand. . . .

The British soldier was gay and careless of death—always. Shell-fire meant nothing to him. If he were killed—well, after all, what else could he expect? Wasn't that what he was out for? The twice-married girl knew a charming boy in the air force. He had made love to her even before Charlie was "done in." These dear boys were so greedy for love. She could not refuse them, poor darlings! Of course they had all got to die for liberty, and that sort of thing. It was very sad. A terrible thing—war. . . . Perhaps she had better give up dancing for a week, until Charlie had been put into the casualty lists.[9]

My mental attitude towards the war had changed. Whatever romance and glamour there may have been had worn off. It was just one long, bitter waste of time—our youth killed like flies by "dugouts" at the front so that old men and sick might carry on the race, while profiteers drew bloated profits and politicians exuded noxious gas in the House. . . .

How *dared* they have valets while we were lousy and unshaved, with rotting corpses round our gun wheels? How *dared* they have wives while we "unmarried and without ties" were either driven in our weakness to licensed women, or clung to our chastity because of the one woman with us every hour in our hearts whom we meant to marry if ever we came whole out of that hell?[10]

The soldier is bitter because civilians see the glamour of war and gloss over its ugliness by beautiful speeches. Remarque's ex-soldiers make reply to the principal of their school in the following passages:

The Old Man's voice sinks to a minor. It puts on mourning, it drips unction. A sudden tremor passes over the black flock of masters. Their faces show self-control, solemnity.——"But especially we would remember those fallen sons of our foundation who hastened joyfully to the defense of their homeland and who have remained upon the field of honor. Twenty-one comrades are with us no more—twenty-one warriors have met the glorious death of arms; twenty-one heroes have found rest from the clamor of battle under foreign soil and sleep the long sleep beneath the green grasses——"

There is a sudden, booming laughter. The principal stops short in pained perplexity. The laughter comes from Willy, standing there, big and gaunt, like an immense wardrobe. His face is red as a turkey's, he is so furious.

"Green grasses—Green grasses!"—He stutters. "Long sleep? In the mud of shell holes they are lying, knocked rotten, ripped in pieces, gone down into the bog—Green grasses! This is not a singing lesson!" His arms are whirling like a windmill in a gale. "Hero's death! And what sort of thing do you suppose that was, I wonder? Would you like to know how young Hoyer died? All day long he lay out in the wire screaming, and his guts hanging out of his belly like macaroni. Then a bit of shell took off his fingers and a couple of hours later another chunk off his leg, and still he lived; and with his other hand he would keep trying to pack back his intestines, and when night fell at last he was done. And when it was dark we went out to get him and he was full of holes as a nutmeg grater.—Now you go and tell his mother how he died—if you have so much courage. . . .

"Mr. Principal," says Ludwig in a clear voice, "you have seen the war after your fashion—with flying banners, martial music, and with glamour. But you saw it only to the railway station from which we set off. We do not mean to blame you. We, too, thought as you did. But we have seen the other side since then, and against that the heroics of 1914 soon wilted to nothing. Yet we went through with it—we went through with it because there was something deeper that held us together, something that only showed up out there, a responsibility perhaps, but at any rate something of which you know nothing and about which there can be no speeches."

Ludwig paused a moment, gazing vacantly ahead. He passes his hand over his forehead and continues. "We have not come to ask a reckoning—that would be foolish; nobody knew then what was coming. But we do require that you shall not again try to prescribe what we shall think of these things. We went out full of enthusiasm— the name of the "Fatherland" on our lips—and we have returned in silence, but with the thing, the Fatherland, in our hearts. And now we ask you to be silent too. Have done with fine phrases. They are not fitting. Nor are they fitting to our dead comrades. We saw them die. And the memory of it is still too near for us to abide to hear them talked of as you are talking. They died for more than that.[11]

How the soldier hates the men of talk, especially those who prattle of ideals and honor and fighting for the right! An explicable attitude? Not at all. Because the soldier has come to believe, and with considerable reason, that those who talk about ideals do not fight for them, and that those who fight for them do not talk about them. The soldier knows that when the nation fights for freedom and for justice in far-flung areas of the world, he must lose his freedom, his comfort, even his identity for the duration of the conflict. The ideals for which he is fighting can have little meaning for any soldier so long as the war lasts, while for those who die and for many of the wounded they can never have any meaning at all. He knows that those who speak so glibly of ideals have no conception of what the process of enforcing those ideals means in terms of pain and starvation and death and horror; perhaps he comes to realize that for many civilian orators, fighting for ideals, being "alert to the danger" was a very good business and a short road to promotion and pay. Perhaps the soldier returning from this war will be told that few of the really vocal Hitler-haters ever managed to get near the front line, that none of them ever missed a meal, and all of them will die in bed after they are heavy with years. Possibly he will hear once more the bitter jest that a patriot is a man who is always willing to lay down his life for his country, while an orator is willing to lay down your life for his country.

When the British had won the great victory at El Alamein, the civilian populace rejoiced, but the sound of their rejoicing as it came in over the radio did not make the soldiers happy. It seemed a little premature to the soldiers, because they were still in the desert, they were still suffering from flies and dirt and heat and cold and hunger, and they were still getting killed by Stukas. For the soldiers victory or defeat meant just another battle with an enemy who was still full of fight.[12]

When the soldier comes home, he hears his victories extolled by an unctuous radio announcer who has taken good care of himself during the conflict, and he thinks that the announcer is just a "cheap chiseller" who is trying to "muscle in" on the soldier's prestige, and it is a little sickening to hear him "make cracks" about what we are doing, have done, or are going to do to the little yellow devils in the Pacific and talk between whiles of bath salts and a superduper cereal which will help the war production.

Perhaps the soldier returns to college, and learns about America's predestined role as the savior of the world from an amiable gentlemen who takes all his opinions from the liberal press—the very best opinions, mind you—who can never be quite sure what he thinks of anything until he has read the latest copy of *The New Republic*, having devoted his best thought for twenty years to just one subject, and that being the best method of cleaning a pipe, a subject upon which he expended all the ingenuity of his fertile brain when the war produced a shortage of implements designed for that purpose. Or perhaps the soldier goes to his philosophy class and learns that human beings must always be treated as ends, and must never, never, never be treated as means; yet he knows very well that while he was a soldier he was only a means and not an end at all, and as for those who died in the war, well, that was an end of their being either an end or a means.

The returned soldier of any mental level is less enthusiastic than he might be about a program to furnish a quart of milk for every Hottentot child when he himself has been living on indescribably vile powdered eggs and an execrable brand of canned meat. If he is intelligent, he may begin to question the whole species of humanitarianism which leads A and B to decide to send C to fight D for the sake of very problematic benefits to E, while A and B, if they really wish to further human welfare, have only to cease and desist from persecuting F and G.

And the veteran knows that these men of words, who irritate him so much and are so often in his way, could not have lasted very long or amounted to much in the world in which he has been living. As one young soldier recently remarked, and as many said in 1919, "A smash of a gun butt over the head would soon dispose of ———, of him and all his thoughts and clever tricks. Such and such, an illiterate truck driver, is a better man than he is."

One day the soldier will be subject once again to men of talk—perhaps he never escapes them at all—but they will be men who express to him his own prejudices, men who talk against talk, politicians who denounce politics, and such men are exceedingly dangerous. In his disdain of men of words, men who make their living through the little shams, poses, and hypocrisies of the world, the soldier is more than half right. But he does not realize that our society could not exist without such men and that the men of talk whom the soldier chooses as his very own are likely to be ten times worse than the others. Here, as elsewhere, the soldier's anger is reasonable, at least nine-tenths justified, but its expression is often unreasonable.

In the end, the soldier is almost certain to feel that his sacrifices have not been fully appreciated. There is a brief period of glory in which those who have done least and come home first play the greater part. The soldier receives the grateful thanks of the nation, and that is all. He finds himself left behind and permanently disadvantaged in competition.

HOW FAR IS THIS BITTERNESS JUSTIFIED?

In considerable part the soldier's bitterness is justified. He has been the victim of the worst injustice that any modern civilized society visits upon its members. He has given everything and received very little in return, nothing in fact except a highly perishable kind of glory. At no point does the conflict between the individual and society become more intense than with regard to military service. A notice of induction is for most young men a sentence to hard labor, and for some a sentence of death; for others, it is a sentence to lose a limb or an eye—disfigurements that no civilized society can now impose as a punishment for crime—at least it is distinguished from these things only by the fact that it is associated not with disgrace but with honor. The concepts of honor and duty have been invented to make such sacrifices acceptable. What, then, if the honor that is the soldier's due in the bargain be withheld? What if the Purple Heart or the Croix de Guerre become equivalent in a few years to the little bronze medal that the eight-year-old child receives for attending Sunday School on twenty-six successive Sundays? What if the veteran, in his need, must pawn his medal for heroism in order to buy food for himself and his children? The windows of America's pawnshops were full of medals for heroism in the nineteen-twenties.

"It is true," says Lorenz von Stein, "that victory brings to the sum total of the State, to the people, the highest profits, whereas at the same time it remains forever unable to restore to the individual what it has taken from him."[13] At the very least, the state has taken from the soldier some years of his youth, and it can never give them back.

The essential injustice to the soldier inheres in the fact that a competitive society decides to fight a war. Less injustice is involved when a socialistic society fights a war. In a hypothetical communist state, which would take from each according to his abilities and give to each according to his needs, there would be no injustice at all in taking a man for a soldier. There is, as Quincy Wright has noted, a natural affinity between socialism and war: "States at war have tended to become socialistic and socialistic states have tended to be at war."[14] Wright comments further that socialistic economies have produced the most warlike states of history, citing, among other examples, the socialistic empires of Assyria and Peru as well as socialistic Sparta.[15] Along the same line is Powell's conclusion that autocracies have seemed to suffer less from veterans' problems than free societies.[16]

The social arrangements of modern America are such as to guarantee that we cannot wage war without inflicting the maximum of injustice upon the soldier. Ours is a competitive society. Every man is supposed to take care of himself.* It is part of the virtue, and almost the whole of virtue, for a man to try to get ahead in the world. The essential American idea is that it is possible for a man to rise to a high position through industriousness, that the status which a man attains in society adequately reflects his ability and conscientiousness. All we ask of the young man is that he work and make the most of his abilities. He is brought up to believe that this is his full social duty. In ordinary times, military service is no part of what one owes to the world. In periods of peace, we are inclined to hold the soldier in disrepute. We turn much of the work of education over to pacifists thus conditioning our young men against military service. What is even more fatal is that the soul of our society is civilianism, which, rather than pacifism, is the true antithesis of militarism.[17]

When war comes, we take these young men trained for peace and

---

*Our society is really a competitive, familistic society, the family being the competing unit, a unit in which competition is not supposed to take place; but that does not matter for the present argument.

send them off to fight. Having conditioned our young men to compete and to look to their own interests, we compel them to sacrifice their personal good and their personal lives to the collective good. They could hardly have been worse prepared for the experience of war. We remove them from the competitive society for which they have been trained, and demand of them services and sacrifices that can really be justified only in a communal society in which each person lives for others. Then, with a pat on the back and some hypocritical words of praise, we return them to competitive society where, for a time at least, they compete at a considerable disadvantage.

If we took all the young men of a generation, that would seem less unfair to the soldier. And though he would still be disadvantaged in comparison with other age groups, his own generation would start even. However, we do not take all the members of an age group by any means. We grant full exemption from military service to many men who have minor physical defects. We reject many others for minor psychoneurotic disorders. We exempt others because they have special skills of use in war production—or are thought to have such special skills—and we excuse many others, less defensibly, because of the essential jobs they hold in war industries, even though their skills are admittedly not particularly great. We grant exemptions to some in special cases because of family obligations. When so many can escape, the one who is ordered to serve has some reason to feel abused. All this, of course, is part of the fundamental injustice of the situation. No one is personally responsible. No one planned it that way. Draft boards and others have done their best to administer our intrinsically inequitable laws in a just manner.

While the man selected for military service is giving his time to the collective effort, others forge ahead in the competitive race of civilian life. Imagine a foot race in which a hundred performers start even, all with high hopes of winning. When the race has just begun, we take a few of the runners out of the race and demand that they fix the track. We keep adding to our labor force in the same way until we have removed about half the contestants. When the work is over and the laborers are fatigued, we release them in the same haphazard way, give them our hearty thanks, and tell them to resume the race. That is the way the system works.

While we were away, as Vera Brittain put it, "others stayed behind and just got on—got on the better since we were away." The absence of the soldiers and the demands of war industries have created the best labor market of a generation. What a labor market! According to information received from confidential sources, the average IQ of persons hired by a large defense plant in late 1943 was in the middle eighties (84)—the average IQ. The average weekly pay of these intellectual giants, who were also, of course, completely untrained, was about $11, at the start, with more to come later, naturally.

What the soldier believes is not, of course, wholly and unqualifiedly true. It is easy to understand why the soldier resents the high wages of war workers, and yet the advantage is not always on the civilian side in financial matters. Many civilians with fixed incomes, notably white collar workers, have been severely pinched by rising prices and taxes. Even the war workers do not fare so well as the gross earnings indicate; there are deductions to be considered: union dues, the social security tax, the withholding tax, and the bond purchases, which are obligatory in most war industries. While the soldier's apparent income is low, allowances for his family are considerable and are free of taxes. Furthermore, soldiers in certain types of service are paid at rates which compare favorably with war industry and some young officers, especially in the air corps, undoubtedly touch more perquisites than they are likely to attain in civilian life for many years. When we consider these things, the comparative position of the soldier is less unfavorable than the uncorrected figures would indicate, although the *net advantage is still on the side of the civilian in the majority of cases*. Furthermore, it is unlikely that the veteran will be interested in refined calculations of comparative advantage. He will be convinced that he has received a raw deal, and there will be evidence enough to support his case.

While stating the soldier's grievances, we should note that it is not necessarily the common soldier who is most set back in the struggle of life. Sometimes the officer is badly used. Doctors who have been taken into the service have often received very unjust treatment. A young doctor, aged thirty-three, was taken from a small city in up-state New York. He had educated himself at his own expense and had struggled for several years to build up a practice. He was, therefore, a business man with a considerable investment. Before the war, his practice was worth about $7000 a year, clear profit. The army made him a first lieutenant at $3300 a year. In order not to break up his family, he is consuming his savings, while his wife and children lead a most unsatisfactory existence in various training camp communities. If he had remained a civilian, his practice would be worth $15,000 a year. When the war is over, he must start again to build it up. Many thousands of other doctors will also be returning to practice, and will compete with him. This young doctor has lost nearly everything, gained nothing, not even, as he believes, any experience of value. If he should be killed in the service, his wife and children would be very poorly provided for.

When the soldier returns to civilian society, he is at a disadvantage for some time. His skills and attitudes are not applicable to civilian life.

Undoubtedly the great majority of soldiers manage to overcome their initial handicap, and perhaps, because of the various preferences given to the veteran, some of them do a little better in competition than they might otherwise have done. A great many soldiers, however, do worse in competition because of their military service. The disabled have been really handicapped; and we recognize this and try to compensate them for it. Others have been injured in more subtle ways, and it is difficult to assess and evaluate their damages.

In every competition, however, some must fail. Some veterans fail because of what war has done to them. Others would fail anyhow. But all have a perfect excuse for failure, more than an excuse—an unsettled claim upon society. Because they once wore the uniform of their country, they feel that their country must take care of them. The problem of justice is to separate those who have a valid claim from those who have not.

HOW LONG DOES THIS BITTERNESS LAST?

As in any other group of people, there is a wide range of variation in the attitudes of veterans. There is a core of anger in the soul of almost every veteran, and we are justified in calling it bitterness, but the bitterness of one man is not the same thing as the bitterness of another. In one man it becomes a consuming flame that sears his soul and burns his body. In another it is barely traceable. It leads one man to outbursts of temper, another to social radicalism, a third to excesses of conservatism. Much depends upon the veteran's temperament, upon where and under what circumstances he served, and upon his experiences after he is released from service.

The veteran who suffers little inconvenience in readjusting to the world of civilian society usually recovers rapidly. If he returns to his former job, and is contented there, that helps, although he may still be angry because others have received promotions while he was away. If his family is undamaged by war, and his community and friends receive him graciously and take care of him, those things help too. If he was originally a stable personality, it is less likely that he has developed an outlook that will seriously interfere with readjustment. If after the war he becomes a success in life, there is little likelihood that he will be permanently embittered.

Even in the most favorable cases, however, it seems probable that the veteran's anger does not disappear altogether. Instead, the residues of resentment are redirected into different channels, usually into channels of class, race, and religious antagonism. Whomever a man would naturally hate, he hates a little more because he has been a soldier. After the war, the soldier's sympathy with the enemy, born of the heat of conflict, apparently weakens for a time and is replaced by hatred, although the veteran's hatred of the enemy is often less keen than his hostility toward his former allies.

If the veteran does not adjust to society, his bitterness persists through the years. Some veterans are unable to adjust because of disability, and it is understandable that they should cherish a lasting resentment because of this fact. Other veterans merely fail in competition and in life for reasons which have nothing to do with military service; they are the improvident, the unstable, the foolish, the stupid and the wrongheaded, the luckless ones who would have failed anyhow, the men who never would have been able to hold their jobs, their friends, their wives, or their self-respect. Now if these men had never been in an army, they would have no socially acceptable excuse for failure. Since they have been in the army, they can hang all their feelings of guilt and resentment upon that peg, blame the war for everything that has gone wrong with their lives, the jobs they lost, the wives who betrayed them, the employers who bullied them, the friends who drifted away. The veterans who made up the Bonus Expeditionary Force of 1932 were just such pitiful maladjusts who had found a good excuse for failure. Failure to help the veteran in the post-war years leaves him with an unsettled claim upon society and thus facilitates this sort of rationalization.

The normal veteran who adjusts well to civilian life usually finds himself thinking rather pleasantly of his war in a few years. He never forgets the comradeship of men at arms and never ceases to think of it with a certain warmth. And, in time, he learns that there are a few real rewards in being a veteran. As a veteran, he has a place in society; some honor comes to him because he once served his country in time of war.

VETERANS ARE IMMIGRANTS IN THEIR NATIVE LAND

The task of assimilating the veteran into the community is one of reincorporating him in the communicative process, placing him economically in such a way as to make the best use of his abilities, tying him down by membership in the family and other groups, and arranging for him to take his part in the political deliberations of the community. When the veteran returns to the civilian world, his situation is a sort of immigrant in his native land. He is like the immigrant because he has no sure and settled place in society and because he derives many, if not most, of his social satisfactions from the company of others of his own kind; partly because he prefers their society and partly because he does not fit in anywhere else.

The analogy with the immigrant suggests that the tendency of veterans to stick together for a time is not altogether unhealthy. Paradoxical as it may seem, the best way for veterans to establish relations with the rest of society may be for them to cling to their own group, to cleave to their own kind, *for a while*. The society of veterans will thus furnish a sort of causeway leading to normal readjustment and the veterans will more quickly attain the goal of normal community relations if they make haste slowly.

Our experience with immigrants demonstrates clearly that groups of aliens tend to be assimilated together, and that it is best that it should be so. Early students of immigration were often concerned over the fact that many immigrants cling to their native culture, settle in their own cultural islands, develop their own institutions, have their own banks, schools, churches, social and business associations and even their own newspapers. In this way they seem to resist assimilation. Many persons still believe that it would be better if these immigrants gave up their old culture at once and immersed themselves immediately in the main currents of American life. However, studies of immigrants have repeatedly shown that a period of clinging to the old culture is useful, and that the associations of the foreign-born can read about American political struggles and become familiar with other American ideas than for the native-born to be completely unable to communicate with the immigrants. Furthermore, these foreign colony institutions lessen the degree of personal disorganization in the immigrant. The priest and the elders of the community must speak to the immigrant in his native tongue if they are to reach him at all, and even his economic adjustment may be easier if he makes it in the company of his countrymen.

The analogy with veterans is clear. We must attempt to assimilate the veterans in groups as well as individually. If veterans form their own organizations, which they have a great penchant for doing, then those organizations can be incorporated into the pattern of community life and the veterans with them. Opposition to the veterans' organizations, which has arisen so often in the past, will not prevent those organizations from existing but it may alienate the veteran group from the rest of society.

A further clue furnished by the immigrant analogy concerns the importance of participation in assimilation. We have learned that the key to the assimilation of the immigrant is participation. Here the contrast between European and American methods of assimilation is illuminating. In Europe embittered struggles have taken place for many generations over just one issue, Who is to oppress whom? When one nation has conquered and annexed another, it has often tried to annihilate the culture of the subject people, that is, to assimilate the conquered people by force to the people of the conquerors. If one thing is clear from the study of history, it is that such methods do not work. The Poles have been Germanized and Russianized for many generations, but they remain Poles, the Czechs are stubbornly Czech no matter what the language of their conquerors. In America, none of that. No force. Opportunity. We allow our immigrants to be as foreign as they wish, but we insist that their children be educated and we permit them to send their children to the public schools. If aliens desire to do so, they may become citizens and vote in our elections, but no one forces them to take this step. If immigrants organize themselves into associations, our politicans will bargain with those associations and thus persuade a whole new group of foreign-born to participate in American life. And so it comes about that a free country—albeit corrupt and materialistic—accomplishes without planning or effort what European despotisms have always been unable to do.

With the veteran also, participation is the royal road to assimilation. Let him organize! Let him make his demands and suggestions! No doubt he will sometimes be unreasonable—as who is not?— nevertheless he will have begun to argue and to participate. The ideal outcome would be a gradually widening sphere of participation for the veterans and their organizations. Starting with themselves and their own concerns, such as veterans' relief and the care of the disabled, the veterans would naturally tend to widen their interests through the years, and would soon find themselves participating in wide areas of civilian life. This is the method of assimilation through participation, the method of a free and democratic society.

NOTES

1. Philip Gibbs, *Now It Can Be Told* (New York: Harper, 1920), p. 549.
2. Edgar L. Jones, "The Soldier Returns," *The Atlantic Monthly*, January 1944.
3. Jules Romains, *Men of Good Will*, Vol. VIII: *Verdun* (New York: Knopf, 1940), p. 430.
4. Erich Maria Remarque, *The Road Back* (Boston: Little Brown, 1921), pp. 252ff.
5. Romains, op. cit., pp. 440–42.
6. Maxwell Anderson, and Laurence Stallings, *What Price Glory?* (New York: Harcourt, Brace, 1926).
7. Ibid.
8. Carl Sandburg, *Abraham Lincoln, The War Years* (New York: Harcourt, Brace, 1939), Vol. II, p. 377; Vol. III, p. 284. The trick, a very shady one, was to count naval enlistments at New York City in the New York quota. Thus when a boy from the Middle West joined the Navy in New York, he was counted toward the New York City quota.
9. Gibbs, op. cit., pp. 333ff.

10. A. H. Gibbs, *Gun Fodder, The Diary of Four Years of War* (Boston: Little, Brown, 1919), pp. 141–44.

11. Remarque, op. cit., pp. 123ff.

12. Jones, op. cit.

13. Quoted by Alfred Vagts, *A History of Militarism* (New York: Norton, 1937), pp. 18–19.

14. Quincy Wright, *A Study of War* (Chicago: University of Chicago Press, 1942), Vol. II, p. 1172

15. Ibid.

16. Talcott Powell, *Tattered Banners* (New York: Harcourt, Brace, 1933), p. 5.

17. See Vagts, op. cit., p. 15, for the contrast between militarism and civilianism.

3

THE "GOOK" SYNDROME: THE VIETNAM WAR AS A RACIAL ENCOUNTER

SEYMOUR LEVENTMAN AND PAUL CAMACHO

After being wounded in Vietnam in 1969, a U.S. Army Special Forces veteran commented, "I liked it better in '65 and '66. Then it was just you against them. Now you just sit back and you get blasted or they do. That ain't no fun" (Glasser 1971, p. 61). The nostalgia of this GI for the "good old days" of the Vietnam War is incomprehensible apart from knowledge of the inner dynamics and changing structure of that confrontation. Not only did the character and quality of the war change militarily, but certain social features changed as well. One of these was the intensification of a factor seemingly so obvious it is often taken for granted in accounts of the war. This is the *racial* difference between the armies involved—the "yellowness" of the North Vietnamese and the "whiteness" of American troops. This chapter focuses on race as a variable critically affecting both the military and social experiences of American troops in Vietnam. We suggest that *race* was a latent though important component in the war that socialized the military experiences and militarized the social experiences for Americans. The racial factor thus ties together varying events and is a key for gaining at least partial sociological understanding of the happenings in Vietnam. We recognize that race alone is socially insignificant unless in fact at least one of the interacting groups attaches meaning and importance to it. Therefore, it is the social definition of race as *race consciousness* that must be examined.

THE VIETNAM WAR AS A RACIAL ENCOUNTER

Classic sociological works suggest an inverse correlation between the degree of technical formalization of social relations and the degree of race consciousness among the members of the interacting groups who are parties to these relationships. This hypothesis has wide application and may be tested in a variety of circumstances. One possible instance is warfare between nations whose armies constitute different racial groups. Under what conditions and to what extent do members of warring armies define their contacts as racial and therefore perceive one another racially? When is a war a *racial* war? At the same time, when are the diverse racial identities of warring armies blurred, considered irrelevant, or even forgotten? Answers to these questions are difficult to obtain. Indeed, certain issues of the World War II period such as the factors behind the Japanese-American citizens' relocation, the particular bloodthirstiness of the Pacific war, and whether or not the United States would have dropped the atom bomb on non-Asiatic peoples all raised questions of possible racial motivation that are still unanswered.

Post-World War II events (the Korean War and particularly the Vietnam War) afforded new opportunities for testing some of these ideas. In fact, war is an excellent test context precisely because it is so difficult an experience to formalize completely, whether by mathematical formula or computer design. As the Prussian military strategist Karl von Clausewitz and others have pointed out, warfare is a context of chance, accident, and uncertainty in the most extreme and threatening circumstances (Barnett 1971; Leonard 1967). At the same time, some wars are less informal than others as in the differences between wars involving official and/or professional armies and those involving unofficial "peoples units" commonly called "guerrillas." As we will show, combat circumstances may differ so much, even within the same war, one may observe possible effects of these variations on the relationships between the warring groups. Vietnam was unusual in that it consisted of two types of wars, an early one lasting from 1964 to 1968, and a late one lasting from 1968 to 1972. The early one was largely conventional and involved the usual confrontation of opposing armies, each attempting to capture or retain predefined military objectives. From the American GI's viewpoint, the enemy was the North Vietnam Army (NVA)* whose members could easily be recognized, defined, and hence

---

*The Vietnam communist fighting forces consisted essentially of two units; the North Vietnamese Army (NVA) and the National Liberation Front, commonly known as the Viet Cong (VC). The anticommunist army of South Vietnam was the Army of the Republic of Vietnam (ARVN).

killed legally. This war involved neither complex moral judgment by American troops nor administrative indecision and therefore could be called the "good war." The later type involved the confrontation between American troops and Vietnamese guerrillas as well as civilians who sometimes shielded troops or military objectives. Booby traps and mines planted by an invisible enemy inflicted high casualties among American troops. Yet GIs had few guerrilla or NVA bodies to show for their efforts. In fact, much of the contact between Americans and Vietnamese occurred randomly in "search and destroy missions" that took place in and around local villages as part of no clear-cut military goal or plan (Fitzgerald 1973, pp. 167, 502). This situation, compounded by the high rate of civilian casualties, resulted in great moral, psychic, and physical strain for GIs as well as strategic turmoil for military authorities, all of which contributed to producing the "bad war." Of course, we are not suggesting here that any war could ever be "good" in the moral or humanitarian sense. All wars are indeed "bad" in these terms. In using these labels, we wish to call attention to distinctions between those wars that are legally declared and receive rather full social support and those undertaken by secret commitment and/or executive order that receive partial support or are outrightly opposed by groups of citizens. Furthermore, we use the designations "good" and "bad" heuristically to identify special social and structural features of wars that are relevant for purposes of our analysis.

The history of the Vietnam War from actual military involvement by the United States in 1964 to official American withdrawal and the cease-fire in 1973 reveals that the war shifted from good to bad around 1968 with the Tet counteroffensive by the NVA and Vietcong (Oberdorfer 1971, pp. 158–96). This offensive, which in itself consisted of conventional-type battles, eventually led to a heightening of guerrilla warfare by the VC and the crystalization of a limited war policy by American commanders (Oberdorfer 1971, pp. 280–327). All wars are bounded and restricted by political considerations both at home and overseas.

Although ostensibly a strategy to show "determination" and maximize honor, the "no win" or stalemate policy accurately reflected the questionable nature and vague political purposes of the American presence in Vietnam. Thus, Vietnam was also a "no goals" war. Yet in waging a war that official policy has already determined could not or should not be "won" in the usual sense of forcing the enemy to surrender, Americans nevertheless went through the motions of deploying massive ground forces. This only added to the frustrations and anxieties of troops as they attempted to fight by the nagging and complex rules of a predefined stalemate. Compounding the ambiguity was knowledge of the turmoil in American society reflected in a highly

centralized administration, a weak Congress, and a growing disenchantment with the war by the general public as well as the various
radical movements of the 1960s. Moreover, accounts suggest that when
the Vietnam War was good, Americans related to the enemy NVA as
cofunctionaries and to the indigenous population as civilians (noncombatants). In the period 1964 to 1966, for example, GIs could relate easily
to Vietnamese villagers, talk to them, eat with them, or perhaps barter
with them. And in that period, ARVN were seen as "fledgling but
spunky" fighters, they needed only time and training to come up to par
(Sheehan et al. 1971). But when the war became bad, Americans began
to view all Vietnamese, whether soldier or civilian, as the enemy, seeing
them for what they "really" were all along—racially inferior gooks!
(Fitzgerald 1973, p. 498).

The following description may illustrate some of the dynamics
involved in the bad war that produced the prototype conditions for My
Lai occurrences:

> A platoon is on patrol, on another hot, dusty, 120° Vietnam day.
> While working their way across open fields and rice paddies they
> begin to receive the inevitable sniper fire from a nearby village. They
> take one or two casualties before they start to assault and envelop the
> village, hoping to capture the VC where they are hiding among the
> villagers. Anxiety begins, they start the assault but almost immedi-
> ately they are halted. "Mines! God damn booby traps." Mortar fire;
> nine buddies are dead or bleeding to death. A rear guard stays with
> the dead and wounded and the rest of the platoon continues on to the
> village. At this point there are a number of things on every soldier's
> mind. They are: fear, frustration, hate and above all revenge. The GIs
> enter the village. "Where are the VC," they ask. "Who are the VC,"
> they ask again? There is no answer. Nobody knows anything about
> VC. Everyone is a civilian. There are no VC in this village. The GIs
> stare at the villagers who are all staring at the GIs. The representa-
> tives of two widely separated cultures and races are staring at each
> other with mutual distrust, fear and hate. (Camacho 1970)

Since initial contact in Vietnam occurred in relatively formalized
warfare activity, Americans' race awareness then lay dormant while the
Vietnamese played fairly conventional roles as allied or enemy troops
and as civilians. However, when the enemy receded into the civilian
countryside to fight a guerrilla war of ambush, mines, and booby traps,
the entire structure of group contact shifted as the war changed from
good to bad. In a sense, these changes resulted in closer contact with
Vietnamese people blurring the previous clear-cut role distinction
between soldier and civilian. The tensions and ambiguities thus produced for GIs what Robert Park would have called "race prejudice," a

release of race consciousness previously embodied in the conventions of the social order. All Vietnamese were then transformed into "gooks," which redefinition became a basis for different kinds of impersonal and formalized relations between American troops and the local peoples. With the disintegration of a conventional system of intergroup relations, one type of categorical relationship (a technical one) was replaced by another (a racial one). Military objects were replaced by racial objects and the impersonal killing now included civilians as well as the officially defined (though often invisible) enemy. In this way, group contact became race contact, that is, when changed conditions transformed perspectives from one type of impersonal relation to another. Thus, the NVA and Vietcong troops were then evaluated for what they did— fight. South Vietnamese and civilians were then evaluated for what they were—gooks. We are not suggesting that from 1968 on only the ARVN and civilians were racially stereotyped. The situation was a relative one. That is, with the transformation of the war from good to bad, American troops came to intensify their racial conceptions of some Vietnamese more than others, that is, ARVN and civilians more than VC and NVA. The latter were still racially perceived but comparatively less so than the former. Thus, race consciousness was indeed a *variable* closely correlated with the changing social nature of the war in Vietnam.

The term "race consciousness" here refers to a frame of reference by which members of one group in contact with members of another define the latter ethnically as being everlastingly "different" and inherently inferior. Members of the former then attempt to separate themselves from the "inferior" group by establishing patterns of social distance appropriate for maintaining their presumed moral superiority and sense of historic perpetuity.* In a good war, armies meet on a prescribed battlefield where group conflict is regulated by clear-cut norms. Here the maintenance of social distance patterns is not an issue since intergroup contacts are formally prescribed. But in guerrilla warfare, where group contact is informal, sporadic, and comparatively unregulated, and criteria for defining friends and enemies became difficult to establish, there was resulting "danger" for Americans of being absorbed by the alien environment of Vietnam. So when contacts with Vietnamese became closer and more frequent, race consciousness (or prejudice) became a way for GIs to distinguish themselves socially from the local people and maintain a sense of their own "true"

---

*Since little data are available on the racial views of Vietnamese regarding Americans, all generalizations and contentions regarding race consciousness in this chapter apply only to Americans.

identity and link to "civilization." The "we-they" feeling, was especially strengthened for Americans during the bad war. "Just look how they lived in the shacks and the filth . . . they were all 'gooks,' after all" (Fitzgerald 1973, p. 595). The role of official military authorities in encouraging and supporting race consciousness among American troops in Vietnam should not be ignored. One observer reports that the headquarters of General William Westmoreland contained separate toilet facilities for Vietnamese and Americans (Bourne 1971, p. 466).

This chapter hypothesizes race consciousness of American troops to be a response to the later, bad war phase of the Vietnam experience.[1] In the early, good war phase, race consciousness was present but remained latent or assumed the benignity of a "white man's burden" frame of reference. Indeed, one of the many paradoxes of the Vietnam War was that as it progressed, American troops came to deracialize and increase respect for the official enemy while mistrusting and racially dehumanizing allies and civilians. We have depicted these relationships in Figure 3.1.[2]

FIGURE 3.1: Race Consciousness of American Troops and Phases of the Vietnam War

	Good War	Tet 1968	Bad War
Race Consciousness	O		X
No Race Consciousness	X		O

This is not to say that the race consciousness of American GIs began with their arrival in Vietnam.[3] Rather, they brought with them the standard American race consciousness that, especially in the case of special fighting units such as the Marines, had been intensified in brainwashing routines as part of basic training.* Referring to his training experiences, an Army Sergeant reports: "Then I was sent on to advance genocide training down at Ft. Polk, Louisiana . . . this is where I started to hate, hate anything that wasn't like me. Anything that wasn't a fighting machine. Gooks" (Thorne and Butler 1971, p. 38). Similarly, a Marine First Lieutenant describing his 32 weeks' basic training, comments, "Phrases like 'Gook' and 'link the Chink,' 'Luke the Gook' stuff we used in training got solidly into my head. I had Gooks on my mind when we flew into Danang Airport. As I was getting off the plane I suddenly found myself surrounded by Gooks. It was horrifying" (Thorne and Butler 1971, p. 96). A Nisei Marine Corporal reports being identified as a gook in his training class: "I was used as an example of a gook. You go to class and they say you'll be fighting the VC or the NVA. But then the person who was giving the class will see me and he'll say, 'He looks just like that, right there'" (Thorne and Butler 1971, p. 42). Such experiences seem to have been a part of military training both in the early good war and late bad war periods.

The Gook Syndrome

Initial contact with Vietnamese people reinforced these perspectives, especially upon viewing the latter's "obvious" technological and moral inferiority. The racial dehumanization of the Vietnamese as supported by American cultural beliefs eventually led to a pattern, the "gook syndrome," which became so ingrained as to form a normative aspect of American troops' subculture.[4] References to "gooks" and "dinks" were so constant and ubiquitous, "Just trying to avoid the gook syndrome made one abnormal in that environment . . ." writes Robert Lifton (1973, p. 202). Those GIs attempting to break away from the syndrome and humanize the Vietnamese risked social isolation from their buddies that could literally threaten survival, especially in combat. In its component elements—race consciousness, ethnocentrism, victimization, and a sense of technological superiority—the gook syndrome came to represent a quintessential experience for GIs. Eventually they felt impelled to demonstrate not their mission to the war but to that racial complex. After all, race-conscious persons react to their race as a social object toward which they develop a sense of loyalty, obligation, and willingness to fight (Brown 1931, p. 92). Lifton (1973, p. 212) even

---

*Earlier training probably also perpetrated these kinds of attitudes since Marines have always been trained for "bad" or "dirty" wars, as in the Pacific theater during World War II.

suggests that from a researcher's or outsider's viewpoint, one could not "feel with" Americans fighting the war without entering the "gook syndrome."

The syndrome attained special significance as the Vietnam War degenerated from good to bad. Thus, although all Vietnamese were gooks from the start, some became gookier than others. In the beginning, it was the official combatants, the NVA and the VC, who were the "real" gooks. South Vietnamese and civilians were then friends of Americans, allies, or neutrals and their gook qualities were low in visibility and significance. But around 1967 when the war began to go bad, and especially after Tet 1968, this rank order of gookiness was reversed. VC and NVA troops, while still gooks, became viewed primarily as respected and dedicated fighters, ideologically motivated to defend their homeland without benefit of modern technology and a huge war machine. "They've got balls," was the GI consensus (Starr 1973, p. 21). At the same time, South Vietnamese troops (ARVN) and especially civilians were reevaluated downward in worthiness in the gook hierarchy, that is, they became viewed primarily as "despicable gooks." The relationships between the changing character of the war and the racial redefinition of Vietnamese according to their respective positions in those changes we illustrated in Figure 3.2.

FIGURE 3.2: Race Consciousness of American Troops, Phases of the Vietnam War, and the Gook Hierarchy

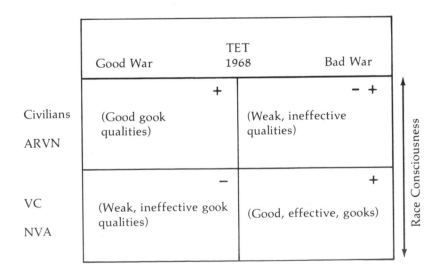

Source: Compiled by the authors.

This gook hierarchy is a racial status ranking of Vietnamese by Americans. Our main thesis contends that racial awareness of Americans was exacerbated by the bad war. This variable also shifted in intensity from certain groups of Vietnamese to others.* The key question remains, however, if all Vietnamese were seen as gooks, why was the racial component of this perception more salient for American troops in relation to some gooks than others? A close student of American fighting men, Charles Levy (1971, pp. 18–27) raised the same question. If all Vietnamese are racially indistinguishable, he asked, why were GIs more hostile to the ARVN than toward the VC/NVA? Levy argued it was because Americans believed the ARVN were "faggots."

The ARVN weren't always faggots; they became faggots as the war turned sour and conflicts for Americans increased over goals, purposes, and strategies. In that context faggot may have been equivalent to a racial epithet since the label functioned to redefine the ARVN as moral inferiors, thereby separating them from "civilized" Americans. The latter then had a basis for maintaining a "safe" social distance from cultural and moral taint. GIs felt they had good reason to do so. Americans became especially bitter about fighting "their" war while South Vietnamese refused risks and fought little and badly—"They just don't give a shit." Originally friends and allies, the ARVN became "little yellow bastards"† whose perceived incompetence and weakness was contrasted with NVA and VC capability. So Levy's account requires consideration of broader stresses experienced by GIs fighting in Vietnam that have already been alluded to and are embodied in our typology of the good war/bad war.

---

*These changes occurred over time, indeed, each year from 1964 to 1973 was different. So the situation of the war varied even within our categories of good and bad. Since tour of duty for most GIs was one year, it was highly unlikely for the same group to experience all the variations referred to. Moreover, since we cannot say that GIs serving in Vietnam themselves varied from one time period to another, we can infer it was the structure of the war situation that itself varied. GIs serving, say, in 1966 experienced different relationships to the war and to the Vietnamese than did those serving, say, in 1970. Finally, we have assumed here that whether troops served in the Marines or the Army, their experiences were essentially similar with respect to the gook syndrome and the good war/bad war distinction.

†American technology also came to reflect this negative race consciousness or "racism." In the late 1960s a major electronics firm on the Route 128 industrial complex just west of Boston developed a high-powered rifle, electronically triggered by a polaroid-type camera sensitized to skin color. A yellow-skinned person coming into view set off the device with deadly accuracy. Some "bugs" developed in producing this death machine and apparently it was never actually used. In this connection, one is reminded of I. F. Stone's statement: "The most frustrating thing about this war for Americans is that the Vietnamese refuse to be killed off by the rules of the war games devised by the Rand Corporation."

Before 1968, American relationships with various Vietnamese groups existed along fairly clear-cut lines. Racial awareness was ever-present but remained dormant to be superseded by essentially functional and nonracial considerations. Thus the North Vietnamese were the authentic enemy engaged by Americans in conventional-style combat. The South Vietnamese were officially friendly allies and civilians were passive and neutral onlookers. With the Tet offensive of 1968, as we have indicated, NVA activity and particularly VC guerrilla operations were stepped up (Fitzgerald 1973, pp. 495ff). Specifically, VC troops would enter villages and mingle with civilians while sniping at Americans and planting booby traps and mines. In fact, the VC became part-time civilians. In this situation, the VC would "hit and run" and rarely engage in sustained conventional combat. Furthermore, the VC often used civilian informants as, for example, in having children tending buffalo mark American troop positions on the ground with sticks for the VC to discover. Injuries resulting from this kind of combat were especially infuriating and frustrating since the weaponry was personally directed by an invisible force against which it was impossible to retaliate directly.

In a resulting search for alternative targets, widespread scapegoating processes were generated. Jean Paul Sartre (1971, pp. 546–47) remarked that in colonial wars civilians are always the most visible enemies. Frustration by foreign troops over this "unorthodox" situation then turns to hatred of the indigenous peoples. In Vietnam it was the civilians who, because they got in the way of the good war, bore the brunt of GI bitterness over a frustrating and stalemated situation. Civilians were ever-present to blame for casualties, disillusionment, and generalized feelings of hopelessness at even being in such a forsaken place. Civilians thus became surrogate targets for an invisible enemy and suffered mistaken or intended killings, burnings of their villages and/or crops, and a generalized dehumanization at the hands of GIs. The reduction of these people to objects was also revealed in the compulsive reporting of the "body count." This came to epitomize efforts by the American military to discover technical criteria for measuring success and accomplishment in a war otherwise difficult to assess (Lifton 1973, p. 41). An Army Sergeant tells of an officer in Vietnam requesting that his platoon's body count be passed on to the higher command. "We can confirm the body count of that company. There's nine women, three children and one baby" (Thorne and Butler 1971, p. 84). Stripped of their benignity as peaceful farmers by the circumstances of war and an aroused American race consciousness, Vietnam civilians were ultimately reduced to racial objects—gooks.

Another source of stress for American troops in Vietnam was

indigenous to the very structure of the military operation there. This was the organization of the tour of duty itself. The tour was a year long and consisted of four 90-day cycles with three assigned operations per cycle and three or four days' rest per operation. These operations could involve two activities: being stationed at a base subjected to air or ground attacks, searching for and destroying the enemy in the bush (jungle), village, or wherever he might be. The latter was particularly stressful in requiring a proper balance between aggression and caution, readiness to attack while watching for mines and booby traps, to say nothing of ambush. Because of their training for spontaneous aggressive warfare and difficulty in utilizing passive tactics, American troops were particularly susceptible to booby traps that thus became a major source of casualties in Vietnam (Levy 1971, pp. 23–24; Starr 1973, pp. 15).

Furthermore, the rotation system itself was problematic for GIs, especially in affecting their sense of unit solidarity. Since men had different "Days of Expected Return from Overseas (DEROS)" as a GI passed from one 90-day cycle to another approaching DEROS, his original unit and reference group became increasingly depleted, thus effectively reducing his primary group support. This became a critical deprivation since the "hit and run" tactics of the "enemy" required constant awareness and great dependency by GIs upon fellow squadron or platoon members for information and protection. The "grunt" or ground trooper had to be constantly aware of where he and his unit were on the map, especially friendly and supporting units. He had to watch his fellows and, because of the nature of his task, have extraclose relations with them. So great was the need for mutual dependency among GIs that intense emotional outbursts often resulted when buddies were killed or injured since this broke the protective chain and shield against death and loneliness. This alienation from the community of "civilized" peers was another factor exacerbating Americans' racial conceptions of the Vietnamese. And so it is the "gook hierarchy" that emerges as a construct of factors enabling us to further refine some of our original contentions concerning the Vietnam War as a racial encounter. Although Americans always knew all Vietnamese were gooks, particular circumstances modified this conception. From 1964 to 1968, while the NVA and VC were seen as "warrior gooks," the South Vietnamese and civilians were seen as "good gooks." But from 1968 on, the South Vietnamese and civilians became "bad gooks" while the NVA and VC became "gook warriors." Although as official enemies, the NVA and VC were indeed seen as cofunctionaires throughout the war, their relative "gookiness" varied. Early on, as "dupes" of Communist China, they seemed more "yellow" in comparison with the ARVN and civilians then seen as outposts of democratic civilization. Later on, however, the highly motivated and achievement-oriented NVA and VC grew less "yellow" compared to the South Vietnamese and civilians whose "yellowness" increased as Americans grew increasingly disillusioned with the latter's "uncivilized" ineptitude and underachievement.

A final observation concerns the post- "bad" phase of the Vietnam War. The earlier transformation of the war from good to bad had led to military failure and revulsion at home. So it was necessary either to withdraw and stop the war, or make it good again. Since American leaders did not want to opt for the first, they tried to "clean it up." This was "accomplished" by withdrawing ground troops, thereby eliminating problems of civilian involvement in face-to-face informal combat while relying instead upon massive air and naval bombings and bombardments. In these ways, the war was formalized and depersonalized again, albeit through technological means. American troop involvement in the Vietnam War thus concluded on this "clean" note and "peace with honor" could then be achieved.

SUMMARY AND CONCLUSIONS

The following is offered to highlight the critical variables in the relationships between race consciousness and warfare as a social encounter.

Good Wars	Bad Wars
1. Formalized confrontation between opposing forces	1. Informal confrontation
2. Classic and conventional military operations and engagements	2. Unconventional warfare involving civilians
3. Predictable re military tactics and strategy	3. Increasingly unpredictable
4. Clear distinction between combatants and non-combatants	4. Blurred distinction between combatants and noncombatants
5. Legitimate killing and destruction	5. Illegitimate killing and destruction
6. Combat at a distance involving large forces	6. Face-to-face, more one-on-one combat though enemy may sometimes be invisible
7. Specified militarily obtainable goals	7. Uncertain or absent goals
8. Conflict between societies	8. Socities with radically different

with generally similar cultural traditions*	cultures
9. Conflict between societies at same general level of development	9. Conflict between societies at different levels of development
Therefore: little or no race consciousness	Therefore: strong race consciousness

In short, when these kinds of variables come together in certain combinations, a good war is transformed into a bad war, giving rise to racial consciousness that functions to justify military and quasi-military actions subsequently taken. More generally, we have tried to show that when two groups meet, the likelihood of one attaching racial significance to the identity of the other depends in large part upon the nature and conditions of the contacts. Generally, the more formalized and functionalized the contact, the less the probability of the contact being perceived as "racial" by the groups involved. When these conventionalized contacts break down, and relations become more personalized and unpredictable, a struggle for predominance ensues, increasing the likelihood that traditional racial perceptions will be newly intensified. In Vietnam the ground war was an extraordinarily complex type of racial contact that we have simplified here for purposes of analysis. As a result of prior general cultural conditioning and the specific conditioning of military training, all Vietnamese were initially viewed by Americans as members of a racially inferior group. The nature of the specific contacts, however, modified this race consciousness particularly as the war shifted from good to bad, that is, conventional to unconventional.

Furthermore, even though the NVA, especially the VC, began using the "unfair" military tactic of hiding among civilians, it was the latter who bore the brunt of GI frustration. Thus, race-conscious aggression came to be directed mainly against the Vietnamese farmers, women, and children who got in the way of the war. The infamous massacre at My Lai and other such events were not motivated solely by ordinary pent-up frustrations and aggressions. At his court martial, Lieutenant Calley testified that the "wasting" of civilians at My Lai was

---

*We called the Vietnam War good even though the American and North Vietnamese armies hardly represent societies of similar cultural traditions or levels of technological development. For our purposes, however, we felt that from 1964 to 1968, points 1 through 7 outweighed points 8 and 9 in such a characterization. We are also suggesting that when armies of varying civilizations meet in combat, every war, no matter how good at first, contains the seeds of becoming bad. Our typologies are designed as working models to highlight critical variables and not necessarily to hypothesize the empirical "purity" of one type of situation or another.

"no big deal." In Vietnam the aggressive responses were given special force and direction by the racial character of the victimized group.* How else to explain why peasants defending themselves aroused such massive retaliatory responses from Americans (Slater 1970, pp. 41ff)? Or, how else to explain the American use in Vietnam of chemical warfare techniques considered anathema even in World War II, that is, defoliants, napalm, phosphorus, and antipersonnel bombs that destroyed nothing but people?

EPILOGUE

One of the most telling aspects of the war in Vietnam, especially the bad phase from 1968 on, was how closely American experience there paralleled trends back home. The purposelessness and meaninglessness of avowed goals, the mixture of bureaucratic fantasy and absurd actuality, dependency on drugs as a routinized escape from boredom, the sporadic nature of violence mutually expressed by "victimized" officials and their "victimized" clients, the intensification of interethnic tensions, a mixture of profound distrust of authority with a need for loyalty and trust, a growing sense of powerlessness in the face of unseen forces of intimidation and destruction, and a disbelief in political and ideological rhetoric as explanations and policies—surely counterparts existed for all these features both in Vietnam and in American society. In a sense, therefore, experiences of GIs in Vietnam were good preparation for the life they were to experience upon returning to civilian society.

There is an ironic postscript to this chapter. With the fall of South Vietnam to the North Vietnamese in the spring of 1975, the Vietnam War came to an actual conclusion. The U.S. government then evacuated and resettled large numbers of Vietnamese refugees in various sections of the United States. Considerable resistance was then expressed by some Americans, which prompted a cartoon by the political satirist of the Boston Globe, Paul Szep. In it he portrayed the Statue of Liberty with the caption, "Give me your healthy, your wealthy, your white, your select few . . ." and instead of the lamp in the Statue's upstretched right hand was a sign reading, "NO GOOKS."

---

*Such patterns also occurred at home in the 1960s and 1970s. National Guard and police units were then called upon to fight unconventional "bad wars" against the "enemies" of the period, protesting students and blacks. Supported by much of public opinion, these units conceived of their "foes" as inferior beings and therefore expendable. One result was official killing of both students and blacks at Kent State, Watts, Jackson State, and Attica prison.

NOTES

1. This hypothesis is also predictive of several other conditions that developed into problems of major proportions in Vietnam. They are drug traffic and drug use by American troops, and "khaki collar" crime in the military, specifically the embezzlement of massive funds from the PX system by army officers. Both drug use and PX crime became endemic with the bad war. See Alfred McCoy et al., *The Politics of Heroin in Southeast Asia* (New York: Harper & Row, 1972); also, *Fraud and Corruption in Management of Military Club Systems—Illegal Currency Manipulations Affecting South Vietnam*, U.S. Senate, Hearings of the Committee on Government Operations, Vols. I–VIII, (Washington, D.C.: U.S. Government Printing Office, 1969–71). Racial tensions between black and white American troops also increased in the bad war period. See Wallace Terry, "Bringing the War Home," in *Vietnam and Black America*, ed. Clyde Taylor (New York: Doubleday, 1973), pp. 200–19. Another pattern correlated with the good war/bad war distinction was "fragging," the pointed killing by American troops of despised officers. While this tactic seems to have occurred during the entire period of the war, its character changed from one phase to another. According to one observer, fragging in the early period was "classical," that is, it was an emotionally motivated act rationalized as protective for the security of the unit and most often committed during contact with the enemy. "Modern" fragging occurred in the later stages of the war. In contrast, this pattern seemed "irrational" in that it often occurred arbitrarily in rear areas away from formal danger. It was aimed at the "new enemy," one's own military authority, and was meant to intimidate as well as kill. It included ordinary grenadings or more "exotic" means such as booby trapping toilet seats where bowls filled with jet fuel instead of the usual diesel oil produced predictable results when lit to dispose of waste. See William Corson, *Consequences of Failure* (New York: W. W. Norton 1974), pp. 87–89, 99. See also Charles Levy, *Spoils of War* (Boston: Houghton Mifflin, 1974), pp. 35–37, 42–46.

2. To be sure, this model requires further refinement in light of the complexity of actual events. Specifically, the Vietnam War did not become bad all at once in 1968. There was a middle period in which the transitional war occurred from 1967 to 1969. It was in this period that several developments signaled the transformation of conventional combat into an ambiguous conflict lacking clear-cut purpose. First was the splintering of ARVN loyalties during the Buddhist Nationalist uprising in 1966. This "proved" ARVN's ineffectiveness, thus paving the way for greater American involvement in hostilities. Second was the dissolution of NVA and VC mainforce units due to heavy combat and the subsequent infiltration by VC personnel of civilian populations. Third was the "light at the end of the tunnel" imagery ostensibly projected to signify eventual American victory but actually a euphemism for a limited war strategy that indeed prevailed for the duration. See, especially, Daniel Ellsberg, *Papers on the War* (New York: Simon and Schuster, 1972).

3. We have assumed here that the American fighting force, though racially diversified, represented a unity with respect to sharing the gook syndrome. That is, we contend that GIs, whether black, Indian, Hawaiian, or of Chinese or Japanese extraction, all entered the syndrome either out of social necessity or to demonstrate their loyalty to America and "prove" themselves to their white buddies. This was especially true before 1968. We recognize that as the war became bad, however, blacks began to form cliques as expressions of race pride and of opposition to "racist America's killing colored Vietnamese brothers of blacks." Though a significant problem, the differing perceptions and relations of the various racial groups composing the American military force to the Vietnamese, whether VC or civilian, would require much more detailed evidence than is available to us. Therefore, we believe that for present purposes, our analysis that portrays race relations in Vietnam as occurring essentially between two groups, Americans and Vietnamese, is

valid within the limitations noted. See Lifton (1973, p. 204); and Taylor, *Vietnam and Black America*, op. cit., especially "Vietnam: A Brother's Account," by Gerald Snead, pp. 223–41, and "Memphis-Nam-Sweden," by Terry Whitmore, pp. 242–53.

4. We are indebted to Robert J. Lifton for this concept. Although "gook" seems related to the American slang term meaning slime or filth, it has Korean linguistic origins and was first used by American troops in that war. In actual usage by Americans in Vietnam, "gook" served as a combined racial and nationalistic epithet. See Lifton's "The 'Gook Syndrome' and 'Numbed Warfare,'" *Saturday Review*, December 1972, pp. 66–72.

REFERENCES

Barnett, C. 1971. "How Not to Win a War." *Horizon* 13 (Summer): 49–53.

Bourne, P. G. 1971. "From Boot Camp to My Lai." In *Crimes of War*, ed. R. Falk, G. Kolko, and R. Lifton. New York: Vintage Books.

Brown, W. O. 1931. "The Nature of Race Consciousness. *Social Forces* 10 (October): 90–97.

Camacho, P. 1970. Unpublished Field Notes, Vietnam 1968–69.

Fitzgerald, F. 1973. *Fire in the Lake*. New York: Vintage Books.

Glasser, R. 1971. *365 Days*. New York: George Braziller.

Leonard, R. A. 1967. *A Short Guide to Clausewitz on War*. New York: Capricorn Books.

Levy, C. 1971. "ARVN as Faggots: Marines View Their Allies." *Transaction* 8 (October): 18–27.

Lifton, R. 1973. *Home From the War*. New York: Simon and Schuster.

Oberdorfer, D. 1971. *Tet!* Garden City, N.Y.: Doubleday.

Parsons, T. 1965. "Full Citizenship for the Negro American? A Sociological Problem." *Daedalus* 94 (Fall): 1009–54.

Sartre, J. P. 1971. "On Genocide." In *Crimes of War*, ed. R. Falk, G. Kolko, and R. Lifton. New York: Vintage Books.

Sheehan, N. et al. 1971. *The Pentagon Papers: The Secret History of the Vietnam War . . . as published by The New York Times*. New York: Bantam Books.

Slater, P. 1970. *The Pursuit of Loneliness*. Boston: Beacon Press.

Starr, P. 1973. *The Discarded Army*. New York: Charterhouse Books.

Thorne, D. and G. Butler. 1971. *The New Soldier*. New York: Collier Books.

4

SURVIVING THE WAR IN VIETNAM

CHARLES MOSKOS

By the end of the American involvement in Vietnam it was evident that the ground combat forces of the United States were plagued by breakdowns in discipline. Mass media accounts were quick to report occurrences of troop insubordination, murder or "fraggings" of non-coms and officers, atrocities against Vietnamese civilians, endemic racial violence, widespread drug abuse, and corruption of military personnel. Even if the incidence of these indicators were overstated in such accounts, it was nevertheless privately acknowledged by the command hierarchy that the mission capabilities of the U.S. ground forces were being brought into question. It was also generally agreed that the morale of the American Army in Vietnam changed markedly over three rather distinct and successive periods: 1965–67, relatively high cohesion and morale; 1968–69, a transitional time of mixed cohesion and demor-alization; and 1970–72, widespread demoralization.

My purpose here is to offer a sociological assessment of these historic events by bringing to bear available data and relevant theoreti-cal considerations on the processes that affected the cohesion and demoralization of the American forces in Vietnam.

That men too often find themselves fighting wars is a depressing commentary on both history and contemporary life. That many of these same men endure situations where they can be killed and kill others is a perplexing fact of human behavior. It is not surprising, then, that interpretations of the motivations of men in combat are many. From among diverse explanations, however, we can distinguish some recurring themes.

The viewpoint with perhaps the earliest antecedents finds combat motivation resting on the presumed national character of the general populace. The varying effectiveness of different national armies has often been popularly ascribed to the putative martial spirit of their respective citizenries. The use of national character explanations of military effectiveness, however, is not unique to popular folklore. In recent American history, certain prominent spokesmen invoked such broad cultural determinants to explain the alleged poor performance of American prisoners of war in the Korean War as a result of a "softening" of the American character (Kinkead 1959). Similarly, during the Vietnam War the deterioration in military discipline was often ascribed to diffuse social phenomena such as "youth culture" or "generation gap."

A contrasting viewpoint sees combat performance as resulting essentially from the operation of the formal military organization. Combat motivation results from effective military leadership and discipline and unit *esprit de corps*. Although such a viewpoint is typically associated with traditionalist military thought, the importance of military socialization is similarly emphasized—albeit from different premises—by commentators concerned with the assumed deleterious consequences of military life on personality development. Thus, we frequently find both supporters and opponents of the goals of the military organization giving great weight to the total or all-inclusive features of military life (a synthesis of this perspective is found in Gabriel and Savage 1978).

Another interpretation of combat behavior holds that the effective soldier is motivated either by a sense of national patriotism or by a belief that he is fighting for a just cause. Such a viewpoint holds that combat performance depends upon the soldier's commitment to abstract values or the symbols of the larger society. The effective soldier, in other words, is an ideologically inspired soldier.* Combat performance directly varies with the soldier's conscious allegiance to the stated purposes of the war. It is usually assumed in this regard that such allegiance preexists the soldier's entry into the formal military organization.

---

*A striking example of extremely ideological combat groups was the appearance of microrevolutionary groups in several Western parliamentary societies in the 1970s.

A quite different explanation of combat motivation, largely arising from the social science studies of World War II, deemphasizes ideological considerations (and, to a lesser extent, formal organizational factors as well) (Shils and Janowitz 1948; Shils 1950; Little 1964; Shirom 1976). It focuses attention instead on the role of face-to-face or "primary groups" and explains the motivation of the individual soldier as a function of his solidarity and social intimacy with fellow soldiers at small group levels. Significantly, the rediscovery of the importance of primary groups paralleled those accounts given by journalists, novelists, and other combat observers. In its more extreme formulation, combat primary relationships were viewed as so intense that they overrode not only preexisting civilian values and formal military goals but even the individual's own sense of self-concern.

My own early research on American combat soldiers, while making reference to national character and military socialization explanations, was directed essentially to considerations raised in the ideological and primary-group interpretations of combat performance (Moskos 1970). This research was based on field observations and in-depth interviews of combat soldiers in Vietnam during 1965 and 1967. Put most concisely, I concluded that combat motivation arises out of the linkages between individual self-concern, primary-group processes, and the shared beliefs of soldiers. In particular, my findings sought to document and to demonstrate how important modifications and rethinking were required in those social science viewpoints that deemphasized the salience of ideological considerations and that stressed instead the determinative features of primary relations in combat groups.

In concrete terms, my research revealed that the intensity of primary-group ties so often reported in combat units are best viewed as mandatory necessities arising from immediate life-and-death exigencies. Much like the Hobbesian description of primitive life, the combat situation also reaches the state of being nasty, brutish, and short. To carry the Hobbesian analogy a step farther, one can view primary-group processes in the combat situation as a kind of rudimentary social contract; a contract that is entered into because of advantages to individual self-interest. Rather than viewing soldiers' primary groups as some kind of semimystical bond of comradeship, they can be better understood as pragmatic and situational responses. This is not to deny the existence of strong interpersonal ties within combat squads, but only to reinterpret them as derivative from the very private war each individual is fighting for his own survival.

It was found, moreover, that although the American soldier had a general aversion to overt ideological symbols and patriotic appeals, this should not obscure those salient ideological factors that serve as preconditions in supporting the soldier to exert himself under dangerous conditions. For the individual, behavior and small-group processes occurring in combat squads operate within a widespread attitudinal context of underlying value commitments; most notably, an antipolitical outlook coupled with a belief—evident during the time of my field research in the early years of the Vietnam War—in the worthwhileness of American society. Correspondingly, when changes in these value commitments occurred in the later years of the Vietnam War, this had indirect but important consequences on military cohesion. These values—what I term "latent ideology"—must therefore be taken into account in explaining the combat performance of American soldiers in Vietnam.

THE COMBAT SITUATION

Despite a commonly held view that danger to American soldiers was widespread throughout Vietnam and pervasive for all echelons, in fact in any large-scale military organization—even in the actual theater of war—only a fraction of men under arms personally experience combat. As in other modern American wars, nearly all casualties in Vietnam were suffered by that small group of men in the front or first echelon of the military organization, the soldiers taking part in patrols, major battles, and air operations. As has been true in other if not all wars, the front-echelon soldier in Vietnam—the "grunt"—made a sharp distinction between his position and that of rear-area servicemen.

To understand the way the soldier's attitudes and behavior are shaped, one must try to comprehend the extreme physical conditions under which he must manage. Only in that context can one appreciate the nature of the primary-group processes developed in combat squads. Within the network of interpersonal relationships with fellow squad members, the combat soldier is also fighting a personal war, a war that he hopes to leave alive and unscathed.

The concept of relative deprivation, as an interpretive variable, suggests that an individual's evaluation of this situation can be understood by knowing the reference group of comparison. We should not, however, lose sight of those extreme situations where deprivation is absolute as well as relative, where in the most literal sense the individual's social horizon is narrowly determined by his immediate life chances. The combat soldier, as an absolutely deprived person, responds to direct situational exigencies. He acts pragmatically to maximize short-run advantages in whatever form they exist. Though combat soldiers rarely display what C Wright Mills termed the "sociological imagination" (that is, relating personal situations to broader societal conditions), this is not simply a default in political sophistication. Rather, for the soldier concerned with his own day-to-day survival, the decisions of state that brought him into combat become irrelevant. It is in this sense that the pros and cons of the basic issues of national policy are meaningless to the combat soldier.

In the combat situation, the soldier not only faces the imminent danger of loss of life and, more frightening for most, limb, he also witnesses combat wounds and deaths suffered by buddies. Moreover, there are the routine physical stresses of combat existence: the weight of the pack, tasteless food, diarrhea, lack of drinking water, leeches, mosquitoes, rain, torrid heat, mud, and loss of sleep. In an actual fire-fight with the enemy, the scene is generally one of utmost chaos and confusion. Deadening fear intermingles with acts of bravery and, strangely enough, even moments of exhilaration and comedy. If enemy prisoners are taken, they may be subjected to atrocities in the rage of battle or its immediate aftermath. The soldier's distaste of endangering civilians can be overcome by his fear that Vietnamese of any age or sex can be responsible for his own death.

Once the combat engagement is over, the soldier still has little idea in a strategic sense of what has been accomplished. His view of the war is limited to his own personal observations and subsequent talks with others in the same platoon or company. The often-noted reluctance of combat soldiers to discuss their experiences when back home is not present in the field. They make a conversational mainstay of recounting fire-fights and skirmishes with the enemy. They engage in such discussions not so much for their intrinsic interest but, more importantly, to specify tactical procedures that may save lives in future encounters with the enemy.

In ground warfare an individual's survival is directly related to the support—moral, physical, and technical—he can expect from his fellow soldiers. He gets such support largely to the degree that he reciprocates it to others. Much of the solidarity of combat squads can be understood as an outcome of individual self-interest within a particular situational context.

Do the contrasting interpretations of the network of social relations in combat units—the primary groups of World War II versus the essentially individualistic soldier in Vietnam—result from conceptual differences on the part of the investigators, or do they reflect substantive differences in the social cohesion of the American soldiers being described? If substantive differences do exist, some of this variation can be accounted for by the effects of the rotation system introduced in the Vietnam War. In World War II, men served for the duration. In Vietnam, on the other hand, Army enlisted men served a 12-month tour of duty (13 for Marines).

SOLDIERS AND THE COMBAT CYCLE

It would be hard to overstate the soldier's constant concern with how much more time—down to the day—he had remaining in Vietnam. For the individual American soldier the paramount factor affecting combat motivation in the Vietnam War was the operation of the rotation system. Barring his being killed or severely wounded, every soldier knew his exact departure date from Vietnam; his whole being centered on reaching his personal DEROS (Date Expected Return Overseas).

Within the combat unit itself, the rotation system had many consequences for social cohesion and individual motivation. The rapid turnover of personnel not only hindered the development of primary-group ties but also rotated out of the unit men who attained combat experience. Furthermore, because of the tactical nature of patrols and the somewhat random likelihood of encountering the enemy, a new arrival might soon experience more actual combat than many of the men in the same battalion who were nearing the end of their tour in Vietnam.

During his one-year tour in Vietnam, the combat soldier underwent definite changes in attitude toward his situation. Although such attitudes varied depending on individual personality and combat exposure, they typically followed this course. Upon arrival to his unit and for several weeks following, the soldier was excited to be in the war zone and may even have looked forward to engaging with the enemy. After the first serious encounter, however, he lost his enthusiasm for combat. From about the second through the eighth months of his tour in Vietnam, the soldier operated on a kind of plateau of moderate or dutiful commitment to the combat role.

Toward the ninth and tenth months, he began to regard himself as an "old soldier." It is usually at this point that a soldier was generally most effective. But as he began to approach the end of his tour in Vietnam, the soldier noticeably began to withdraw his efficiency. He became reluctant to engage in offensive combat operations. Stories were repeated of men killed the day they were to rotate back to the United States. "Short-timer's fever" was implicitly recognized by the others and demands on short-timers were informally reduced. The final disengagement period of the combat soldier was considered a kind of earned prerogative that those earlier in the rotation cycle hoped eventually to enjoy. In other words, short-timer's fever was a tacitly approved way of cutting short the soldier's exposure to combat dangers.

Overall, the rotation system reinforced an individualistic perspective that was essentially self concerned. The end of the war was marked by the individual's rotation date and not by its eventual outcome—whether victory, defeat, or negotiation. Whatever incipient identification there might be with abstract comrades in arms was circumvented by the privatized view of the war fostered by the rotation system.

The long-term consequences of the rotation system on American combat performance in Vietnam are difficult to assess, but it does appear that something like the following occurred. During the period that the war was on the upswing, the rotation system contributed positively to the morale of the individual combat soldier. Contrarily, once the war was defined as on the downswing—the start of the American withdrawal—the rotation system served to work against combat effectiveness. Not only did the withdrawal of efficiency associated with short-timer's fever begin to appear earlier in the combat cycle, but the whole elan of the American forces was undercut by the knowledge that the Vietnam War was coming to some kind of inconclusive end. Indeed, the quite rational feeling of not wanting to be the last man killed in a closing war that characterized the low morale of the American ground forces after 1969 can be regarded as a kind of short-timer's fever writ large.

CLEAVAGE AND CONFLICT IN COMBAT GROUPS

The most valuable source of information on the World War II serviceman is found in the volumes of *The American Soldier* (Stouffer et al. 1949). Never before or since have so many aspects of military life been studied so systematically. It would take us far afield to give a detailed summary of the findings of *The American Soldier*. It is important, however, to note that the two basic generalizations were complimentary in their understanding of social cohesion in soldier's groups. First, *The American Soldier* documented the widespread discontent among enlisted men in World War II toward the "caste" system of the Army. Indeed, it appears that resentment toward the differential treatment of officers generated the strongest negative feelings about Army life among enlisted men. How with all this malcontent among the rank and file could the American soldier give a good account of himself in combat? The answer was not because soldiers believed in the stated purposes of the war. Quite the contrary, the findings revealed a profoundly non-ideological soldier: "The broad picture . . . is one of a matter of fact adjustment, with a minimum of idealism or heroics in which the elements which come closest to the conventional stereotypes of soldier heroism enter through the close solidarity of the combat group" (p. 191).

The "Lifers" and the "Brass"

Yet, starting in the Cold War era and becoming particularly pronounced in the Vietnam War, the structural source of conflict in soldiers' groups began to take a new form. Where internal Army cleavages formerly derived from the basic distinction between enlisted men and commissioned officers, the new distinction became that between single-term soldiers—whether officer or enlisted—and career soldiers—whether officer or enlisted. Where the enlisted man of World War II directed his primary animus toward the officer corps, the younger enlisted man of the Vietnam War focused his resentment on the career noncom. The term "lifer" (that is, senior sergeants) in GI parlance took over the pejorative quality accorded "the brass" by the World War II soldier. Generational factors, that is, in the Vietnam period overrode the traditional differences between enlisted men and officers.

Symptomatic of the cleavage between single-term service and career soldiers—with consequences on social cohesion—were the opposing views of the two groups toward drugs and alcohol. The younger enlisted men were favorably disposed toward the newer drugs, most notably marijuana, while the career soldiers tended to take much more tolerant views of alcoholic indulgences. In picturesque soldiers' language, these contrasting sentiments were referred to as the "heads" versus the "juicers" (Helmer 1974).

Situational Race Tensions

Beyond drug use, there was a more pervasive internal conflict confronting the American military in Vietnam. That black soldiers might find they owed a higher fealty to each other than to the U.S. Army was a possibility that haunted commanders. The 1948 Executive Order of President Truman abolishing racial segregation in the armed forces was an impressive instance of directed social change. By the 1950s this integration policy was an accomplished fact, thus bringing about a far-reaching transformation in the makeup of a major American institution in a remarkably short period of time. In fact, extending through the middle 1960s, the degree and quality of racial integration in the armed forces stood in marked and favorable contrast with that of civilian society. But the era of harmonious race relations in the military dissipated by the end of the 1960s. The Vietnam period was characterized by polarization and even violence between the races within the context of formal integration. Less dramatic than overt race conflict, but ultimately more significant, was the emergence of race consciousness throughout the rank and file of black soldiers. At one level the new race consciousness took the form of symbolic cultural behavior, for example, involved handshakes or the "dap," the wearing of "slave" bracelets, and rhetoric of "brother-me" and "nation-tie." Although close living and common danger mitigated racial conflict in combat units in the field, self-imposed informal segregation in the noncombat environment became almost *de rigueur* on the part of lower-ranking black and white servicemen. And it was largely in such off-duty situations that embroilments between the races became a common occurrence in Vietnam.

Fragging

Although beginning as early as 1965, it was not until after 1968 that the antiwar movement in America began to have noticeable effects within the active-duty service population. Outside of Vietnam there was much mass media coverage of antiwar entertainment troupes and the growing number of draft evaders and military deserters. In Vietnam itself, breakdowns in Army discipline were reflected in incidents ranging from "talking it out" (when leaders tried to persuade reluctant soldiers to go out on combat operations) to "fraggings" (violent often lethal reprisals against noncoms and officers). Outbreaks of fraggings reached epidemic proportions toward the last years of the Vietnam War. It goes without saying that a definitive sociological treatment of the fragging phenomena is handicapped by the unavailability of participant data. Yet an interpretive analysis of the accounts of several score former members of Vietnam units where fraggings occurred allows for a partial understanding. From these accounts two broad categories of fraggings emerge.

Personal Vendetta Fraggings

The first type, probably accounting for less than one in five of all incidents, were the acts of solitary individuals pursuing a kind of personal vendetta. Such individuals developed a diffuse resentment against the whole military system rather than toward a specific person—though a particular noncom or officer might come symbolically to represent the system. These were the cases in which the perpetrator was likely to be personally unbalanced or psychologically disturbed at the time he resorted to violence. In this type of fragging no collusion with others was involved, little if any warning was given, the lethal instrument was usually one's personal weapon, happenstance often determined the ultimate victim, and the culprit made little effort to hide his identity.

Group–Engendered Fraggings

The second and much more common type of fragging systemically involved small-group processes. These fraggings occurred in response to soldiers' groups believing their integrity had been violated in some way. Three variants of such group-engendered fragging can be specified: racially inspired fraggings, typically by blacks against what was regarded as a racist white superior; "dope hassle" fraggings arising from informal groups of drug users seeking reprisal against enforcers of antidrug regulations; and fraggings in combat groups against a noncom or officer who was seen as too "gung-ho" in risking the lives of his subordinates.

Whatever their concrete motivation, group-engendered fraggings involved covert knowledge if not collusion on the part of other members of the group; had a specific individual as the intended target; often were characterized by escalatory threats; and usually involved some form of grenade explosive. Unlike the personal vendetta fragging, moreover, the actual perpetrator of the group-engendered fragging was rarely readily identifiable. It is an irony of sorts that the primary-group processes that appeared to sustain combat soldiers in World War II are close cousins to the social processes that underlaid the vast majority of fraggings in Vietnam.

Rebellion and Discontent

Such typically small-scale sporadic or anomic troop behavior toward the end of the war in Vietnam coincided with the emergence of concerted groups actively seeking to organize servicemen to the antiwar cause. The American Servicemen's Union and the Movement for a Democratic Military were the two principal organizations that had discernible yet ultimately limited consequences on fostering subversion within the ranks. Most likely, commentators in the future will look back upon the troop dissent movement of the Vietnam era as a notable failure in social movements. Much more due to its own internal contradictions rather than any effective counteraction by the military command, the troop dissent movement failed to crystalize the inchoate resentments of many of the lower ranks into a mass antiwar force. Several of the more obvious contradictions were as follows: the failure to bridge broad ideological issues with immediate troop discontent arising from the military system; the opposing appeals of the counterculture versus radical political ideology; the castigation of career noncoms; and the inability of white radicals to resonate with the long-term concerns of black servicemen. Most fundamentally, the troop dissent movement of the latter years of the Vietnam War was never of clear purpose as to whether its goal was to revolutionize the military or to radicalize a youth cohort. On these dialectic shoals the troop dissent movement foundered.

IDEOLOGY AND MILITARY EFFECTIVENESS

The remaining and most elusive question is what were the effects of the antiwar movement at home on the cohesion and demoralization of the American Army in Vietnam. The discussion up to this point has generally stressed the transideological factors (for example, the rotation system, drug abuse, race strife, survival concerns of combat soldiers) that contributed to the deterioration of military discipline in Vietnam. It is also probably the case that much of the decline in military order in Vietnam reflected that general weakening of morale that always seems to accompany an army coming to the end of a war.

Nevertheless, some account must be given of the political impact of the antiwar movement in the United States on soldiers in Vietnam. I have proposed that the concept of latent ideology is an important though indirect variable on combat motivation. It follows that changes in belief systems of soldiers will have observable consequences on military cohesion and performance. Thus prior to 1968 the modal reaction of combat soldiers toward peace demonstrators was one of undisguised hostility. This in turn contributed to military cohesion. Yet once antiwar sentiment at home gained momentum, there was a corresponding drop in troop morale in Vietnam. It was patently evident that soldiers assigned to Vietnam after 1969 differed noticeably from their predecessors in that they were coming from an antiwar milieu that contrasted markedly with that of the early years of the Vietnam War.

However, and this must be heavily stressed, the vast bulk of popular questioning of the American involvement in Southeast Asia after 1969 was not congruent with the widely publicized moral and political arguments against the war typified by the pacifists, intellectuals, academics, and leftists who made up the basic constituency of the organized antiwar movement. Rather than being persuaded by moral and political issues, as Howard Schuman has shown in a detailed study of antiwar attitudes, American public opinion was moved after 1969 by such pragmatic consideration as the unanticipated strength of enemy forces, the adoption of a "no-win" military policy, and, most important, distress over continuing American casualties (Schuman 1972). In fact, one interpretation of the survey data is that the moral–political stance and tactics of the organized antiwar movement may have actually retarded American popular opposition to the Vietnam War.*

The point being made here is that although overt moral considerations or political ideological factors did not have significant consequences on American combat soldiers' motivation, the concrete belief systems of soldiers must nevertheless be included in any understanding of combat cohesion. It was not that American soldiers after 1969 had become antinational or less patriotic, but rather that they themselves reflected a basic change in the national perspective toward the Vietnam War. And it must be noted that despite the post-1969 troop malaise, the fundamental commitment of the combat soldier to the worthwhileness and broad legitimacy of the American system persisted. The American Army in Vietnam did not disintegrate, it did not suffer mass defections, it was not receptive to subversive political forces. This conception of combat motivation—summarized in the notion of latent ideology—bridges the gap between the level of microanalysis based on individual behavior and the level of macroanalysis based on variables common to political sociology.

Furthermore, the underemphasis of ideological factors in the combat studies of World War II can in hindsight be explained on the grounds that public questioning of the war was probably of a low order and in any event severely controlled. That is, ideological support for World War II—at least at elite political and intellectual levels—was a constant. This was not to be the case during the Vietnam War and therefore the salience of ideological factors became a fluctuating variable. Because of the ideological conformity of World War II, the positive role of primary groups in sustaining combat soldiers became overly interpreted. During the later years of the Vietnam War, on the other hand, soldiers' primary groups probably contributed as much to subverting as to supporting the formal goals of the military organization. In sum, the ideological and primary-group explanations are not necessarily contradictory. Rather, an understanding of the combat soldier's motivation requires a simultaneous appreciation of the linkages of small groups and underlying value commitments as they are shaped by the immediate combat environment.

POSTSCRIPT: THE VIETNAM VETERAN

The passions of the Vietnam War carried over into the popular

---

*A comprehensive overview of national survey data pertaining to support and opposition to World War II, the Korean War, and the Vietnam War is found in John E. Mueller, *War, Presidents and Public Opinion* (New York: John Wiley, 1973).

imagery of the returning serviceman. Vietnam veterans were the first to fight in an American war that could not be recalled with pride. In television, movies, novels, and scholarly studies, veterans were stereotyped variously as crazy, guilt ridden, drug addicted, violence prone, allienated, and bitter. Yet, as the Vietnam War recedes into the past, a more balanced picture has began to emerge. Figures referring to veterans who suffered mental breakdowns after discharge may, in part, reflect the greater acceptance of mental illness and the corresponding greater willingness to seek professional help than in times past. They almost certainly reflect the growing tendency of the "helping professions" to define a population in need of attention. A definitive study has shown that the vast majority of soldiers who had become addicted to narcotics in Vietnam, a small proportion to begin with, had abandoned their drug habits upon return to the United States (Robins, Davis, and Goodwin 1974). Careful survey analyses of the social and political attitudes between the veterans and comparable civilian groups conclude that there were few discernible differences, except that the veterans displayed a slightly greater tendency to have positive attitudes toward the military and the American government (Jennings and Markus 1977; Schreiber 1978).

The really striking fact has been the lack of concrete appreciation on the part of the American government toward those who served in the Vietnam era. The postwar amnesty program was less generous to soldiers who received bad discharges than to civilian draft evaders. To be sure, educational benefits were given to Vietnam veterans, but they contained—in constant dollars—less than half of the benefits of the GI Bill of World War II (Army *Times* 1974). Yet the federal government found the wherewithal in the 1970s to expand grants and loans to college students who had not served in the military. In 1978 the administration sought to curtail veterans' preferences in the civil service, a step that would most affect Vietnam veterans. It almost seemed as if the federal government was intent on placing Vietnam veterans at a disadvantage with those who had stayed out of the service. That the public had a more reasoned attitude was revealed in an extensive national poll conducted in 1972 at the height of the disillusionment with the Vietnam War (New York *Times* 1972). Ninety-five percent believed Vietnam veterans "deserve respect for having served their country in the armed forces," and 83 percent disagreed when asked whether "the real heroes of the Vietnam War are the boys who refused induction and faced the consequences." Of course, the true magnitude of those who did not serve in the Vietnam period was found in the widespread *legal* avoidance of military service on the part of America's more privileged youth (Baskir and Strauss 1978).

The Vietnam War was singular in that it produced an antiwar veterans' movement. The inordinate attention given to these groups by opinion shapers and intellectuals probably speaks more to the rationalizations of those who opposed the war than to how much the antiwar veterans represented the views of the mass of Vietnam veterans. In some paradoxical ways, however, the antiwar veterans did display parallels with more conventional veterans' groups. Stories of atrocities witnessed or committed often seemed to be the functional equivalent of heroic war stories. Both gave the soldier's participation in war an exaggerated meaning that could resonate with certain elements of the public back home. It may be that the impassioned antiwar veterans were taking a long detour in the quest for respect that, finally, would win them the admiration and deference from Americans they were otherwise denied. Vietnam veterans' groups, as is true of those of other wars, can find their best purpose neither in glorifying war nor in belittling their service but in commemorating those who died or suffered in battle.

If there is to be any ultimate solace for the Vietnam veteran it may have to be in a reappraisal of the American role in Southeast Asia. Certainly the American soldier had to do a job he neither liked nor understood; but he might take a joyless statisfaction that events in Indochina since his departure show his mission there had some moral justification.

REFERENCES

Army *Times*. 1974. November 22, p. 13.

Baskir, Lawrence M., and William A. Strauss. 1978. *Chance and Circumstance*. New York: Knopf, pp. 14–61.

Gabriel, Richard A., and Paul L. Savage. 1978. *Crisis in Command*. New York: Hill and Wang.

Helmer, John. 1974. *Bringing Home the War*. New York: The Free Press.

Jennings, M. Kent, and Gregory B. Markus, 1977. "The Effect of Military Service on Political Attitudes: A Panel Study." *American Political Science Review* 71 (March): 131–47.

Kinkead, Eugene. 1959. *In Every War But One*. New York: W. W. Norton.

Little, Roger W. 1964. "Buddy Relations and Combat Performance." In *The New Military*, edited by Morris Janowitz. New York: Russell Sage, pp. 191–224.

Moskos, Charles, C., Jr. 1970. *The American Enlisted Man*. New York: Russell Sage, pp. 134–56.

New York *Times*. 1972. January 6, p. 10.

Robins, Lee N.; Darlene H. Davis; and Donald W. Goodwin. 1974. "Drug Use by U.S. Army Enlisted Men in Vietnam: A Follow-Up on Their Return Home." *American Journal of Epidemiology* 99: 235–49.

Schreiber, E. M. 1978. "Enduring Effects of Military Service: Opinion Differences Between U.S. Veterans and Nonveterans." Unpublished paper, Latrobe University, Melbourne, Australia.

Schuman, Howard. 1972. "Two Sources of Anti-War Sentiment in America." *American Journal of Sociology* 78 (November): 513–36.

Shils, Edward A. 1950. "Primary Groups in the American Army." In *Continuities in Social Research*, edited by Robert K. Merton and Paul F. Lazarsfeld. New York. The Free Press, pp. 16–39.

———. and Morris Janowitz. 1948. "Cohesion and Disintegration in the Wehrmacht in World War II." *Public Opinion Quarterly* 12 (Summer): 280–315.

Shirom, Arie. 1976. "On Some Correlates of Combat Performance." *Administrative Science Quarterly* 21 (September): 419–32.

Stouffer, Samuel A. et al. 1949. *The American Soldier.* Vol. I: *Adjustment During Army Life*; Vol. II: *Combat and Its Aftermath*. Princeton, N.J.: Princeton University Press.

5

HIDDEN INJURIES OF WAR

NORMA WIKLER

How does one qualify to be counted among the wounded in the Vietnam War? From the official point of view only those with either physical disabilities or symptoms of a classically defined psychiatric illness are counted. According to authoritative sources, including those who have collaborated on this volume, there are many invisible wounds of war that are as yet undetected. These hidden injuries or residue from the events of the war in Vietnam have been associated with considerable postmilitary adjustment problems. These hidden injuries are the focus of this chapter, which is part of my study (Wikler 1973) on the effects of the war on the political thinking and consciousness of Vietnam veterans. The study was conducted between 1970 and 1972 in the San Francisco Bay Area. The sample included a range of enlisted men of different races, from various social classes and branches of service. I asked them questions to elicit their estimates of self-concept before, during, and after their war experiences. From my interviews it was clear that the Vietnam War led many men to experience painful dissonance of self-conception and personal identity that frequently led to difficulties later in their personal and social readjustments to civilian life styles.

THE DEVELOPMENT OF THE SELF

Few if any of the analyses of the war experiences of American soldiers take into account the age of the enlisted man. This, despite the fact that the meaning of the war, in terms of both psychological and political impact, is certainly influenced by the special features of the particular psychosocial stage of development being experienced. In general, the men in Vietnam were younger than soldiers in previous American wars. Most of the first-term enlistees entered the service between the ages of 17 and 19 and served in Vietnam during that year or the following. In terms of the psychosocial life cycle, those ages fall in the stages of late adolescence or early adulthood.

According to widely accepted theories of developmental psychology, each stage in the life cycle entails a set of specific tasks or "crises" through which the individual must pass in order to successfully mature into adulthood. According to Erik Erikson (1950), the specific crisis of adolescence is the resolution of "identity versus role confusion"; and for young adults, the crisis is that of "intimacy versus isolation."* Though treated variably by society at large, it is generally recognized that the resolution of these specific crises and the general maturational task of establishing an adult identity involves a certain amount of experimentation and the trying out of various social roles.†

The military has usually been considered a special context in which to work out questions of identity and to effect changes in personality and behavior. A number of the veterans interviewed mentioned that one of their expectations of military service was that they would "grow up" and "become a man." Even those who had had reservations about the war prior to service admitted that in some sense they saw the military as an opportunity to discover certain things about themselves, their various competencies, strengths, or courage. When asked to comment on their parents' reaction to their entering the service, several veterans said their fathers, especially, liked the idea because "it would straighten them out a bit." And finally, of course, those Solomonic judges who give delinquents the choice of jail or military service have assumed that the military could serve the purpose of "building character."

---

*See Chapter 7 in this volume by John P. Wilson for a related discussion.

†Erikson points out that society's recognition of this need is reflected in America by the generally accepted period of "psychosocial moratoria" during which (within limits) youths are expected and allowed to experiment with life styles and personal roles before assuming the responsibility or stable identity of adulthood.

One of the essential points to be made about the ordinary civilian setting in which most youths typically forge their identities is that self-discoveries occur as forms of behavior are tried out, as new social relations are developed, and as different physical and mental tasks are engaged. It is unlikely that these new discoveries will be dissonant from previous self-conceptions because of the selective continuity in the process of forging an identity. That is to say, the fundamental issue of the identity crisis—"who am I?"—when tested in ordinary, civilian settings is not likely to lead to startling or unexpected insights especially dissonant from previously held self-conceptions.

In an extraordinary situation—and war, especially the combat situation, may be the most extraordinary of all—there is a great likelihood that the individual will discover aspects and capacities that challenge preconceived notions of himself. In civilian life and in the context of war, the *process* of self-discovery is the same, but the conditions that provide the *concrete experiences* through which the discoveries of the self are made are radically different. Through participation in concrete events, through the development of personal relationships, and in reflection and private thought, young soldiers and young civilians affirm and revise (consciously and unconsciously) their sense of personal being and their various self-conceptions. Part of one's self-conceptions cover the range and depth of emotional response. Such emotions as hate, love, guilt, courage, or terror cannot be imagined; they must be experienced. Once experienced, they may become a part of one's self-concept. Knowledge of one's capacity to experience and express certain emotions may sometimes be flattering and increase self-esteem; in other instances, self-knowledge may be painful, humiliating, and lead to shame and self-hate.

Equally important with the knowledge of one's emotional capacities is the awareness of the kinds of acts one would or would not commit. Few could reasonably argue with common sense that "you really don't know what you would do in a situation until you're actually in it." Fortunately, for most middle-class civilians, everyday life does not generally place men or women in situations where decisions of great moral weight are demanded. There are exceptions, of course. An intruder enters the home, and the owner may have to decide to shoot or not to shoot; and more concretely, whether to "try out" killing or wounding. For the most part, however, civilians are spared the opportunity to discover in themselves the capacities for action that, if done, would be highly dissonant and perhaps intolerable to previously held conceptions of the self. Historically, and even more so in modern times, that is one of the many reasons we delegate most "dirty work" to policemen and others.

A distinctive feature of war is that men are called upon to commit acts that challenge conventional notions of morality and that if committed by civilians would be considered criminal as well as immoral. One of the functions of basic training is to substitute a military morality for a civilian morality and thereby minimize or stifle the resistance of young recruits to doing soldier's work—killing and maiming. If success is measured by the ability to insure that soldiers will consistently and effectively carry out orders, then it must be acknowledged that the military in Vietnam has had very few failures, for apparently most soldiers went competently about their business.

From the point of view of the individual, however, the meaning and consequences of military training are quite different and more complicated. Consider the combat situation as a setting for older adolescents or younger men to forge their adult personalities and to work through the crises of "identity versus confusion" and "intimacy versus isolation"; and to develop a moral component of the self.

THE VIOLENT ESSENCE OF WAR: A WITNESS

The military is the nation's organized instrument of international violence and soldiers are the executors and the victims of violence and its retaliation. Though not everything men find out about themselves in the context of war is directly related to violence, and despite the peaceful appearance of many day-to-day activities, the theme of violence pervades and colors their social world. To understand how pervasive violence is in the military world it will be helpful to first consider the soldier's experience as a *witness* to death and destruction.

It is difficult for those of us who have not been to war to understand the meaning of what Price (a pseudonym), a black ex-Marine captain, called "an arena surrounded by death." No matter how great our powers of empathy, they are insufficient to bring us close to a subjective understanding of that phrase and the phenomena it covers. Nevertheless, through the materials from the veterans' interviews we are able to approach some distant sensitivity to that horrifying arena of war. Recollecting aspects of the war's lasting impact on some of the men in his unit, Price stressed their reaction to this feature of the combat situation:

> When you're in that setting it's like being in an arena surrounded by death. It's hard to explain what happens once you start seeing people die. That's something as civilians, that *something we don't do*. We just don't see people die. We might see it on T.V. or see it in the movies,

but that's all. We very seldom hold a guy and watch him die like soldiers do in Vietnam. Maybe here, kids'll see their parents or their grandmother dead, but they look at them *after* they're dead. But in Vietnam there are so many feelings, and you think, oh my God, look at 'em, what is this, I could be next, just look at the people out there.

The trauma of seeing buddies die was intensified by being witness to the destruction of the Vietnamese people. Speaking of his combat experience as a Marine, Underwood remembered the reaction of his buddies who were sent to check a village that had been "accidentally" bombed by the U.S. Air Force several years before. Most of them came back sick, just sick, white, and completely torn apart because they had never seen such a gross destruction of man, woman, and child."

The soldiers' trauma of seeing their buddies being killed and wounded came not only from the shock and grief of the loss of young lives but also from the frustration and pain of being impotent to help them. Gillen was a medic and saved many lives but he said that of all of his experiences in the field, he remembers most vividly the incident described below:

When I went into the field, the first casualty was a Marine, about nineteen years old with his legs blown off, and he said "Doc, doc, I'm gonna live! You're gonna save me, aren't ya doc?" And I said, "Yeah, yeah babe, you're gonna live." And then he dies in my arms, so I cried and there was nothing I could do but go to the next guy that was hurt, and then the next guy, and then the next.

Nelson was a quiet, soft-spoken black Army veteran. During the interview he rarely displayed emotion, but when he spoke of witnessing the death of his buddies, he did not conceal his nervousness and pain.

Yeah, I saw a lot of it, a lot of it, and it's weird, you know, to see, well here you are, two guys in a hole, and there goes a guy's head, you know, and he's really hurt, really hurt bad, and there's nothing you can do at the time, you know, you've gotta keep fighting, you just know that you have to. You have to shine it on, look over it, forget it. Put it out of your mind, because you can't take care of it, you can't stop in the middle of a fight, even though you want . . . then maybe sometimes you can just glance over and quick put something over the hole, or try to tie a tourniquet around it to stop the bleeding, and that's all you can do, 'cause you're right in the middle of the fight, and you have to keep your mind on what you're doin', on that one thing.

Increasing the terror for American soldiers in the field was the fear of being blown to bits by mines and bobby traps. Already engaged in fighting an "invisible enemy," land mines, and booby traps—staple weapons of guerrilla fighters—increased the tension and anxiety in areas of active combat and even throughout the allegedly pacified countryside. Not infrequently the explosions from the mines activated by a footstep killed soldiers in front or behind the man who stepped on the mine. When the soldier who activated the mine survived and the others did not, "survivor guilt" was a distinct possibility. When Peters stepped on a rock mine, he was wounded, but his buddy in front was killed. He hesitantly described the incident.

> Well, I stepped on a rock mine—that's like an antipersonnel mine, except that instead of using metal they use rock. I got rocks in my thigh; a few went in my arm and my foot, and my ankle's pretty well blown up. Well it happened about the fifth day out on patrol. I stepped on the mine, and it blew up in front of me and my buddy in front of me, he got killed. Shrapnel hit 'em in the back of his head. He lived for twenty-four hours, but, it killed him, you know, the guy in front of me. All he was doing was walking but that was it. And he . . . I just felt bad about that 'cause it killed him and he didn't have nothin' to do with it. He was just walking in front of me.

Peters said that after two years of intense guilt and depression following discharge from service he began to see a minister and to talk about the war experience. After a few months of counseling, he said he felt much better. For those soldiers who do not successfully resolve the guilt incurred by such experiences, it would be hard to believe that there are not serious consequences on the developing self-concept and sense of personal identity (see Chapter 7).

Nevertheless, some of the self-discoveries reported by veterans can be interpreted as possibly enhancing the quality of their future lives. Nearly all believe that in some way or other they had "grown up" in Vietnam and learned things about themselves that they could not have possibly experienced had they not been in war. Kirk said that this was probably true for all of the men who had been in Vietnam, but especially those in combat:

> It could happen to anybody, but it happens definitely much more when you're in a combat area. You know, it's a survival type of situation, it's really life or death. You see people dyin' around you and you realize that you still might make it, and, uh, there's no place for self-delusions or anything like that. I think it was a good experience really, you know, it opened my eyes to quite a few things.

When Underwood first became a Marine he felt, like most of the men, that it was unmanly to express any kind of emotion. Through his own combat experience, he saw through this restrictive American myth. "I think it's ridiculous that men aren't supposed to show any emotion," he reported. "When my best friend in Vietnam was killed, I sat and cried and cried. I had to bring him back, and all that kind of stuff, it's really tough. You should cry when there are things that you feel really deeply about, it's only a human thing to do."

Generally speaking, the experiences of war are likely to create strains and difficulties in the soldiers' attempts to resume normal civilized activities and social relationships. Of all the problems of readjustment to civilian life discussed by veterans, none was more common or troubling than that of reestablishing close personal ties. Perhaps this is not surprising when we consider that the traumatic experience of the loss of close friends or even acquaintances sustained in Vietnam came at the crucial developmental stage when problems of intimacy were dominant. Veterans themselves attributed their readjustment problems regarding relationships to the Vietnam experience. Griffin said of Vietnam:

> You learn not to have friends—not close friends. You don't get too close to anybody, 'cause it might kill you . . . say you have a friend and you go on patrol and something happens and he gets pinned down. If you were really close to him you might go and help him, and if you're in some command position you can't do that. It would get you in trouble. Besides that, if he got killed it could depress you pretty bad, and cause you to do things you shouldn't. You have to have some friends, but as far as getting real buddy-buddy, you try not to do that.

The same sort of personal experience influenced French to come to define a close relationship as one where "you depend on that person more than you should." He elaborates this view following a description of the death of a member of his unit.

> You don't have no friends, no buddies over there, just acquaintances. You don't get attached to people because he may be gone tomorrow, and there's no room in combat, no room in Vietnam or anywhere except for the fightin'. You know, John Doe, he got shot, you know, he's dead, and you're not gonna sit around for the next two or three days holding the weight. It doesn't work . . . at first it's natural to try to make friends, but after you've been there two or three combat missions and you see a couple of people shot down, you know, and blown away, and they don't come back, you get used to it. You say, well, it was just a casual acquaintance, or a "military acquaintance"

that's all . . . you learn not to have close friendships, 'cause close friendships are where you get so you depend on that person, you know, more than you should.

THE SOLDIER IN ACTION

The experiences of war just described afforded the soldier—sometimes forced upon him—new self-knowledge. As long as the soldier was a *witness* to rather than an *agent* of violence, destruction, or war, it is unlikely that his most basic self-conceptions would be assaulted or called into question. It was while *doing* that American soldiers experienced the deeper dissonance of self. Veterans know this well and, understandably, they signify the first time they killed a person as a crucial transition point: "The worst feeling in the world is the first time you ever had to kill anyone, ah, it kinda shakes you up, you know, it makes you think; and you go into yourself and think about yourself" (Underwood).

The first experience of killing a person is often an occasion of intense (though generally fleeting) self-reflection. The soldier's discovery of his own capacity to so easily and automatically execute such a deed may take him by surprise. Smith, a disabled veteran, recalls his surprise and embarrassment:

> The first time I killed . . . the first time I shot someone over in Vietnam, I dropped my gun, fell to my knees, and started crying 'cause I had shot somebody . . . it happened so fast and I didn't realize what I had done. I stayed like that on my knees for a minute or so, then he [the sergeant] came up and kicked me in the butt and told me to get up.

Nearly a year after his return from Vietnam, Witt was still unable to adjust to the fact that he had killed other human beings. Indeed, this was the dominant theme of his lengthy interview. Perhaps his reaction was all the more intense and disorganizing because that experience led to a sudden sense of betrayal by the Marine Corps that had promised through combat experience to "make him into a man":

> I can see the people with me, I remember saying, "Wow, I don't think that's the good guy," 'cause like I was in the militarized zone. Well, you've got twenty yards to decide [laugh] on what your reaction's going to be. My first thought was to try to get them to surrender. I said, *chu hoi*, you know, which means "give up." I could see them but they couldn't see me, and as soon as the first one got down I could see

the second one and I said, *chu hoi* again. And the guy just looked startled and he threw the bag at me and I started shooting, and I was carrying an M-14 gun. And, uh, so my fingers were on the trigger and I just blew him up, I blew both of 'em up, and that's all the shooting there was. Just the noise of my gun and then quiet.

Then the guys next to me were jumping and rolling down the hill, it was happening so fast. My squad leader was there and he said, "Come on, let's go after 'em, maybe there's more." And I said, "You go after them, I don't want to." Both of the guys were laying there, dead, not even moving, not even twitching. And then I said to myself, "So this is what it's all about," and I went up and grabbed the first one and I carried him all the way down the hill, and then I laid him in front of my lieutenant and I said, "Well, lieutenant, I guess this means I'm a *man* now, huh?"

That's all I really had to say. It was like, well, you know, to be a Marine means like doin' well in combat, it makes you a man. When I said that to him, as a sarcastic remark, because I sure didn't feel like I had done anything great, I sure didn't feel like I had become a man.

He told me I had to search the guy, you know, because I was the one who killed them and that was my responsibility, and I had to report the whole thing, so I did, and I was looking through the guy's wallet, you know, and I saw a picture of his wife and a picture of girls and guys with writing on them, you know, like a school picture trip, with writing on the back, and I just said, wow, this guy was a real live human being. And it made me realize, you know, how totally screwed up being a human being is. It's just a bunch of bullshit . . . I don't think human beings are less of an animal than a tiger.

For some soldiers, like Witt, the act of killing provoked a profound sense of dissonance and a personal moral crisis. However, it would be quite misleading to suggest that this was the most common response of soldiers; it was not.

The most impressive fact to emerge from discussion of this topic with veterans was the very wide range of their responses. Leonzi represented a very different reaction, perhaps at the other end of the spectrum. Discovery of his capacity for violence seemed to enhance his self-esteem. He found combat an exciting game:

The first time you shot at somebody, you get excited . . . I got excited, too, I don't know why, I couldn't say whether it's being scared or just plain excited. My heart started beating faster, no, it wasn't an upsetting experience . . . I just made it into a game; that's the enemy and you're the opponent and you go and git 'em . . . it was just a game. If they just happened to be out at night, you know, they got shot. It may sound prejudiced, but you don't even think of them as people when you're shooting at them, you know, they're just an enemy, well, they're not an enemy, either, they're just an opponent. It's like in the daytime they're people but at night they're not.

Perhaps Detrick's description is most representative. He initially responded with surprise at his own reflexes (both to shoot automatically and to get sick afterward) but he found that after the first time, it was quite easy. Detrick's personal account seems to exemplify J. Glen Gray's (1970, p. 181) insight that "becoming a soldier was like escaping from one's own shadow. To commit deeds of violence without the usual consequences that society visits upon the violent seemed at first a bit unnatural but for many not unpleasant. All too quickly it could become a habit." As Detrick recounts,

> The first time I ever shot anybody I got sick. It was such an automatic reaction, you know, I didn't even stop to think about it at first. By the time I realized, I already shot him. The zip had come over the top of the hill and he had a rifle like this. I saw him and he saw me, and I picked it up and shot him. I didn't realize at first, I didn't get sick till after I had come back to look at him ten, fifteen minutes later when all the shooting had stopped. . . .
>
> And I did get to thinking "How can I do that?" You know, but it was easy. I just did it without thinking. He had come running up the bank, I picked up the gun and shot him and put it back down. . . . But, you know, what amazed me the most was, you know, I did it without even thinking, you know, it was just something automatic. I don't think anything passed through my mind, it was just, you know "snap" that quick. Then, there were some incidents that happened after my outfit was wiped out, and they didn't bother me one way or the other. Like, once we were going through a village and got some fire. We caught 'em out in the open running across the rice paddies, and everybody was firing, and I says, "Should I fire or shouldn't I?" you know, I had a perfect opportunity not to fire; nobody would've thought much of it, but I knelt down and started bangin' away at a few of 'em. It was none of this "kill or be killed" you know, he was just runnin' away and I got him. It was not a life or death circumstance on my part. It was different, you know, not really personal. That was very impersonal, but even when it was up close, it didn't seem to bother me. After the first time it didn't bother me at all.

There were other aspects of combat behavior that seem to be almost as brutalizing and costly to one's self-conception as that of killing another person. Some soldiers discovered that unexpectedly and unaccountably they would strike out in senseless acts of brutality that would later produce shame and guilt. Yamada relates an incident that involved his best buddy:

My buddy said that he felt kind of bitter, you know, when he looked at this dead guy he said maybe he had wounded four or five of our guys, and maybe he would have wounded some more if he hadn't been killed, you know that's war and what can you do about it. Anyway, my buddy went past him and *kicked him*, you know. He was tellin' me about this later, and I say, I said, "What'd you do that for, you know?" and he goes, "I don't know, I seen Rod get hurt, and I know that guy's dead but I kicked him anyway." He was kind of ashamed that he had kicked a dead person, even though it was the enemy he kicked, you know. He didn't show it on the outside too much, because he wasn't that type of fellow, but deep down, you know, he thought maybe it was kind of wrong to do that even though the person was dead and the enemy. He didn't know what to make of himself for doing that, because he just wasn't the type, the type to be real violent and have a built-in hatred for the enemy, like some folks do.

Not all veterans found their capacity for brutality or violence disconcerting. Even for those like Kirk who are reflective and introspective, it is possible that their self-conception will be maintained despite their combat behavior. Whether justification or rationalization, Kirk's ability to accept the necessity for his own combat activities spared him the agony of doubt, confusion, and guilt that some other soldiers suffered. Here he explains why his first experience of killing the enemy was not especially traumatic:

I didn't feel that it was traumatic. I mean, I was, you know, you're ready for it, you know, you see T.V. and movies all your life, you know what to expect. Maybe, maybe not completely conscious of all the implications of it when it happens. But, like at the time it's a necessary thing, you know. Like the attitude was, if somebody died, you know, if they killed the gook, that was a good thing, you know. Like, if they run into somebody and they get 'em before he had a chance to get away, that was good, you know.

And one day I caught myself, you know, "Oh, we got 'em!" you know, somebody says, uh, "Yeah, good!" you know. And, uh, I caught myself thinking, you know, "well, this is really *strange*, you know, you just killed some guy, o.k., what's good about it, you know." But, uh, I was thinkin' about it, you know, in that situation, it was a good thing for them to be dead, you know. . . . it was not a personal thing or anything. It just, for them to be dead was a good thing, you know. It was good for you, because it was protecting your life.

In *The Warriors*, Gray (1970) probes the reasons why many men both hate and love combat. He speaks (p. 27) of the way in which war, especially combat, forces the transition from soldier to "fighting man":

They may write home to their parents and sweethearts that they are unchanged, and they may even be convinced of it. But the soldier who has yielded himself to the fortunes of war, has sought to kill and escape being killed, or who has even lived long enough in the disordered landscape of battle, is no longer what he was. He becomes in some sense a fighter whether he wills it or not—at least most men do.

Gray admits that "beyond doubt there are many who simply endure war, hating every moment, . . ." but he does argue that in the context of combat, many other soldiers who never suspected in themselves the impulse to kill and destroy their own kind will discover their capacity not only to perform brutal deeds but to enjoy them as well.

The soldiers' realization that they could derive pleasure from such destruction led to the most painful kind of dissonance of self-conception. This was the most terrible secret that some young GIs were forced to confront—sometimes while in Vietnam, more often after their return to civilian life. Very few veterans spoke of their own reactions of pleasure in combat, although most would talk about others they knew—the "killer types," as they were referred to, the men who "really got into it." "killer types" or "hard-core" were not those who simply excelled in combat skills. Instead, they were those who really seemed to enjoy their work, getting "kicks" or "highs" from killing.

One veteran who talked freely about the process of "getting into it" [killing] was Kempton:

By the time I got to the artillery unit, I had become really hard-core, you know, I just hated, hated the VC, and I can't say it was a hate for shooting my friends, because by then I had become calloused, that's how I felt, just calloused. I didn't care anymore.

You said that earlier you had actually begun to enjoy the killing?

Yeah, I wanted to kill, I really did, and when I went off to artillery, these guys were in infantry and they weren't supposed to be killing anybody—I would just sneak out at night and go on ambush and patrol with the infantry . . . they did have a couple of skirmishes and all the other guys were hiding under the bunk, and I just started to kill. They were hiding but I thought, wow, this is a field day, and I actually dug it. I ran out with my rifle and I was just all smiles from here to there.

Did you hate the VC?

No, I couldn't say I hated them. I didn't know them, so I couldn't hate them. But I wanted to kill them. It wasn't that I wanted to kill an individual person. I can't say who I wanted to kill, but I wanted to shoot somebody. Still, I never was like they were in the Recon unit I had just left. They really wanted it. That was their whole life. And I wanted it, to kill, but I could never be as hard-core as they were.

Could you tell me a bit more about the actual feelings you had at that time?

Well, mentally it was like, a good time, a good party, you know, like this is party time, let's get going. That's the way I felt. "Bang, all right, let's shoot somebody," that's the way I felt. But, I didn't really know that I was getting this way. I really never noticed it until the last six or seven months. Then finally I noticed it, you know, and I couldn't figure out how come I wanted to kill, and I can't still figure that out. I mean I was going from a very mellow trip to a violent trip and I couldn't figure it out.

THE QUESTION OF WILL

In addition to providing the opportunity to discover one's capacity for killing another human being and the "morality" to enjoy such acts, the combat situation poses still another challenge to the self-conception of the individual soldiers. The purpose of the endless drills and repetitious maneuvers of basic and advanced military training is to insure automatic, reflexive responses to commands in or out of the combat situation. Though many soldiers were upset by the feeling during training that this conditioning was turning them into a "robot," usually they accepted the fact that such automatic reflex action could save their lives in Vietnam.

Nevertheless, military training insuring automatic response that can and does override and precede conscious reflection may also have severe psychological consequences for the young soldier. The question of "will"—confidence in the ability to control and direct one's own behavior—is vital for the personal identity of all humans. Military training points men, especially the combat soldiers, toward a peculiar dilemma concerning the issue of will and identity. Sometimes soldiers commit acts that later—sometimes only seconds later—they regret. Their subsequent suffering comes not only from the regret regarding the act performed but also from the frightening discovery of the possibility that their own "will" was overpowered and obliterated by their reflexes. One Vietnam veteran described the feeling as being "something like a schizophrenic must feel. You don't know who you are. It's like you have another side to you, another person, and you never know when that other side is gonna take over."

Another veteran, Wilcox, had come back to California and entered junior college. By all outward appearances he was "well adjusted." Throughout most of the interview he maintained a sort of polite indifference. Near the end, however, he became quite visibly upset and began to describe an incident that had happened shortly before his return to the States. Embarrassed by the tears in his eyes, he explained that this was the first time in the eight months since his return that he had spoken of the Cambodian raid. According to Wilcox, his superior officer had wanted a motorcycle that had been spotted in a small Cambodian village. Wilcox was the gunner in the Cobra helicopter and as the "chopper" swooped down on the village, he was ordered to fire on the defenseless civilians. He obeyed. More in an attempt to explain to himself than to me, he said,

> I haven't gotten over it. I still haven't gotten over it. Like I killed that one dude, I know I did, I didn't want to kill him, but it was like just a spontaneous thing. I was two years over there in combat and trained never to hesitate starting to fire, and once firing started I was trained to react and it's really unfortunate, my reflexes got the best of me. I, I know he was dead, I know he was Cambodian and just minding his own business. He came out of his house, his house was on fire. Dear God, of course he's going to run, but these things, they didn't enter my mind. All I saw was him running, and all these dead people, and I just seemed to lose control. I just lost all rationality, and I just *reacted*. How could I have done such a thing?

In Austin's moving description of his killing a young Vietnamese girl while on patrol we see another example of the soldier's discovery of uncontrollable reflexes. However, in this case, the young Marine externalizes the anger and the blame. To the haunting question "How could I have done such a thing?" Austin formulates an answer. Recognizing the reflex to fire drilled into him during training, he concludes that for his act of killing he has his government to thank.

> The turning point for me came when this incident occurred, in which we were coming through a village. We had been on our feet for almost three days, running around doing something worthless. But, ah, we were coming through a village and I can't remember the name of the village and we were spaced apart maybe ten feet and everybody was slogging along. We were dirty, we were tired, we were hungry. We had three or four days' growth of beard on and it was filthy dirty and, ah, we were asleep on our feet.
> Then, this Vietnamese girl—she must have been sixteen, seventeen years old—gorgeous looking girl, ah, stopped me by stepping in

front of me and putting her hands on my chest. Ah, and I looked at *her*, she looked at me and this was the first girl I'd seen in, you know, a long time and it did things to me and if it didn't they'd be something wrong with me. But, ah, it did. She reached up and she touched my face like this and looked into my eyes. It just blew my mind [pause] completely. So I pushed her back and continued forwards and I think, I don't remember how far I'd gone, it couldn't have been very far. She . . . somebody fired a round at me. It went by my ear. And I turned in reflex, in the space of a single breath I turned and had fired half a magazine into this girl, all the way up the front till she was disfigured. You couldn't recognize her. She had no face left. And I, I went over to her and it was then that I decided that the order of things was absurd. That things no longer made sense. That, ah, the way things were happening, this particular incident was a waste, for me, for her, for everything. It served no purpose. It, ah, it promoted no goodness.

I, I blamed, I blamed—I don't know who I blamed for my reflex but I knew that six months before that I would never have done that, turned and done something else, but . . . so I took the cartridge, she had had an M-1 carbine as it turned out. She had, she's the one who had shot at me, but she had stopped me to see the face of the man that she was going to kill. And I took the cartridge from the carbine and I threw the carbine in one of the bushes and I kept the cartridge with me, and every time I see the cartridge, when I reach into my hand, my pocket, for some change, the cartridge always comes out with it. And I see, this is the bullet that almost killed me and *yet*—something happened in her the last minute that made her miss. But when I turned nothing happened inside me. *I killed her.*

But what was it that happened to her that last minute before she fired? That moment of indecision or of consciousness—or of conscience—whichever, that made her pull to the left or pull to the right, so that she missed me? She was maybe ten feet away and a man's back is a pretty massive target. She couldn't have missed me, but something happened. She changed her mind and pulled to the left or the right and missed. But me, when I turned around, the reflex that had been *drilled* into me overrode my conscience, my thought, everything. And I had killed her before I realized what happened to me.

So I figured that I would carry this cartridge and all these I.D. cards and photography and everything else until I could look at them and not feel guilty about them. Until I could look at them and say, "Um, it's all right. You know, no one's going to hold it against you." And so, I have them all at home, and I don't look at them often, but when I do . . . when someone says, "Do you have any photographs of Vietnam?" I show them these and to them, it's just a bunch of pictures. But, ah, when I look at them I feel that this is the fact of my life *and for this I have my government to thank.*

In the interviews many combat veterans stated that since their return to the United States they shunned any situation where violence could result. Sometimes they explained this by saying, "I have seen enough violence" and other times by admitting "I don't know what I might do." They were uncertain whether or not they could control themselves. Thus, the question of the extent to which automatic reflexes instilled in training and combat would continue to override willful attempts at self-control became another one of the problems to be dealt with in the soldier's attempts to consolidate his self-conception and sense of identity.

THE VETERANS COME HOME

It is possible that for some soldiers the war experience did not yield any dissonance of self-conception, and that even among those for whom it did, some were able to successfully reconcile the dissonance. Nevertheless, there remains an unknown proportion of soldiers for whom the impact of the assaults on the self ranged from painful, though tolerable, to utterly devastating. For these men, leaving Vietnam did not necessarily diminish their trauma. The resolution of the dilemmas of personal identity and self-conceptions posed by the war depended upon the personal and postwar conditions they encountered upon their return. In this postwar era, as in no other, the injuries were likely to persist.

Surely soldiers of all American wars were subjected to conditions similar to those in Vietnam. They, too, endured military training and served as both witnesses to and agents of destruction. What was it about the Vietnam experience that exaggerated and intensified the dissonance of self-conception? And what were the postwar features that impeded its resolution?

Guilt and doubt may be common feelings of soldiers in every war, but some elements peculiar to the Vietnam war compounded and confused these feelings. In conventional wars it is not difficult to distinguish combatants from noncombatants. In the Vietnam war, however, the distinctions were not so clear. Americans had contact with Vietnamese civilians in a number of settings—on base compounds where there were maids, barbers, and other civilians; in towns and cities and in the villages and hamlets throughout the country. Everywhere the question for the GI was the same, "Whose side are they on?" Repeated incidents of civilians firing on Americans, setting roadblocks, and laying mines led to the widespread belief that all Vietnamese were or could be Vietcong. Thus, women and even small children were redefined as "enemy" and this new definition facilitated the killing of civilians. From the interviews it was clear that the typical rationale, "If you don't get them now, they'll get you later, was in many cases insufficient to assuage the guilt that came from killing Vietnamese civilians.

For many soldiers the justification for the destruction in Vietnam lay in their belief that the United States was "helping" the people of South Vietnam. The films they had seen in basic training showing new schools, roads, and hospitals built by teams of Vietnamese and Americans had motivated some to serve in Vietnam. However most of the GIs interviewed saw no evidence of such American aid programs once they got to Vietnam, and for many soldiers, maintaining the definition of the activities of the U.S. troops they observed and served in as "aid" required a kind of logic so convoluted it often proved to be untenable. The famous remark, "We had to destroy the village in order to save it," was a model for this kind of thinking. Especially in the later war years, soldiers increasingly came to doubt the effectiveness and moral justification of the war. As the enterprise waged by their government came under question, some men were led to confront the implications of their own acts; their disillusion with the American government often entailed a comparable disillusion with themselves.

One of the structural features of the Vietnam War that played a part in sustaining the injuries of these soldiers was the system of rotation and demobilization. In contrast to World Wars I and II when soldiers generally served for the duration and were released from service at the end of the war with members of their unit, each soldier in Vietnam, serving a 12-month tour of duty, had his individual DEROS (Date Expected Return Overseas) from Vietnam. When his tour was completed he returned, usually alone, to the United States. Not uncommonly, a soldier in Vietnam would get on a plane in Saigon, travel 15 hours crossing 12 time zones, arrive at an air base in the United States and six to eight hours later be on the street as a civilian. Such procedures disallowed the possibility of veterans collectively "working through" their war experiences and possibly resolving or coming to terms with the injuries of self.

Never before had America's fighting men returned home so quietly and so unwelcomed. Much has been made of the fact that there were no "victory parades" for the veterans of Vietnam, but little consideration has been given to the consequences of this fact for the soldiers' personal identity. While in Vietnam soldiers were aware of the "divided homefront," and regardless of their own convictions "for" or "against" the war, the lack of support from home was a source of distress and usually anger. Once in the United States they discovered that they had become the visible symbols of this unpopular and unvictorious war. Many found their status of "veteran" a stigma rather than a source of pride. In contrast to veterans of other wars (especially World War II) for whom the role of veteran enhanced self-conception, the men back from Vietnam tended to reject the role. Few joined the veterans service organizations and many shunned the Veterans Administration.

The men we interview often spoke of their fear of hostility and blame from their peers for having participated in the war and of the lack of respect accorded them by older veterans who reproached them for not having won "their" war. The image of Vietnam veterans put forth by the media did not help them restructure a positive civilian identity. Television, especially, portrayed Vietnam veterans as crazed killers coming back hooked on drugs or disposed toward uncontrollable violence (see Chapter 13).

The postwar periods of all the twentieth-century American wars, except Vietnam, had prosperous economies that were able to absorb the demobilized troops into the labor force. During the war and in the postwar period, unemployment among Vietnam veterans was high and persistently above the rates of nonveterans of the same age group. In early 1971, for example, the rate of unemployment among Vietnam veterans was 11 percent, two points higher than for nonveterans of the same age group (the rates for the disabled, disadvantaged, and minority veterans were much higher, of course). The restricted opportunity in the labor force exacerbated the reentry process and prolonged the period of civilian readjustment.

A job, almost any job, helps to ease the transition from soldier to civilian in a number of often subtle ways. Civilian language and habits are more easily regained, and informal social controls through day-to-day social action involve the veterans in patterns of civilian response that may have been lost or diminished through military training and the experience of war. Without a new civilian role—student* or worker—the young veteran is likely to find that his continued attempts to work through the identity crisis are once again impeded or frustrated. The transition from soldier to civilian depends partly on having a social role that can serve to enable answers to the question central to the identity crisis "Who am I?" Since that question, for the most part, is answered in terms of "what I do," a man who does nothing generally discovers a humiliating answer.

Resolution of the crisis of "intimacy versus isolation" was forestalled partly because the age of these veterans meant that, compared to

---

*Many who would have chosen to go to school found their GI benefits too low to support themselves entirely without additional employment.

veterans of other wars, few were married with families of their own. For many, it was not a question of returning home to renew preservice intimate ties, but rather a problem of establishing new ones. However, as we have pointed out in this chapter, the capacity for intimacy was often damaged by the experiences of war. In their attempts to reestablish close relationships or begin new ones, manifestations of their hidden injuries were likely to be most apparent. Though there are no official statistics to document it, individuals who work with Vietnam veterans (and veterans' groups themselves) report a very high incidence of divorce. In personal accounts of returning veterans, severe difficulties in expressing love and sexuality are often described (Eisenhart 1975). It is bitterly ironic that the potentially healing powers of intimacy and love were so often unavailable because the very nature of the veterans' injuries damaged the source of these powers.

What resources were available to the veterans who sought help with problems of readjustment? Though the Veterans Administration was formally charged with handling service-connected disabilities, the veterans' distrust of any facility attached to the government made it unlikely that they would turn there. Civilian mental health professionals encountered some of these men, but because of the particular response syndromes engendered by the special characteristics of the Vietnam experience, their treatment has not been notably effective (Horowitz and Solomon 1975). Probably the rap groups that were begun by the Vietnam Veterans Against the war to provide for a collective appraisal of the war experience were the most successful means of resolving or at least reducing the injuries to self and identity (Lifton 1973; 1978). Such groups were, unfortunately, available to only a few.

Most Vietnam veterans were left to cope alone, for better or for worse, with the personal aftermath of the war. To the Americans killed in Vietnam and the more than 300,000 wounded we must add the tens of thousands among us who bear the hidden injuries of war.

REFERENCES

Barnes, Peter. 1972. *Pawns: The Plight of the Citizen Soldier*. New York: Alfred Knopf.

Bims, Hamilton. 1971. "The Black Veteran: Battle on the Homefront." *Ebony*, November.

Bourne, Peter G. 1970. *Men, Stress and Vietnam*. Boston: Little, Brown.

Egendorf, Arthur. 1975. "Vietnam Veterans Rap Groups and Themes of Postwar Life." *Journal of Social Issues* 31 (Fall): 111–24.

Eisenhart, W. 1975. "You can't hack it little girl: A discussion of the overt psychological agenda of modern combat training." *Journal of Social Issues* 31: 4.

Erikson, Erik H. 1950. *Childhood and Society*. New York: W. W. Norton.

FitzGerald, Frances. 1972. "Annals of War: Vietnam, Part IV." *New Yorker* 48 (July 22): 53–68.

Gray, J. Glen. 1970. *The Warriors: Reflections on Men in Battle*, 2d ed. New York: Harper & Row.

Grinker, Roy, and J. P. Spiegel. 1945. *Men Under Stress*. Philadelphia: Blackiston.

Havinghurst, Robert et al. 1951. *The American Veteran Back Home: A Study of Veteran Readjustment*. New York: Longmans, Green.

Helmer, John. 1974. *Bringing the War Home: The American Soldier in Vietnam and After*. New York: The Free Press.

Horowitz, Mardi, and George Solomon. 1975. "A Prediction of Delayed Stress Response Syndromes in Vietnam Veterans." *Journal of Social Issues* 31 (Fall): 67–80.

Lifton, R. J. 1978. "Advocacy and Corruption in the Healing Professions." In *Stress Disorders Among Vietnam Veterans*, edited by Charles R. Figley. New York: Brunner/Mazel, pp. 209–30.

———. 1973. *Home From the War*. New York: Simon and Schuster.

McDonagh, Edward C. 1946. "The Discharged Serviceman and His Family." *American Journal of Sociology* 51 (March): 451–54.

Moskos, Charles, Jr. 1970. *The American Enlisted Man*. New York: Russell Sage.

Polner, Murray. 1971. *No More Victory Parades: The Return of the Vietnam Veteran*. New York: Holt, Rinehart and Winston.

Pratt, George K., M.D. 1944. *Soldier to Civilian: Problems of Readjustment*. New York: McGraw Hill.

Starr, Paul. 1973. *The Discarded Army: Veterans After Vietnam*. New York: Charterhouse.

Stouffer, Samuel A. et al. 1949. *The American Soldier*: vol. 1, *Adjustment to Army Life*; vol. 2, *Combat and Its Aftermath*. Princeton, N.J.: Princeton University Press.

Strange, Cdr. Robert E., and Dudley E. Brown, Jr. 1970. "Home From the War: A Study of Psychiatric Problems in Viet Nam Returnees." *American Journal of Psychiatry* 127:4 (October): 488–92.

U.S. Congress. Senate. 1971. Committee on Labor and Public Welfare. *Unemployment and Overall Readjustment Problems of Returning Veterans: Hearings Before the Veterans' Affairs Subcommittee*. 91st Cong. 2d sess. Washington, D.C.: U.S. Government Printing Office.

U.S. Department of Labor. 1971. "Employment Situation of Vietnam Era Veterans: Third Quarter 1971." *News* (October, 15).

Vietnam Veterans Against the War. 1972. *The Winter Soldier Investigation: An Inquiry into American War Crimes*. Boston: Beacon Press.

Veterans World Project. 1972. *Wasted Men: The Reality of the Vietnam Veteran*. A report prepared by the Veterans World Project, Southern Illinois University, Edwardsville.

Waller, Willard. 1944. *The Veteran Comes Back*. New York: Dryden Press.

Wikler, Norma. 1973. "Vietnam and the Veterans' Consciousness: Pre-Political Thinking Among American Soldiers." University of California, Berkeley.

SECTION II

THE RETURNING VETERAN

CONFUSED, HATED, IGNORED, AND DISHONORED: AN INTRODUCTION TO SECTION II

Charles R. Figley

This second set of chapters examines the special problems of those who returned from Vietnam. Beginning with the classic analysis of the homecomer by Alfred Schuetz, the chapters proceed from a careful theoretical discussion of the unique emotional burdens of the Vietnam veterans in the chapter by John Wilson, to an overview of the various adjustment problems uncovered by the research of Figley and Southerly and expanded in terms of employment by Kohen and Shields, to examination of veterans' political feelings and activities in separate chapters by Loch Johnson and Fred Milano.

Chapter 6, by Alfred Schuetz, an abridged version of his post-World War II article in the *American Journal of Sociology*, is both timely and timeless. The "homecomer," as he points out, is, in effect, someone who feels like a stranger at home: "The home to which he returns is by no means the home he left or the home which he recalled and longed for during his absence. And, for the same reason, the homecomer is not the same man who left. He is neither the same for himself nor for those who await his return." As Schuetz notes, the returning war veteran is a particularly good example of a homecomer. We hear this theme throughout this volume: The veteran homecomer expects little change but finds considerable; those he returns to expect little change but also find considerable.

What may be most difficult for the homecomer is the transition from one world view and resultant pattern of life away from home (for example, in the military and in war) to another view and pattern at home. Adjustment is often difficult. Thus, as Schuetz correctly concludes, we need to prepare not only the veteran for his new life as a civilian but also the civilian environment for his return. Neither, of course, was done for the Vietnam veteran.

One of the most frequently quoted authorities on the Vietnam veteran is John P. Wilson. In Chapter 7 he relates the history of his involvement with Vietnam veterans, first as a teacher, then as a researcher, and eventually as counselor and spokesman. The thrust of the chapter is to draw upon extant theories of human development to create a "holistic look at how the Vietnam war affected the veterans' reentry into the mainstream of society. . . ."

Wilson addresses such questions posed by Vietnam veterans as: "Why can't I feel more at home now?" "Why do I feel depressed even though I've survived?" Drawing upon his data and theoretical perspectives, Wilson answers these and other questions. For example, he notes that because most Vietnam veterans spent part of their late teen and early adult years away from home, they were denied the normal period of moratorium from adult responsibilities, since they were expected to be men during as well as following military service. Moreover, this period is a critical time in male sex role development and the formation of ego-identity.

Wilson concludes from his research and theorizing that Vietnam veterans who entered the military, served and fought in Vietnam, and were released into a hostile American society were severely handicapped in terms of either ego-retrogression (associated with severe estrangement and identity diffusion that may manifest in mistrust and self-doubt) or psychosocial acceleration (premature, precocious ego development that may manifest in, for example, acute anxiety and periodic self-estrangement), or all of these patterns.

Chapter 8 continues the attempt to explicate the individual and collective problems of Vietnam veterans trying to adjust to postmilitary life in the explosive years surrounding the end of the Vietnam war decade. Charles Figley and William Southerly present the findings of a large survey of randomly selected Vietnam veterans living in the multicounty region of southern Illinois surrounding East St. Louis. Their data are cold and startling, yet somewhat reassuring. Except for significant unemployment problems among combat veterans, the vast majority of Vietnam veterans have adjusted miraculously well following their military experiences. This chapter provides an important empirical perspective on the "clinical" status of Vietnam veterans and, though providing relatively few interpretations, includes a considerable amount of data. Based on 1974 data collected immediately following the war, the sample demographics appear to match the population of Vietnam veterans quite well: mostly white, mostly young, mostly married, mostly living in urban areas, mostly having at least a high school education. Again, similar to the national profile, most Vietnam veterans in the sample served in the Army and about half were draftees. All but a small percentage had honorable discharges. (Nationally, however, there are nearly 800,000 Vietnam-era veterans with "bad paper" discharges they received without trial.) And, similar to national trends, only a relatively small number of Vietnam veterans are members of the large, traditional veterans' service organizations.

Although initially bitter about being drafted, most of the draftees appear to have gotten over their resentment. Most claim that their military experiences have been beneficial, overall, though most who went to Vietnam appear significantly less well adjusted emotionally compared to non-Vietnam veterans.

In contrast with those who never went to Vietnam, those who served in a combat role had significantly more frequently recurring dreams and nightmares that woke them up, made them fear or fight sleep, and were so bad that they felt the need to consult professional help. This finding is particularly depressing in view of the acute shortage of trained clinicians who can effectively help the Vietnam combat veteran with combat-related stress reactions—a fact that prompted the Consortium on Veteran Studies to publish *Stress Disorders among Vietnam Veterans: Theory, Research and Treatment* (New York: Bruner/Mazel, 1978).

Drug problems among Vietnam veterans since the war now appear to be less acute than first suspected. Unemployment, on the other hand, was at its peak during 1974. Nearly one out of four Vietnam veterans interviewed in the study was unemployed; while one out of three of those presently unemployed had had no permanent job since leaving the military. Figley and Southerly note that blacks, however, account for a large segment of the unemployed in the sample, with an unemployment rate of 40.2 percent. The major factor accounting for the high unemployment rate was the *time of release* from the military. Those lucky enough to get out of the service prior to 1970 were able to avoid the major job crunch that occurred during the recessionary period of the early 1970s. This chapter in many ways serves as an important backdrop for viewing the other chapters in the section, most of which focus on some facet of political alienation and dissatisfaction.

In Chapter 9 Andrew Kohen and Patricia Shields carefully consider the homecomer Vietnam veteran in terms of his relative success in the labor market. Drawing upon the National Longitudinal Surveys of Work Experience project's sample of over 5,200 young males interviewed between 1966 and 1971, the authors posed and answered three broad questions: What factors determined who served in the military during the Vietnam war era (1964–71)? What were the relative effects of this service on civilian labor market experiences? How do veterans feel the military helped or hindered their civilian careers?

Their findings were generally as they predicted. They found that the probability of serving in the military was much lower for those men with health problems, those with dependents, and those from either the highest or lowest levels of intelligence and education. When these factors were controlled, however, racial differences disappeared, which challenges many of those theorists who believe that nonwhites were significantly overrepresented.

In terms of the relative contribution of military service, or veteran status, to employment (that is, hourly earnings, employment, and occupational status) the picture was clear: Veterans enjoyed few benefits. "When earnings or status is the criterion, young white veterans were found to have paid a substantial cost for their military service in terms of foregone civilian work experience." If, however, the recently released veteran went to college or was able to find employment that matched his work in the military, he was better off than his nonveteran counterparts. For blacks, veterans status generally made no difference either way.

Although these bleak findings would lead to the assumption that veterans would have a rather negative attitude toward military service, vis-a-vis postservice employment, over half believed that "armed forces experience had helped their career."

Chapter 10, by Loch Johnson, focuses on the homecoming of veterans physically disabled by the war in Vietnam and in particular the degree to which they feel politically alienated and estranged from American society. Johnson's data tend to refute commonsense beliefs, since characteristics of being wounded and the severity of the disability were not found to be significant factors in terms of political alienation and estrangement, though rank, military entrance status, and attitudes toward the war were related. Beyond the neatly rounded correlation coefficients, however, Johnson found considerable resentment and frustration among his sample of disabled Vietnam veterans: feelings of being "used and discarded," frustration over the "waste of human resources," and violent dreams of the war that nobody understands.

In the last chapter in this section, Fred Milano uses the film, *The Deer Hunter* as a medium for focusing on the readjustments of a small sample of Vietnam combat veterans who returned to a small industrial town in Pennsylvania. According to some informal surveys, Vietnam veterans consider *The Deer Hunter* to be the most meaningful movie about their experiences compared with the six or so others on Vietnam that have come out as of this writing. Prior to *The Deer Hunter*, Vietnam veterans were mostly depicted by the entertainment media as caricatures, primarily bad, violent men.

Prior to discussing his study, Milano suggests that the military, by its very nature and due to its socializing effect, has a significant influence on men who spend varying amounts of time in it. Among other things, Milano suggests that military service affects political attitudes and behaviors of the veteran. He draws upon military sociology to support this contention, and in the process he takes issue with Moskos's (see Chapter 4) contention that all combatants are politically indifferent. Milano argues that observations by objective sociologists within the battle zone may be an artifact of the climate all combatants collaborate to maintain: high priority to the mission and surviving their tour, in addition to their natural distrust of researchers.

Among his small sample, Milano found that the veterans were more political than the nonveterans. Although not running for political office, veterans in the sample exercised their political rights through unions and social organizations and churches. Although the data provide limited generalizable findings, they do support the notion that military service is a political attitude incubator. Few social milieus can match military service in bringing together in one place at one time so many people from various social backgrounds and cultural and personal beliefs. Such an environment acts as an overwhelmingly powerful change agent for any young man with limited experiences and social networks. It is a place where political attitudes are forged as well as attitudes toward religion, women, sexuality, and many other aspects of adulthood.

6

THE HOMECOMER

ALFRED SCHUETZ

The Phaeacian sailors deposited the sleeping Odysseus on the shore of Ithaca, his homeland, to reach which he had struggled for 20 years of unspeakable suffering. He stirred and woke from sleep in the land of his fathers, but he knew not his whereabouts. Ithaca showed to him an unaccustomed face; he did not recognize the pathways stretching far into the distance, the quiet bays, the crags and precipices. He rose to his feet and stood staring at what was his own land, crying mournfully: "Alas! and now where on earth am I? What do I here myself?" That he had been absent for so long was not the whole reason why he did not recognize his own country; in part it was because goddess Pallas Athene had thickened the air about him to keep him unknown "while she made him wise to things." Thus Homer tells the story of the most famous home-coming in the literature of the world.[1]

To the homecomer home shows—at least in the beginning—an unaccustomed face. He believes himself to be in a strange country, a stranger among strangers, until the goddess dissipates the veiling mist.

This is an abridged version of an article of the same title that appeared in the *American Journal of Sociology* 50 (1944–45): 369–76. Reprinted with permission. Copyright © 1945 by the University of Chicago Press.

But the homecomer's attitude differs from that of a stranger. The latter is about to join a group which is not and never has been his own. He knows that he will find himself in an unfamiliar world, differently organized than that from which he comes, full of pitfalls and hard to master.[2] The homecomer, however, expects to return to an environment of which he always had and—so he thinks—still has intimate knowledge and which he has just to take for granted in order to find his bearings within it. The approaching stranger has to anticipate in a more or less empty way what he will find; the homecomer has just to recur to the memories of his past. So he feels; and because he feels, so he will suffer the typical shock described by Homer.

These typical experiences of the homecomer will be analyzed in the following *in general terms* of the social psychology. The returning veteran is, of course, an outstanding example of the situation under scrutiny. His special problems, however, have recently been widely discussed in many books and articles,[3] and it is not my aim to refer to them otherwise than as examples. We could refer also to the traveler who comes back from foreign countries, the emigrant who returns to his native land, the boy who "made good" abroad and now settles in his home town.[4] They all are instances of the "homecomer," defined as one who comes back for good to his home—not as one returning for a temporary stay, such as the boy spending the Christmas vacation with his family.

What, however, has to be understood by "home"? "Home is where one starts from," says the poet.[5] "The home is the place to which a man intends to return when he is away from it," says the jurist.[6] The home is the starting-point as well as terminus. It is the null point of the system of co-ordinates which we ascribe to the world in order to find our bearings in it. Geographically "home" means a certain spot on the surface of the earth. Where I happen to be is my "abode"; where I intend to stay is my "residence"; where I come from and whither I want to return is my "home." Yet home is not merely the homestead—my house, my room, my garden, my town—but everything it stands for. The symbolic character of the notion "home" is emotionally evocative and hard to describe. Home means different things to different people. It means, of course, father-house and mother-tongue, the family, the sweetheart, the friends; it means a beloved landscape, "songs my mother taught me," food prepared in a particular way, familiar things for daily use, folkways, and personal habits—briefly, a peculiar way of life composed of small and important elements, likewise cherished. *Chevron*, a Marine Corps newspaper, inquired what United States soldiers in the South Pacific miss most, outside of families and sweethearts. Here are some of the answers. "'A fresh lettuce and tomato sandwich with ice-cold fresh milk to wash it down.' 'Fresh milk and the morning paper at the front door.' 'The smell of a drugstore.' 'A train and the engine whistle.'"[7] All these things, badly missed if not available, were probably not particularly appreciated so long as they were accessible at any time. They had just their humble place among the collective value "homely things." Thus, home means one thing to the man who dwells far from it, and still another to him who returns.

"To feel at home" is an expression of the highest degree of familiarity and intimacy. Life at home follows an organized pattern of routine; it has its well-determined goals and well-proved means to bring them about, consisting of a set of traditions, habits, institutions, timetables for activities of all kinds, and so on. Most of the problems of daily life can be mastered by following this pattern. There is no need to define or redefine situations which have occurred so many times or to look for new solutions of old problems hitherto handled satisfactorily. The way of life at home governs as a scheme of expression and interpretation not only my own acts but also those of the other members of the in-group. I may trust that, using this scheme, I shall understand what the other means and make myself understandable to him. The system of relevances[8] adopted by the members of the in-group shows a high degree of conformity. I have always a fair chance—subjectively and objectively—to predict the other's action toward me as well as the other's reaction to my own social acts. We not only may forecast what will happen tomorrow, but we also have a fair chance to plan correctly the more distant future. Things will in substance continue to be what they have been so far. Of course, there are new situations, unexpected events. But at home even deviations from the daily routine life are mastered in a way defined by the general style in which people at home deal with extraordinary situations. There is a way—a proved way—for meeting a crisis in business life, for settling family problems, for determining the attitude to adopt toward illness and even death. Paradoxically formulated, there is even a routine way for handling the novel.

. . . There still are means of communication, such as the letter. But the letter-writer addresses himself to the type of addressee as he knew him when they separated, and the addressee reads the letter as written by the person typically the same as the one he left behind.[9] Presupposing such a typicality (and any typicality) means assuming that what has been proved to be typical in the past will remain relevant, the same degree of intimacy in personal relationships will prevail, and so on. Yet by the mere change of surroundings, other things have become important for both, old experiences are re-evaluated; novel ones, inaccessible to the other, have emerged in each partner's life. Many a soldier in the combat line is astonished to find letters from home lacking any under-standing of his situation, because they underscore the relevance of things which are of no importance to him in his actual situation, although they would be the subject of many deliberations if he were at home and had to handle them. This change of the system of relevance has its corollary in the changing degree of intimacy. The term "inti-macy" designates *here* merely the degree of reliable knowledge we have of another person or of a social relationship, a group, a cultural pattern, or a thing. As far as a person is concerned, intimate knowledge enables us to interpret what he means and to forecast his actions and reactions. In the highest form of intimacy, we know, to quote Kipling, the other's "naked soul." But separation conceals the other behind a strange disguise, hard to remove. From the point of view of the absent one the longing for re-establishing the old intimacy—not only with persons but also with things—is the main feature of what is called "home-sickness." Yet, the change in the system of relevance and in the degree of intimacy just described is differently experienced by the absent one and by the home group. The latter continues its daily life within the customary pattern. Certainly, this pattern, too, will have changed and even in a more or less abrupt way. But those at home, although aware of this change, lived together through this changing world, experienced it as changing in immediacy, adapted their interpretative system, and ad-justed themselves to the change. In other words, the system may have changed entirely, but it changed as a system; it was never disrupted and broken down; even in its modification it is still an appropriate device for mastering life. The in-group has now other goals and other means for attaining them, but still it remains an in-group.

The absent one has the advantage of knowing the general style of this pattern. He may from previous experiences conclude what attitude mother will take to the task of running the household under the rationing system, how sister will feel in the war plant, what a Sunday means without pleasure driving.[10] Those left at home have no immedi-ate experience of how the soldier lives at the front. There are reports in the newspapers and over the radio, recitals from homecomers, movies in technicolor, official and unofficial propaganda, all of which build up a stereotype of the soldier's life "somewhere in France" or "somewhere in the Pacific." For the most part, these stereotypes are not spontaneously formed, but are directed, censored for military or political reasons, and designed to build up morale at the home front or to increase the efficiency of war production or the subscription of war bonds. There is no warrant whatsoever that what is described as typical by all these sources of information is also relevant to the absent member of the in-group. Any soldier knows that his style of living depends upon the military group to which he belongs, the job allotted to him within this group, the attitude of his officers and comrades. That is what counts, and not the bulletin "All quiet on the western front." But whatever occurs to him under these particular circumstances is his individual, personal, unique experience which he never will allow to be typified. When the soldier returns and starts to speak—if he starts to speak at all—he is bewildered to see that his listeners, even the sympathetic ones, do not understand the uniqueness of these individual experiences which have rendered him another man. They try to find familiar traits in what he reports by subsuming it under *their* preformed types of the soldier's life at the front. To them there are only small details in which his recital deviates from what every homecomer has told and what they have read in magazines and seen in the movies. So it may happen that many acts which seem to the people at home the highest expression of courage are to the soldier in battle merely the struggle for survival or the fulfillment of duty, whereas many instances of real endurance, sacrifice, and heroism remain unnoticed or unappreciated by people at home.[11]

The home to which he returns is by no means the home he left or the home which he recalled and longed for during his absence. And, for the same reason, the homecomer is not the same man who left. He is neither the same for himself nor for those who await his return.

This statement holds good for any kind of home-coming. Even if we return home after a short vacation, we find that the old accustomed surroundings have received an added meaning derived from and based upon our experiences during our absence. Whatever the accompanying evaluation may be, things and men will, at least in the beginning, have another face. It will need a certain effort to transform our activities again into routine work and to reactivate our recurrent relations with men and things. No wonder, since we intended our vacation to be an interruption of our daily routine.

Homer tells of the landing of Odysseus' comrades at the island of the lotus-eaters. The lotus-eaters devised not death for the intruders but gave them a dish of their lotus flowers; and as each tasted this honey-sweet plant, the wish to return grew faint in him: he preferred to dwell forever with the lotus-eating men, feeding upon lotus and letting fade from his mind all longing for home.

To a certain extent, each homecomer has tasted the magic fruit of strangeness, be it sweet or bitter. Even amid the overwhelming longing for home there remains the wish to transplant into the old pattern something of the novel goals, of the newly discovered means to realize them, of the skills and experiences acquired abroad.

But—and here we touch upon a chief problem of the homecomer—

it is unfortunately an unwarranted assumption that social functions which stood the test within one system of social life will continue to do so if transplanted into another system. This general proposition is especially applicable to the problem of the returning veteran. From the sociological point of view, army life shows a strange ambivalence. Considered as an in-group, the army is characterized by an exceptionally high degree of constraint, of discipline imposed authoritatively upon the behavior of the individual by a controlling normative structure. The sense of duty, comradeship, the feeling of solidarity, and subordination are the outstanding features developed in the individual—all this, however, within a frame of means and ends imposed by the group and not open to his own choice. These features prevail in times of peace as well as in times of war. However, in times of war they do not regulate the behavior of the members of the in-group in relation to members of the out-group—that is the enemy. The combatant's attitude toward the enemy in battle is, and is supposed to be, rather the opposite of disciplined constraint. War is the archetype of that social structure which Durkheim calls the state of *"anomie."* The specific valor of the fighting warrior consists in his will and adroitness in overcoming the other in a desperate struggle of power, and it cannot be easily used within that pattern of civilian life which has prevailed in Western democracies. Moreover, the homecoming soldier returns to an in-group, the homeworld in the postwar period, which itself is marked by a certain degree of *anomie*, of lack of control and discipline. He finds, then, that *anomie* is no longer to be the basic structure of his relations with the out-group but is a feature of the in-group itself, toward the members of which he cannot apply the techniques permitted and required within the *anomie* situation of battle. In this civil world he will have to choose his own goals and the means to attain them and can no longer depend upon authority and guidance. He will feel, as Professor Waller puts it, like a "motherless chile."

Another factor supervenes. In times of war the members of the armed forces have a privileged status within the community as a whole. "The best for our boys in the service" is more than a mere slogan. It is the expression of prestige deservedly accorded to those who might have to give their life for their country or at least to those who left family, studies, occupation, and the amenities of civil life for a highly valued interest of the community. The civilian looks at the man in uniform as an actual or future fighter; and so, indeed, the man in uniform looks at himself, even if he performs mere desk work in an army office somewhere in the United States. This humbler occupation does not matter; to him, too, the induction marked a turning-point in his life. But a discharged homecomer is deprived of a uniform and with it of his privileged status within the community. This does not mean that he will lose, by necessity, the prestige acquired as an actual or potential defender of the homeland, although history does not show that exaggerated longevity is accorded to the memory of glory. This is partly because of the disappointment at home that the returning veteran does not correspond to the pseudo-type of the man whom they have been expecting.

This leads to a practical conclusion. Much has been done and still more will be done to prepare the homecoming veteran for the necessary process of adjustment. However, it seems to be equally indispensable to prepare the home group accordingly. They have to learn through the press, the radio, the movies, that the man whom they await will be another and not the one they imagined him to be. It will be a hard task to use the propaganda machine in the opposite direction, namely, to destroy the pseudo-type of the combatant's life and the soldier's life in general and to replace it by the truth. But it is indispensable to undo the glorification of a questionable Hollywood-made heroism by bringing out the real picture of what these men endure, how they live, and what they think and feel—a picture no less meritorious and no less evocative.

In the beginning it is not only the homeland that shows to the homecomer an unaccustomed face. The homecomer appears equally strange to those who expect him and the thick air about him will keep him unknown. Both the homecomer and the welcomer will need the help of a Mentor to "make them wise to things."

NOTES

1. The presentation follows the translation of Homer's *Odyssey* by T. E. Lawrence ("Lawrence of Arabia") (New York: Oxford University Press, 1932).

2. Cf. the present writer's paper "The Stranger," *American Journal of Sociology* 49, no. 6 (May 1944): 500–07.

3. We mention, in the first place, Professor Willard Waller's *The Veteran Comes Back* (New York: Dryden Press, 1944), an excellent sociological analysis of the civilian made into a professional soldier and of the soldier-turned-veteran who comes back to an alien homeland; also—Professor Dixon Wecter, *When Johnny Comes Marching Home* (Cambridge, Mass.: Houghton Mifflin, 1944), with valuable documents relating to the American soldier returning from four wars and very helpful bibliographical references; finally, the discussion of the veteran problem in the New York *Herald Tribune*, "Annual Forum on Current Problems," October 22, 1944 (Sec. VIII), especially the contributions of Mrs. Anna Rosenberg, Lieutenant Charles G. Bolte, and Sergeant William J. Caldwell. See also the very interesting collection of servicemen's *Letters Home*, arranged and edited by Mina Curtiss (Boston: Little, Brown, 1944).

4. Cf. the fine analysis of this situation in Thomas Wolfe's short story, "The Return of the Prodigal," in *The Hills Beyond* (New York: Harper & Bros., 1941).

5. T. S. Eliot, *Four Quartets* (New York: Harcourt, Brace, 1943), p. 17.

6. Joseph H. Beale, *A Treatise on the Conflict of Laws* (New York: Baker, Voorhis, 1935), I, 126.

7. Quoted from *Time*, June 5, 1944; other examples can be found in Wecter, op. cit., pp. 495.

8. This term has been discussed in the aforementioned paper on "The Stranger," loc. cit., pp. 500.

9. Cf. Georg Simmel's excellent analysis of the sociology of the letter in his *Sociologie, Untersuchungen über die Formen der Vergesellschaftang* (Leipzig, 1922), pp. 379–82.

10. This, of course, does not hold in case of a violent destruction of the home by catastrophes or enemy action. Then, however, not only may the general style of the pattern of home life have changed entirely but even the home itself may have ceased to exist. The absent one is then "homeless" in the true sense and has no place to return to.

11. "Without exception GIs most dislike tinhorn war and home-front heroics" is the summary of a poll by *Time* correspondents: "What kind of movies do G.I.'s like?" (*Time*, August 14, 1944).

7

CONFLICT, STRESS, AND GROWTH: THE EFFECTS OF WAR ON PSYCHOSOCIAL DEVELOPMENT AMONG VIETNAM VETERANS

JOHN P. WILSON

In 1975 I began to explore the question of how the Vietnam War had affected the lives of the men who saw military duty in Southeast Asia. My interest in this issue came from several sources. As a social psychologist I was particularly concerned with the fact that many veterans in my classes became emotionally upset when we discussed Stanley Milgram's (1974) famous experiment on obedience to authority. In Milgram's study, naive subjects are asked to administer increasingly severe levels of electric shock to an innocent victim who is ostensibly participating in an experiment concerned with the effects of punishment on learning. Milgram found that about 60 percent of the participants willingly obeyed the authority and administered 450 volts to the learner even though they suffered a great deal of emotional tension and moral conflict over this action. In the course of class discussion I suggested that Milgram's study had real-world implications for understanding such events as the Nazi holocaust, the My Lai atrocity, and the Watergate break-in of the Democratic national headquarters. It was at this point in our discussion that several veterans left class in a state of

The author gratefully acknowledges the support of a three-year research grant from the Disabled American Veterans Association. (807 Maine Ave., S.W. Washington D.C.)

anguish. Later I would learn from them that the issue of obedience to authority raised many unresolved questions in their minds about their actions in the Vietnam conflict. Even though the war was over they continued to feel as emotionally distressed over their role in Vietnam as did Milgram's subjects in the obedience experiment. It seemed that they were strongly conflicted over the fundamental moral dilemma of individual responsibility and personal conscience as the basis of action versus obedience to authority and reliance on external values and normative sanctions.

A second consideration that further involved my interest in understanding the influence of the war on the psychosocial well-being of the veteran stemmed from my dissatisfaction with the field of social psychology. Stated simply, there has not been much effort made by social psychologists to study major social problems in society or to apply existing empirical knowledge to the paramount social crises of our time. And of all the fields of psychology, the social-personality area is the one with the greatest potential to make significant contributions to the solution of these problems. When thinking about the Vietnam War, then, it seemed to me that we should attempt to understand more fully the nature of the social psychological processes that underlie such phenomena as distortion in decision making by political and military leaders, the antiwar movement, the emergence of the "counterculture," the My Lai atrocity, as well as the consequences of these events in society and in the day-to-day lives of individual veterans.

PRELIMINARY INTERVIEWS

The veterans in my classes at the university wanted to talk about their experiences in Vietnam with someone who was trustworthy and empathic. So together with Chris Doyle, a combat veteran and psychology student, I began interviewing about 60 men who had volunteered to talk to us. Initially, we simply asked the men to tell us about their military experiences, beginning with basic training and then moving on, chronologically, to Vietnam and from then to the present time. We explained that we were beginning a research study to examine how the Vietnam War had affected their lives and that we wanted to explore with them their feelings about their experiences and how they might have changed as a result of them. What we did not anticipate was how intense, emotional, and dramatic the interview sessions would prove to be. It seemed to us that each man wanted to come to grips with the Vietnam experience but found it difficult to create a personal perspective of the war that made sense while also providing some resolution for his tensions. They welcomed the opportunity to do so through the interview. There were often visible signs of catharsis, relief, and the freeing of emotional burdens and pent-up frustrations. Fully 75–80 percent of the men cried or expressed deep-seated anger or anguish as they relived, remembered, and recounted the events of Vietnam. It was an emotionally trying and exhaustive experience for them and for us. Many of the men had been profoundly affected by Vietnam; it had changed their sense of identity and ideological perspective of society. This fact struck me as especially significant in light of several contemporary theories of personality and life-span development. Therefore, in the fall of 1976 we began a large-scale investigation to determine more precisely how the Vietnam War affected the process of psychosocial development among Vietnam era veterans (Wilson 1977; 1978).

BASIC METHODOLOGY AND THEORETICAL RATIONALE

The basic methodology used in the study is described in detail elsewhere (Wilson 1977; 1978). Briefly, however, we interviewed about 400 veterans who were selected from a potential pool of over 800. This sample included black and white combat and noncombat Vietnam veterans from all branches of the military who were matched with cohorts who saw active duty during the era outside of Southeast Asia. Of the 400 interviewed, 356 men successfully completed the entire interview procedure, which typically lasted between two and four hours. During the interview the veteran was questioned about himself and his experiences in the military. In addition, each participant completed an extensive set of questionnaires that included biographic and demographic information, a set of personality scales to measure moral reasoning, motivation, and values, as well as a specially constructed questionnaire with 110 items designed to assess six areas of experience pertinent to the major hypotheses under investigation. These areas of experience included personality characteristics and personal attributes (for example, drug use), interpersonal relationships and adjustment, moral reasoning and ethical beliefs, military experience, political attitudes and ideology, and perception of society and its institutions. The questionnaire consisted of a number of Likert-type scales in which the veteran was asked to assess himself at three time intervals: upon entering the military, during active duty, and at the time of discharge. Factor analyses performed on the questionnaire data reproduced our classificatory scheme for the six areas assessed and demonstrated its internal consistency and validity (Wilson 1978). Thus the data reported in this chapter as well as the theoretical ideas on the patterns of adjustment and personality integration, are derived directly from the two years of interviews and the results of the statistical analyses reported in earlier papers (Wilson 1977; 1978).

Ultimately, of course, any comprehensive analysis designed to study changes in personality and psychosocial development among Vietnam-era veterans will require a longitudinal analysis of the type used by Block (1971) in his landmark work, *Lives Through Time*. It is the specific purpose of this chapter, however, to combine psychosocial theories of personality and life-span development into a framework that permits a more holistic look at how the Vietnam War affected the veterans' reentry into the mainstream of society. Specifically, this framework will be used to understand the veterans' problems of identity formation, interpersonal intimacy, alienation, and intrapsychic conflict in the process of personality integration itself.

THE IMPACT OF THE VIETNAM WAR
ON PSYCHOSOCIAL DEVELOPMENT

Two years of extensive interviews with Vietnam-era veterans produced an extraordinary amount of transcript that is rich in detail and psychological significance. Based on this data, it seemed to me that the various social, moral, political, and psychological conflicts encountered in the line of duty in Vietnam were powerful forces of change in the lives of the veteran. Upon returning home from military duty, the individual veteran frequently felt a disquieting sense of uncertainty, alienation, and estrangement from himself and society. While he was happy to be alive and "back home," something did not seem quite right or in its place. The men in our sample reported that they had trouble "fitting in" and in finding a niche in society. They often said that their sense of self-sameness and continuity with the past was changed in confusing ways. Future goals and commitments were unclear and intangible. At this point, usually within the first year and a half after coming home, the individual veteran began questioning himself and his role in the war as never before. Typically, the veteran found himself grappling with questions central to his sense of identity and belief system. He struggled with ideological incongruities, moral dilemmas, and philosophical valuing. The questions most often asked were: What's the war really about? For what did my buddies die? Who am I and what do I want out of life? Why can't I feel more at home now? Why do I feel depressed even though I've survived? Why must I feel so much guilt and pain for an unjust war? Why should I have to struggle to live on the GI Bill? Why does everyone think I'm a killer and dope freak? Why don't people listen to us about the reality of Vietnam? To what should I commit myself and who can I trust anymore? These and other questions seem to reflect the conflicts that Erik Erikson (1968) describes for the developmental task of identity versus role confusion that normatively occurs in late adolescence. Thus it seemed to me that the experiences of war had intensified the normal developmental process of identity integration. What we sought to understand then, in a much broader context, were the effects of the Vietnam War on the process of personality development. If the war experience could affect the process of identity integration in both positive and negative ways, then it could theoretically affect all stages of personality development in the life cycle. Therefore, we decided to employ Erikson's conceptualization of personality development in our study for a number of interrelated reasons. First, it most closely approximates the descriptions the veterans gave of their problems, concerns, and joys in life. Second, the epigenetic nature of Erikson's theory is supported by a good deal of the literature in developmental psychology (for example, Newman and Newman 1975) and therefore has much theoretical and clinical utility. Third, it is possible to integrate Erikson's theory with those of Kohlberg (1971), Lifton (1976), and Maslow (1970) in order to establish a more inclusive theoretical base for understanding changes in psychological functioning with respect to motives, moral judgments, and psychoformative processes. Fourth, this larger, integrative model based on Erikson's theory permits a more precise analysis of the stress-producing events in Vietnam. Finally, an epigenetic model enables us to detail the different, if limited, patterns of personality integration and adjustment as well as to speculate on how future psychosocial stages of development will proceed in the years ahead.

GENERAL THEORETICAL OVERVIEW

Before exploring the nature of the stress-producing events in Vietnam and their effect on personality development, it is necessary to gain a basic overview of Erikson's (1968) theory of psychosocial development. Erikson is one of the few personality theorists who has conceptualized age-specific developmental stages for the entire life cycle. Although he had had a long-standing interest in the problem of identity and ego development, Erikson became interested in disruptions of ego-identity after World War II when he was observing and treating psychiatric patients whose problems did not seem to fit neatly into traditional psychiatric disorders variously labeled traumatic war neurosis, hysterical reaction, and the like. He states (p. 17):

> Most of our patients, so we concluded at that time, had neither been "shellshocked" nor become malingerers, but had through the exigencies of war lost a sense of personal sameness and historical continuity. They were impaired in that central control over themselves for which, in the psychoanalytic scheme, only the "inner agency" of the ego could be held responsible. Therefore, I spoke of a loss of ego-identity.

Taking a lead from Erikson it seemed plausible, for a number of reasons to be detailed later, to make ego-identity the keystone of our analysis. If it is useful then all the results should be linked to it theoretically and empirically. It should allow us to see how strengths and weaknesses of the ego were exacerbated by the experiences of Vietnam. This is so because ego-identity is a core process within the personality structure that links emotional, motivational, and cognitive processes essential to the well-being and growth of the organism. If the construct is superfluous we shall find that it adds little or nothing at all to the coherence of our theory and research findings.

IDENTITY FORMATION, INTEGRATION, AND IDEOLOGY

Erikson (1968) states that the process of identity formation begins at birth and progresses in increasing differentiation until death. Briefly, Erikson states that there is a universal sequence of human development that is epigenetic in nature. The epigenetic sequence means that there is a constant interplay between genetically based aspects of personality and the presses of culture and family that shape the personality and motivational attributes of the person. Each stage of development contributes something toward the organism's adaptive competence. Each stage of development adds something to the overall configuration of identity, ego-vitality, or ego-strength, that is, to new modes of adaptive behavior, new cognitive capacities, new motivational attributes and capacities for interpersonal involvement. Epigenesis implies, in part, that each succeeding stage of development, with its intrinsic growth crisis, is determined by the outcome and form of integration of the stages that precede it. This organismically based ground plan, together with socializing influences, combine to form a series of psychosocial crises. In essence, a psychosocial crisis refers to a critical period of development that will contribute some attribute to the final form of the identity structure. What gets contributed to the mature, adult identity is a function of how well a particular crisis is resolved. Erikson writes (p. 96):

Each successive step [in psychosocial development] then is a potential crisis because of a radical change in perspective. Crisis is used here in a developmental sense to connote not a threat of catastrophe, but a turning point, a crucial period of increased vulnerability and heightened potential, and therefore, the ontogenetic source of generational strength and maladjustment.

In his theory Erikson details eight psychosocial crises or "stages" of human development. Table 7.1 presents an outline of Erikson's psychosocial model of personality. Inspection of the table indicates that there are age-related psychosocial crises that, depending on their outcome, result in different degrees of ego-strength or cognitive-emotional capacities to master reality. Each stage also leads to the formation of personality "traits" that characterize the idiosyncratic modes of need satisfaction. Thus, the crisis of trust versus mistrust characterizes infancy and the need for a predictable and relatively consistent form of interaction with others. In the play age children learn varying degrees of self-control through motor coordination, language acquisition, and more sophisticated interpersonal relationships. By age five the child builds on his autonomy to engage in more self-initiated activities that bring a sense of self-esteem at being able to be more independent. During the school years the developing cognitive capacities enable him to broaden the basis of personal and social competence through advanced learning. With adolescence, puberty, and increased maturation comes the pressing need to establish an identity unique to oneself and apart from the earlier identifications acquired during the formative years. Later in adulthood and the life cycle, the psychosocial stages focus on the need for intimacy, generativity, and personal integrity that will be discussed in more detail later in the chapter.

Most central to our discussion, however, is the fifth psychosocial crisis, identity versus role confusion, which normatively occurs in late adolescence and young adulthood. This developmental period has as its "task" the need to form a more stable and enduring personality structure and sense of self in order to assume the various roles of adulthood and to meet adequately the demands that accompany them. This crisis is especially important since the doubts, uncertainties, insecurities, as well as personal and social competencies of a person must be interwoven into a more coherent and enduring sense of self that links the historical past in continuity with the present. It is a time of emancipation from parents, increased responsibility, career choice, early attempts at mutual intimacy, and the recognition of one's abilities

TABLE 7.1: General Outline of Erikson's Psychosocial Theory

Psychosexual Zones	Psychosexual Modes	Psychosocial Zones	Psychosocial Modality	Psychosocial Crisis	Ego Quality "Virtues"	Related Aspects of Social Order
Oral, respiratory, sensory Kinesthetic	Passive incorporative / Active incorporative	Maternal person	To get / To take	Trust versus mistrust	Hope	Cosmic order
Anal-urethal muscular	Retentive / Eliminative	Paternal person	To hold on / To let go	Autonomy versus shame-doubt	Will	Law and order
Infantile Genital Locomotor	Intrusive 0 / Inclusive 0	Basic family	To make (going after)	Initiative versus guilt	Purpose	Ideal prototype
(Latency)		Neighborhood School Community	To make things / To make things together / To know how	Industry versus inferiority	Competence	Technological elements
(Puberty)		Peer groups and out-groups models of leadership	To be oneself (or not to be) / To share being oneself	Identity versus role confusion	Fidelity	Ideological perspectives

(Genitality)	Partners in friendship, sex, coopera-tion, and competition	To lose and find oneself in another	Intimacy versus isolation	Love	Patterns of cooperation and compe-tition
	Divided labor and shared	To make be 0 To take care of 0	Generativity versus stagnation	Care	Currents of education and tradition
	Mankind My kind	To be, through having been to face not being	Integrity versus despair	Wisdom	Wisdom, liter-ature, and oral philosophy

Source: Adapted from Richard Jones, *Feeling and Fantasy in Education*, New York: Harper Colophon, 1978.

and limitations. Since the issue of forming a coherent sense of ego-identity is of paramount significance to core organismic processes (indeed it is part of the developmental schema itself), most cultures grant to youth at this time a "psychosocial moratorium" in which to explore oneself in the process of working out the identity structure. Although the moratorium may take different forms in different cultures, it shares a common thread in that there is usually a culturally tolerated latitude of acceptance to engage in many activities without necessarily making commitments to them or prematurely defining an adult set of roles and responsibilities. If all goes well, then childhood identifications get transformed into a more or less crystallized sense of identity and emotional stability. Erikson (1968, p. 50) comments:

> But here it is necessary to differentiate between personal identity and ego-identity. The conscious feeling of having a personal identity is based on two simultaneous observations: the perception of self-sameness and continuity of one's existence in time and space and the perception of the *fact* that others recognize one's sameness and continuity. What I have called ego-identity, however, concerns *quality* of this existence. Ego-identity then, in its subjective aspect, is the awareness of that fact that there is a self-sameness and continuity to the ego's synthesizing methods, *the style of one's individuality*, and that this style coincides with the sameness and continuity of one's meaning for significant others in the immediate community.

IDENTITY DIFFUSION AND DISRUPTION OF THE PSYCHOSOCIAL MORATORIUM

In young adulthood not everyone is so lucky to have an ideal moratorium that has the proper conditions or experiences to work out residual conflicts, existential dilemmas, or value choices that make knowing oneself easier. Where the identity process is disrupted, delayed, or made extremely difficult due to personal, social, or cultural reasons, then a sense of role confusion or identity diffusion may predominate the individual's subjective sense of self-sameness and continuity in time and space. For such unfortunate persons, the choice of career becomes difficult to settle upon; time seems unmanageable, fleeting, and uncontrollable; the residual doubts and uncertainties about one's ability to control important aspects of behavior loom in the forefront of consciousness and contribute to a heightened self-consciousness; there is a sense of being "fixed" into roles and frustration in not meeting ideal expectations; intimate relations are avoided or difficult to establish since the lack of self-esteem makes commitment a potential threat. In general, the person with a sense of identity diffusion experiences strong anxiety and, at times, alienation from age-mates against whom self-defeating comparisons are made. Thus, the struggle of identity versus role confusion will persist until some balance is reached that establishes a relative degree of self-sameness and continuity.

One of the cognitive changes that occurs during the stage of identity versus role confusion is that of ideological commitment. According to Erikson, the problem of "pledging fidelity" to a system of values is an integral part of the process of identity integration. In the most basic sense the individual needs some system of beliefs to help guide the direction of identity. As ego-identity becomes more crystallized and less diffuse, the pursuit of some system of values constitutes an integral part of the entire process of having a sense of "self-sameness and continuity." To the extent, then, that the system of values is confused, unclear, or yet to be integrated, identity diffusion is experienced. When this is the case, the problem of commitment to ideological beliefs, values, and moral principles becomes a difficult psychosocial task. Thus, the basic choice of a career, marriage, or advanced education implies long-term continuity into the future. The emergence of adulthood demands, sooner or later, that choices be made as to the roles one will occupy within the culture. Clearly, the choice of those roles reflects individual identity and its psychosocial development. Where identity is strong and the individual has a broadly based sense of personal competency, self-esteem, and a supportive social milieu, the issue of commitment is less frightening and less unpredictable than where this is not the case.

DISRUPTION OF THE PSYCHOSOCIAL MORATORIUM

The period of the psychosocial moratorium varies in length according to the complexity of a culture, the number of role choices available to an individual, and the idiosyncratic pattern of psychosocial development up to the normative crisis of identity versus role confusion. In our culture we tend to have an extended period of time for the moratorium, ranging somewhere from late adolescence to the late twenties. We must ask the question, however, as to a traumatic and sudden disruption of the moratorium. More specifically, how does involvement in war affect the entire crisis of identity versus role confusion? What happens to a young man where the normal moratorium is prematurely shortened by circumstances beyond his control? Here we shall do well to remember that the soldier in Vietnam was typically between the ages 17 to 25, with the average age being closer to 20. Clearly, being drafted or volunteering for military service may stress or facilitate the entire identity process, depending, of course, on the kind and quality of experience. Under the best circumstances one would hope for good role models, a clear sense of purpose or mission, a moral and political cause worthy of commitment, the opportunity to broaden one's geographic-historic world image, the opportunity to believe in the trustworthiness of authority and leaders, collectively share experiences with age-mates such that a more positive sense of self emerges, and, finally, to come to a more profound and complex understanding of cultural processes and prevailing technologies. We hypothesized that these things would be difficult for the soldier in Vietnam since there was not a full-fledged commitment by the government of the United States to the war effort. There was reasonable doubt about the moral and political legitimacy of the war within the country. The clear-cut national commitment that characterized World War II was absent in the era of Vietnam. Rather, there was a good deal of controversy over U.S. involvement in Vietnam that spawned widespread antiwar protests. The country was ambivalent about the war, a fact that would make more difficult the soldier's task of forming an ideological perspective to guide his involvement in the conflict. Our earlier study (Wilson 1977) indicated that most men initially believed that the ideological purpose of Vietnam was to stop communist aggression or to help the South Vietnamese toward democracy. However, this set of beliefs would undergo significant, if not profound, modification *after* the Vietnam experience in which he would encounter a series of stress-producing psychological conflicts. And while all wars have death, atrocities, and human degradation, few have placed the soldier in an existential quagmire of such intensity or absurdity so as to render ideological justification nearly impossible short of psychological delusion.

STRESS-PRODUCING EXPERIENCES AND THEIR EFFECT ON EGO-IDENTITY AND PERSONALITY

It is possible to conceptualize many of the experiences in Vietnam as stress-producing events. In one sense there is nothing really new in this idea for it is common knowledge that war taxes a person's ability to maintain optimal adjustment, reality testing, and moral sensibility. However, several studies (for example, Shatan 1978; DeFazio 1978) have indicated that the Vietnam War was different from those of the past in several significant ways. In brief, the lack of a strong moral and political ideological justification for the war, coupled with its guerrilla nature in which it was difficult to discern friend from foe, led to a psychological situation that made it difficult for the soldier to maintain a healthy sense of control and predictability over the events occurring around him. Table 7.2 presents a summary of the common stress-producing events that the typical combatant encountered in the line of duty and their relationship to different aspects of ego-identity and personality integration.

From the theoretical perspective of psychosocial development, it is possible to view these stress-producing events as influencing ego-identity in three basic ways:

The stress-producing events can lead to retrogressive ego-integration or dissolution by stressing defensive modalities of adaptation beyond an optimal level of functioning. In this case, the negative polarities of each nuclear growth crisis may manifest a regressive form, that is, strong mistrust, doubt, guilt, inferiority, and identity diffusion.

The stress-producing events may intensify the predominant psychosocial crisis of a person. For most soldiers in Vietnam this was usually identity versus role confusion. Intensification means that the process of assimilation and accomodation of experience into a coherent self-structure with a clear ideological perspective was impeded.

The stress-producing events can lead to psychosocial acceleration or progression. In this case, the normal course of maturation and ego-development is accelerated in a way such that the individual begins to assimilate and accomodate the experience into an identity structure that normatively would occur later in life. In this sense, there is an awareness of a broader set of human values, motivations, and modes of integrating experience. More specifically, each of the adult stages of ego development emerges into ascendancy prematurely. Thus, the individual now becomes concerned not only with identity but intimacy, generativity, and integrity as well. In some respects psychosocial acceleration parallels ego-retrogression since both generate acute anxiety over the meaning of the stress-producing events and the ego's capacity to integrate the experience in a healthy manner. However, ego-retrogression frequently is associated with traumatic war neurosis while psychosocial acceleration is not. This distinction will be discussed in more detail later in the chapter.

EGO-RETROGRESSION: ACUTE IDENTITY DIFFUSION

Severe stress during the process of identity integration may precipitate the appearance of retrogressive components of ego-identity. Where the stress overpowers the individual's ability to meet the

TABLE 7.2: Relationship of Stress-Producing Events to Qualities of Ego-Identity and Personality Integration

Common Stress-Producing Events in Vietnam and Afterward	Psychosocial Stage and Personality Attribute Affected by Stress-Producing Event (Retrogression)
Guerilla nature of war	Mistrust: time confusion Shame-doubt (lack of control and predictability)
Inability to fulfill warrior role and authority-based killing	Shame-doubt (self-doubt; will) Guilt (role-fixation; lack of purpose) Inferiority (competence; sense of futility)
Repeated loss of territory Failure of ARVN to make full-scale commitment to war	Inferiority (sense of futility) Guilt (lack of purpose) Identity diffusion (lack of ideological commitment)
Rotation in duty: 12–13 month tour of duty	Guilt (lack of purpose) Identity diffusion (lack of ideological commitment)
Ineffective military leadership	Mistrust (lack of trust in authority) Identity diffusion (lack of ideological commitment)
Technological warfare— de-humanization of war	Identity diffusion—industry (depersonalization of self, dehumanization of the enemy)
Death of buddies and atrocities	Identity (sense of existential guilt; search for meaning; Ideological confusion) Isolation (emotional distantiation; loss of self-respect) Despair (meaning of life)
Black-market operations	Identity-initiative (lack of a sense of purpose)
U.S. social-political controversy over war in Vietnam	Identity (ideological confusion)
Homecoming: social integration Stigmatization of veteran Inadequate GI Bill Difficulty entering labor force	Identity diffusion—intimacy— Isolation (ideological confusion; problems of intimacy; search for authenticity)

Source: Compiled by the author.

demands confronting him, a retrogression to earlier modes of conflict resolution may occur. Specifically, psychosocial "fixations," or negative polarities of each nuclear growth crisis (for example, mistrust, doubt, shame, guilt, and so on) may dominate the consciousness of the person. Erikson (1968, p. 183) has called this process identity diffusion.

> We also diagnosed identity-consciousness among the ingredients of identity-confusion, and we meant by it a special form of painful self-consciousness which dwells on discrepancies between one's self-esteem, the aggrandized self-image as an autonomous person and one's appearance in the eyes of others.

Clearly, it is possible that the stress of combat or other experiences in Vietnam may precipitate acute identity consciousness. Table 7.3 summarizes the relationship of psychosocial development to the process of identity diffusion, estrangement, and retrogression among Vietnam veterans.

If we return for a moment to Table 7.2 and the list of stress-producing events, we can examine in more detail how each of these events, singularly or in combination, affected the process of retrogression. First, there was often a sense of time confusion. In the intensity of jungle warfare the soldier frequently felt as though time stood still; that temporal continuity with the past was broken, which led to a sense of separation in psychoformative processes (Lifton 1976). It was as if the war occurred in a vacuum or time warp. The war seemed to exist in a plane of reality separate from that governing life elsewhere in the world. Within this temporal void, the soldier often felt that all was hopeless; nothing could be trusted or counted on to provide temporal continuity necessary to a feeling of connectedness or self-sameness.

A pseudo-sense of self-certainty emerged from the structured regimen of military life. Military custom, the hierarchic mechanism of authority and social regulation, the symbols of rank, duty, and status all helped create an illusion of "a mission" of certainty. In short, the soldier could only "hide" in his unit in the most superficial sense; the vestiges of military order could only buffer a sense of doubt or shame for participating in the war for a short while. Eventually, many men began questioning their role in the war and its purpose in much more basic and profound ways. At first, questions centered around the difficulty of actualizing the warrior role as a highly competent fighter since the guerrilla warfare made definitive victories ephemeral and obtuse. The repeated loss of territory paid for with the lives of buddies often made the war seem futile and senseless. Ultimately, the extreme self-doubt concerning the legitimacy of the war led to a sense of helplessness and the need for some sense of predictability and control over the events of

TABLE 7.3: The Relationship of Psychosocial Stages to Ego-Retrogression and Identity Diffusion among Vietnam Veterans

Life Stage	Psychosocial Crisis	Ego-Strength	Ego-Retrogression	Identity Diffusion	Psychoformative Mode After Lifton 1976	Self-Process
Infancy	Trust versus mistrust	Hope (Drive)	Hopelessness, dependency, anxiety, withdrawal	Time confusion	Separation	
Play Age	Autonomy versus shame/doubt	Will (Control)	Overcontrol, impulsiveness, order, structure, predictability, helplessness	Self-doubt	Stasis	
	Initiation versus guilt	Purpose (Direction)	Guilt, loss of rootedness, need for protectors, loss of purpose	Role fixation	Stasis, separation	
School Age	Industry versus inferiority	Skill (Method)	Sense of futility, work paralysis, incompetence	Work paralysis	Stasis	
	Identity versus identity diffusion	Devotion (Fidelity)	Self-consciousness, lack of commitment, prolonged moratorium	Ideological confusion	Separation Disintegration	Survivor guilt Decentering Psychic numbing

Young Adulthood	Intimacy versus isolation	Love (Affiliation)	Distantiation, loss of self-respect	Bisexual confusion	Separation	Animated guilt
Adulthood	Generativity versus stagnation	Care (Production)	Narcissism, depression, exploitation	Authority confusion	Stasis	Uncentering
Senescence	Integrity versus despair	Wisdom (Renunciation)	Despair, helplessness, withdrawal, absence of meaning	Confusion of values—ultimate meaning	Disintegration	Ungrounding, concern with symbolic immortality

Source: Compiled by the author.

the day. When a sense of helplessness occurred, the individual's psycho-formative processes reflected stasis: the lack of the ability to autonomously regulate the events of one's immediate psychological space.

If the military order provides an external authority system and hierarchic chain of command—a cybernetic control unit—then it also provides an arena for ritualistic role experimentation. For most men it was a pseudo-form of role experimentation since conscription precluded free choice as to the kinds of experiences that would enable the strengths of the ego to cohere into a stable, internalized control system. To the extent that role experimentation was regimented and limited by the exigencies of war would the individual struggle to have a sense of initiative, purpose, and direction without a sense of guilt over the inability to pursue self-chosen ideals. But the nature of war constrains and defines the domain of initiative: successful initiative is to kill with a purpose. Yet, justifying both the killing and the purpose for it was not to be an easy thing to do. It was often difficult to discern the enemy, especially in villages where older men, women, and youths sometimes collaborated against American troops. This set of circumstances typically generated high levels of anxiety and feelings of helplessness since it was nearly impossible to control or predict who was friend or foe. Further, the typical tour of duty (rotation) was 12–13 months. For many men, especially "short-timers," the paramount goal was survival before commitment to the war effort. Additionally, the factor of frequent rotation (designed to reduce combat stress) and the sophisticated technological nature of modern warfare further served to create doubt and confusion over the purpose of the war itself. In short, these factors affected the individual's sense of rootedness and contributed heavily to a sense of survivor and personal guilt. In survivor guilt the individual wonders why he lived when someone else died, whereas in personal guilt he suffers a loss of self-esteem for committing acts inconsistent with his self image. A passage from Caputo's *A Rumor of War* (1977, p. 321) illustrates this well:

> They walked off. I stayed for a while, looking at the corpse. The wide glowing glassy eyes stared at me in accusation. The dead boy's open mouth screamed silently his innocence and our guilt. In the darkness and confusion, out of fear, exhaustion, and the brutal instincts acquired in the war, the marines had made a mistake. An awful mistake. They had killed the wrong man. That boy's innocent blood was on my hands as much as it was on theirs. I had sent them out there. My God, what have I done? I thought. I could think of nothing else. My God, what have we done? Please God, forgive us. What have we done?

This sense of guilt, then, may create a strong need for authentic human contact, for reassurance, for mutual, positive, and constructive intimate involvement with others. It may also lead to a strong sense of role fixation, a fear to venture forth again with a zealousness of purpose, the fear that to trust oneself to pursue self-chosen ideals may again lead to catastrophic results.

In the process of questioning the purpose of the war and in the struggle with animated and survivor guilt, the soldier (and later veteran) often came to feel that the entire enterprise was futile. While the preparation for combat had instilled a sense of pride and competence in his abilities (for example, physical endurance, marksmanship, coordination within a fighting unit, and so on) the individual in the field often began to grapple with the problem of being "locked into" a job that served no valid apprenticeship outside the war zone. Upon returning home, the question of "futility" and his war efforts took on added significance since many age-mates who had not been drafted had pursued advanced education or job training in preparation for a tangible position in the labor force. All of this adds up to the potential estrangement from a sense of industry, work paralysis, and the strong feeling of inferiority in comparison to peers who did not have their psychosocial moratorium disrupted by the war. In acute identity diffusion, the inability to make commitments is a common problem among veterans suffering partial or complete psychic numbing (Lifton 1976).

THE RELATION OF EGO-RETROGRESSION AND IDENTITY DIFFUSION TO TRAUMATIC WAR NEUROSIS AND THE DELAYED STRESS SYNDROME

In earlier research both Shatan (1978) and Horowitz and Solomon (1978) note that the onset of stress-related neurotic symptoms (traumatic war neurosis) was delayed for the Vietnam veteran. There are many reasons why the frequency of stress-related disorders has been increasing steadily and has yet to reach an asymptote. First, our research has shown that there is widespread mistrust of authority, of the U.S. government and, in particular, of the Veterans Administration (Wilson 1978). Hence, there is a reluctance to go to the VA hospitals for medical treatment. Second, many individuals feel exploited, rejected, and stigmatized for their military service in Vietnam (Wilson and Doyle 1978). Third, evidence indicates that many individuals found it difficult to obtain higher education and job-related training on the GI Bill and currently have disproportionately higher rates of unemployment (Figley 1978). Fourth, Horowitz and Solomon (1978), Shatan (1978), and

Wilson (1977) found that most men rarely, if ever, discussed their war experiences with others. These factors suggest that following the war the process of reintegration into society was often difficult and constituted an additional source of stress.

In the simplest sense, it is possible to view the veteran as having had to face a series of stress-producing conflicts that did not terminate automatically upon coming home. As a consequence, therefore, these experiences may have overpowered ego-defenses and the ability to cope effectively with the normal demands of living and mastering age-related developmental tasks. As our research found, the combat veteran was significantly different from his cohorts on all major areas of social-psychological functioning (Wilson 1978). In brief, he is more alienated and has significantly more problems in establishing intimate relationships. Thus, the stress-producing events encountered seem to have an effect roughly proportional to the degree of conflict experienced. In retrogression, however, the veteran typically manifests a broad range of symptoms that are connected, psychodynamically, to his predominant psychosocial crisis and to regressive components of the ego.

Traditionally, traumatic war neurosis has been thought of as similar to hysteria in terms of the underlying mechanisms of defense and adaptation to intrapsychic conflict. In fact, those who have commented on the delayed stress syndrome (for example, DeFazio 1978; Horowitz and Solomon 1978) cite Breuer and Freud's (1895) *Studies on Hysteria* in which there is a discussion on ego-regression, dissociation, and symptom formation. In traumatic war neurosis, the regression to a hysteric-like neurotic condition enables the ego to assimilate the trauma through a form of "repetition-compulsion" or what Kris (1952) termed regression in the service of the ego. When retrogression occurs as part of a traumatic war neurosis, the individual typically reports several of the following symptoms: anger, apathy, anxiety, alienation, cynicism, denial, depression, defensiveness, emotional numbness (psychic numbing), fear, "flashbacks," guilt, impatience, insomnia, inability to concentrate, lethargy, mistrust, repression, regression, recurring dreams and nightmares, repetition compulsion or repetitive tendencies, psychological stasis, sleep disorders, social introversion, and withdrawal. From our perspective, what is impaired is indeed a dimension of ego-control and resiliency (Block and Block 1978). There is a constriction of ego control processes governing attention, memory, rational thought, perceptual vigilance, and so on, and a lack of interconnectedness of these processes to effective information processing of external reality (ego-resiliency). Clearly, these ego processes are central to the maintenance of a sense of ego-identity as characterized by Erikson (1968). Traumatic war neurosis is thus more than an overpowering of the ego due to a specific event or set of experiences. Rather, it must be understood as a trauma that produces retrogression and affects the core organismic processes of ego-identity, motivation, and moral judgment (Kohlberg 1971). In retrogression the total set of stress experiences seems to shatter a sense of self-sameness and continuity to the point of severe self-estrangement. It becomes difficult for the person to trust himself and others in a way that would lead to more ego-integration and coherency. Hence, the person is not merely seeking to "work-through" the trauma but to restore a much more fundamental aspect of himself. Retrogression is regression in the service of ego-integration; to restore ego-strength to master the trauma and to promote organismic vitality for age-related psychosocial crises. What most psychotherapists treating Vietnam veterans have failed to recognize is just how profoundly the war affected the veteran's sense of ego-identity as the age-related and developmentally defined configuration of ego-processes. To successfully treat traumatic war neurosis necessitates an understanding of the symptoms associated with retrogression within a much more inclusive perspective of human development.

INTENSIFICATION OF PSYCHOSOCIAL DEVELOPMENT WITHOUT RETROGRESSION: THE POST-VIETNAM SYNDROME

It is abundantly clear from medical records and current research that the majority of Vietnam veterans do not suffer a form of retrogression or traumatic war neurosis (Figley 1978). In fact, the majority of men seem to be adjusting quite well by conventional societal yardsticks. They are holding steady jobs, raising families, and watching Monday night football. Superficially, all seems well with these men. But beneath the persona of the self there often resides a continued struggle with ego-identity and the existential search for meaning in life. This highly personalized search for authenticity is often an attempt to prolong a psychosocial moratorium in order to more fully integrate the precipitates of the stress-producing events into the self-structure. As noted earlier, the conditions society (high inflation, unemployment, and stigmatization) as well as the individual need to find meaning and purpose to past actions in the military combined as factors that intensified the need to establish a firm sense of ego-identity. Unfortunately, these very same conditions precluded a culturally supported extension of the psychosocial moratorium. Establishing a clear sense of identity and finding a niche in society thus became a pressing demand if role-confusion, estrangement, and despair were to be avoided. Clearly, this problem of interfacing the self within the nexus of society eventually led to enough cognitive conflict and dissonance to force a reexamination of ideological beliefs. Our findings supported this idea in that there was a left-wing shift in ideology and a loss of faith in political leaders, democratic political processes, and loss of belief in the trustworthiness of authority and institutions (Wilson 1977). It is of little wonder then that they found it difficult to trust leaders and their ideologies since that form of naive trust previously involved them in a war they came to hate. The various stress-producing events in Vietnam were too profound not to generate a process of ideological reexamination. Hence, a simple set of conventional values could no longer be subscribed to with naiveté. The moral dilemmas posed by atrocities and fraggings, the senseless and unjustifiable deaths of buddies, the controversy over the war, and so on, produced within the individual a significant amount of cognitive dissonance and disequilibration that lay dormant until a moratorium could be constructed to permit the conflicts to be assimilated into a more inclusive perspective. It is no surprise then that the paramount philosophic issues centered around conceptions of authority, power, trust, legitimacy, equity, fairness, justice, love, and altruism. These basic beliefs and values, central to human existence, had been violated too many times by the exigencies of war. The meanings of these principles and values were now no longer academic abstractions. Rather, they resonated deep within the conflicted and anguished soul of the returning veteran. What was important now was the need to reestablish self-trust in order to make personal commitments to trustworthy authorities, politics, and institutions who would somehow safeguard liberty, justice, fairness, and provide equitable opportunities for a meaningful involvement in society.

If it is given that the psychosocial moratorium was disrupted by the war, then the problem of making personal commitments to a system of values compatible with ego-identity was an understandably difficult process. Frequently, the individual veteran felt confused and directionless during the first year or so after discharge. On the one hand, the old ideological beliefs were not quite sufficient or adequate enough to meet the presses of existence. On the other hand, there was not a highly visible or widely endorsed alternative system of values either. Thus, in the process of maintaining a sense of self-sameness and continuity the veteran had to weather the rebuffs of an apathetic and ambivalent society while assimilating new values. In the struggle to achieve self-coherency and unity many individuals found themselves troubled in perplexing ways that they did not comprehend. This struggle, then, gave rise to an interconnected set of "symptoms" now known as the postcombat syndrome. As Shatan (1978) indicates, this syndrome included feelings of guilt and the need for self-punishment, aggressive impulses and fantasies (see also Wilson 1977), psychic numbing (Lifton 1973), alienation, mistrust, and difficulties in intimate relationships.

IDENTITY DIFFUSION AND THE POST-VIETNAM SYNDROME

Intensification of the nuclear growth crisis of identity versus role confusion, or its successor, intimacy versus isolation, means that these crises were made more difficult than is typically the case for most persons in society. Where the effects of delayed stress and reentry exacerbated the predominate psychosocial stage, elements of the post-Vietnam syndrome occur. However, intensification of the age-related psychosocial stage of maturation differs from traumatic war neurosis and retrogression in several important respects. First, there is an absence of debilitating neurotic symptoms. If the person chooses to, he can work productively, sustain love relationships, and manage his anxieties reasonably well. Second, there tends to be less "acting-out" of traumatic conflicts. Although the individual may have nightmares, "flashbacks," images, or thoughts of a hostile, aggressive, and retaliatory nature, they rarely get externalized into overt action. Third, there is a somewhat cyclical nature to the appearance of acute symptoms. Months may pass before there is depression, guilt, or existential questioning of life's meaning. Fourth, while there is a general reluctance to freely discuss the war experience, he will do so with a compassionate, empathic, and accepting person. There is very little blocking of visual images and painful memories. He can recall in detail a large number of war-related incidents. Fifth, supportive group discussions ("rap sessions") with other veterans about their concerns in life and their residual conflicts emanating from the war are often sufficient to transform survivor guilt into animated guilt and to produce a general cathartic and therapeutic effect (for example, Lifton 1973; Shatan 1978). Sixth, the dominant attributes or symptoms of psychosocial intensification are stage-related rather than predominately regressive or the result of preidentity infantile fixations. The most pressing conflicts tend to be age-specific, developmental concerns that are overlayed by the characteristics of the post-Vietnam syndrome. Clearly, this would seem to imply that the individual is attempting to assimilate unresolved conflicts, moral dilemmas, or value-conflicts into his current life-structure (Levinson 1978).

If we return to Table 7.3 for a moment, it is possible to state with more precision how psychosocial development and the post-Vietnam syndrome are interrelated. Since Erikson's (1968) theory is epigenetic and implicitly hierarchic, we can see by inspection of the table that each emerging psychosocial crisis incorporates the one that preceded it. Thus, under the column entitled "Identity Diffusion," we can see that there are problems associated with intimacy that include bisexual confusion, emotional distantiation, and loss of self-esteem. Similarly, the identity crisis contributes ideological confusion, difficulty in maintaining commitments, and self-consciousness. Problems of career choice and occupational fulfillment sometimes culminate in a form of work paralysis and an inability to find purpose or meaning in one's job. Finally, the individual will periodically experience a profound sense of guilt about his past actions that feeds self-doubt, anxiety, and a sense of hopelessness. When viewing these emotional and motivational attributes psychosocially, we can see clearly that postcombat stress intensifies stage-specific ego-development by taxing ego-control and resiliency (Block and Block 1978). The post-Vietnam syndrome is thus not simply a variation of traumatic war neurosis. On the contrary, it is an ego-process in which the entire life-structure and configuration of self-hood is undergoing a profound struggle to achieve coherency and individuation within the limits set by the laws governing organismic growth.

THE RELATION OF PSYCHOSOCIAL ACCELERATION TO THE COMMON STRESS-PRODUCING EVENTS IN VIETNAM AND THE DELAYED STRESS SYNDROME

The third and least-explored consequence of the common stress experiences is that of psychosocial progression or acceleration. By this it is meant that there is a premature acceleration of all the postidentity life stages and psychosocial crises that are described by Erikson (1968) and Levinson (1978). In an earlier study (Wilson 1978) I described this process of psychosocial acceleration as a kind of psychological time warp since the questions the men asked of themselves, their ultimate concerns in life, their interpersonal orientation and view of society were characteristic of those that normatively emerge later in the life cycle. This process of acceleration is illustrated in *A Rumor of War* in which Caputo (1977, p. 192) says:

> I was twenty-four when the summer began; by the time it ended, I was much older than I am now. Chronologically, my age had advanced three months, emotionally about three decades. I was somewhere in my middle fifties, that depressing period when a man's friends begin dying off and each death reminds him of the nearness of his own.

What personality characteristics do individuals with psychosocial acceleration possess? First, they all appear to be highly courageous persons who are honest to the point of "testing the limits" of the norms governing social transaction. They are extremely intense individuals who are actively determined to live an existentially valid existence. In fact, they live their day-to-day lives with a good deal of creativity, emotional intensity, and integrity. They present themselves bluntly, directly, assertively, and are unusually sensitive to phoniness, deceit, cruelty, callousness, inequity, and injustice. Their psychoformative images and symbols, their philosophical and psychological orientation simultaneously center around the psychosocial stages of identity, intimacy, generativity, and integrity. Specifically, they are deeply concerned with altruistic action and the need to contribute meaningfully to society. They are responsible and concerned with ethical principles of a universal nature and the need to live with personal integrity. As a result of this basic motivation to be more Protean, to give birth to new inner forms of experience, the individual frequently experiences intense anxiety (of short duration) that results from a postconventional level of moral judgment with high degrees of self-esteem. In some respects, this existential anxiety is connected with the awareness that their ultimate goals and concerns are not typical of other individuals their age. Thus, the war created a paradox for these men. It was an existential vacuum where time, space, and meaning had little, if any, continuity with the past. It was a surrealistic absurdity that produced massive psychoformative decentering (Lifton 1976). However, once removed from this plane of existence, psychosocial acceleration became evident in the personality structure. At its best, the psychosocially accelerated person recognized that he marched to the beat of a different drummer. At its worst, and in stark contrast, the retrogressed individual felt nothing but numbness to life since the continuity of his existence had been shattered by death. These different patterns of adjustment are explored in the next section.

PATTERNS OF ADJUSTMENT AND PERSONALITY INTEGRATION AMONG VIETNAM VETERANS

By now it is a truism to say that there are different patterns of adjustment and personality integration following a war. All veterans are not alike and neither was the effect of the stress-producing events in their lives.

Based on our extensive interviews with a cross-section of Vietnam-era veterans, as well as the theoretical considerations discussed above, it is now possible to consider in a broader perspective on how the war affected the individual's pattern of personality integration. Specifically, we can view this process as cross-cutting the domain of personality functioning in at least four ways: the predominant psychosocial crisis in a critical period of development, the cognitive psychoformative processes, the organization of the belief system and ideological referents, and the affective-motivational components. Table 7.4 summarizes these elements of personality integration and adjustment.

Acute Identity Diffusion—Psychic Numbing

The individuals most severely and negatively affected by their war experiences suffer psychic numbing. Clearly, the trauma of war overpowered their healthy coping patterns and their capacity to effectively manage stress. As a consequence, all domains of the personality structure show a diminution of humanness, a constriction of being, and the organismic process of self-actualization.

In terms of their psychosocial attributes, the psychically numbed individuals manifest impairments of ego-strength, as well as regressive qualities from earlier periods of psychosocial development. Typically, these men evidence high degrees of mistrust, anxiety, doubt, shame, survivor guilt, inferiority, isolation, withdrawal, stagnation, and despair. They have a deep-seated conviction that nothing matters anymore; that they are helpless against the external forces of fate that helped create their outlook of hopelessness and the incapacity to experience life richly, fully, and in the gut. They rage against this perceived state of doom with anger or depressed resignation but have no ideological conviction to give direction to this emotional turmoil. Rather, the overall configuration of their belief system and the psychoformative processes is that of confusion and blockage, a prevailing sense of stasis, separation, and disintegration. It is not surprising then that many of these men are loners who isolate themselves from others that they so desperately need.

Exploitative-Opportunistic Orientation

In the exploitative orientation the individual suffers partial psychic numbing and identity diffusion. These are the angry veterans who have not been able to fully "work through" the war experience in a manner that would result in a strengthening of the ego and the quality of interpersonal relationships. These men are anomic extroverts (Block 1971) who are typically emotionally unreactive, impulsive, and egocentric. They tend to be opportunistic, Machiavellian, and conform to social norms, rules, and laws only when expedient and necessary to the maintenance of a socially desirable, conventional facade. It is not

TABLE 7.4: Personality Integration and Patterns of Adjustment in Vietnam Veterans

Dimensions of Personality Structure	Postconventional Humanistic Orientation	Conventional Orientation	Exploitative-Opportunistic Orientation	Psychic Numbing
Psychosocial attributes	Psychosocial acceleration beyond identity; concern with intimacy, generativity, and integrity. Manifest virtues of fidelity, care, acceptance of others, and so on.	Concern with normative psychosocial crises, for example, intimacy versus isolation. Strongly oriented toward intimate interpersonal involvement.	Partial identity diffusion, difficulty in establishing intimacy. Regressive aspects of development salient; mistrust, doubt, inferiority, and so on; egocentric, immature.	Acute identity diffusion characterized by mistrust, doubt, inferiority, work paralysis, despair, stagnation, isolation; withdrawal, bisexual confusion, ego-regression.
Psychoformative processes (after Lifton 1976)	Protean style; creative recentering; maintains sense of vitality; connectedness; integrity movement; continuity without self-sameness.	Has a sense of grounding and centering but does not risk decentering; maintains self-continuity with sameness.	Partial psychic numbing; sense of separation, disintegration but capable of movement; often uncentered.	Blockage of psychoformative processes; strong sense of uncentering; stasis; separation and disintegration.
Belief system	Left-wing ideological orientation; concern with universal values and ethics; major themes justice, equity, altruism, honesty; utilitarian use of power and authority.	Conventional ideological world view; concerned with conforming to or upholding normative values inherent in social order; family, home, work.	Preconventional-conventional; opportunistic; function primarily on principle of instrumental exchange. Anomic extroverts; conform to norms, rules, and so on, only when expedient.	Ideological confusion; confusion of values and lack of commitment to coherent belief system.

Table 7.4 (continued)

TABLE 7.4 (continued)

Affective motivational components	Existential anxiety. Associated with positive psychosocial acceleration and Protean style; strong self-esteem; periodic depression over existential dialectic to remain authentic; manifests elements of post-Vietnam syndrome coupled with philosophical questioning.	Generally has positive outlook on self and others; seeks approval; affiliation and belongingness to a meaningful community. Occasionally manifests elements of post-Vietnam syndrome.	Machiavellian; emotionally unreactive, exploitative with others; impulsive. Heavy use of alcoholic and psychoactive substances; post-Vietnam syndrome.	Feelings of hopelessness and helplessness, rage, anger, guilt, depression, low self-esteem; high anxiety; withdrawal, safety-oriented, emotionally unresponsive; traumatic war neurosis.

Source: Compiled by the author.

surprising, then, that their belief systems and moral judgment structures are preconventional (Kohlberg 1971) and oriented toward principles of "fair exchange," getting a good deal, and enhancing their needs
in a narcissistic way that only minimally has concern for others' needs
and values. Perhaps part of this exploitative-opportunistic orientation is
the consequence of psychoformative blockage with respect to a sense of
connectedness and integrity (Lifton 1976). These men frequently feel
uncentered but do have some sense of direction in their lives. Indeed, it
is this drive or persistence to have some feeling of on-going "process" or
aliveness that propels them to action. Thus, any negotiation is justifi-
able if it enhances the sense of continued function as an organism, even
if it is *without* a sense of self-sameness and continuity. Clearly, these
men are preconsciously aware of the fact that cessation in striving, no
matter how opportunistic and self-centered, is tantamount to a symbolic death. Moreover, they equate immobility, loss of freedom to
maneuver, to "deal," to "make something happen" with death and its
imprint in memory of lost buddies. After all, death, if nothing else, is
immobility and disintegration.

In the most basic sense, opportunistic functioning reflects a strong
sense of insecurity, doubt, mistrust, and anxiety in connection with the
ability to be masterful as a person. In this orientation the basic
weakness is compensated for by an unfeeling "macho" show of power
and the capacity to influence events. However, this style of coping with
the vaguely perceived threats of personal insecurity and death is not
conducive to harmonious and intimate love relations. On the contrary,
these men have much difficulty establishing and maintaining mutually
satisfying intimate relationships. Ultimately, this egocentric orientation
forces a premature ending to an affair that, in turn, further fuels the
entire motivational syndrome all over again. When the stress produced
by this motivational syndrome exceeds the person's capacity to manage
it effectively, they usually drink heavily or use psychoactive substances
in the search for tension release. The combination of drugs and psychic
tension is usually sufficient to numb the ego and release the stored
anger in a vain attempt to rectify the feeling of having been exploited
for service in Vietnam and denied the full opportunity to have an
alternative sense of ego-identification.

Conventional Orientation

Among the entire group of Vietnam veterans, the conventional
orientation represents the largest number of individuals. These men are
fundamentally well-adjusted and well-integrated into the social fabric
of American life. In contrast to the other forms of personality integra-

tion, these men are developmentally "on schedule," that is, they are currently concerned with the psychosocial crisis of intimacy versus isolation and have achieved in some measure the ego strength of fidelity, the ability to commit themselves to ideals and a way of life compatible with their life experiences. In many ways these men are not very different from their age mates who did not enter the military service or those who saw military duty outside of Vietnam. Typically, the conventionally oriented veteran is concerned with establishing or deepening love relationships and securing a place of belonging in an organization, institution, or community. He tends to have a sense of grounding and centering (Lifton 1976) that maintains a sense of self-sameness and continuity. However, he is not a risk taker and shies away from decentering unless it is necessary for ego-vitality. It is not surprising that this belief system tends to subscribe to a conventional set of ideological principles characterized by conformity to the normative social order. They seek acceptance and approval from those they see as models of success, and frequently they feel anxious to make up for the "lost time" spent in Vietnam. Periodically, they manifest the post-Vietnam syndrome but not with much intensity or direction. Indeed these individuals seem to want to forget the war and go on with the business of raising a family and succeeding in their careers. Curiously, however, their view of the war is negative and similar to that of their cohorts but without the deep-seated alienation and resentment. Unlike the other patterns of adjustment, these men do not struggle much with anomie, existential estrangement, or being beyond the conventional social order in one form (psychosocial acceleration) or another (exploitative orientation). Rather, they want to be successful and happy within the American way of life.

Postconventional, Humanistic Orientation

The postconventional humanistic orientation grows out of the existential search for meaning when the individual has experienced a psychological time warp and acceleration of the postidentity growth crisis. In many ways these men represent the most extreme distance from conventionality and the normative social order. Psychosocial acceleration produces profound changes in all of the interconnected domains of the human personality structure. These changes, detailed below, lead to very special problems in reentering the mainstream of society.

Psychosocial Acceleration

To begin with, it is necessary to explain the idea of psychosocial acceleration in more detail. This is especially important because the phenomenon of psychosocial acceleration presents interesting questions to many contemporary theories of personality and human development. If we recall for a moment our discussion of Erikson's epigenetic principle of human development, we note that it assumes that personality development proceeds in a *linear* fashion with one stage following the next in a prescribed sequence that itself is determined by organismic changes. In theory, then, a 25- or 30-year-old veteran could not be concerned with the psychosocial crisis of, say, generativity versus stagnation or integrity versus despair since the normative period (life stage) had not been reached to permit these organismic capacities to "unfold." Furthermore, the special qualities of awareness (ego-strengths) associated with a life stage or critical period of development would not emerge since the individual would not have had the experiences necessary for this more mature form of ego-synthesis to occur. What psychosocial acceleration implies, however, is that this linear sequence is either accelerated beyond the normative pattern of personality development or somehow short-circuited altogether. While both possibilities are intriguing, I favor the view that the normal, linear organismic sequence is in fact accelerated. The alternative view might argue, however, that there are no life stages or critical periods of development after the formation of ego-identity. In other words, given the pattern of intellectual and emotional growth up to the time of young adulthood, those persons possessing the ability to reason abstractly and who are characterized by high degrees of ego-strength, self-esteem, frustration tolerance, positive temperamental traits, and so on, may potentially acquire cognitive *and* motivational systems typically called "generative" or "integrity" by virtue of experiencing conflicts centered around the most basic processes of being human—the omega point issue of life, death, and the existential creation of meaning and identity.

While I do not totally rule out the competing hypothesis, I think that there is now a respectable body of research (for example, Levinson 1978) to document that there are adult stages of ego development that correspond to Erikson's model. Additionally, research in moral development, while less than complete, also favors the view of organismically determined, universal stage of moral judgment (cognitive) structures (for example, Kohlberg 1971). Therefore, the organismic view implies that personality, in part, is the unique organization of more or less stable attributes of ego function that result from socialization. Therefore, each organismically rooted stage of personality usually has a normative period of ascendancy but may potentially emerge prematurely under certain highly conflicting, stressing, catastrophic, or cataclysmic experiences. What determines whether the individual experiences psychosocial acceleration, psychic numbing, or some other personality outcome is determined, in part, by the degree of ego-strength, self-esteem, and the intellectual capacity to resynthesize and reorganize cognitive precepts in order to create existential meaning in one's life, a point that Bettelheim (1943) and Frankel (1959) have made as well.

Psychosocial acceleration causes the individual to have new psycho-formative modes that are characterized by the strong need for continual Protean functioning, that is, decentering and recentering images and forms that define the self. One of the consequences of this process is that the individual's cognitive structure undergoes a significant and large degree of reorganization. Specifically, his concepts of time, space, and causality are dramatically changed. In many respects, it is possible to speak of the men as existing in a different temporal-spatial plane of existence, that is, they no longer subscribe to many of the traditional, conventional, or orthodox views about reality, life, the social order, and its rule of goverance. They possess many of the characteristics of the self-actualizing person as described by Maslow (1970), especially in the realm of values. Typically, they are strongly concerned with such values as integrity, justice, equity, altruism, the utilitarian use of power and authority, harmony, truth, honesty, dignity, courage, reality, ultimate goodness, and so on. Furthermore, they are intense people who seem to live each moment fully, cherishing life's richness. Their self-concept is that of an on-going process oriented toward the continued creation and recreation of ultimate meaning ("integrity"); Tao-like love for others, mature-love ("intimacy"); creative fulfillment in being productive and caring qualitatively about life now and in the future ("generativity"). As I see it, psychosocial acceleration allows the individual to live *beyond* the fear of death, the death imprint, and the finality of existence itself. Paradoxically, the encounter with death seems to open new doors of perception, to invert death's usual significance in life to permit full humanness to emerge as the essence of organismic centering within a more "cosmic" grounding of being.*

---

*This point has been made recently by Terrence Des Pres in his book *The Survivor* (1976). He writes (pp. 201–03):

Much of the behavior of survivors may thus be traced to the biosocial roots of human existence; and not their behavior merely, but also extraordinary stubbornness of will which characterizes action in extremity—the furious energy of a will impersonal and stronger than hope, which in an accurate, unmetaphorical sense can only be that of life itself. But survivors do more than maintain moral

Negative Effects of Psychosocial Acceleration

While the individual who has undergone psychosocial acceleration generally views the changes as positive and subjectively desirable, there are a number of problems generated by these changes in personality. First, the individual often experiences acute existential anxiety. I call this form of anxiety existential to differentiate it from neurotic anxiety or character-based anxiety more typically associated with basic need deprivation or psychological threat to ego defenses. Existential anxiety is experienced as the tension emanating from the need to live authentically as a person with dignity, integrity, and "wisdom." It is the anxiety that results from the continual partial suspension of the temporal, spatial, and emotional planes of being that constitute the bases of centering (Lifton 1976). Thus the decentering—recentering psychoformative process in itself produces a special kind of anxiety. This concept is similar to the Piagetian idea of horizontal decalage in which changes in intellectual judgment (logical ability) generalize from one categorical area to another. Cognitive disequilibration or changes in the psychoformative modes (Lifton 1976) generate energy (existential anxiety), which motivates the process of organizing a new set of cognitive structures and modalities of perception, thinking, and action. For the veteran, this process of change in psychoformative modes centers around integrating in a more mature form the newly acquired ego virtues associated with "intimacy," "generativity," and "integrity." Obviously, this is no simple task; the individual must come to terms with the fact that the normative expectations that others and society have of him are no longer congruent with his own expectations, ideologies, and moral judgment perspectives. Clearly, his sense of identity, values, and perception of ultimate meaning are beyond the conventional, normative order, that is, postconventional and humanistic in orientation. However, because of his age (presently about 33) it is unlikely that he has a completely internalized sense of self-worth or self-esteem. In other words, while his motivational striving is largely based on the need for greater organismic competence, there are still residues of the need for esteem which have not been gratified to the

---

sanity and establish bonds among themselves. They struggle to preserve dignity as something which cannot be dispensed with. This too may be the specifically human enactment of a biological imperative. . . . But just as much, they struggle fiercely for an existence apart, for an integrity absolutely unbreachable. That is the basis of dignity, of personality, of the egoism which fuels creation and discovery, and finally of the sense of individual "rights." . . . On the human level, this activity of keeping whole and inviolate, this constant resistance to the penetration of others, is the essence of dignity.

extent where a more mature and integrated form of self-acceptance is possible. Therefore, one source of conflict and frustration centers around the belief or expectation that others (society) should see the validity of his world view, goals, ideals, and commitments. Yet, the conventional order cannot give to him the rewards he seeks precisely because they do not fully comprehend what he is saying and striving toward as a person. For many Vietnam veterans this "wailing against the established order" is a source of depression, anger, and existential frustration until they learn that many people really do not care about their ideological perspective. It is only when they reach the conclusion that there will always be irresolvable differences among people in their values that a greater inner peace comes to pass. Until that time, the veteran knows that he marches to the beat of a different drummer and feels moderately alienated from those who have not experienced similar changes in personality. It must be remembered that these are basically strong healthy persons who do not wallow in self-pity or maladaptive forms of being. If they are alienated, they tend to accept it as an inevitable outcome of what they have experienced. However, unlike the psychically numbed or exploitative veterans, their positive ego-strength leads them to accept that there are many paradoxes in life that have no rational or logical solution. Rather, they come to accept without furor, depression, or infantile demandingness that their dignity stems from the process of creating personal meaning while maintaining a positive self-judgment perspective of the entire life cycle when repeatedly confronted with the absurdities and paradoxes of existence.

PSYCHOSOCIAL DEVELOPMENT IN ADULTHOOD: FUTURE CRISES AND PROBLEMS ASSOCIATED WITH THE WAR EXPERIENCE

As noted above, the typical veteran is in his early to mid-thirties. According to theories of ego development, he is now in the stage of life in which the crisis intimacy versus isolation is at the center stage of personality development. In future years the individual will enter other stages of the life cycle until death ends this organismic process. Since many of the participants in our study were at the age where the formation of intimate relationships was a central part of their lives, we thought it important to look at this issue more closely. To state the major question simply, Are those individuals who were exposed to stress-producing events in combat more likely to have difficulty in establishing successful love relationships and intimate friendships than their cohorts who were not in combat or Southeast Asia?

Before examining some of the research evidence on this question, it is important to gain an overview of the psychosocial crisis intimacy versus isolation (Erikson 1968). In the stage of genitality, the psychosocial crisis centers around the capacity to form mutually satisfying intimate relationships and affectional bonds. In general, we can state that to the degree that one has a strong ego-identity, one will be able to "take chances" with that identity by fusing and counterpointing it with another person (Newman and Newman 1975). A strong psychosocial sense of intimacy is the capacity to establish, maintain, and involve oneself with another in a way that brings affection, sexual pleasure, love, affiliation, and to enjoy the by-products of this involvement (for example, children, cooperative ventures, and so on). A sense of isolation, on the other hand, is a form of estrangement from intimate contact and commitment. Where identity is so diffuse that self-doubts, feelings of inadequacy, confusion, lack of directedness, purposelessness, anxiety, and dependency predominate consciousness, the need for intimacy constitutes an ambivalently valued goal. Erikson (1968) has termed this state as one of distantiation. Distantiation or isolation refers to the estrangement created by withdrawal from attempts to fuse ego boundaries. The individual fears further loss of identity and self-esteem; he fears being rejected and therefore prematurely rejects others or disengages from intimate contact to avoid emotional hurt. As a consequence of this self-doubt and disengagement the individual may suffer bisexual confusion, which is a form of doubt as to what it means to have a sex-role identity as a man or woman.

Where there were problems of crystallizing a sense of ego-identity into a coherent self-structure the veteran frequently reported maladaptive or nonconstructive forms of dealing with interpersonal difficulties (Wilson 1978). Included in these nonconstructive forms of coping are the frequent and heavy use of various psychoactive substances, especially alcohol; fits of anger, rage, and hostility; emotional ambivalence and distance toward loved ones; and irresponsibility with respect to commitments demanding some measure of propriety, reliability, and trustworthiness. Clearly, the diffusion of identity makes it particularly difficult for the individual to successfully fuse ego boundaries with others. In some instances, the capacity to feel emotion, especially affection and warmth, was numbed through confrontation with killing and the witnessing of death in combat. The individual's pattern of coping seems to follow a logic that dictates: "If I don't get close, I don't have to suffer the pain of loss (of my good buddy; of myself)." This paradigm of estrangement was sometimes initiated by the first encounter with the reality of death in war. In *A Rumor of War*, Phil Caputo (1977, pp. 162–63) says:

I came to understand why Lemmon and the others had seemed so [emotionally] distant. It had nothing to do with my no longer belonging to the battalion. It was, rather, the detachment of men who find themselves living in the presence of death. They had lost their first man in battle, and, with him, the youthful confidence in their own immortality. Reality had caught up with them, with all of us. . . . Some combat veterans may think I am making too much of a single casualty. Later, I was to see fairly active fighting, and I know that experiencing heavy or constant losses tends to diminish the significance of one individual's death. But at the time we lost Sullivan, casualties were still light; it was the "expeditionary" period of the war, a period that lasted roughly March to September, 1965. The loss of even one man was an extraordinary event. Perhaps, too, we were less emotionally prepared for death and wounds than those who came later; . . . They had been together for years and assumed they would remain together until the end of their enlistment. It upset the sense of unity and stability that had pervaded life in the battalion. . . . Later in the war, that sort of feeling became rarer in infantry battalions. Men were killed, evacuated with wounds, or rotated home at a constant rate, then replaced by other men who were killed, evacuated, or rotated in their turn. By that time, a loss only meant a gap in the line that needed filling.

Thus, this paradigm of interpersonal involvement, *purposeful distantiation*, served a survival function in Vietnam but became maladaptive after demobilization. Many men lost the capacity to discriminate when to "turn off" the switch controlling ones degree of distantiation or isolation from others. Furthermore, the delay of the psychosocial moratorium demanded that identity-integration take precedence among the psychosocial tasks. Yet, as one of the consequences of war, purposeful distantiation would exacerbate and confound the crisis of identity as well. The partial psychic numbing indigenous to distantiation contributed to identity diffusion since the individual would, at times, block images or emotional modes of relating that would enable ego integration to occur (Lifton 1973; 1976). Hence, the complex problem of balancing the positive and negative poles of the crisis identity versus role confusion.

Perhaps more than anything else the returning veteran needed social support, love, affection, and a positive welcome from his community in order to "work through" the war experiences while establishing his sense of identity. As we now know, this did not occur in the majority of cases. More typically, the ambivalence of society toward the war was conveyed bluntly and subtly by the realities of the economic marketplace and the social stigma of having matriculated from higher education in the rice paddies and jungles. For many men this tacit rejection or thinly disguised ambivalence was tantamount to emotional apathy or indifference from those they needed to rely on for emotional and social support (Wilson 1978). Psychologically, it is possible to view these events as a form of deprivation of intimate contact and a sense of belonging that was needed to not only work out identity but to feel a rich sense of psychic vitality, wholeness, and unity in the self. While the confrontation with death and the realities of war led to purposeful distantiation, it also created a need to know oneself more fully and to be genuinely close to others. Yet, this learned modality of interpersonal involvement that maintained a psychologically safe distance did not extinguish upon coming home from the war. Rather, the social conditions of the time contributed to its prolonged use even though purposeful distantiation was not conducive to healthy psychosocial growth and development. Where this strategy of interpersonal involvement persisted the individual was likely to have difficulties in establishing intimate relationships and a sense of belonging and rootedness in a community meaningful to him. In its extreme form, the consequence of purposeful distantiation is loneliness and alienation.

PROBLEMS OF INTIMACY AMONG VIETNAM VETERANS

The results of our research indicate that combat veterans, in total, had more problems in interpersonal relationships than their cohorts and that the findings were not limited to a single person (for example, father) but tended to involve significant others in his life at various points in time, starting initially with fellow soldiers (the paradigm of purposeful distantiation) and extending to friends, family, and members of the opposite sex. Moreover, the results revealed that the constructiveness of the combatant's coping patterns did not change with the tenure of his military duty. Rather, it tended to stay in a realm of ambivalent functioning with respect to others, whereas his cohorts tended to become more positive. This fact is consistent with the finding that the combatant believed that others saw him as conflicted and having personal difficulties. While this may be nothing more than an attribution process or a form of externalization of motives and attitudes, it does suggest that the individual was aware of the problem of intimacy in interpersonal relationships and perceived that others recognized these difficulties as well. All of this must be considered from the perspective that at the time of entry into the military there were no significant differences in the quality of interpersonal relationships by place of duty. Thus, we can conclude that it was the experience of combat that contributed strongly to the observed change in interpersonal relationships (Wilson 1978).

The findings discussed above may imply that the nature of the Vietnam War was such that many veterans suffered a deprivation of the psychosocial moratorium when it was most critically needed in order to form a coherent sense of ego-identity. However, once home from the war it was often difficult to have the time to explore different areas of the self before making commitments to a career, another person, or oneself. Deprivation of the moratorium may lead, in turn, to a premature foreclosure of ego-identity or identity diffusion. Where this is the case, the individual veteran, especially the combatant, may not have had enough time to work through the complexities of his experience in order to gain a healthy perspective of himself and his involvement in the war in a way that would lead to a free choice of identity and future possibilities. For many Vietnam veterans the consequence of this deprivation and identity foreclosure is the urgent need to feel a part of a community and to have a sense of being able to love and be intimate with others. For them a sense of connectedness and rootedness is perceived as necessary to feel vital and intact as a person of integrity. But where identity diffusion or identity foreclosure predominate, the veteran simultaneously wants intimacy but fears further loss of identity or potential hurt by getting too close to someone he loves. This typically seems to result in strong ambivalence that counterbalances purposeful distantiation on the one hand, and the need for intimate contact and personal acceptance on the other hand. Where the attempt to fuse and counterpoint individual identities tips toward the negative critical ratio, the result is estrangement, isolation, distantiation, and a feeling of alienation from family, friends, and loved ones. This is particularly sad since genuine acceptance, love, and a sense of belonging to a meaningful community would do much to heal the psychic wounds that stemmed from the encounter with death and absurdity in Vietnam and the subsequent need for purposeful distantiation.

FUTURE PSYCHOSOCIAL STAGES

Generativity versus Stagnation

In Erikson's (1968) schema of the life-cycle the next crisis is that of generativity versus stagnation (see Table 7.1). This stage is described as a period of actively guiding the next generation. What seems clear is that the concern is with providing care to one's children and those parts of society for which responsibility has been assumed. The emphasis here is on a special kind of productivity: the need to become responsible for the quality of succeeding generations, the results of one's career, one's institutional organization, and its output.

In midlife and the crisis of generativity, the emphasis on quality and meaningfulness indicates that what is being described are relationships in which the psychological elements have to do with a mature form of self-esteem rather than intimacy. It appears that Erikson is pointing out that by this time an individual can achieve a firm sense of self-worth so that no longer do the earlier comparisons of being "better than" have any importance. Rather, at this stage there can be a growth of involvements and the assumption of greater depths of responsibility for the successful development of others and a concern for the quality of their achievement.

For the Vietnam veteran the crisis of generativity versus stagnation will raise anew the problem of existential meaning in life. It is likely that they will remember vividly their experiences in Vietnam and how they influenced life afterward, the struggle to understand themselves in terms of self-sameness and continuity, and the problem of overcoming distantiation in forming intimate relationships with others. In the fourth decade of their lives the men will be faced once again with the issue of authority and its appropriate exercise in society. Since many of the men will have a residual mistrust of authority and its institutionalized form as well, it will be a difficult task to evolve a new psychological configuration of themselves as *the* agents of authority, those responsible for the quality of the next generation, the administration of justice, the construction of new social values and functional ideological principles. What will make this task especially difficult is that by then so many individual veterans will have established social patterns of an apolitical nature characterized by partial disengagement from the conventional order, the established and prevailing systems of authority, and corporate responsibility. Yet, to attain a full sense of vitality at this point in life (that is, not to suffer further identity diffusion, distantiation, or stagnation), the veteran will have to counterbalance postidentity modalities of being with the new demands to be the authority leading those in need of ideological confirmation, to be good adult role models, and to be the torch bearers of essential value principles and orientations. All of this will require a reexamination of the war experiences and their role in shaping the newly emerging configuration in the life structure. Based on Levinson's research (1978), this crisis will have its turning point between the ages of 40 and 45 and once again at age 50.

Integrity Versus Despair

The last life stage is senescence and has as its nuclear growth crisis integrity versus despair. As the individual approaches the end of his life cycle he has to face nonbeing and death. This stage of life is character- ized by the need to find meaning and achieve self-acceptance after the "triumphs and disappointments" of life, the need to find meaning and worth in what has been experienced. In essence, the psychosocial task of this stage is to construct a new configuration or perspective of oneself and the entire life cycle. When an individual has true self- acceptance and when the psychological configuration concerns itself with matters of ultimate concern and acceptance of the varities of coping and expressive behavior, differences in value orientations, physical decline, and the inevitability of death, we speak of a sense of integrity. When there is unhappiness, frustration, denial, the lack of acceptance of oneself, the course of life cycle, resignation, and with- drawal from the *process* of being vital, we speak of a sense of despair as the final psychosocial configuration.

For the Vietnam veteran the issue of integrity versus despair will demand a final synthesis and perspective of the war and its role in his life. In the face of nonbeing and death it is likely that he will recall his first encounter with death in Vietnam and the difficulties associated with making sense out of it. He may become somewhat anxious (that is, existentially anxious) to live the last years with a full measure of dignity and integrity. If he was severely numbed by the war experiences and purposely distantiated, then the existential concern may center around the fear that he may become numbed and distantiated again when facing his own death. Although the young combat veteran witnessed death many times, its psychological significance was different than it will be at the last stage of life since once again there are new possibilities and new opportunities for achieving selfhood and psychosocial vitality. The struggle for integrity will have to counterbalance the need for healthy self-acceptance of himself, his life cycle, and its events against the tendency to despair and believe that truly nothing was sacred, important, meaningful, or significant in life. The despairing tendency is a form of premature grieving over the loss of one's self through death, as well as an incapacity to understand why others died earlier in the war. In a sense, the earlier struggle with the existential absurdity of the war is renewed here and expanded into questions about the absurdity of life itself. Where survivor guilt, a fragmented identity, distantiation, and stagnation predominate, it is likely that the individual will feel despair that his life cycle never quite unfolded in the way he had hoped it would as a young adult. To cite Erikson (1968, pp. 140–41):

> ... Evidence suggests that the lack or loss of this accrued ego interac- tion is signified by disgust and by despair: fate is not accepted as the frame of life, death not as its finite boundary. Despair expresses the

feeling that time is short, too short for the attempt to start another life and to try out alternate roads to integrity. Such a despair is often hidden behind a show of disgust, a misanthropy, or a chronic contemptuous displeasure which, where not allied with the vision of a superior life, only signify the individual's contempt of himself.

To whatever abyss ultimate concerns may lead individual men, man as a psychosocial creature will face, toward the end of his life, a new edition of an identity crisis which we may state in the words "I am what survives me."

Thus, the numbed veteran fears that nothing of meaning will survive him because he is already a survivor whom death robbed prematurely of the opportunity for a full and vital life cycle. Perhaps it was the confrontation of death long ago in Vietnam that precipitated an early form of despair. In *A Rumor of War*, Caputo (1977, pp. 230–31) says:

The hallucinations I had had that day in mess, of seeing Mora and Harrison prefigured in death, had become a constant waking nightmare. I had begun to see almost everyone as they would look in death, including myself. Shaving in the mirror in the morning, I could see myself dead, and there were moments when I not only saw my own corpse, but other people looking at it. I saw life going on without me. The sensation of not being anymore came over me at night, just before falling asleep. Sometimes it made me laugh inside; I could not take myself seriously when I could already see my own death; nor seeing their deaths as well, could I take others seriously. We were all victims of a great practical joke played on us by God or Nature.

Despairing could be doubly difficult to manage during this last stage of life because it might be an amplification of earlier forms of despair against which he may have struggled since death's forceful entrance into his existence in Vietnam. Clearly, this final stage of life counterbalances the concern for ultimate meaning against nothingness and absurdity.

SUMMARY

Two years of research and extensive interviews with a cross-section of Vietnam veterans formed the basis of the ideas presented in this chapter. From this set of data it appeared that the Vietnam War had a profound effect on the identity and ideology of the veteran. To understand the psychological nature of these changes in personality it is necessary to know how the various stress-producing events of combat affected the process of psychosocial development as characterized by Erikson (1968).

In his theory, Erikson notes that the growth crisis identity versus identity-diffusion normally occurs in late adolescence and young adult-hood. It is then followed by other stages of adult development, the first of which he calls intimacy versus isolation. The typical combatant in Vietnam was at the stage of life when the issue of forming a coherent personality structure was the predominant developmental task. Fur-ther, a complex set of social, political, and economic factors undermined the period of the psychosocial moratorium that usually permits an individual to unify elements of ego-identity. In Vietnam, then, the young soldier came face-to-face with a series of stress-producing events that strongly affected the process of identity integration and the formation of an ideology. As we now know, however, the stresses of the war came home with the veteran and contributed to problems of reentry into society and to the unification of personality. Thus, the delayed stress syndrome can be viewed as affecting the entire process of psychosocial development in several specific ways. First, in ego-retrogression there is severe estrangement and identity diffusion characterized by high levels of mistrust, self-doubt, purposelessness, inferiority, and confusion. Frequently there is also traumatic war neurosis that overlays identity diffusion and problems in coping with stage-specific developmental tasks. Second, in identity-intensification the veteran attempts to prolong the psychosocial moratorium in order to assimilate the war experiences into the self-structure. These veter-ans show symptoms of the post-Vietnam syndrome but do not manifest traumatic war neurosis or ego-retrogression. Rather, they attempt to construct a prolonged psychosocial moratorium in order to achieve unity and coherency within the self. Thus, the predominant crisis of development is intensified and most characteristically centers around the need to know oneself and live with meaning and authenticity. Third, in psychosocial acceleration the normal course of ego develop-ment is accelerated and there emerges prematurely some or all of the remaining stages of adult development (that is, intimacy, generativity, or integrity). Psychosocial acceleration, like retrogression or intensifica-tion of ego development, is accompanied by acute periods of anxiety and periodic self-estrangement. These veterans have the special problem of assimilating into their life structure elements of ego-strength that normatively would occur later in their lives. For this reason, then, they experience existential tension over the need to live responsibly, crea-tively, and with integrity as a moral agent in society.

The analysis of how the war affected ego-identity made it possible to integrate Erikson's theory of development with that of Lifton (1976) and Kohlberg (1971) to specify the patterns of personality integration and adjustment among the veterans. Four patterns of adjustment have been observed that confrom to predictions from psychosocial and psychoformative theory: psychic numbing, exploitative-opportunistic, conventional orientation, and postconventional-humanistic orientation. These were discussed as personality syndromes and then related to future issues of personality development in the life cycle.

REFERENCES

Bettelheim, B. 1943. "Individual and Mass Behavior in Extreme Situations." *Journal of Abnormal and Social Psychology*. Vol. 38, pp. 417–52.

Block, J. 1971. *Lives Through Time*. Berkeley: Bancroft Press.

Block, J. H., and J. Block. 1978. *The Role of Ego-Control and Ego-Resiliency in the Organization of Behavior*. New York: Lawrence Earlbaum.

Breuer, J., and S. Freud, 1885. *Studies on Hysteria*. Standard Edition, 2, London: Hogarth Press, 1955.

Caputo, P. 1977. *A Rumor of War*. New York: Holt, Rinehart and Winston.

DeFazio, V. J. 1978. "Dynamic Perspectives on the Nature and Effects of Combat Stress. In *Stress Disorders Among Vietnam Veterans*, ed. C. R. Figley. New York: Brunner/Mazel.

Des Pres, T. 1976. *The Survivor*. New York: Oxford University Press.

Erikson, E. H. 1968. *Identity, Youth and Crisis*. New York: W. W. Norton.

Figley, C. R. 1978. *Stress Disorders Among Vietnam Veterans*. New York: Brunner/Mazel.

Frankel, V. 1959. *From Death Camp to Existentialism*. Boston: Beacon Press.

Horowitz, M. J., and G. F. Solomon. 1978. "Delayed Stress Response Syndromes in Vietnam Veterans." In *Stress Disorders Among Vietnam Veterans*, ed. C. R. Figley. New York: Brunner/Mazel.

Kohlberg, L. 1971. "From Is to Ought." In *Cognitive Psychology and Epistemology*, ed. T. Mischel. New York: Academic Press.

Kris, E. 1952. *Psychoanalytic Explorations in Art*. New York: International University Press.

Levinson, D. 1978. *The Season of a Man's Life*. New York: Knopf.

Lifton, R. J. 1976. *The Life of the Self*. New York: Simon and Schuster.

———. 1973. *Home from the War*. New York: Simon and Schuster.

Maslow, A. H. 1970. *Motivation and Personality*. New York: Harper and Bros.

Milgram, S. 1974. *Obedience to Authority*. New York: Harper & Row.

Newman, B., and Newman, P. R. 1975. *Development through Life*. Homewood. Dorsey Press.

Shatan, C. 1978. "The Emotional Content of Combat Continues." In *Stress Disorders Among Vietnam Veterans*, ed. C. R. Figley. New York: Brunner/Mazel.

Wilson, J. P. 1978. "Identity, Ideology and Crisis: The Vietnam Veteran in Transition, Part II." *Psychosocial Attributes of the Veteran Beyond Identity. Patterns of Adjustment and Future Implications*. Unpublished Monograph. Cleveland State University.

———. 1977. "Identity, Ideology and Crisis: The Vietnam Veteran in Transition, Part I." Unpublished Monograph. Cleveland State University.

———. and C. Doyle. 1978. "Stigmatization of the Vietnam Veteran." Unpublished monograph. Cleveland State University.

8

PSYCHOSOCIAL ADJUSTMENT OF RECENTLY RETURNED VETERANS

CHARLES R. FIGLEY AND WILLIAM T. SOUTHERLY

Several years ago the Veterans Service Center (VSC) of Southwestern Illinois (Alton, Illinois) was funded by the Office of Economic Opportunity to conduct a large, comprehensive research project focusing on the Vietnam veteran.[1] The major thrust of the study was to provide the most up-to-date, comprehensive, and unbiased information about the Vietnam veteran's postmilitary service adjustment. Of primary importance was to profile and contrast veterans who were employed, unemployed, or underemployed following recent reentry into civilian life. Specifically, the study attempted to provide a picture of demographic and social characteristics of the Vietnam-era veteran; his personal adjustment, including indexes of emotional fall-out resulting from combat; substance use and abuse; and characteristics of the employed and unemployed veteran. The VSC employed 40 interviewers to collect the data. The interview schedule used was developed specifically for the study. The VSC contracted with the Survey Research

This chapter was originally presented at the American Psychological Association meetings in San Francisco, August 1977. Support from the National Institute of Mental Health (No. MH 29384-01-1R03-MSM) is gratefully acknowledged.

Center (University of Michigan) to refine the measure and train the interviewers.

Other than a brief report to the Illinois Governor's Advisory Council on Manpower (VSC 1975), this chapter is the first report of the findings. Future reports will present the findings based on more sophisticated multivariate statistical analyses. In this report we will present a portion of the initial data analysis employing only nonparametric statistical formulas due, in part, to the characteristics of the data.

METHOD

Sample

Subjects were drawn from a list of 12,000 Vietnam veterans generated from the Veterans Administration's out-reach lists for the Metro-East region of southwestern Illinois and lists from two county clerk's offices within the region. Only veterans released from military service since 1964 were included. Approximately 2,000 names were randomly selected from the master list stratified by branch of service, separation date, and sex based on a national demographic profile of the Vietnam veteran population in 1971 (U.S. Senate 1972) and by race based on the racial profile of Vietnam veterans within the region.

Among the initial list of 2,000 potential subjects, approximately 29 percent were unavailable (for example, moved away, hospitalized), approximately 16 percent refused to participate in the study, approximately 10 percent were not interviewed because no additional subjects were needed from their group (for example branch of service, separation date). Thus, 906 veterans were interviewed (45 percent) from the initial list of potential subjects. The Results section of this chapter includes a complete description of the sample.

Procedure

Approximately 100 letters per week were mailed to randomly selected names from the master list. The letter briefly described the project and told the veteran he would receive a phone call from the VSC in the near future. If the letter was not returned, the veteran was called to establish an interview date. If the letter was returned by the postal service because of an incorrect address, various procedures were followed to locate the veteran. A weekly log was kept of completed interviews. The log contained the race, sex, branch of service, and separation date of each veteran and was used to facilitate meeting the originally established sample criteria as noted earlier.

Interview Schedule

The interview instrument attempted to include items that appear to be intuitively, theoretically, or empirically related to postmilitary adjustment. Each interview lasted approximately 90 minutes and included the following: (1) A General Demographic Information Section obtains socioeconomic information regarding the veteran's family background. (2) The Service Data Section is primarily concerned with information related to military service. Items focus on, for example, how the veteran entered service, feelings about military service, branch of service and training. (3) Less-Than-Honorable Discharge Section is designed only for veterans with less-than-honorable discharges. Items deal with the contributing factors related to the discharge, whether or not attempts had been made to have the discharge upgraded, and problems experienced because of the discharge. (4) The Employment Section gathers information related to work experience before and after service, including, for example, type of workplace, wages, hours worked, occupation. (5) The Education Section includes items related to the amount of preservice and current education, and how schooling was and is now financed. (6) The Adjustment Section deals primarily with the veteran's overall emotional adjustment and the attitudes and feelings related to military service. (7) The Drug Use Section focuses on drug use and drug-related troubles. Court martial information, drug usage, and frequency of usage, as well as addiction data, are included in this section. (8) The Wrap-Up Section gives each veteran an opportunity to discuss problem areas that had not previously been dealt with during the interview. (9) The Interviewer's Overall Ratings of the Veteran Section allow interviewers the opportunity to assess the validity of the data obtained from each veteran.

RESULTS

Demographic and Social Characteristics

The veteran sample appears to be representative of the national profile of the Vietnam veteran, except for race.

Race: The overall sample was 72.9 percent white, 26.9 percent black, and .02 percent Mexican-American. Although nationally only 11 percent of those in the military service from 1964 through 1973 (U.S. Senate 1972) were black, the study sought a 30 percent black sample to obtain a closer approximation to the Greater East St. Louis region of Illinois where the sample was drawn.

Age: The mean age of the sample was 27.2 years old. Overall, 91 percent of the sample was between 21 and 31 years of age. The mean age of the group at the time of their separation from the service was 22.2 years.

Marital Status: A total of 70.7 percent of the sample was married at the time of interview or had been married at one time. Of this group, 8.9 percent had been married at least twice. Slightly over half (50.6 percent) of the veterans who married did so after they left the service. Also, the married veterans had an average of 1.27 children. At the time of interview, 11.2 percent of the veterans who had married were not living with their wives, while 15.3 percent of this group had been divorced. In both instances, the major reason given for the separation was incompatability. Of the veterans who had been divorced, 51.6 percent had remarried.

Home Town: The largest part of the sample (43.9 percent) grew up in small cities (population 10,000–50,000) while 26.6 percent came from large cities (population greater than 50,000), and 24.6 percent came from town settings (population less than 10,000). At the time of interview, 46.6 percent of the sample lived in small cities, while 25.6 percent lived in towns, and 24.1 percent lived in large cities.

Education: The average education of the sample before they entered the service was 12.5 years, while the education level at the time of interview was 13.06 years. Overall, 83 percent of the sample had high school diplomas before they entered the service. At interview, 92 percent of the sample had at least a high school education. The number of veterans with college degrees increased from 4.5 percent before the service to 13.9 percent at interview.

Branch of Service and Entry Status: Overall, 63.3 percent of the veterans served in the Army, 14.4 percent in the Navy, 13.3 percent in the Air Force, and 8.6 percent in the Marines. A little less than half (48.2 percent) of the sample was stationed in Vietnam. The majority of the sample entered the service through enlistment (52.3 percent) while 41.2 percent were drafted.

Service Discharge Status: The sample has a less-than-honorable discharge rate of 7.3 percent, of which 3.9 percent are general, 2.9 percent undesirable, 0.3 percent bad conduct, and 0.2 percent dishonorable.

Membership in Veterans' Organizations: Only 17.1 percent of the veteran sample belonged to veteran organizations. Of this group, 50.3 percent belonged to the Veterans of Foreign Wars and 34.8 percent belonged to the American Legion. The two main reasons given for not joining veterans' organizations were "not interested/not a joiner" and "don't have time."

Personal Adjustment: Good News and Bad News

The majority of the veterans adjusted well in most areas. Almost half (47.8 percent) of the veterans who were drafted had "bad feelings" about being drafted at induction. At interview, only 14.8 percent had bad feelings about being drafted, while 54.5 percent had good feelings about being drafted. Further, the majority of the veterans (82.9 percent) felt they had their "head straight" when they returned to civilian life. In fact, 68.4 percent reported their military experience helped them know themselves better.

Despite adjustments made by most veterans, however, a substantial number (43 percent) had a dream or nightmare about their military experience. Another 81 percent of this group, or almost 35 percent of the total sample, had had recurring dreams or nightmares. Even more revealing is the fact that 26.3 percent of the total sample felt the need to consult a professional person to counsel or treat them for a recurring dream or nightmare. (Recent estimates [Figley 1979], unfortunately, show that only a small percentage of mental health specialists are adequately trained to treat Vietnam combatants.) In other words, about one-fourth of the total sample felt the need to seek professional help for recurring dreams or nightmares. Because these symptoms have been associated with combat-related stress disorders (Figley 1978), the sample was stratified by degree of combat stress experience, using the chi square formula.

The sample was divided into four categories by the degree of combat stress experience: wounded—those wounded in daily combat; combatant—those in daily combat, but not wounded; Vietnam veteran—those who served in Vietnam, but were not in daily combat; and Vietnam-era veteran—those who did not serve in Vietnam.

The two groups associated with the most stressful experience (the two combat groups) consistently reported significantly more dreams/nightmares and associated problems. Overall, 65.8 percent of the wounded and 60.5 percent of the combatants experienced dreams/nightmares about their military experience, while only 43.2 percent of the Vietnam veterans and only 33.9 percent of the Vietnam-era veterans experienced the same.

The wounded and combatant groups experienced more recurring dreams/nightmares, more dreams/nightmares that woke them up, were more likely to fear or fight sleep because of the possibility of having a dream/nightmare, were more likely to feel the need to consult a professional person for help, and are more likely to be still having dreams/nightmares than the Vietnam veteran and the Vietnam-era group. (Maybe even more important is the fact that the wounded and the combatants more frequently had nightmares rather than dreams about military experiences, while the other two groups more frequently had dreams.)

Drug Use

The veteran sample had tried a variety of drugs and had had some problems associated with using them. In fact, 13.6 percent of the veterans indicated they tried to quit using alcohol or other drugs, and 7.1 percent had been in trouble with the authorities for drug-related offenses.

Alcohol (78.2 percent) and marijuana (39.6 percent) are the drugs that were tried most frequently. The following is a list of other drugs and the percentages of the sample who tried these drugs: amphetamines (14.8 percent), mescaline (13.5 percent), LSD (12.4 percent), cocaine (11.3 percent), barbiturates (9.9 percent), opium (9.3 percent), tranquilizers (7.8 percent), and heroin (6.2 percent). At interview, only alcohol and marijuana were being used to any extent. In fact, half of the sample (54.1 percent) used alcohol and almost one-quarter (22.7 percent used marijuana at least once a week.

Employment

Our definition is based on the one used in the *1973 Handbook of Labor Statistics* and is as close an approximation as is possible with the given design of the interview instrument. Included in our unemployment category are "unemployed and looking for work" and "unemployed" (includes full-time students). The last category is adjusted so as to exclude students (n = 62) from the unemployed category. Given the small number of part-time workers in our sample (n = 42), this group is also excluded from the following calculations. The exclusion of students and part-time workers allows us to make the "purist" distinction between employed and unemployed veterans within the limits of our sample and interview schedule. Thus, the following calculations are based on an adjusted sample size of 802.

The overall unemployment rate for the sample was 15.0 percent. There were significant racial differences: blacks had an unemployment rate of 30.0 percent, while whites had an unemployment rate of 9.5 percent. If an adjustment is made to account for the high proportion of blacks in the sample, the unemployment rate drops to 11.8 percent. (The adjustment involves computing a weighted unemployment rate using the national figures for each race—blacks, 11 percent and whites, 89 percent—and the unemployment rates for each group in the sample.) Even adjusted, the unemployment rate was extremely high. In fact, 40.2 percent of the unemployed had no permanent jobs since leaving the service. This raises the question why so many veterans are unemployed and how do the employed veterans differ from the unemployed veterans? The following section will attempt to contrast the employed group versus the unemployed group by way of several preservice, service, and postservice variables.

Preservice Variables

Family Background: The unemployed veteran came from a larger family whose total family income was not adequate to meet the family's needs and, therefore, more likely to receive government assistance than the employed veteran's family.

Home Town Size and Work Experience: The unemployed veteran was less likely to have worked as a child or a year before he entered the service than the employed veteran. This finding is possibly related to where the unemployed veteran grew up. Over half of the unemployed (52.1 percent) grew up in large cities, while only 20.7 percent of the employed grew up in large cities. The employed veterans were more likely to have grown up in a small setting. Large cities typically have the highest unemployment rates; therefore, the unemployed were less likely to find a job. If they found one, they were more likely to contribute to the family income because their families tended to need all the assistance they could receive.

Service Variables

Entry and Exit Dates: Starr (1973) and Kohen, Grasso, Myers, and Shields (1977), as well as Chapter 9 (Kohen and Shields) in this volume, have suggested the importance of age and separation dates in explaining the Vietnam-era veteran's unemployment. Our data appear consistent with these observations. The unemployed veteran entered the service later, left the service later, and was younger at the time of separation than the employed veteran.

The mean entry date for the employed veteran was 1966.4 and only 9 percent of the employed veterans entered the service after 1969. The mean entry date for the unemployed veterans was 1967.8 and 34.5 percent of them entered after 1969. The mean exit date for the employed veteran was 1969.2, while for the unemployed veteran it was 1970.8. Overall, only 10.6 percent of the employed veterans left the service after 1971, while 36.8 percent of the unemployed group left after 1971. The mean age of the employed group at the time of separation from the service was 22.29, while for the unemployed group it was 21.8 years of age. In fact, only 44.9 percent of the employed group were 21 years or younger when they left the service, while over 57.5 percent of the unemployed were 21 years or younger at the time of their separation from the service.

Conduct in the Military: During the service, the unemployed veteran was more likely to refuse orders and be involved in antiwar activity.

This seems to be reflected by the larger number of unemployed veterans who received less-than-honorable discharges. Overall, 95.7 percent of the employed received honorable discharges, while only 76.7 percent of the unemployed received honorable discharges. Also, the unemployed veteran earned less than the employed veteran while in the service.

Postservice Variables

Marital Status: The unemployed veteran was less likely to have ever been married than the employed veteran. Only 47.9 percent of the unemployed veterans had ever been married, while 78.4 percent of the employed had been married. If the unemployed veteran did marry, he was more likely to be presently *not* living with his wife and more likely to be divorced.

Education: The unemployed veteran had less education before he entered the service and has less education at interview than the employed veteran. The employed veteran had an average of 13.0 years of schooling, while the unemployed veteran had 12.2 years of schooling.

Current Residence: As indicated in the preservice section, the unemployed veteran was more likely to have grown up in a large city, while the employed veteran primarily grew up in small city settings. This same difference exists for their residency at interview. In fact, 48.7 percent of the unemployed veterans presently lived in large cities compared to 18.9 percent of the employed veterans. Almost half of the employed group (49 percent) lived in small city settings, while only 34.5 percent of the unemployed lived in this type of community.

Drug Use: The unemployed veteran was more likely to have tried a variety of drugs including LSD, mescaline, heroin, cocaine, and opium. Alcohol is the only drug the employed veteran had a greater probability of trying than the unemployed veteran. The unemployed veteran reported a significantly higher physical or psychological addiction to either drugs or alcohol than the employed veteran. In fact, 21.3 percent of the unemployed reported they had been physically or psychologically addicted to either drugs or alcohol, compared to 7.0 percent of the employed group. These findings are further supported by the fact that 26.3 percent of the unemployed reported they had tried to quit using alcohol or drugs compared to 12.1 percent of the employed veterans.

Toward Causal Models of Postmilitary Adjustment: A Progress Report

We have focused our attention upon three major variables—employment, sleep problems, and drug use after the service. Each major variable is being utilized in an in-depth analysis of the determinants and consequences of problems within each area (Figley and Southerly, 1979a, 1979b).

Utilizing regression analysis, discriminant analysis, and automatic interaction detection (AID), we have completed our preliminary investigation. The following sections will briefly identify and discuss the preliminary findings for each major variable.

Employment

For our advanced statistical analyses, employment is a five-category ordinal-level variable. The following categories are utilized: working full time and happy with the job, working full time and unhappy or looking for another job, working part time, unemployed for four months or less, and unemployed for more than four months.

Though this analysis is in its preliminary stages, the following groups have been identified as potentially valuable classes of variables for understanding employment problems of veterans: race—black versus white; job patterns before and after the service, such as the establishment of permanent or temporary job patterns; psychologically related variables, that is, the veteran's own perceptions of his mental state at discharge; military experiences, such as final pay grade and type of discharge; family variables, such as marital status and family background; and job-entry variables, including education level, age, and the number of months in the job market.

Indications are that this group of variables will account for approximately 25–35 percent of the variance in employment, while discriminant analysis suggests that this group of variables may lead to successfully classifying veterans into employed/unemployed groups on the average of 75–85 percent of the time.

Our AID analysis is being utilized to helpfully identify subsets of our sample that may have particularly high unemployment problems or who are characterized by no unemployment problems. Also, due to the importance of race in our present analysis, we are presently examining the possibility of developing separate regression models for each race.

Sleep Problems

Sleep problems represent the present level of reported problems, as indicated by a group of nine questions exploring various aspects of sleeping disorders. Preliminary analysis indicates that five variables are of major importance in determining sleep problems in Vietnam-era veterans: race (black versus white), the degree of exposure to combat-related stress, the veteran's perception of his own mental state at time of discharge, the total range of drug use in the service, and the establishment of temporary job patterns.

Generally it can be stated that veterans with sleep problems are white, were exposed to more combat stress, tried more drugs while in the service, reported their "head was not straight" when they were discharged, and established temporary employment patterns since leaving the military.

Through a series of regression analyses, these five variables accounted for approximately 21 percent of the variance of our dependent variable. Our estimates suggest that our final model will account for 20–30 percent of the variance associated with sleep disorders. Once again, the AID analysis hopes to identify subsets of our sample that are characterized by acute problems or characterized by a total lack of problems.

Drug Use after the Service

This concept involves a measure of the range of daily drug use after the service. A veteran was given a "one" for every drug he reported using at least once a day. Not surprisingly, our preliminary analysis indicates that drug-related variables offer the most explanatory power. Included in the drug-related variables are daily drug use before the service, daily drug use during the service, the total number of drugs tried, the number of drugs addicted to, and drug use for nerve problems. Among the potentially important nondrug-related variables are education level, age, and trouble with the authorities for nondrug offenses.

Once again, regression analysis, discriminant analysis, and AID will be utilized to help determine the antecedents of drug problems. Though our early analysis indicates there may be problems with multicollinearity among our drug-related variables, preliminary findings suggest that our final model may account for approximately 40–50 percent of the variance.

DISCUSSION

Based on VA estimates, the sample appears to match the national profile of Vietnam-era veterans. Although black veterans were over-represented in the sample based on national criterion, they were slightly underrepresented by regional standards. Based on the demographic and social characteristics, the following profile emerges: Typically, the Vietnam-era veteran at the time of the interview was 27 years old, white, out of the service for about five years, had one child, and lived in a moderate-sized urban area. He had had one year of college, served honorably in the Army, but did not belong to a veterans' organization.

Personal Adjustments

An important finding of the study was that the majority of the veterans adjusted very well to military service in general and the transition back to civilian life in particular. Even though a considerable number of the draftees were angry initially, most did not regret the experience. In fact, over two-thirds of the sample believed that their years in the military helped them to know themselves better.

Another important discovery was in the area of dreams and nightmares. Viewed as a group, the veterans appeared to have adjusted well to the stress of military service. At closer inspection, however, the residue of combat service in Vietnam appeared to have left its mark. In contrast to noncombat veterans, the combatants reported significantly more nightmares that were related to military service in general, that were recurring, that woke them up, that made them fear or fight sleep, and that are still occurring now. Even though significantly more combatants compared to noncombatants felt the need to consult a therapist for help related to their nightmares, only 27 veterans actually got help. These findings appear to coincide with the results reported elsewhere (for example, Archibald and Tuddenham 1969; Figley 1977, 1978; Grinker and Spiegal 1945; Wilson 1977, 1978).

Drug Use

Although a sizable percentage of veterans tried to kick a drug habit (13.6 percent), while fewer (7.1 percent) had gotten in some kind of legal trouble using drugs, drug use was primarily confined to alcohol and marijuana at the time of interview. These results confirm earlier findings that most Vietnam veterans are not hooked on drugs— particularly narcotics (Johnston 1973; Robins 1974; Stanton 1976 and Chapter 14, this volume). Figley (1978) has noted that the Vietnam veteran has been maligned by the press as a sick dope fiend who cannot be trusted. The bad press was not simply bad for morale, but created even more obstacles to finding a job. As Stanton (1976, p. 177) has observed, "some men were refused employment simply because they had served in Vietnam, that is, employers considered this a prima facie evidence of drug addiction."

Employment

Our sample's high unemployment rate (15 percent) indicates that unemployment continues to be a problem for the Vietnam-era veteran, even several years after release from the service. This is especially true for the black veteran who, in our sample, had an unemployment rate of 30 percent in contrast to the 9.5 percent for whites.

The Vietnam-era veterans were returning home at a time when the economy was tight and jobs were scarce. Our results tend to suggest that the *employed* veteran may have missed this recessionary crunch since they returned earlier than the veterans who are presently unemployed. Other factors seem to be associated with the veterans' employment status at time of interview. The unemployed appeared to be younger, have less work experience, have less education, and were more likely to live in large cities than employed veterans in our sample.

CONCLUSIONS

Based on initial data analysis of in-depth interviews of 906 Vietnam veterans, our general conclusion is that these men are apparently coping well in mainstream America. They are coping in spite of inadequate government programs, in spite of the political, economic, sociological, and psychological pressures and adversities unique to the Vietnam veteran that have been discussed elsewhere (see Figley 1978 and 1979a,b,c; Mantell and Pilisuk 1975; Starr 1973). Section III addresses these inadequacies and suggests some immediate ameliorative programs and policies.

NOTE

1. The authors gratefully acknowledge the contribution of the data by the Veterans Service Center, including the individual assistance of the following interviewers:

Joel Berrey	Lee Lancaster	Joseph Hoyle
Paul Burkhart	Jim Dugan	James Lowry
Mike Davenport	Terry Hall	Edward Moore
Don Duey	Paula Johnson	Timothy G. Richards
Poncho Green	John Dwiggins	Michael Smith
Medardo Jo	Thomas DeDell	Wayne Spencer
Terry Kelly	Bernard Bolden	Trent Turner
John Revenburgh	Phyllis Brockman	Kenneth Williams
Jim Seib	Gregg Cooper	James Windett
Tom Sorbie	Tommy Davis	Ed Musgrove
Roger Watkins	Wallace A. Fingal, Jr.	Clifford Simmons

John Welle   James Henley   Linda Flatt
Bob Zipprich   Eddie N. Howard   Rita Collins
James Steele

The continuing assistance and encouragement of the entire VSC staff is greatly appreciated. The project was made possible in part by a grant to VSC from the Office of Economic Opportunity (OEO 59130) and to C. R. Figley by the National Institute of Mental Health (MH 29384-01-1R03-MSM) and the Indiana Agricultural Experiment Station.

REFERENCES

Archibald, H. D., and R. D. Tuddenham. 1979. "Persistent Stress Reactions Following Combat: A Twenty-year Follow Up." *Archives of General Psychiatry* 20: 78–81.

Figley, C. R. 1979a. The Spartans and the Spartacans and the Vietnam Veterans. Invited address to the students and faculty of the Wabash College, Crawfordsville, Indiana.

Figley, C. R. 1979b. Combat as disaster: Treating the Vietnam veteran as survivor. Invited address to the American Psychiatric Association, Chicago, May 14.

Figley, C. R. 1979c. Delayed stress reactions and overreactions. Invited address at the First National Symposium on the Issues of Vietnam Veterans. Sanomo State University, Santa Rosa, California.

Figley, C. R., ed. 1978. *Stress Disorders Among Vietnam Veterans: Theory, Research and Treatment.* New York: Brunner/Mazel.

———. 1977. "Symptoms of Delayed Combat Stress Among a College Sample of Vietnam Veterans." *Military Medicine* 142: 107–10.

———. 1975. "The Returning Veteran and Interpersonal Adjustment: A Review of the Research." Paper presented at the annual meeting of the National Council on Family Relations, Salt Lake City, August.

Figley, C. R. & Southerly, W. T. 1979a,b,c. Casual models of Vietnam veterans' post-military adjustment: I, Sleeping Problems. II, Employment Problems. III, Drug Use. Forthcoming.

Grinker, R. R., and J. P. Spiegel. 1945. *Men under Stress.* New York: Blakiston.

Johnston, L. 1973. *Drugs and American Youth.* Ann Arbor: Institute for Social Research.

Kohen, A. I.; J. T. Grasso; S. C. Myers; and P. M. Shields. 1977. *Career Threshholds: Longitudinal Studies of the Educational and Labor Market Experiences of Young Men.* Center for Human Resource Research, College of Administrative Science, The Ohio State Unversity, Columbus, Vol. 6, March.

Lifton, R. J. 1973. *Home from the War.* New York: Simon and Schuster.

Mantell, D. M., and M. Pilisuk, eds. 1975. *Soldiers in and after Vietnam.* Special issue of the *Journal of Social Issues* 31, no. 4.

Robins, L. N. 1974. "Veterans' Drug Use Three Years after Vietnam." St. Louis: Department of Psychiatry, Washington University School of Medicine.

Shatan, C. R. 1974. "Through the Membrance of Reality: Impacted Grief and Perceptual Dissonance in Vietnam Combat Veterans." *Psychiatric Opinion* 11: 6–15.

Stanton, M. D. 1976 "Drugs, Vietnam and the Vietnam Veteran: An Overview." *American Journal of Drug and Alcohol Abuse* 3: 557–70.

Starr, P. 1973. *The Discarded Army: Veterans after Vietnam.* New York: Charterhouse.

U. S. Senate. 1972. "A Study of the Problems Facing Vietnam-era Veterans." Senate Veterans Affairs Committee Print No. 7, 92d Cong. 2d sess. January 31.

VSC 1975. *Special Report to the Governor's Advisory Council on Manpower: Information on Manpower Services to Veterans.* Alton, Illinois Veterans Service Centers, Inc.

Wilson J. P. 1978. "Identity, Ideology and Crisis: The Vietnam Veteran in Transition, Part II, "Psychological Attributes of the Veteran Beyond Identity, Patterns of Adjustment and Future Implications. Unpublished monograph, Cleveland University.

———. 1977. "Identity, Ideology and Crisis: The Vietnam Veteran in Transition, Part I." Unpublished monograph, Cleveland University.

9

REAPING THE SPOILS OF DEFEAT: LABOR MARKET EXPERIENCES OF VIETNAM-ERA VETERANS

ANDREW I. KOHEN AND PATRICIA M. SHIELDS

Most of the young men under study here were in the midst of the transition from adolescence to adulthood during the turbulence produced by the Vietnam War. For many, this war intervened directly in the transition process as they became the manpower that staffed the American armed forces. (Clearly, the Vietnam War and the concomitant draft entered the decision calculus of many young men who never entered the armed forces. However, our data provide no direct way of determining the extent to which college attendance was a method of draft evasion. Johnston and Bachman [1972, p. 111] report that "20 percent of the college youth mentioned avoiding the draft among their three most important reasons for entering college.") Most of those who survived the conflict in Southeast Asia reentered the civilian population as Vietnam-era veterans. In their roles as soldiers and veterans, these men were an integral part of the American experience of the 1960s.

In the early 1960s, when the U.S. military efforts in Southeast Asia were receiving overall public support, the draft was generally accepted

This chapter has been adapted from Chapter 6 of *Career Thresholds*, vol. 6, by A. I. Kohen, J. T. Grasso, S. C. Myers, and P. M. Shields. U.S. Department of Labor, R & D Monograph No. 16 (Washington, D.C.: U.S. Government Printing Office, 1977).

and was the cornerstone of the military recruitment process. While the draft was not the main method of inducting men into military service, its presence often led to the decision to enlist. (A 1970 Defense Department study estimated that 50 percent of all Army and Air Force volunteers were "reluctant volunteers" [Helmer 1974, p. 3]. Clearly, over the history of the Vietnam conflict the proportion of reluctant volunteers varied.) However, the equity of the draft became a widely debated national issue as draft calls increased with the intensification of the war and the growing number of reported weekly casualties (see Useem 1973, pp. 44–113). Deferments for college students were seen as the means of placing the burden of the fighting on young men from the lower and lower-middle social classes. Eventually, military manpower policy was changed with the enactment of the lottery in 1969 and the end of the draft. Although the young men who served during this total period probably were not the "Poor Man's Army" (see Helmer 1974, pp. 3–10; Ladinsky 1976), it seems clear that military service during the Vietnam conflict was not randomly distributed among young men in the relevant age range. (Some young men who served during the Vietnam era entered the military prior to 1964. While the war spanned ten years, those who were discharged in the early war years may have been much different from those who entered during periods of heavy combat. Of the young men used in this study, 267 were Vietnam veterans at the time of the 1966 survey.) It is therefore important to inquire who these men were and from what socioeconomic groups they came.

While the debate over the equity of the draft continued, the experiences of the young men returning from the armed services also began to draw national attention. In the early years (1964–66), a relatively steady flow of veterans reentered a healthy civilian economy. This made their assimilation into the labor force relatively easy. However, this changed dramatically as the economy slumped, the war intensified, and the number of men discharged annually began to rise (Figure 9.1). Veterans and their readjustment problems became the focus of national attention. Newspapers, magazines, and television emphasized major themes such as the frustration of unemployment and the psychological readjustment problems of the returning soldiers (see Lifton 1973; Starr 1973; U.S. Senate 1974). As compared to white veterans, black veterans were thought to find assimilation even more difficult. They experienced higher rates of unemployment, on average, and had to cope with returning to a society and economy plagued by racial tensions (Fendrich and Axelson 1971; Michelotti and Gover 1972).

In response to veterans' needs, Congress passed several laws aimed

FIGURE 9.1: Number of Entrants, Draftees, and Separatees, 1964–72

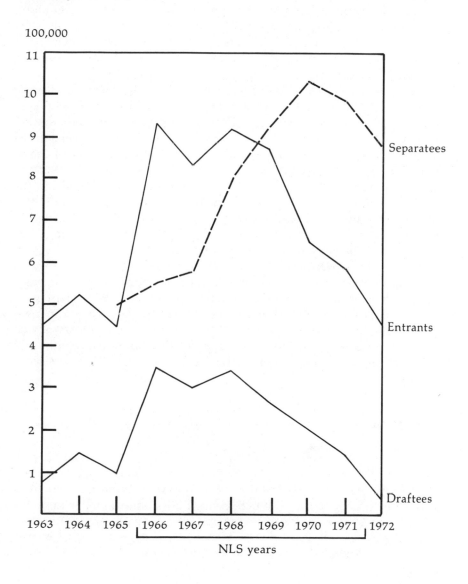

100,000

Sources: U.S. Bureau of the Census, *Statistical Abstract of the United States 1960–1972* (Washington, D.C.: U.S. Government Printing Office, 1973); and *Data on Vietnam Era Veterans: A Report Prepared by the Veterans Administration submitted to the Committee on Veterans' Affairs United States Senate*, Committee on Veterans' Affairs, 1976.

at easing the transition from military to civilian life. As a result, veterans received preferential hiring into government jobs, increased educational assistance allowances, special counseling for both employment and drug abuse, and access to many other special benefits. The readjustment problems of veterans also stimulated interest within the social science community and led to research devoted to many aspects of the assimilation process.

This study has two objectives: to explore the factors affecting entrance into the armed forces during the Vietnam era and to investigate the links between military service and subsequent labor market experiences. (Most of the veterans in the sample used here served in the military for less than four years. Contributing to the incidence of short-term service during the 1966–71 period were the draft and lottery conscription methods.) The next section describes the data used in the study. The third section focuses on the first objective by starting with a theoretical framework used to explore the factors affecting service in the armed forces and concluding with the application of the data to this framework. The fourth section explores several issues related to the labor market experiences of the Vietnam-era veterans. The first focus is the impact of service in the military on a young man's earnings, occupational status, and unemployment experience in 1971. Then more subjective measures of the impact of service in the military are investigated; namely, the veterans' self-reports of the effects of service on their civilian careers. In the final section of the chapter the findings of the preceding sections are summarized and their implications are highlighted.

THE DATA

This study is based on data from the National Longitudinal Surveys (NLS) of Work Experience.* The members of the sample who provided the information were selected to be representative of the approximately 16 million young men in the U.S. civilian noninstitutionalized population who in 1966 were between the ages of 14 and 24. The sample was drawn by the U.S. Bureau of the Census, whose experienced interviewers also conducted the annual interviews (1966–71) of the panel. In

---

*These surveys have been designed by the Ohio State University Center for Human Resource Research under a contract with the Employment and Training Administration of the U.S. Department of Labor. The sample design, field work, and the initial stages of data processing are the responsibility of the U.S. Bureau of the Census under a separate contract with the Employment and Training Administration. For a more complete description of the surveys see Kohen et al. (1977).

order to provide sufficient numbers of observations for reliable inter-color comparisons, the sampling ratio for blacks was about three times as high as that for whites. Thus, the sample of over 5,200 youths originally interviewed in 1966 included 3,734 whites and 1,438 blacks. Although the statistics reported in the tables show numbers of sample cases rather than blown-up population estimates, all calculations were performed by weighting the observations so as to represent accurately the population being studied.

Stated most succinctly, the data collected during the course of the NLS include a detailed record of educational experience, information concerning first job after leaving school, a detailed work history during the period covered by the surveys, information about any military service experience, and information about a variety of social, psycholog-ical, and economic characteristics that are expected to influence labor market behavior.

While detailed description would serve no purpose here, the analyt-ical potential of the longitudinal nature of the data merits attention. The fact that the data were collected at six points in time over a five-year period makes it possible to examine the extent and character of change in important aspects of the labor market status of the youth. This in itself is a substantial contribution, because such data are relatively uncommon. Much more important is the ability to relate an individual's characteristics at one point in time to his characteristics or status at a later point and to examine changes in one set of characteris-tics in light of changes in another. This allows analysis of directions of causation that can be accomplished in no other way. This application of such data to the labor market experiences of Vietnam-era veterans is both natural and unprecedented.

DETERMINANTS OF WHO SERVED IN THE ARMED FORCES

As has been indicated above, the draft played a key role in the recruitment process throughout the Vietnam era. By definition, a conscripted individual who wished to remain a citizen in good standing had no feasible alternative to entering military service. In a period of armed conflict during which risk of injury and death associated with membership in the armed forces increases, the question of who serves takes on new significance.

From the demand side of the picture, it is important to recognize that young men of the Vietnam era were born and reached maturity during a period characterized by frequent international crises (World War II, Korea, Berlin, Cuba). These crises provided the climate in which the draft was viewed as a necessary policy tool. It permitted able men to be drawn quickly into service in the event of an emergency. In addition, the military pay scale was kept below the civilian wage, thereby holding down defense expenditures.

On the supply side, the post-World War II "baby boom" provided a large pool of eligible young men from which to draw. Therefore, the Selective Service had the freedom to develop multiple criteria for either exempting or deferring young men from military service. Because these criteria were felt to systematically exclude upper class youth to the detriment of the lower classes (see Helmer 1974), the draft classification scheme came under attack. The model used here to explain the likelihood of serving in the armed forces during the Vietnam conflict draws heavily on criterion measures established by the Selective Service (see National Advisory Commission on Selective Service 1967), descriptive material about who served (see Helmer 1974; Useem 1973), and studies that have examined only the personal decision to enlist (see Johnston and Bachman 1972).

Conceptual Framework

A healthy young man of this period could not make realistic decisions about future plans without taking into account the Selective Service System, because the armed services legally had a prior claim on him.* However, if a young man did not meet certain minimum physical and mental health standards,† he was automatically excluded. Also, young men who could meet specific criteria established by Selective Service regulations were deferred (that is, were not liable to the draft while so classified). Although the criteria for deferment were revised several times during the Vietnam era (see Useem 1973), hardship and student deferments remained relatively stable. The hardship deferment was based primarily on the presence of a child and was a permanent

---

*For separate analysis of who enlisted and who was drafted, see Shields (1977).

†Until the inception of Project 100,000 (1966), young men were not eligible to serve in the armed forces if they scored below the tenth percentile on the Armed Forces Qualification Test (AFQT) or they scored between the tenth and thirtieth percentiles and failed the minimum requirements on the Army Classification Battery (ACB) or the Army Qualification Battery (AQB) (Karpinos 1966). Project 100,000 was begun as a part of the Defense Department's War on Poverty. The minimum mental test score requirements were lowered in order to give low-scoring men the chance to learn skills in the military. The new minimum standard was a score as low as the tenth percentile on the AFQT if the youth was a high school graduate or he received a minimum score on one of seven aptitude tests (Wool and Flyer 1969). Note that while the minimum mental requirements were lowered, they were not abolished. These "new standards" men comprised 9 percent of the entrants to the armed forces between 1966 and 1968.

deferment that depended mainly on there being enough alternative manpower to maintain a minimum level of national security. The student deferment, on the other hand, was *designed* to be temporary.* Upon graduation or withdrawal from school a II-S classification almost automatically was converted to a I-A, placing the former student in the pool of young men eligible for the draft. However, student deferments could be converted into de facto exemptions through subsequent occupational or hardship deferments.

Aside from Selective Service criteria, there are various personal characteristics that may reasonably be expected to be associated with the likelihood of serving in the military. Since the question addressed here had never been dealt with directly, heavy reliance is placed on literature that focuses on factors related to a young man's decision to enlist.† However, the enlistment decision is only one important component of the participation by a young man in the armed forces. Thus it is important to consider possible countervailing effects of some factors that would decrease the likelihood of serving, even if they increase the likelihood of enlisting.

The literature indicates that a young man's enlistment decision stemmed from a variety of sources. Included among these are draft pressures, opportunities for training and the GI Bill, and several personal background characteristics. It is clear that the draft did induce enlistments during this period. Enlistment often reduced the likelihood of combat duty. It also offered a greater degree of choice of branch of service, type of training, military occupational specialty, and number of

---

*The precise criteria for a student deferment changed throughout the Vietnam era. Until 1966, enrollment in a graduate or undergraduate program insured deferment. For a short time (1966) the II-S was based on class standing. Graduate student deferments (except for students in medical or related fields) were abolished in 1967, while undergraduates making "normal progress" toward a degree continued to be protected. In 1969 the lottery was established and student deferments were no longer extended to incoming students. However, existing deferments were continued until graduation or withdrawal from school.

†The draft and problems associated with it led the Defense Department to sponsor several research studies that looked exclusively at the enlistment decision. Hence, unlike the broad question of the likelihood of entering, there is a substantial body of literature from which to draw for enlistment explanations. In addition to the obvious distinction between enlistment and induction, these studies tend to address even more narrow criterion measures. For example, Johnston and Bachman (1972) explore the enlistment decision only in the year following high school graduation. Hence, this study departs even further from theirs because they include as enlistees young men who attempted to enlist but were rejected and they exclude young men who enlisted after the year following high school graduation. Enlistment studies prepared for the President's Commission are also narrower in that they limit the question to specific branches of service (Cook 1970; Fechter 1970; Cook and White 1970) or to specific ranks (Altman and Barro 1970).

years of obligation. Indeed, for some individuals enlistment may have offered relatively more attractive options than the civilian labor market.

In addition, it has been hypothesized that the military is a potential vehicle by which a young man may (temporarily) escape an unpleasant environment. For example, individuals who have experienced or expect to experience racial or social class discrimination would be more likely to enter the armed forces, other things being equal. Although the military traditionally has been viewed as an avenue used by blacks to escape racial discrimination, the greater likelihood of black inductees scoring very low on the mental examination serves to reduce the rate of conscription for blacks. (Between 1964 and 1965, 59 percent of the black inductees failed the mental examination as compared to 25 percent of the white [Karpinos 1966].) In 1966 the armed forces attempted to increase participation among blacks by lowering the mental ability requirements through Project 100,000. This hope seems to have been realized; as of 1968, 33 percent of the New Standards men were blacks (Wool and Flyer 1969). This in turn contributed to the popular belief that blacks were more likely to serve during the latter part of the Vietnam conflict (Helmer 1974; U.S. Senate 1974).

Some observers have suggested that there is a relationship between geographic region of residence and the decision to enlist. First, some studies of enlistment behavior have hypothesized, but have not confirmed, a higher likelihood of enlistment by young men from the South. (The hypothesis was grounded in the popular notion that the traditions of the South are congenial to the pageantry of the military. For elaboration and empirical results see Johnston and Bachman [1972, p. 105].) An examination of AFQT disqualification rates by state reveals a pattern that may explain why earlier studies did not confirm the hypothesis. That is, the more rural Southern states show higher-than-average rejection rates.* perhaps because of lower-quality educational systems. Thus, an above-average propensity to enlist in the South may be offset by an above-rate of failure on the AFQT among rural Southern youth. Another reason to expect that region will be related to the likelihood of serving in the armed forces is that, during the Vietnam War, college students in the Northeast were influenced by the high level of protest against the war and were less likely to enlist (Altman and Barro 1970, p. II-10). In order to investigate these hypotheses, the research model includes a variable representing the interaction between urbanicity and region of residence.

---

*Even controlling for race, Karpinos (1966), p. 102) found that draftees from the South were half again as likely as all youth to be rejected for mental reasons. His data also indicate that AFQT failure rates in the predominantly rural Southern states were twice the national rate.

Since the student deferment was central to controversy over the draft, it is necessary to examine variables associated with its impact. Johnston and Bachman (1972) found that some variables predict enlistment solely because they are inversely related to college entrance. For example, men with high measured mental ability and successful high school careers were less likely to enlist. In addition, their study indicated that young men of higher socioeconomic levels were more likely to attend college and, thus, more likely to avoid entering military service. These findings are consistent with the popular notion that members of the middle and lower social classes actually served in disproportionate numbers. Therefore, an explanatory variable representing socioeconomic status of parental family is included in the model.

Finally, the intensity of the war effort played an important role in the likelihood of a youth entering the armed forces. If a young man became eligible for the draft between 1966 and 1968, he entered a draft pool from which the proportion drawn had grown significantly. This, in turn, increased the probability of his serving. Therefore, a variable indicating the intensity of the war is included in the model.

Empirical Model and Results

In order to examine the issues raised in the preceding discussion, the data used refer to all young men in the sample who could have become veterans during the Vietnam era. The era is defined as the period from 1964 to 1971. Operationally, the dependent or criterion variable is a dichotomy. It distinguishes between those who served in the armed forces during the Vietnam era and those who did not, irrespective of whether they were discharged by late 1971.*

In review, the explanatory variables used in the analysis can be divided into two broad categories: Selective Service criteria and other "demand" factors, and personal characteristics associated with the student deferment and the enlistment decision. Selective Service criteria include health condition at age 18;† a below-average level of

---

*The sample excludes veterans who were discharged prior to 1964 and thus is consistent with most published statistical accounts of Vietnam-era veterans. Since the Vietnam War ended in 1973, this study understates the total proportion of young men in the age cohort who served by excluding those who entered in 1972 and 1973. However, the declining entrance rates after 1971 and the age of the NLS cohort (the youngest respondent was 19 in 1971) make it unlikely that the results would change substantially if 1972 and 1973 entrants were included. For confirmation of this see Shields (1977).

†In preparing the data for the study, it was necessary to construct variables that utilize individual characteristics at a common "age" reference point, that is, at a time prior to entrance into the service. This is essential because predicting the likelihood of serving demands preservice traits as the relevant criteria. The characteristics as of a young man's

measured mental ability; the presence of dependents at age 18; and the student deferment (that is, educational attainment at age 18). The other "demand" factor is a variable indicating the intensity of the war at the time that the youth became 18 years of age.

Personal characteristics associated with the student deferment include above-average socioeconomic level of parental family and above-average level of measured mental ability. In addition, the following characteristics are included in the analysis because of their hypothesized relationship with enlistment behavior: residence in the rural South, the urban South, or the Northeast at age 18; and race. For reasons discussed above, parabolic (inverted U-shaped) relationships are expected between the likelihood of serving in the military and levels of measured mental ability and education completed at age 18. That is, high and low values on both variables are expected to be negatively associated with participation in the armed forces.

Methodology

The hypotheses described in the preceding section are tested by means of Multiple Classification Analysis (MCA), a version of multiple regression analysis with all the explanatory variables expressed in categorical form.* The MCA technique permits one to calculate the mean value of the dependent variable for each category of a particular explanatory variable, "adjusted" for the effects of all other variables in the model. Differences in these values among the several categories of a variable may be interpreted as indicating the "pure" effect of that variable upon the dependent measure. For example, the MCA technique allows one to calculate for each education category of youth what proportion would have served, if the members of that category had been "average" in terms of all the other variables entering into the analysis.

Results

Most of the hypotheses presented in the preceding section are

---

18th year were chosen because eligibility to serve without parental consent and draft registration both occur at the 18th birthday. For additional discussion of the methodology, see Kohen et al. (1977, p. 164).

*In order to maximize the data cases available for analysis, codes of NA (not available) on IQ, socioeconomic level, and type of residence at age 18 were included in the MCA, but the coefficients are not analyzed. For elaboration on the statistical implications of this procedure, see Kohen et al. 1977, p. 165.

supported by the analysis (Table 9.1). Having health problems and/or dependents at age 18 reduced the likelihood of serving in the armed forces, although the former is statistically significant only among whites. A parabolic relationship was expected for mental ability (IQ) and for education at age 18. Both variables exhibit this relationship, although education demonstrates it more forcefully. That is, respondents with only elementary education and those with at least some college training were much less likely than average to enter the military.

Of special interest is the finding that socioeconomic status per se was not related to military service during the Vietnam era, once the effects of education and mental ability are taken into account. Of course, it is true that social class background had an indirect impact on the probability of serving because it influences both measured mental ability and educational attainment at age 18. It is also noteworthy that a variable representing the war's intensity when the young man reached age 18 displays a strong relationship with the likelihood of his serving. Obviously, participation in the military service in the presence of the conscription system depends on the unpredictable nature of American foreign policy and the fortunes of war. Finally, as expected, geographic area of residence was related to the probability of having served in the military. Young men from the urban South were more likely than average to serve and those from the Northeast were less likely than average to serve.

Overall, a somewhat larger percentage of white than of black youths served in the armed forces between 1964 and 1971 (29 versus 26 percent of those eligible for military service), although this difference shrinks when other factors are controlled and is not statistically significant. However, the racial differences in the effects of some of the factors explaining service in the military are worthy of note. The most pronounced of these is that the health variable is not statistically significant among black youth, whereas it is very powerful among whites. While it is only speculation, it may be that the greater attractiveness of the military as compared to the civilian labor market led black youths with subtle or minor health problems (for example, allergies) to waive their right to nonservice more frequently than similarly afflicted whites.

Another racial difference appears for youths who had completed fewer than 12 years of school. While entering the service was negatively related to an elementary education of age 18 for both races, the absolute difference between blacks and whites in this category is very large. Whites were twice as likely as blacks (22 versus 10 percent) to enter the military. For youths who dropped out of high school or had

TABLE 9.1: The Likelihood of Serving in the Armed Forces during the Vietnam Era: MCA Results
(F-ratios in parentheses)

Characteristic	Whites		Blacks	
	Number of Respondents	Adjusted[a] Likelihood of Serving	Number of Respondents	Adjusted[a] Likelihood of Serving
Total or average	3,627		1,432	
Mental ability		(6.56)[b]		(4.08)[b]
Above average	809	27.9[c]	27	28.2
Average	1,534	32.7	264	33.0[c]
Below average	301	27.9	314	26.0
NA	983	24.9[c]	827	23.0[c]
Socioeconomic status		(0.41)		(0.78)
Lower	629	28.7	701	25.9
Middle	1,439	30.1	444	27.3
Higher	1,403	28.7	100	21.4
Education at age 18		(10.44)[b]		(22.76)[b]
0–8 years	235	21.7[c]	234	9.6[c]
9–11 years	922	29.9	594	22.8[c]
12 years	1,844	32.2[c]	508	35.9[c]
13–15 years	626	22.0[c]	96	20.5
Residence at age 18		(2.67)[b]		(4.66)[b]
Northeast	876	27.0[d]	156	20.6[d]
North Central	1,082	29.8	216	24.2
South-urban	456	33.7[c]	442	32.4[c]
South-rural	572	24.9[c]	498	24.2
West	554	31.1	57	10.0[c]
Health condition at age 18		(35.37)[b]		(2.04)
No health problems	3,429	30.2[c]	1,367	26.0
Health problems	198	10.5[c]	65	17.7
Dependents at age 18		(7.68)[b]		(9.08)[b]
None	3,511	29.6[c]	1,329	26.6[c]
Some	116	17.8[c]	103	13.2[c]
War intensity at age 18		(46.18)[b]		(24.69)[b]
Intense period	1,236	36.5[c]	548	33.6[c]
Not intense period	2,391	25.7[c]	884	21.9[c]
Grand mean		29.2		25.7

R^{-2}	.04	.09
F-ratio	9.45	9.70

Universe: Respondents 19 to 29 years old in 1971 who were not discharged from the armed forces prior to 1964.

ᵃAdjusted by multiple regression technique of holding constant all other variables shown in the table.

ᵇStatistically significant at .05 level.

ᶜCategory is significantly different from the grand mean at .05 level.

ᵈCategory is significantly different from the grand mean at .10 level.

Source: Compiled by the author from computer analysis of NLS data.

not graduated by age 18, the likelihood of serving was below average for blacks but not significantly different from average for whites. Thus, minority youths who perhaps had most to gain from the service were least likely to enter.*

The geographic background variable also exhibits some interesting racial differences. While the likelihood of serving was higher than average for all young men from the urban South, the reasons probably differ for whites and blacks. For whites the popular notion of the congeniality of military traditions and Southern culture is most plausible. For blacks, it seems that the military maintained its potential as a way of escaping racial discrimination in the labor market even during the Vietnam conflict. Among young whites (but not blacks) from the *rural* South the rate of participation in the armed forces was significantly below average. This strong negative effect among whites probably derives both from availability of occupational (agricultural) deferments and from lower-quality schooling leading to higher failure rates on the AFQT. The weaker effect among black youths may be due to an above-average propensity to enlist in order to escape discrimination, which partially offsets the negative effect of lower-quality education. Finally, the absolutely and relatively lower likelihood of a young black than a young white serving if he resided in the Northeast or West may be due to lower levels of racial discrimination in those regions. That is, these lower levels of discrimination may have provided labor market opportunities that made the armed forces relatively less attractive. Or

---

*The racial differences discussed in this paragraph may arise from the fact that for both educational categories blacks had completed fewer years of schooling than had whites. Within the elementary school category a black youth was approximately twice as likely as a white (36 versus 19 percent) to have completed fewer than seven years of school by age 18. Within the group who had attended but not finished high school at age 18, equal proportions (that is, 17 percent) of the color groups had only nine years of schooling but fewer blacks than whites (49 versus 57 percent) had completed eleven years. Hence, on average, whites had accumulated more human capital and were better equipped to pass the AFQT.

they may have provided an environment more sensitive to the dangers and political issues associated with participation in the wartime armed forces.

LABOR MARKET EXPERIENCES OF YOUNG VETERANS

A young man's military experience is an interruption in his life plans with unknown consequences. On the one hand, being a veteran may make a young man more attractive to employers relative to nonveterans, resulting in an increase in short-run and long-run earnings. On the other hand, military experience may serve only as a discontinuity in human capital accumulation with negative consequences for long-run success. The overriding question investigated in this section is whether service in the armed forces during the Vietnam era had any *net* (independent) effect on the subsequent civilian labor market experiences of young men. As serious students of this question have realized, to date neither theoretical nor empirical studies have produced unambiguous conclusions about the direction of such an effect (Beusse 1974; Browning, Lopreato and Poston 1973; Cutright 1973; Jurkowitz 1968; O'Neill, Ross, and Warner 1976; Weinstein 1969).

On the one hand, a young man's service in the armed forces has the potential of adding to his human capital in many forms. He may acquire new specific vocational skills, increased general educational credentials, broadened geographic horizons, "improved" work habits (for example, punctuality, adherence to instructions, teamwork), and additional resources with which to get civilian education and training (that is, GI Bill benefits). Also, while the draft was in effect, the potential cost of turnover to employers was smaller for youths who had fulfilled their military obligation. In addition, national campaigns to hire returning veterans led to some preferential hiring due to a moral sense of indebtedness to young men who fought on behalf of the nation. The same result was generated more formally in the public sector through veterans' preference rules under civil service systems.

On the other hand, military service also implies a loss of at least two years of potential civilian labor market exposure and experience,* even though legislative and collective bargaining actions have at-

---

*Strictly speaking, the period could be less than two years if, for example, a young man was severely wounded and discharged early, or if he was in combat for an extended period and "earned" an early discharge. The operational definition of a veteran used here requires active duty for a minimum of only six months.

tempted to minimize this loss. For example, the Selective Service Act of 1967 stipulated that a young man holding a nontemporary job was guaranteed the right to return to that job after military service and that he did not lose any seniority status accumulated up to the time of entering the armed forces (Waldman 1970). Some unions, through collective bargaining, extended these rights to include additional accumulation of seniority and even promotions and pay increases while a young man was in the military service. Another potentially negative impact of military service on later labor market experience is the increased likelihood of physical disability, which limits the type and/or amount of work a young man can do. Last, but certainly not least, is the psychological damage that afflicted some young veterans of the Vietnam era (see Figley 1978). To the extent that they were stigmatized for participating in the war and/or felt personal guilt about their associations with the military establishment, veterans may have developed attitudes that reduced their productivity in job search and on the job.

While the military's intervention into a young man's life was felt by all who entered the armed forces, the effect may have been more pronounced among minority and disadvantaged youth. On the one hand, the military traditionally has been viewed as a means of escaping discrimination and achieving status advancement. In this sense the military experience would be perceived as a cause of later labor market success. For example, some have suggested that the armed forces creates a "bridging environment" that aids successful minority group assimilation into the civilian labor market (Browning et al. 1973). Minority youth often live in enclaves isolated from mainstream society, and service in the military tends to reduce their dependence on racial or ethnic enclaves by cutting community ties.

On the other hand, this type of positive effect of service may have been less likely in the Vietnam era because of the widespread feeling that U.S. involvement in the war was unjust. In addition, black youths were less likely to receive valuable training and more likely to participate in combat than their white counterparts (U.S. Senate 1974; also see Phillips, Chapter 18, this volume). It also has been suggested that in the black community traditional sentiments about the military changed dramatically as the war intensified. That is, why should a black youth die in Southeast Asia to save democracy that does not really exist? (Fendrich and Axelson 1971). This, in turn, led to a greater degree of political alienation among returning black veterans. Finally, disadvantaged youths were less likely to take advantage of programs (for example, the GI Bill) that eased the assimilation process.

Clearly, "military experience" and its impact on later civilian labor market experiences are not the same for all. Among the potentially important sources of differences are branch of service, type of military occupation, length of active service, and type of formal training. A long-standing recruiting technique has been to emphasize the uniqueness of one branch of the armed forces in contrast to the others. One study found that Navy veterans more easily transferred their skills to the civilian sector than did Army veterans (Weinstein 1969). It was speculated that this resulted from philosophical differences among the branches of the armed forces—namely that Navy training was designed to be more general and to be applied to a wider range of job situations. However, that study was based on a sample of pre-Vietnam-era veterans. A later study using data on Vietnam-era veterans found no consistent net association between branch of service and later labor market success, although civilian earnings were found to be relatively lower among Army veterans in some military occupation groups (O'Neill et al. 1976).

Another source of differentiation in the military experience is type of training. For example, one study found that the labor market payoff to training in the armed forces differs by type. That is, the higher the status of the civilian counterpart of the training, the more likely the training is to be positively associated with earnings (O'Neill et al. 1976). Length of active service is another factor contributing to differences in the effects of military experience. That same study discovered no positive association between subsequent earnings and length of military service, except for veterans who had been electronic equipment repairmen in the military.* A more limited case study did find more occupational progress among Army veterans than corresponding nonveterans (Katenbrink 1969).

The labor market implications of military service extend beyond income and occupational attainment. There has been considerable policy concern about the process by which a newly discharged veteran becomes a fully participating member of the civilian sector. For some veterans the process involves long spells of unemployment. In early 1970 unemployment among veterans began to rise, and it continued to do so through 1971, reaching 11.4 percent in the final quarter of that year (Michelotti and Gover 1972). For the younger veterans this was one-third again as high a rate of unemployment as that experienced by nonveterans of the same age and race, a difference that persisted through 1977 (*Employment and Training Report of the President* 1978, pp. 194–95).

---

*According to a personal communication from John Warner (one of the study's authors), the lack of a generally positive association may have resulted from inclusion of a variable representing highest military paygrade, because this variable is highly correlated both with length of service and with postservice earnings.

Perhaps the most important factors contributing to increased unemployment among veterans were the coincident rising level of general unemployment and the peaking of the discharge rate in the 1969–71 period. The relative youth of the Vietnam-era veterans at the time of discharge probably also contributed to the higher-than-historic incidence of unemployment. The average age at discharge of Vietnam-era veterans was 23 in contrast to 25 for Korean War veterans and 27 for veterans of World War II. Thus the Vietnam-era veterans had had relatively less time to accumulate meaningful labor market experience prior to entering the armed forces (Showell 1975).

Obviously, during the Vietnam era the Defense Department focused on winning the war and, therefore, on producing "soldiers." Clearly, "soldier" is an occupation with relatively few nonmilitary applications. There was little, if any, concern for the civilian manpower implications of military training. This placed veterans at a competitive disadvantage upon their reentrance to the civilian labor market. Even though reemployment rights were guaranteed, few veterans took advantage of this right (Werner and Radcliff 1973).

However, there also were forces that tended to inflate artificially the unemployment rate among veterans. First, virtually all veterans were eligible for unemployment insurance benefits. It was technically true that a veteran had to be looking for work during the benefit period. Yet, as a practical matter, state veteran employment representatives relaxed standards for recently discharged veterans, allowing them several weeks to readjust to civilian society (*Manpower Magazine* 1971). Second, it has been suggested that the educational benefits of the GI Bill tended to inflate the rates (Werner and Radcliff 1973). Because the educational system is typically divided into 10- to 15-week periods, veterans waiting to enroll had to seek temporary employment and were faced with employer reluctance to hire them because of their planned return to school.

Models and Empirical Results

Models

In order to address the first two questions about the effects of military service on later labor market experience, rather conventional regression models are used. They are models of the determination of earnings and occupational status but contain additional measures to identify various categories of veterans. To illustrate, the regression model to explain hourly wages includes traditional human capital variables, environmental variables, and job context variables. (The human capital variables are education, civilian occupational training, mental ability, civilian work experience, length of service with current employer, and health condition. The environmental variables are urbanicity and region of current residence. The job context variable is one that distinguishes between private employees and government employees.) Several alternative sets of variables to distinguish veterans are also included in the equation. First, categories of veterans are separately identified by variables indicating whether training was received in the military and in which branch of service the veteran served. For example, Army veterans with training are differentiated from Army veterans without training. Second, an alternative equation is estimated by including, as substitutes for the variables representing training and branch of service, variables indicating whether the veteran's military and postdischarge jobs were in the same major occupational group. As a third alternative, these variables are replaced by one measuring the total number of months of active military duty. In each of the three specifications, the total amount of civilian work experience is divided into two portions—experience prior and subsequent to military service. (Obviously, all nonveterans receive a value of zero on the latter variable and on the one measuring months of active military duty.) Finally, each equation includes a variable specifying whether a veteran returned to school after being discharged.

Because of the well-documented racial differences in the determinants of wages and occupational status, separate equations are estimated for blacks and whites. This permits evaluation of whether the effects of military service differ according to race. The universe for which the equations are estimated consists of 19- to 29-year-old men who were both out of school and employed in 1971.

Turning next to the impact of service in the armed forces on personal unemployment experience, regression analysis is again employed. The equations control for several variables expected to be related both to unemployment and to the status of being a veteran. Because the "proper" dependent variables cannot be specified unambiguously, two alternatives are presented: the probability of experiencing at least one week of unemployment during 1971 and the proportion of time in the labor force during 1971 that was spent unemployed.*

The models for explaining the incidence and extent of joblessness are nearly identical to those for earnings and occupational status described above. The major change is the addition of a variable designating those veterans discharged from the armed forces during 1971.

---

*The first is a variable coded "1" if the respondent experienced any full weeks of unemployment and "0" otherwise. The second is the ratio of weeks unemployed in 1971 to weeks in the civilian labor force in 1971.

Another change is deletion of the analysis based on comparing the military and civilian occupations because some of the veterans whose unemployment could be studied had not secured a postservice job by the time of the 1971 survey. The new variable is added because having been recently discharged is expected to increase the likelihood of joblessness. First of all, few veterans exercised their reemployment rights. Second, veterans were virtually automatically eligible for unemployment compensation due to minimal requirements to search. It is also expected that recency of discharge would artificially increase the proportion of labor force time spent unemployed, because it increases the numerator (weeks unemployed) and decreases the denominator (weeks in civilian labor force) of the ratio.* The universe for the analysis of unemployment consists of 19- to 29-year-old men who were not enrolled in school at the time of the 1971 survey.

As a supplement to analyzing the objective consequences of military service on civilian labor market experiences, it is useful to examine the veterans' perceptions of these consequences. All veterans in the sample were asked (in 1971) whether they believed that their service in the armed forces had helped or hurt their (civilian) careers. Overall, slightly more than one-half of them reported that it had helped their careers and one-sixth reported a deleterious effect. The remaining three-tenths felt that their military experience had no impact on their later experiences in the civilian labor market. As might be expected, these response patterns were far from uniform across all types of veterans. For example, ex-Marines, veterans with very brief periods of service, and those who received no training with civilian application were relatively less likely to report positive effects of their military service. Similarly, college graduates, draftees, and those discharged in 1971 were relatively more likely to report negative effects.

In order to examine more carefully the sources of variation in the reported effects of the military service, MCAs were performed using two dependent variables. The first distinguished those who perceived positive effects from all others. The second differentiated those who reported negative effects from all others. Using the identical set of explanatory variables permits identification of the net distribution of responses to the question for each category of young veterans, where

---

*There is also reason to believe that the diligence of the census interviewers contributes to an artifically high proportion of a veteran's time spent in unemployment. That is, if it was learned that a respondent was unavailable at the initial attempt to contact him but that he would be discharged from the military service before the close of the survey period, the interview was probably conducted. Thus, the total amount of time in the civilian population for such a veteran will be minimal (less than two months), which artificially inflated the proportion of time unemployed if he sought work and/or applied for unemployment compensation.

"net" means "adjusted for the variation in the response due to other characteristics." Moreover, using the same explanatory variables demonstrates the nonsymmetric nature of the responses. That is, a given characteristic may induce an above-average positive response rate but not a below-average negative response rate.

Some of the explanatory variables included in these analyses are similar to those used in the analyses of earnings, occupational status, and unemployment. However, because the term "career" is somewhat vague, the hypotheses underlying these variables are more tentative than in the earlier analyses and may best be viewed as exploratory. For example, it is of interest to know whether the perceived impact of the military on civilian careers depends on the veteran's level of human capital. This knowledge would assist in evaluating military service as a source of producing human capital. Especially in light of programs such as Project 100,000 and Project Transition, it seems reasonable to expect that the least-well-educated young veterans had the most to gain from military service in terms of acquiring skills. Thus, the amount of schooling completed by the veteran prior to entering the military is included in the analysis. For similar reasons the following are included in the MCAs: whether the respondent's military and postservice jobs were in the same major occupation group, whether the respondent returned to school after being discharged from the service, and a comparison between the respondent's health status before and after military service.

The nature of a veteran's experience during his tour of military duty may be expected to influence his perception of its impact on his postservice career. Some of the variables in the equations are designed to represent this set of factors. These include method of entry to the armed forces, duration of military service, type of training received in the military, branch of service, and date of discharge. The hypotheses underlying this set of variables deserve brief explanation. First, it is anticipated that those who served involuntarily would be less likely to exhibit positive reactions and more likely to express negative reactions to their military experience. Second, longer periods of service are more likely to have been voluntary and, therefore, are expected to produce more positive perceptions about the impact of service. Third, it is anticipated that those who received training with some potential transferability to civilian jobs would be relatively more positive about the effect of their military experience.

The branch of the armed forces in which a young man served is included for exploratory purposes, with no a priori hypotheses. While gross differences in the response patterns of Army, Navy, Air Force, and Marine veterans are observed, they may simply reflect differences in voluntariness of service and/or differences in training. The date of discharge is included for three reasons. First, the question about the impact of military service was asked of all veterans in 1971 (rather than, say, at the first interview after discharge), and it may be that the perceived impact of military service is stronger the more recent the tour of duty. Second, veterans who returned to civilian life in 1970 or 1971 entered a much less buoyant economy than was true of those discharged in the middle or late 1960s. Third, growing societal disenchantment with U.S. military involvement in Vietnam over the period 1966-71 probably made a difference in the general acceptance of the veteran according to when he reentered the civilian labor force.

Results

Overall, the statistical results of analyzing the effect of military service on civilian earnings and occupational status are mixed (Table 9.2). Since the effect does apparently differ substantially between the races, the findings are discussed separately for whites and blacks.

For young white men, all of the variables identifying veterans exhibit positive associations with current hourly earnings, but there are only two effects that attain statistical significance, namely returning to school after being discharged and doing the same kind of work after discharge as was done while in military service. (It should be noted that the latter effect may represent either the impact of specific types of occupational training in the military or the identification of young men who held the same [high-paying] occupations before, during, and after military service.) While each month of active military duty seems to increase current wages, the impact is minuscule (about $0.002/hour/ month of service) and not statistically significant. Indeed, comparing the size of the effect to the effect of civilian work experience implies that, on average, the time spent in the military is detrimental to later success in the labor market. To be more specific, the regression results imply that the wage payoff per year of military service was only about $0.025 hour in contrast to more than $0.11/hour per year of civilian work experience. Hence, for white veterans it seems that only those young men who availed themselves of the subsidy to pursue postservice additional schooling received monetary payoffs from their military experience.

In contrast, the impact of armed forces service is less clear among young black men. First of all, there are too few (fewer than 10) respondents who returned to school after leaving the armed forces to have confidence in the estimated effect of this behavior on civilian wages. Second, none of the variables identifying veterans attains statistical significance in any version of the equation. Finally, the estimated effect of a year of military service (about $0.08/hour) is

TABLE 9.2: Net Effects of Selected Aspects of Military Service Experience on Civilian Hourly Wage and Occupational Status, 1971, by Race

Version of the Equation and Aspect of Military Service Experience	Hourly Wage (dollars/hour)		Occupational Status (Duncan Index)	
	Whites	Blacks	Whites	Blacks
Version I				
Recipient of training in the military—Army	0.11	-0.15	-1.3	-1.2
Recipient of training in the military—other branch	0.18	b	-1.8	b
Nonrecipient of training in the military—Army[a]	0.30[c]	-0.16	-0.7	-4.9
Nonrecipient of training in the military—other branch[a]	0.10	0.13	-3.2	-3.3
Returnee to school after military discharge	0.85[d]	b	11.8[d]	b
Version II				
Military and 1971 occupations—same	0.51[d]	b	1.8	b
Military and 1971 occupations—different	0.12	0.03	-2.4	-3.6
Returnee to school after military discharge	0.82[d]	b	11.6[d]	b
Version III				
Per month of active military duty	0.002	0.007	-0.1	0.0[e]
Returnee to school after military discharge	0.89[d]	b	11.7[d]	b

Universe: Employed respondents 19–29 years of age in 1971 who were not discharged from the armed forces prior to 1964.

Note: The effects are net in the sense that other variables that determine wages (occupational status) are held constant by the regression, including those variables associated with being a veteran. Each version of the equation was estimated separately and contained only those variables characterizing veterans that are shown. For example, Version I contains interactive dummy variables for veteran status, receipt of military training, and branch of service along with a dummy variable indicating the return to school, but it excludes the occupation comparison variables and the duration of service variable.

[a] Strictly speaking, these veterans received only basic training and/or training only in a military (combat) job.
[b] Coefficient based on fewer than 25 respondents.
[c] Statistically significant at .10 level.
[d] Statistically significant at .05 level.
[e] Indicates nonzero value rounded to zero.

Sources: Compiled by the authors; full regressions appear in Kohen, P. I., et al. *Career Thresholds* 6, U.S. Department of Labor, R & D Monograph No. 16. Washington, D.C.: U.S. Government Printing Office, 1977.

greater than the estimated value of a year of premilitary work experience (about $0.02/hour) but less than that of a year of postmilitary work experience. If one takes the estimate at face value and ignores the lack of statistical significance, then the results imply that, whether it represents the acquisition of cognitive skills or productive work habits, the time a young black man spent in the armed forces paid off in increased civilian earnings.

Contrary to expectations, there is no evidence for either racial group that training in the armed forces that is potentially applicable to civilian jobs had a demonstrable, significant return.* With one exception, all of the preceding inferences about hourly earnings apply equally to the analysis of occupational status. The exception is that there is no evidence that black veterans received any payoff to their military service in terms of occupational status.

The impact of being a veteran on unemployment experience in 1971 is more straightforward. The evidence for both racial groups indicates that young veterans were significantly more likely than nonveterans to suffer unemployment during 1971 (Table 9.3). Surprisingly, this conclusion does not apply to black young men who were veterans of the Army infantry. Among white veterans this effect was somewhat reduced for those who returned to school. Partly in contrast to expectations, the veterans discharged in 1971 did not have a higher likelihood of being unemployed, but they did spend significantly larger proportions of their labor force time without jobs. Examination of the full results also reveals that the differential unemployment experience of veterans eventually disappears, other things being equal. For example, a veteran's susceptibility to unemployment in 1971 was much lower if he had been discharged in, say, 1968 than in 1970. Thus, it seems that time in reacclimation to the civilian labor market is the principal source of a "solution" to the unemployment "problem" of veterans.

Turning to the analysis of the employed veterans' perceptions of the effect of their military service, the results of the MCA's provide support for some of the hypotheses (Table 9.4). Since the results for whites and blacks differ, they are discussed separately. Relative to enlistees, white draftees were less likely to report a positive career effect and more likely to report a negative career effect, although only the latter is statistically significant. Finding any statistical significance in this instance is especially noteworthy because branch of service and length of tour of duty are controlled for, and because some of the enlistees were of the draft-induced variety, making their service less

---

*It is noteworthy that approximately three-fifths of the veterans in the sample used here report having received training other than basic or combat training. This is in close accord with published data (U.S. Senate 1971, p. 140, Table 37).

TABLE 9.3: Net Effects of Selected Aspects of Military Service Experience on Unemployment Experience, 1971, by Race

(effects shown in percentage points)

Version of the Equation and Aspect of Military Service Experience	Probability of Being Unemployed 1971		Proportion of Time in Labor Force in 1971 Spent Unemployed	
	Whites	Blacks	Whites	Blacks
Version I				
Recipient of training in military—Army	11.6[c]	25.8[c]	5.1[c]	7.1
Recipient of training in military—other branch	13.7[c]	[b]	3.7	[b]
Nonrecipient of training in military—Army[a]	11.4[c]	-1.9	0.9	-5.6
Nonrecipient of training in military—other branch[a]	14.9[c]	28.6[c]	4.3[c]	5.6[d]
Returnee to school after military discharge	-9.2	[b]	-0.2	[b]
Discharged in 1971	-9.3	-23.9[b]	10.8[c]	3.8
Version II				
Per month of active military duty	0.4[c]	0.6[c]	0.2[c]	0.2[b]
Returnee to school after military discharge	-7.2	[b]	0.7	[b]
Discharged in 1971	-8.6	-10.3	10.2[c]	6.5

Universe: Respondents 19–29 years of age and interviewed in 1971 who were not discharged from the armed forces prior to 1964 and who spent at least one week in the labor force in 1971.

Note: The effects are net in the sense that other determinants of the likelihood of being unemployed are held constant by the regression, including those variables associated with being a veteran. Each version of the equation was estimated separately and contained only those variables characterizing veterans that are shown. For example, Version I contains interactive dummy variables for veteran status, receipt of military training, and branch of service along with a dummy variable indicating the return to school, but it excludes the occupation comparison variables and the duration of service variable.

[a]Strictly speaking, these veterans received only basic training and/or training only in a military (combat) job.

[b]Coefficient based on fewer than 25 respondents.

[c]Statistically significant at .05 level.

[d]Statistically significant at .10 level.

Source: Compiled by the authors. Full regressions appear in Kohen, A. I., et al, *Career Thresholds* 6, U.S. Department of Labor R & D Monograph No. 16, Washington D.C.: U.S. Government Printing Office, 1977.

than entirely voluntary. Also, young white veterans who received training in the armed forces showed above-average positive reports of their military experience.

The long-service group of white veterans forcefully demonstrates the nonsymmetric nature of the perceptions being studied. That is, they had significantly higher-than-average rates of reporting both negative and positive effects of military service on civilian careers. Thus, long-service veterans were the least likely to express ambivalence and those who served for one year or less were the most likely to report no effect on their civilian careers.

As expected, the date of discharge had a strong regular effect on the probability that a young white veteran would report a negative effect of his military service. That is, the probability is much higher the more recently he was discharged. This may reflect one or more of several forces. First, the recency of negative *military* experiences may induce strong negative reports about anything related to those experiences. Second, the loss of a few years of civilian labor market exposure may have been more of an impairment in the relatively depressed labor market of 1971 than in the tighter labor markets of the middle 1960s.

There is one apparent discrepancy between the analysis of the veterans' perceptions and the earlier conclusions. That is, the analysis of perceptions does not show significant differences between white veterans who returned to school and those who did not, whereas the earlier findings showed higher earnings and better jobs among those who returned to school. The discrepancy may be explainable if those who returned to school would have continued their education in any event and, thus, perceived the military experience as an interruption in their prior plans to achieve higher earnings and status. While this is purely speculative, it is consistent with the following facts: those with higher levels of education prior to military service were more likely to return to school after being discharged, and college graduates had significantly below-average reports of positive effects and above-average reports of negative effects of military service.

In general, it is almost impossible to draw any confident conclusions from the analysis of the self-reports by young black veterans. In the main this probably is due to the small number of respondents who comprise many of the categories used in the analysis. Comparable to the findings for whites, there is a strong significant positive relationship between duration of active duty and the likelihood of reporting a positive effect. The small intercolor differences of blacks perceiving both more positive and less negative effects is not uniform across all categories of the veterans. Finally, when all is said and done, young black veterans and young white veterans do not diverge systematically

TABLE 9.4: Perceived Effects of Military Service on Civilian Career: MCA Results (F-ratios in parentheses)

Characteristic	Whites Number of Respondents	Whites Adjusted Percent Reporting that Military Service Was Positive	Whites Negative	Blacks Number of Respondents	Blacks Adjusted Percent Reporting that Military Service Was Positive	Blacks Negative
Method of entry to service		(0.76)	(2.69)		(1.68)	(1.07)
Drafted	152	50.7	21.5[c]	75	53.8	15.5
Enlisted	303	52.7	14.1	50	54.8	9.8[e]
Other	66	59.3	11.8	3	[e]	[e]
Branch of service		(0.30)	(0.64)		(2.63)	(2.67)
Navy, Coast Guard	95	52.4	14.7	8	[e]	[e]
Army	317	54.4	16.9	96	57.1	15.2
Air Force	58	50.5	10.5	11	[e]	[e]
Marines	51	48.4	18.4	13	[e]	[e]
Duration of service		(15.81)[f]	(5.54)[f]		(6.62)[f]	(1.94)
0–12 months	87	20.8[d]	24.4[d]	15	[e]	[e]
13–24 months	234	60.9[d]	10.0[d]	76	41.0[d]	10.0
25–36 months	95	55.2	14.3	25	82.8[d]	10.6
37 months or more	105	60.1[c]	23.6[c]	12	[e]	[e]
Date of discharge		(0.76)	(7.12)[f]		(0.69)	(0.90)
1971	101	49.3	27.6[d]	33	56.9	20.3
1970	117	57.6	18.8	41	63.3	9.4
1968–69	109	49.7	16.0	31	49.1	16.6
1967 or earlier	194	54.0	7.9	23	50.3	8.1
Training in military		(9.18)[f]	(0.53)		(0.38)	(0.17)
None or military only	306	47.4[d]	15.0	104	53.9	13.6
Some training	215	60.3[d]	17.3	24	59.9	10.7

	N			N		
Military and post service occupation		(0.56)	(0.14)		(0.26)	(0.28)
Same	104	49.8	14.8	11	e	e
Different	417	53.8	16.2	117	55.9	12.4
Health condition in 1971		(1.99)	(1.56)		(0.75)	(0.44)
No health limitation	479	54.6[d]	15.2	120	56.3	12.4
Limitation, began before service	15	e	e	2	e	e
Limitation, began during service	16	e	e	6	e	e
Limitation, began after service	11	e	e	0	e	e
Education prior to service		(1.36)	(3.99)[f]		(0.54)	(1.93)
0–8	16	e	e	4	e	e
9–11	91	47.8	10.9[c]	30	57.3	19.9
12	280	53.5	14.8	77	56.7	8.1[c]
13–15	92	59.2	16.8	16	e	e
16–18	42	42.2[c]	34.6[d]	1	e	e
Returned to school post service		(1.72)	(0.51)		(5.67)[f]	(0.56)
No	407	51.5	16.6	114	58.6	13.7
Yes	114	58.1	13.9	14	e	e
Grand mean		53.0	16.0		55.3	12.9
R^{-2}		.07	.06		.14	.00
F-ratio		2.97	2.60		2.03	0.84
Total number of respondents	521			128		

Universe: Respondents who were Vietnam-era veterans and who were employed in 1971.

[a] The percentages are adjusted by the multiple regression technique of holding constant all other variables shown in the table.

[b] Includes those who entered the armed forces through ROTC or OCS and those whose method of entry was not ascertained.

[c] Significantly different from the grand mean at .10 level.

[d] Significantly different from the grand mean at .05 level.

[e] Adjusted percentage not shown where category contains fewer than 20 respondents.

[f] Significant at .05 level.

Source: Compiled by the authors from computer analysis of NLS data.

in their views of the impact of their military service on their subsequent civilian work experiences.

SUMMARY AND CONCLUSIONS

This study was conducted because the experiences of Vietnam-era veterans are integral to understanding the transitions by young men from adolescence to adulthood and from school to work during the late 1960s. As a starting point it focused on the factors determining who served in the U.S. Armed Forces during the Vietnam era (1964–71). In doing so the study departed substantially from earlier research that focused almost exclusively upon the decision by a young man to enlist in the military service. The analysis confirmed many intuitive answers to the question of who served, including the following: young men with health problems and/or dependents were less likely to serve and veterans were less likely to come from the ranks of both the least and the most capable young men than from the group with average educational achievement and mental ability.

Importantly, the findings also demonstrate that while socio-economic background obviously indirectly influenced who served (that is, through measured mental ability and educational attainment), it exercised no independent direct effect once these factors were taken into account. Equally important is the finding that there was no significant racial difference in the likelihood of serving in the armed forces during the Vietnam era. Finally, the results indicate regional/racial differences in the probability of entering the armed forces that are interpreted as evidence that the military was used as an avenue of escape from racial discrimination in the civilian labor market even during the Vietnam conflict.

The second objective of the study was to examine the effects of being a veteran on civilian labor market experiences. In order to consider a broad range of such experiences, regression analyses were performed on hourly earnings, occupational status, and unemployment during 1971. The models were designed to isolate those specific characteristics of veterans that were expected to affect labor market achievements, while simultaneously controlling for other determinants of those achievements.

When earnings or status is the criterion, young white veterans were found to have paid a substantial cost for their military service in terms of foregone civilian work experience. That is, the labor market apparently did not evaluate time in the armed forces as equivalent to time in civilian work in terms of producing human capital. The exceptions to this generalization were the minorities of young white veterans whose military and subsequent civilian jobs were in the same occupational group and those who took advantage of the GI Bill to return to school. For young blacks the interpretation of the results is less straightforward. None of the variables identifying veterans attain statistical significance. However, the estimated earnings payoff to each year on active military duty exceeded the payoff to each year of civilian work experience *prior to* service. For neither race group do the results provide clear support for the hypothesis that there is a significant carryover of military training into civilian jobs.

The most succinct summary of the results of analyzing unemployment among young men is that soon after their discharge veterans evidently experience significantly more joblessness than their nonveteran peers. But this disadvantage disappears with time. That is, reacclimation to the civilian labor market over time appears to be the "solution" to the unemployment "problem" of veterans.

Analysis of veterans' perceptions of the effect of military service on their civilian careers revealed rather more positive attitudes than would be suggested by the analysis of veteran/nonveteran differences in actual labor market achievements. More than half of the employed veterans reported that the armed forces experience had helped their careers. While there was no objective evidence to support it, this positive attitude was relatively more common among those who had received training while in the military service. Some of this dissonance may be due to vagueness in the meaning of "career." Or it may be due to a longer time horizon for the veterans' subjective evaluation than for the evaluation based on 1971 actual experiences. Furthermore, some consistency is evident. First, the results indicated that veterans who reported that military service was a detriment to their careers had significantly lower occupational status. Also, reports of negative effects declined with the length of time since leaving the armed forces, and this is consistent with the finding that (some) labor market disadvantages of veterans disappear with time. Finally, combining the analyses of objective and subjective assessments of the impact of military service leads to the conclusion that there may have been a slightly greater payoff to the young black veterans of the Vietnam era than to their white peers.

REFERENCES

Altman, S. H., and R. J. Barro. 1970. "Model of Officer Supply Under Draft and No Draft Conditions." In Studies Prepared for the President's Commission on an All-Volunteer Armed Force. Washington, D.C.: U.S. Government Printing Office.

Beusse, W. E. 1974. *The Impact of Military Service on Low Aptitude Men.* Washington, D.C.: Manpower and Reserve Affairs Office of the Assistant Secretary of Defense.

Browning, H. L., S. C. Lopreato, and D. L. Poston, Jr. 1973. "Income and Veteran Status: Variations among Mexican Americans, Blacks, and Anglos." *American Sociological Review,* 38 (February): 74–85.

Cook, A. A. 1970. "Supply of Air Force Volunteers." In Studies Prepared for the President's Commission on an All-Volunteer Armed Force. Washington, D.C.: U.S. Government Printing Office.

Cook, A. A., and J. P. White. 1970. "Estimating the Quality of Airman Recruits." In Studies Prepared for the President's Commission on an All-Volunteer Armed Force. Washington, D.C.: U.S. Government Printing Office.

Cutright, P. 1973. *Achievement, Mobility and the Draft: Their Impact on the Earnings of Men.* Washington, D.C.: U.S. Department of Health, Education and Welfare.

Employment and Training Report of the President 1978. Washington, D.C.: U.S. Government Printing Office.

Fechter, A. E. 1970. "Impact of Pay and Draft Policy on Army Enlistment Behavior." In Studies Prepared for the President's Commission on an All-Volunteer Armed Force. Washington, D.C.: U.S. Government Printing Office.

Fendrich, J. M., and L. J. Axelson. 1971. "Marital Status and Political Alienation among Black Veterans." *American Journal of Sociology* 77, (July): 245–61.

Figley, C. R. 1978. *Stress Disorders Among Vietnam Veterans.* New York: Brunner/ Mazel.

Helmer, J. 1974. *Bringing the War Home: The American Soldier in Vietnam and After.* New York: The Free Press.

Johnston, J., and J. G. Bachman. 1972. *Youth in Transition.* Vol. 5. Ann Arbor: Institute for Social Research, University of Michigan.

Jurkowitz, E. L. 1968. "An Estimation of the Military Contribution to Human Capital." Ph.D. dissertation, Columbia University.

Karpinos, B. D. 1966. "The Mental Qualifications of American Youth for Military Service and Its Relationship to Educational Attainment." 1966 Social Statistics Section, Proceedings of the American Statistical Association, pp. 92–111.

Katenbrink, I. G. 1969. "Military Service and Occupational Mobility." In *Selective Service and American Society,* ed. R. W. Little. New York: Russel Sage Foundation.

Kohen, A. I.; J. T. Grasso; S. C. Myers; and P. M. Shields. 1977. *Career Thresholds: Longitudinal Studies of the Educational and Labor Market Experiences of Young Men.* U.S. Department of Labor R & D Monograph No. 16. Washington, D.C.: U.S. Government Printing Office.

Ladinsky, J. 1976. "Vietnam, the Veterans, and the Veterans Administration." *Armed Forces and Society* 2 (Spring): 435–67.

Lifton, R. J. 1973. *Home from the War.* New York: Simon and Schuster.

Manpower Magazine 1971. "Mobilizing Jobs for Veterans." April, pp. 9–13.

Michelotti, K., and K. R. Gover. 1972. "The Employment Situation of Vietnam Era Veterans." *Monthly Labor Review* 95 (December): 7–15.

National Advisory Commission on Selective Service. 1967. *In Pursuit of Equity: Who Serves When Not All Serve*: Washington, D.C.: U. S. Government Printing Office.

O'Neill, D.; S. Ross; and J. Warner. 1976. "The Effects of Military Training and G.I. Bill Training on Civilian Earnings: Some Preliminary Results." Unpublished paper. Center for Naval Analysis.

Shields, P. M. 1977. "The Determinants of Service in the Armed Forces During the Vietnam Era." Ph.D. dissertation, Ohio State University.

Showell, C. H. 1975. "Labor Market Experiences of Vietnam-Era Veterans in Franklin County, Ohio." Ph.D. dissertation, Ohio State University.

Starr, P. 1973. *The Discarded Army*. New York: Charterhouse.

U.S. Bureau of the Census. 1973. *Statistical Abstract of the United States 1960–1972*. Washington, D.C.: U.S. Government Printing Office.

U.S. Department of Defense. 1976. *Selected Manpower Statistics*. OASD (Comptroller) Directorate for Information Operations and Control. June. Washington, D.C.: U.S. Government Printing Office.

U.S. Senate. 1974. "A Study of the Problems Facing Vietnam Era Veterans on Their Readjustment to Civilian Life." Senate Committee Print No. 7, Committee on Veterans' Affairs. Washington, D.C.: U.S. Government Printing Office.

———. 1971. Hearings Before the Subcommittee on Readjustment Education and Employment of the Committee on Veterans' Affairs. 92d Cong. Senate Committee on Veterans' Affairs. Washington, D.C.: U.S. Government Printing Office.

Useem, M. 1973. *Conscription, Protest and Social Conflict*. New York: John Wiley.

Waldman, E. 1970. "Viet Nam War Veterans—Transition to Civilian Life." *Montly Labor Review* 93 (November): 21–29.

Weinstein, P. A. 1969. *Labor Market Activity of Veterans: Some Aspects of Military Spillover*. Washington, D.C.: Department of Health, Education and Welfare.

Werner, W. E., and J. A. Radcliff. 1973. "The Vietnam Vets' Battle— Unemployment," *Journal of Employment Counseling* 10 (December): 187–91.

Wool, H., and E. S. Flyer. 1969. "Project 100,000." In *Programs to Employ the Disadvantaged*, ed. P. B. Doeringer. Englewood Cliffs, N.J.: Prentice-Hall.

10

SCARS OF WAR: ALIENATION AND ESTRANGEMENT AMONG WOUNDED VIETNAM VETERANS

LOCH JOHNSON

It is hardly news that the toll of death, mutilation, and suffering from all wars has been high. Soldiers and poets have reminded us of this throughout history. War, wrote Robert Service, is a "stupid crime" and the "devil's madness"; for Robert E. Lee, his war was "terrible"; for William Tecumseh Sherman, it was "hell."

Others, however, have viewed war as a grand event. To Mussolini, it was "noble"; Shakespeare's Othello thought it "glorious"; Edward Young recognized it could bestow "immortal fame"; and Thackeray knew that "bravery never goes out of fashion." Writing on nineteenth-century French society, historian William L. Langer (1969, p. 77) offers a similar description:

> Musset, in his *Confessions*, recalled the stirring days when warrior fathers returned home bedecked with medals and covered with glory, while Vigny declared that the dream of his generation was to make war, win the *Croix de guerre* at twenty, become a colonel at thirty, or die gloriously in the interval.

Napoleon himself apparently believed "there are no greater patriots than those good men who have been maimed in the service of their country" (Donovan 1970, p. 27).

But how do soldiers—perhaps particularly those who have been maimed—feel about the polity when, upon their homecoming, they are not "covered with glory"? When, instead, the government and the citizens are indifferent or even hostile toward their military exploits? The Vietnam War was not popular; there were, as Polner says in the title to his book, *No Victory Parades* (1971). This chapter examines the attitudes of wounded veterans toward the government that sent them into an unpopular war in Southeast Asia.

Between January 1965 and January 1972, U.S. military forces suffered 303,598 injuries from enemy action; over half of these men (153,291) required hospital care. The study reported in this chapter examines the association between selected war-related factors and levels of political alienation among Army veterans hospitalized from wounds incurred while serving in Vietnam.

Those who are politically alienated often express attitudes that show estrangement or separation from the political system (see Schwartz 1973). If a sufficient number of citizens are alienated from their political leaders and institutions, seeds of revolution may sprout in the fertile soil. When the alienated consist of well-trained and experienced military veterans knowledgeable in the arts of guerrilla warfare, deepening erosion of support for the polity forbodes ominous possibilities for the existing regime. In 1962, for example, alienated French officers ultimately revolted against the government of Charles de Gaulle rather than accept humiliating defeat in Algeria (Macridis and Brown 1963). For a society such as ours, based upon the Lockean principle that a government may properly rule only with the consent and support of the people, the degree of alienation among soldiers returning from the war is a serious matter.

METHODOLOGY

A Measure of Alienation

A multidimensional alienation scale was constructed to measure political alienation among a group of Vietnam veterans. The Political Alienation Scale (PAS) is composed of a series of Likert-type questions measuring frustration in readjustment to civilian life, a sense of political anomie or normlessness, rejection of prevailing social mores, and distrust of established political authorities. The PAS includes a total of 30 items drawn from the work of Fendrich and Axelson (1971), Finifter (1970), and Seeman (1959).

Measurement Validity

Items within each of the four subscales were moderately to strongly correlated on the average, and these interitem correlations within a subscale were higher than the average correlations with items on all other subscales, indicating subscale validity. Moreover, all subscale total scores were significantly related to one another and to the total 30-item score, indicating internal consistency of the entire scale. For the entire PAS, the split-half equivalence coefficient was .70, ($\overline{X}$ = 75.31, SD = 12.56). Though the possible range of scores is 30 to 123, the range of scores found for this sample was from 44 to 103.

A comparison of the split-half equivalence with the subscale interitem correlations shows that the validity of the subscale measures is greater than the homogeneity of the full scale, but not at the expense of reliability for the complete PAS. (This suggests that while the various dimensions of alienation tapped by the four subscales are distinct and separable, an underlying unity also exists [Sellitz, Jahoda, Deutsch, & Cook 1967]).

Items comprising the PAS were interspersed on the questionnaire with a large number of unrelated questions. All items were coded so that negative experiences, evaluations, and expectations (alienation) received high scores.

Data Collection Procedures

Following a brief pilot of the PAS among a group of 50 Vietnam veterans at a large military hospital in 1972, the PAS was sent to 256 Vietnam veterans in early 1973. These men were randomly selected from a list of Vietnam veterans who had passed through the hospital between 1968 and 1972. The initial response rate was 42 percent. Following a second mailing of the questionnaire, the response rate was increased to 65 percent of those contacted, or 166 Vietnam veterans who completed the PAS.

In terms of the severity and circumstances surrounding the veterans' physical injury, most were the result of hostile enemy fire (57 percent) or mines or booby traps (28 percent). A small number of men were wounded by "friendly fire" (8 percent) or noncombat-related accidents (7 percent). (Veterans with strictly or mainly neuropsychiatric symptoms, drug addiction, or those whose injuries resulted in loss of sight or severe burning were usually treated elsewhere and were not included in this study.) The injuries ran the gamut from broken bones and relatively minor cuts to multiple amputations. The sample is primarily white (91 percent), though there appeared to be no difference between the 15 blacks in the study and their white cohorts. See Johnson (1976) for a more detailed discussion of the methodology.

HYPOTHESES

As suggested by Figley (1978) and others (for example, Moskos, Chapter 4 of this volume), there are several factors that combine to make combat stressful. For the purposes of this study, we selected the nature of the combat-related injury, circumstances of the injury, and time since the injury as major factors associated with combat-related stress. Moreover, we also included such factors as avenue of entrance into the military, commitment to the official purpose behind the Vietnam War, and military rank. Our central focus, however, is on the relationship between these factors and the veterans' present political alienation and estrangement.

Nature of the Wound

Napoleon suggested that the war wounded were least likely to be alienated. On the contrary, we expected to find that in an unpopular war, the more severe the injury of a veteran, the more likely he was to be alienated. We made the assumption that veterans wounded severely enough to disrupt the normal pattern of their prewar life style would be angry, bitter, and estranged from the polity. Unlike those Americans returning from popular crusades like World War II (see Stouffer et al. 1949), the wounded Vietnam veterans have not been compensated for their losses by a hero's welcome and widespread respect. Moreover, Vietnam veterans receive fewer benefits than their counterparts who fought in World War II and the Korean War (New York *Times* 1974, p. 1). The severely wounded veteran was more apt to be alienated, we hypothesized, because he faces greater physical and psychological obstacles on the road to civilian readjustment than does the less-severely wounded soldier.

Circumstances of Wound

Some felt that being injured in Vietnam by a mine or booby trap was an especially ignoble fate. If one had to be injured, the place for it to happen was in fierce battle, not as a passive "booby" victim to a contraption placed by a long-vanished enemy. Lifton (1973, p. 47) writes: "The name given to the devices suggests the sense in which they not only maim the victim, but make him into a hoodwinked fool—they are a 'trap(s) for the booby.'" In light of this norm among some soldiers, it was hypothesized that the circumstances of injury might influence later attitudes about the wound. Heroic wounds might be more easily justified, and might encourage a justification of the war itself to insure meaning for the heroic deed. "Accidental" wounds, we reasoned, should increase alienation.

Time Since Wound

Some evidence also suggests that alienation among wounded Vietnam veterans may not set in until after a period of time away from the hospital environment. Figley (1979) has suggested, for example, that Vietnam veterans, like survivors from other disastrous experiences, pass through various stages of adjustment to their emotionally stressful confrontations with death and destruction, and that the realization of their experiences requires many years of adjustment. This would seem particularly true for recently released veterans in our sample due to the hospital setting itself. Injuries and disfiguration within the hospital are a commonplace. Hospitalized veterans, in fact, feel a very strong bond among themselves because of their war wounds. This comment of a wounded veteran is characteristic: "I was closer to people [in the hospital] even than to people in the war, because we were even more in the same boat" (Browne 1973, p. 180). Once away from the hospital, a supportive environment may no longer be available to check feelings of loneliness, frustration, and despair. We hypothesized, therefore, that the more recent the veteran's wound, the less likely he would be to possess attitudes of alienation.

Entrance into Military

The avenue of entrance into the military may also help to explain the presence or absence of alienation among returning veterans. The wounded draftee or reluctant volunteer who joined because he believed he was about to be drafted may feel a greater sense of frustration regarding a war injury since he did not wish to be in the service in the first place. The eager or adventurous volunteer may decide that it was his decision to join and, therefore, the consequences of that decision are more directly his to bear. So we hypothesized that wounded draftees or reluctant volunteers were more likely to be alienated than wounded volunteers who wished to join the service.

Commitment to the War

Also we hypothesized that "hawkish" veterans convinced of the need to fight communism in Southeast Asia might be significantly more willing to support the political system that sent them into war than those cynical about the American presence in Vietnam (see Helmer 1974).

Military Rank

Finally, since surveys have shown lower commitment to military life among the lowest-ranking enlisted men (Moskos, 1970, p. 198), we hypothesized that wounded enlisted men in general were more likely to feel more alienated than wounded officers. Their lower sense of dedication to the service might also make injuries more difficult to accept.

FINDINGS

The responses to the questionnaire items measuring Vietnam veteran alienation are reported in Table 10.1. Among these veterans, an

TABLE 10.1: Responses to the Alienation Scale (in percentages)

	Response	
Item	Agree	Disagree
	(n = 166)	
Readjustment to civilian life		
1. Friends and family did everything they could to make you feel at home again. (disagree)	90	4
2. Most people at home respect you for having served your country in the armed forces. (disagree)	77	16
3. When you got home, you didn't want any thanks for what you had done for your country. (disagree)	74	16
4. People at home made you feel proud to have served your country in Vietnam. (disagree)	48	38
5. People at home just didn't understand what you've been through in Vietnam. (agree)	79	12
6. Having been away for a while, you feel left out of everything that was going on at home. (agree)	60	35
7. When you finally got home, all you wanted was to be left alone. (agree)	48	42
8. The president and his administration are doing all they can to help the veterans readjust to civilian life. (disagree)	46	45
9. Readjustment to civilian life was more difficult than most people imagine. (agree)	62	33
10. Coming home was a big letdown because so few people appreciated the service you had put in. (agree)	39	53
11. Those people at home who oppose the Vietnam War often blame veterans for our involvement there. (agree)	32	55

Normlessness
1. Politics in America is a dirty and corrupt
   business. (agree)   51   22
2. The majority of political officials work for the
   common good rather than their selfish interests.
   (disagree)   28   36
3. Generally speaking, the best men get to the top
   in politics. (disagree)   15   62
4. On the whole, political decisions in America benefit
   most of the people most of the time. (disagree)   33   40
5. The political system can weather the present turmoil
   in the country without being destroyed. (disagree)   55   16
6. In general, our system of government and politics
   is the best that can be devised for this country.
   (disagree)   40   28
7. The government, as set up by the American Constitu-
   tion, is essentially sound and workable and does
   not need significant change. (disagree)   46   33

Societal Restraints
1. The prohibition against marijuana is reasonable
   and fair. (disagree)   31   64
2. The pressure that you be married before you can
   live with another person is reasonable and fair.
   (disagree)   23   75
3. Abiding by laws you don't agree with is
   reasonable and fair. (disagree)   71   24

	Distrust	*Trust*
Distrust of authority		
Labor leaders	70	20
Political party leaders	69	20
President Nixon	57	36
Local politicians	54	31
Military officers	53	35
Congressmen	43	45
Former President Johnson	42	45
Newsmen	42	50
Policemen	26	68

Note: Undecided responses were omitted; alienated responses are in parentheses.

Sources: The questions in the first section of this table are from a Louis Harris &
Associates, Inc. survey reprinted in the Senate Committee on Veterans' Affairs publication entitled *A Study of the Problems Facing Vietnam Era Veterans on Their Readjustment to Civilian
Life* (Washington, D.C.: U.S. Government Printing Office, 1972), pp. 10–13. The other
questions were derived from the alienation literature, particularly Fendrich and Axelson
(1971); Finifter (1970, 1972); Schwartz (1973); and Seeman (1959).

average of 42 percent registered alienated responses to the 11 questions on readjustment. Political normlessness is defined (Finifter 1970, p. 390–91) as "the individual's perception that the norms or rules intended to govern political relations have broken down, and that departures from prescribed behavior are common." Fewer than half of the veterans in this study believed in the fundamental soundness of the government, expressing a general disgust with politics and politicians. These veterans also rejected traditional views on premarital cohabitation and marijuana smoking, although they viewed the broad legal system itself as legitimate. Finally, local policemen were the only figures of authority trusted by a majority of these men.

In sum, a pronounced degree of cynicism toward public authority can be found in the attitudes of a majority of these returning veterans. While the American public in general has become increasingly more politically alienated (see Harris 1973), for Vietnam veterans the frustrations of war have been added to this common feeling of disenchantment producing a particularly high level of alienation toward the polity for a sizable minority of this sample.

As reported elsewhere, despite their alienation, these veterans were largely uninterested in political involvement and unwilling to sponsor major political changes (Johnson 1976). What concerns us here more than the commitment of veterans to political strategies is the association between political alienation and the several war experiences outlined earlier. Data on these war-related hypotheses are presented in Table 10.2.

Nature of the Wound

The severity of the injury incurred in Vietnam does not seem to be significantly associated with expressions of political estrangement. Still, it is worth noting that some evidence tends to refute our initial hypothesis that those most severely wounded (multiple amputees) are apt to be the most highly alienated. Cowen and Bobrove (1966, p. 869) note that conflict and maladjustment "should be relatively *less* acute among profoundly disabled individuals who are *obliged* to behave accordingly and relatively more acute in individuals of intermediate disability where actual behavioral potential spans a broader range and there is, therefore, greater ambiguity about the consequences of behavior." According to this reasoning, one would expect veterans with extreme disability to be more well adjusted generally than those with more moderate disability. In fact, the data from our study tend to support the notion that, among wounded Vietnam veterans, those with extreme injuries are the least likely to express attitudes of alienation toward the

TABLE 10.2: Selected Military Correlates of Political Alienation among Wounded Vietnam Veterans (in percentages)

	Alienation Level				
	Low	Moderate	High	(n)	
Severity of Injury					
Slight injury	24	40	36	(33)	Gamma = .05 (NS)
Gunshot wound	39	25	36	(81)	
Single amputation	25	28	47	(36)	
Multiple amputation	23	46	31	(13)	
Cause of Injury					
Hostile fire	36	31	33	(94)	X^2 = 2.91, NS; Cramer's V = .1
Booby trap/accident	26	28	46	(68)	
Time Since Injury					
Less than three years	23	35	42	(52)	Gamma = .30 (NS)
Three or more years	35	29	36	(114)	
Entrance Into Military [a]					
Draftee	30	27	43	(86)	Gamma = -.29; P < .01
Soldier of fortune	17	52	31	(50)	
Committed volunteer	72	14	14	(14)	

Table 10.2 (continued)

221

Table 10.2 (continued)

	Alienation Level			
	Low	*Moderate*	*High*	*(n)*
View of War[b]				
Color war hawks	49	26	25	(69)	Gamma = .60; P < .001
Antiimperialists	13	31	56	(45)	
Rank				
Enlisted	28	31	41	(146)	Gamma = -.46; P < .01
Officer	57	21	21	(14)	

[a] Ordinal statistics are used since a continuum exists here, ranging from the reluctant to the committed solider.

[b] Again, ordinal statistics are used since a continuum is present ranging from several cynical responses (for example, "The war is a result of American imperialism") to several "cold warrior" responses (for example, "America must help the cause of freedom in the world").

Source: Based on a mail questionnaire (N = 166); see "methodology" section above.

polity. Cowen and Bobrove (p. 870) further note that, among the physically disabled, "those with intermediate levels of disability may face particular adjustment problems." The data on veterans with a single amputation tend to reinforce this perspective, as these men are the most highly alienated in the sample.

Circumstances of the Wound

The cause of injury is not significantly related in a statistical sense to political alienation, either, although a trend supportive of the original hypothesis is evident. Those injured in a "nonheroic," "passive" manner tend to be more highly alienated than those wounded by hostile fire in "active" combat.

Time Since Wound

The time elapsed since the wound and hospitalization is also of limited significance for understanding who is estranged and who is not, although the percentages run counter to the hypothesized direction. As time since the injury passes, the degree of alienation diminishes somewhat.

Entrance into Military

Of greater statistical significance are the data exploring the link between alienation and degree of commitment to the military. The men who joined the military out of career aspirations or a sense of dedication to fighting communism (the "committed" volunteer) were, as hypothesized, much less likely to be among the highly alienated than those wounded veterans who were drafted or who enlisted in search of adventure.

Commitment to the War

Also, as hypothesized, wounded veterans who viewed the war as a Cold War conflict against communism were much less likely to be highly alienated than those who viewed the purpose of the war in cynical terms (such as: "The war is a result of American imperialism" or "The war was fought to make money for corporate executives").

Military Rank

Lastly, though based on few officers, the posited relationship between rank and alienation is borne out by the data, with officers less-highly alienated than enlisted men.

The findings presented here are tentative. The study is cross-sectional in character and limited to data on wounded veterans. A longitudinal study would permit a more refined examination of the hypotheses, as would comparable data on nonwounded veterans. As an initial look at this subject, however, it is possible to conclude that the selected military factors most associated with high levels of political alienation among these wounded veterans are avenue of entrance into the military (soldiers of fortune and, especially, draftees); view of the war (a cynical point of view regarding the purposes of the war); and military rank (enlisted man).

DISCUSSION

This has been a study of alienation among wounded soldiers in the aftermath of the Vietnam War. It confirms three of the original hypotheses: men who were drafted, who were not committed to the rationale behind the war, and who were not officers were eventually the most likely to be estranged from the polity. They returned from the war with bitterness toward the government that pulled them off the streets of their hometowns to give a part of their lives and bodies in Vietnam.

The actual wounding event itself, contrary to the original hypothesis, bore no strong relationship to subsequent levels of alienation toward the regime (or, for that matter, to strengthened support for the regime, as posited by Napoleon's hypothesis). Some evidence did appear, however, to the effect that moderately wounded veterans (notably single amputees) have had particularly difficult readjustment problems. Increased sensitivity of government policy makers toward these veterans would seem to be in order.

What statistical analyses like this one fail to capture, unfortunately, is the profound suffering of individual veterans. The young men with plastic waste-bags forever strapped to their bodies, those whose faces will always be a jumble of scars and twisted muscles, men whose legs were left behind in a swampy mine field appear only as ciphers in the tables of this chapter. Scholarly research on the Vietnam War can serve a purpose, but it is much more important that the American people and their representatives in the state and federal governments do not forget the terrible costs this war inflicted upon so many individuals.

These costs are evident in the following remarks made by wounded Vietnam veterans on the blank space for "additional comments" within the questionnaire used for this study:

My biggest regret about the whole thing is the lack of concern people show veterans. My experience was not traumatic to the extent I could not cope with it, but I have had to do so on my own. What happens to the vet who cannot handle his emotional experience?

> 22-year-old helicopter pilot
> Severe leg injuries from small arms fire

I wonder how long I'll be able to work as a letter-carrier for the Post Office because of [the pain in] my legs. Jobs for people with service-connected disabilities are hard to find and are very low paying.

> 19-year-old infantryman
> Extensive nerve damage in both legs
> from booby trap

No one understands my feelings of guilt about my wounds, which were minimal compared to those who died or lost arms, legs, and sight.

> 27-year-old forward observer
> Extensive nerve damage in both legs
> from booby trap

The thing I think about most is how it would be to run, walk, play ball like others. . . .

> 22-year-old infantryman
> Leg amputated after truck hit claymore
> mine

Many employers to whom I went to seek employment were unwilling to hire me because of my limitations.

> 21-year-old infantryman
> Collapsed lung, extensive nerve damage
> from mortar round

I feel used and discarded. . . .

> 20-year-old pointman
> Multiple shrapnel wound, shattered leg
> from mortar shell

I feel very bitter. Every time I take a step, I'm face to face with the fact of how the war has changed my life. The leg I gave served no purpose, but made life harder for me. . . . I have found that most people could care less about what I did.

> 19-year-old infantryman
> Claymore mine, leg amputated, facial
> scars

I kind of resent having to give part of my body to a useless war. The war was a continuous waste of human resources. Through newspapers, TV, and movies, people feel they know all about Vietnam. I just wish I could tell them the real truth.

> 19-year-old infantryman
> Small arms ambush, wounds in arm and
> leg

I think about how ugly my stumps are and how beautiful my legs used to be and what a goddamned shame it is. . . . Sometimes I wonder how my wife can stand me being as fucked up as I am.

> 21-year-old infantryman
> Feet blown off by enemy hand grenade,
> deaf in both ears

I have dreams where I'm at war and I'm the only one getting shot, or I can shoot someone at point blank and they don't die and they shoot me. . . . [People] don't understand the adjustments—physical and mental—that we go through. If you wear prostheses or braces, there are stares. They sometimes think the rest of you doesn't work. They think everything should be the same as it was. . . . I got wounded for nothing.

> 21-year-old combat engineer
> Paralyzed in left leg, shrapnel wounds
> from accidental mortar fire by his own
> platoon

Here are voices of quiet despair and resignation. These men don't want $100,000 and a sports car from Uncle Sam. They just want a fair share of recognition from the government that sent them to war and, perhaps most of all, some appreciation and understanding from the American people for whom, ultimately, they made their sacrifice. For they, too, are part of America's future.

REFERENCES

Browne, Corrine. 1973. *Body Shop: Recuperating from Vietnam*. New York: Stein and Day.

Bureau of the Census. 1973. *Statistical Abstract of the United States*. Washington, D.C.: U.S. Government Printing Office.

Cowen, Emory L., and Philip H. Bobrove. 1966. "Marginality of Disability and Adjustment." *Perceptual and Motor Skills* 23: 869–70.

Department of the Army. 1973. *Vietnam Studies: Medical Support, 1965–1970*. Washington, D.C.: U.S. Government Printing Office.

Donovan, James A. 1970. *Militarism, U.S.A.* New York: Scribners.

Fendrich, James M., and Leland J. Axelson. 1971. "Marital Status and Political Alienation Among Black Veterans." *American Journal of Sociology* 77 (September): 245–61.

Figley. 1979. Combat as disaster: Treating the Vietnam veteran as survivor. Invited presentation to the American Psychiatric Association, meeting, Chicago, May.

———. 1978. *Introduction to Stress Disorders Among Vietnam Veterans: Theory, Research, and Treatment* New York: Brunner/Mazel, xiii–xxvii.

Finifter, Ada W. 1970. "Dimensions of Political Alienation." *American Political Science Review*, 64 (June): 389–410.

———. ed. 1972. *Alienation and the Social System*. New York: John Wiley.

Harris, Louis. 1972. *A Study of the Problems Facing Vietnam Era Veterans on Their Readjustment to Civilian Life*. Senate Committee Print No. 7, 92d Cong. 2d sess. Washington, D.C.: U.S. Government Printing Office.

Helmer, John. 1974. *Bringing the War Home*. New York: The Free Press.

Johnson, Loch K. 1976. "Political Alienation Among Vietnam Veterans." *Western Political Quarterly* 29 (September): 398–409.

Langer, William L. 1969. *Political and Social Upheaval: 1832–1852*. New York: Harper & Row.

Levy, Charles J. 1971. "ARVN as Faggots." *TransAction* 8 (October): 18–27.

Lifton, Robert J. 1973. *Home from the War*. New York: Simon and Schuster.

Macridis, Roy C., and Bernard E. Brown. 1963. *Supplement to the de Gaulle Republic*. Homewood, Ill.: Dorsey.

Moskos, Charles C., Jr. 1970. *The American Enlisted Man*. New York: Russell Sage Foundation.

New York *Times*. 1974. April 14, p. 1.

Polner, Murray. 1971. *No Victory Parades: The Return of the Vietnam Veteran*. New York: Holt, Rinehart and Winston.

Schwartz, David C. 1973. *Political Alienation and Political Behavior*. Chicago: Aldine.

Seeman, Melvin. 1959. "On the Meaning of Alienation." *American Sociological Review* 24 (December): 783–91.

Sellitz, Claire; Marie Jahoda; Morton Deutsch; and Stuart W. Cook. 1967. *Research Methods in Social Relations*. New York: Holt, Rinehart and Winston.

Stouffer, Samuel A.; Arthur A. Lumsdaine; Marion Harper Lumsdaine; Robin M. Williams, Jr.; M. Brewster Smith; Irving D. Janis; Shirley A. Star; and Leonard S. Cottrell, Jr. 1949. *The American Soldier: Combat and Its Aftermath*, vol. II. Princeton, N.J.: Princeton University Press.

11

THE POLITICIZATION OF THE "DEER HUNTERS": POWER AND AUTHORITY PERSPECTIVES OF THE VIETNAM VETERANS

FRED MILANO

Michael Cimino's Academy Award-winning film *The Deer Hunter* confronts the American public with a piercing and graphic slice of the Vietnam War and its impact. The movie industry, virtually silent during that devastating era, has now deemed it a "safe" (that is, profitable) topic to pursue. The same mass media that gave us the thinly disguised propaganda of *The Green Berets* has turned its attention to the production of films that are more politically mature in both their style and content. The "Vietnamization of Hollywood" has brought us such recent films as *The Boys in Company C, Heroes, Who'll Stop the Rain, Go Tell the Spartans, Coming Home,* and *Apocalypse Now.* However, some vestiges of the old mentality still remain. In *The Deer Hunter,* the bestial portrayal of the Vietnamese— South as well as North—gives the usual hackneyed message: Orientals do not place the same high value on human life that Americans do. Aside from a few blatant stereotypes, the film has a substantial message to offer.

This is not simply a movie about three young working class men from a small Pennsylvania town who go off to fight "for God and country." Rather, it is a slow progression through three interconnected periods of their lives: before, during, and after their confrontation with war. As close lifelong friends, they enjoy a deep camaraderie—laboring beside the blast furnaces, drinking beer and shooting pool in the neighborhood bar, dancing and carousing at a Russian Orthodox wedding celebration. Their everyday existence has a stability, a sense of security and permanence. Then, abruptly, it is 1968. They leave "the world" (that is, stateside) and immediately find themselves engulfed in the horrors of jungle warfare. Their lives, once orderly, now seem out of control. Survival becomes the all-consuming priority. Then, as if watching time-lapse photography, we see the transformations. One of them returns home a cripple. Trying to cope with the loss of three limbs, he turns inward, his spirit withering away as he hides in a veterans' hospital. Another comes back a reluctant hero. The strongest of the three, he appears to have maintained his sanity. Still, he is disoriented. Unable to face the welcoming party prepared by his friends, he spends his first night home alone in a motel room. The third member of the trio, traumatized by the constant death and mutilation, loses all interest in life. Staying in Vietnam after his hitch, he becomes pathologically fascinated by the death game of Russian roulette, a game in which he eventually kills himself.

Yet *The Deer Hunter* is not a war movie. It denies the fable that war is romantic and gallant. Without being judgmental, it demonstrates how our individual lives can be shaped by larger sociopolitical systems or events and how we become trapped by them. It is a statement, too, on the unmeasurable psychological pain and confusion experienced by the American combatant in Vietnam. A movie as disturbing as *The Deer Hunter* may open a few more doors to understanding the problems and aftereffects (for example, the higher-than-average rate of divorce, suicide, and drug addiction among Vietnam veterans) that linger with us as a result of that war.

BRINGING IT BACK HOME

All of those who returned from Vietnam obviously did not succumb to the same fate as the "Bloodbrothers" portrayed in the movie. What then do they share in common? Are there any patterns that emerge? Perhaps the key question is the degree of change that can occur within the citizen-soldier (the Deer Hunter) as he moves between the two worlds. Though speaking of a different time and a different war, Therese Benedek (1946, pp. 77–78) has poignantly summarized the dilemma faced by veterans:

> In many ways the re-adjustment to civilian life is more difficult than was the adjustment to the Army. . . . The civilian is taught how to

become a soldier, but the soldier is not taught how to become a civilian again. Thus the soldier does not notice how far away from his past he has developed until he comes back and faces the old situation with his present personality.

Admittedly there are a number of forces outside the confines of the local town or neighborhood that can affect the individual. However, in terms of a stratification or hierarchy of human experiences, the military is likely to have a greater impact on the individual consciousness than many other influences. Moreover, for those youths who have not been separated from their community for any appreciable length of time, the military may provide the initial—and perhaps most significant—"fresh contact" with an outside institution. Within this context, then, we ought to consider this proposition: other factors being equal, military service is expected to have a major politicizing effect on the behavior and attitudes of persons in a given community. The term "politicizing," as used here, refers to that process by which an individual undergoes a pronounced restructuring of his outlooks as a result of certain dramatic circumstances occurring within his life. In a sense, the sociopolitical maturation of the soldier is accelerated (that is, relative to his nonmilitary contemporaries) by his exposure to the sharp discontinuity between civilian and military environments (Benedict 1938).

Considered alone, the military in itself could be regarded as exerting a formidable politicizing influence. For instance, the essentially democratic and egalitarian life experiences that characterized the prior civilian life of the soldier are contradicted by an alien caste system of inequalities. In Stouffer's (1949, vol. I, p. 55) words,

the Army was a new world for most civilian soldiers . . . [because] of its many contrasts with civilian institutions: (1) its authoritarian organization, demanding rigid obedience, (2) its highly stratified social system, in which hierarchies of deference were formally and minutely established by official regulations, subject to penalties for infraction, on and off duty, (3) its emphasis on traditional ways of doing things and its discouragement of initiative.

Vidich and Stein (1960, p. 496), on the basis of observations drawn from their own brief military careers, also refer to this marked discontinuity:

The routine repetitiveness of training, the frequent appearance of senseless authority, the investiture of authority in regular noncoms who were frequently less educated than the recruit, the reduction of all training and participation to a common denominator—all of which were supported by established and unquestioned authority—gave pause to the civilian-minded recruit who brought with him a quite different set of attitudes.

The personal tensions triggered by this pattern, and its seeming imperviousness to change, may give way to a resigned tolerance as the individual is gradually assimilated within the military organization. Yet such tolerance is not tantamount to acceptance. The precisely stratified structure of the military, furthermore, may have the effect— unintended, though ironic—of forcing the working-class servicemen into a recognition of or increased sensitization to his relative class position, both within as well as outside the armed forces. The aspect of "class," perhaps not previously encountered in his home community, is now dramatically imposed upon him.

Some of the past studies in military sociology would disagree with this. Stouffer's *The American Soldier* (1949) has stressed the "extraordinary indifference" and "lack of political sophistication" of the average American serviceman of World War II. As substantiation, he points to the apparent continuity, or absence of personal change, following the individual's departure from the military. He concludes that "the attitudes . . . of veterans toward America and the postwar world were in no significant way different from attitudes of men still in the Army" (Stouffer 1949, vol. II, p. 637). (A 1945 survey of 588 recently discharged veterans found that a majority of them held strong negative feelings toward the Army. In another survey conducted in the same year, involving 1,137 former enlisted men, a majority reported that the Army had had a detrimental effect upon them.) According to Stouffer, the antagonisms or hostilities that arose within these men were channeled specifically toward the Army. Allegedly the aftereffects did not carry over into their civilian world. A distinction was concisely drawn between the military organization and the society at large that the veteran was reentering. In addition, the serviceman was depicted as sharing a basic consensus with his nonmilitary contemporaries (for example, a popularly supported war, a united front, a clear ideological identification of the enemy).

That the individual is altered by his experience does not necessarily mean that he will always manifest it in some overt or tangible fashion. Stouffer (1949) and Havighurst (1951), in their respective analyses of World War II veterans, repeatedly allude to their "finding" that the ex-soldier, despite personal dissatisfactions with the military, is not a "reformer" or "social crusader." In somewhat the same vein, Moskos (1970) suggests that there is no perceptible difference between World War II and Vietnam participants as to the degree of their sociopolitical apathy and indifference. Basing his conclusions on interviews with 34 enlisted men stationed in a Vietnam combat zone—half of whom are members of an elite unit—Moskos contends that the data are being collected under natural conditions. However, the soldier occupying a front-line position, and concerned foremost with self-preservation, may certainly appear "politically passive," especially in relation to the ex-soldier who is interviewed in altogether different surroundings. What may *seem* to be absent may be, in actuality, merely assigned low priority because of situational demands. Moreover, the researcher is likely to be viewed with suspicion by the military subjects whom he is studying, for he is not only an out-group member but also a possible "extension" or "ear" of the military hierarchy. The responses given to him may therefore be less than candid.

Unlike his predecessor, the combatant in Vietnam encountered no "cut-off" that effectively separated his military status from his postmilitary status.* Consistent with the thesis of this volume, the Vietnam-era ex-soldier may undergo a prolonged process of politicization, one that is initiated within the military but that extends beyond its boundaries. For example, the rate of unemployment of Vietnam-era veterans throughout the early 1970s remained at almost twice that of nonveterans in the same age group (U.S. Bureau of Labor Statistics 1974).

This negative economic situation has led in turn to other developments. Though a record number of Vietnam veterans are enrolled in college programs, the motive may not be strictly, or even primarily, educational. Unable to find full-time employment after their discharge, many seem to resort to the GI Bill simply as a means of economic survival.

Another postmilitary factor that might politicize the veteran is his representation in the mass media. (The preponderance of Hollywood movies dealing with World War II have shaped many of the popular conceptions of American military life. To a considerable degree, World War II still constitutes the setting for war movies and television combat drama. The effect of this trend has not been without its impact: A 1963 study [DeFleur 1964, p. 58] found that elementary school children believed that Japan and Germany were still the main enemies of the United States.) In seeking new dramatic material the entertainment field has gradually relinquished its dependence on the World War II soldier-model (for example, "McHale's Navy"). In its place there have been increasing portrayals of the Vietnam veteran as a "heavy," in which he is characterized as having antisocial and violent tendencies,

---

*Statistics compiled during and immediately following the Vietnam War reveal a situation unprecedented in America's previous wars: over 500,000 were given less-than-honorable discharges, 60,000 to 200,000 became addicted to heroin while in the service, and 30 percent of inmates currently in state and federal prisons are recent veterans (Kastenmeier 1974; Pilisuk 1975).

relying upon criminal behavior to satisfy his "war-and-drug crazed mind," or turning his guerrilla warfare skills against his own society. One writer reports that during a nine-month period in 1974–75, more than 20 prime-time television series cast the Vietnam veteran in the role of protagonist (Brewin 1975).

THE STUDY

For the reasons given above, it seems worthwhile to investigate the potential impact of military service on political attitudes and participation. In studying effects, the overriding question is whether or not serving in the military had a politicizing influence on those who were exposed to that experience. The military institution is structurally more authoritarian and hierarchic than most civilian organizations and institutions. These differences, in combination with the qualitative difference between the climate of opinion concerning the Vietnam War as compared to prior wars, suggest that military service would have a politicizing effect, be it manifest or latent. In order to pursue this line of inquiry, veterans would have to be compared with nonveterans who are as alike as possible in all important respects with the exception of military service. The major difference between these groups would have to be that one group was exposed to military experience and the other was not.

This study was conducted in a small Pennsylvania steel town (1970 population, 12,300) quite similar to the town depicted in *The Deer Hunter*. As is the case in many industrialized areas, the town contains a highly diverse ethnic population. One-fifth of the inhabitants are black. Among those of European background, the largest groups numerically (in descending order of size) are Italians, Polish, Hungarians, Ukrainians, and Czechoslovakians. The data for this study were obtained by means of in-depth, tape-recorded interviews with 30 randomly selected males (15 Vietnam-era veterans and 15 nonveterans) of the Italian-American subcommunity and by the participant observation of the author. All 30 subjects were interviewed during the period from January through April 1976.

The town itself contains a relatively homogeneous Italian-American population. The major social characteristics shared by the 30 young men in this sample are age (23 to 33 years), ethnicity (Italian-American), socioeconomic background of themselves and parents (working class), religion (Roman Catholic), education (all were graduates from the town's solitary high school), and geographical place of residence (except for short absences such as the military service, all had lived their entire lives within this same town). The only major factor that served to distinguish the two groups was their service or nonservice in the armed forces.

FINDINGS

Political Interest and Voting Behavior

An interest in politics was expressed by a larger proportion of veterans than nonveterans. Among the ex-servicemen, nine indicated a strong interest, one a slight interest, and five no interest at all. Of the nonservicemen, three indicated a strong interest, four a slight interest, and eight no interest whatsoever. In spite of this divergence, almost all of the interviewees shared a common cynicism of political affairs.

Air Force Veteran: Yes, I'm interested, but I'm disgusted with the political system.

In the case of an Army veteran who was unemployed, "politics" carried a more direct and particularly poignant meaning:

Army Veteran: I'm not too crazy about him [the President of the United States] because I'm out in the street right now. I just don't like the way people play politics with jobs and stuff like that. I've got a family and I've been out of work six months. I was laid off [from the mill]. So that's not really too great.

When it came to political party affiliation, the two groups differed sharply. Numerically, each group contained seven registered voters and eight nonregistered individuals. However, all seven of the nonveterans had registered as Republicans, whereas two of the veterans were registered as Republicans and five as Democrats. In explaining their preference, some of the men admitted that they had been guided by "conventional reasons" or by the traditional voting habits of their families. A more frequent reason given for registering with a particular party dealt with the established political power structure within both the town and the county. In such instances, the individual's decision was not prompted by any ideological identification but rather by economic necessity. (Veterans and nonveterans alike told of their resentment at being subjected to coercive measures, especially in cases where party affiliation was used as a precondition for securing a job.)

Nonveteran: Why do I prefer the Republican party? It came about forcibly. I used to work part-time as policeman, and you had to be registered Republican to hold the job.

Army Veteran: I was almost forced into it. I *had* to register Republican. I had to because I did have a job at one time, worked for the county at a county park, and they kind of told you in a nice way how to register. It's a Republican county so I had to finally register that way or I probably wouldn't have had the job.

Army Veteran: If you want to live in this county, you have to register Republican. It was proposed to me like that. I got a phone call; it was right after I got out of the service. And it was just made quite clear that I should register Republican. And it wasn't just like an off-the-wall thing! I *knew* the person. And that's the way the proposal was, quite simple. So I registered at that time. Again, it was during my young impressionable years and I was going for a job.

Involvement in Local Government

In general, the members of both groups demonstrated a relatively low involvement in formal, electoral politics, but this nonparticipation was not consistently practiced; it did not extend, for example, to those situations in which the individual was directly confronted or threatened. Despite being on the periphery of the town's governmental activities, the working class residents sometimes found themselves drawn involuntarily into its affairs.

For some veterans, the involvement in local matters was of brief duration. Their entry was usually prompted by a single event or set of circumstances that directly affected, or related to, their personal lives. For other veterans, the excursion into local issues developed into a long-term commitment rather than a limited and transitory one.

Navy Veteran: They were putting ROTC in the high school, and I joined a group to oppose that measure. But they passed it anyway. I guess I'm still politically motivated, to stop things like that. We wrote letters to the school board and we had a meeting with them to present our views. We just met at different houses, got materials together. We got a lot of information from the Friends Committee in Philadelphia, and one of the representatives came out and helped us with relevant information.

Marine Veteran: I've already supported and initiated petitions. Across the area here, they were going to put up a high-density apartment complex which, after reviewing the builder's plans, showed no indication of a playground for children. With the roadways around here, I just felt it was very hazardous. And drainage problems, too. Everybody's down in the valley! And it was going to be all blacktopped. We just fought it, and the guy gave up.

Attitudinally as well as behaviorally, the ex-servicemen stood apart from their nonservice contemporaries. A comparison of the following remarks suggests that the nonveteran was less inclined than the veteran to act on his grievances against the town's governmental body.

Nonveteran: I try to voice my opinion. Other than that, there's not much we *can* do, because the thing always comes back: if you don't vote, you shouldn't open your mouth. But I find, whether you vote or not, it doesn't make any difference. It's going to happen one way or the other.

Nonveteran: Well, it all depends on what it was. If it was something that upset me terribly, I would do something about it. But if it was something I could live with, I wouldn't do anything about it.

Navy Veteran: I like to go to the city council meetings and see what's going on there. Because when you go to a council meeting, you've got people that are either "for" or "against." So, okay, you can find people that feel the same way that you do at the council meeting. One person's voice alone isn't very strong. But a group of voices sometimes can sway. If enough citizens are concerned at what they're doing . . . well, take fluoridation. Enough people say "No, we don't want fluoridation," and certain areas don't. That's what it takes. People have to get together. People have to act for what they believe in, whether it's fluoridation or what.

Navy Veteran: Let's face it. You've got to keep them on their toes. I believe in getting involved with politics to the extent that, the people you're electing in there, keep them in line. You elect them to do a job. Make sure they do the job you want them to do. And if they don't, get them out and get somebody else in. And if it takes going in there and raising your voice once in a while to do it, then do it, regardless of what they think of you.

Nongovernmental Political Action

The "apoliticalness" of the American soldier is a theme that has been continually reiterated in the decades since World War II. Observers of the military scene such as Stouffer (1949), Shils (1950), Huntington (1957), Janowitz (1960), Little (1965), and Moskos (1970) have attested to the "extreme political apathy" of U.S. servicemen. Following a study of American overseas combat soldiers in the mid-1960s, Moskos (1970) concluded that these were individuals who "refused to espouse overtly ideological sentiments" and who "showed a strong distaste for ideological symbols." Proceeding even further, Biderman (1964) has contended that the average soldier is "antipolitical." (These remarks, however, call into question the meanings and value assumptions that have been attached to the terms "political" and "ideological." Unfortunately, many of the past accounts of the American enlisted man have used these terms interchangeably.) In light of the events of the Vietnam period, some writers have questioned this earlier view:

> Though combat soldiers may not display what Mills [1959] terms the "sociological imagination" [that is, relating personal situations to broader societal conditions], this is not simply a default in political sophistication. Rather, for the soldier concerned with his own day-to-day survival, the decisions of state that brought him into combat become irrelevant (Moskos 1975, p. 28).

What then occurs when this fear of combat or the other constraints of military life have been removed? Once severed from the military environment, does the individual demonstrate a heightened degree of political awareness (that is, a "political self")?

By "political," I refer to that sense in which the individual seeks to achieve a greater measure of control or power over his own life. To this end, the ex-soldier employs those means that are accessible and most suited to his working-class situation. The veteran therefore may not show his "politicalness" in the customary ways; he may openly spurn the practice of voting, or of engaging in local politics, or of running for government office. Instead, he may choose to exert his influence through those organizations in which he fits most comfortably: his labor union and other voluntary associations. As Robert Lane (1962) argues in his analysis of the "American common man," the individual who responds in a way that *seems* ideologically confused or apathetic is generally considered to have no political ideology. Moreover, since an individual's involvement in the formal political process is usually minimal, it is likely that his political attitudes will be organized quite differently from those of ideologues or political theorists. By focusing on underlying value orientations, we may find a set of attitudes having a definite coherence—especially within the context of that individual's life situation.

In order to partially ascertain the "political activeness" of the veterans and nonveterans in this study, the members of each group were asked whether they had ever written or spoken to persons in public office regarding a problem or issue, or had ever participated in a strike, protest demonstration, or political rally.

Among those who had personally contacted a government representative at the local, state, or federal level, five were ex-servicemen and two were nonservicemen.

> Navy Veteran: I've spoken at the council meetings. Environmental issues are basically the big trouble spots. That and property tax increases. Even though I'm not a property owner, it's still something that you've got to take an issue with. Because I'm not today, but tomorrow I may be a property owner.

> Navy Veteran: The problem was snow removal. I felt that they weren't doing their job cleaning the roads out here. Well, they told me they were state roads and naturally the state had to do it. They just sort of brushed me off with that. And that didn't satisfy me. I just kept asking them "Well, you're my elected official. You're my local official and I'm paying you to do this job. Find out from the state *why* they're not doing this. Let's get them down here and get it done. Let's face it, a lot of people travel these roads." One thing led to another and that's when the councilman jumped up and told me I was out of order. That's when I told the councilman he didn't know what "out of order" was, and unless I got some action he was going to find out. And I meant it at the time. They did something before the next snow storm came. Evidently *somebody* got in contact with the state.

> Nonveteran: I wrote to our state representative about some of the campaign promises that he made and didn't fulfill, as far as labor promises. He was supported by our local, and I thought maybe he needed a little bit of enlightening on some of the things he made public and didn't come through with.

A slightly larger proportion of veterans (seven) than nonveterans (five) indicated that they had taken part in labor strikes or political demonstrations.

> Marine Veteran: I was indirectly involved in one; it was a wildcat strike. The union workers went on strike and all the nonunion office workers were running presses and till motors and the whole bit. But they knew where we stood.

Though an equal number of individuals (six) in either group had held office (or had campaigned for others) in their unions or clubs, the veterans were more likely to recognize, and to use, those aspects of power that became available to them.

Navy Veteran, vice-president of a union local: We have an independent union; it's within the company. We call it our union, but it's not
our union. We're not allowed to go on strike. But we have "ways" of
getting things done. Like they took a truck off the road. That means
that that eliminated a foreman's job. Now it affects everybody in the
long run because that's all the more time it'll take you to be foreman.
The more trucks you have, the better off you are really, because then
the guys can branch out more. So anyhow, we couldn't go out on
strike. And nobody liked it. So we just all went together and we said
"When a storm comes up and they call you to come in, you just don't
come in." And that is "problems" for the electric company. That's a
real problem. If they have wires down all over the place and poles are
knocked down and they call you at your house and say, "Hey, Vico,
come to work," you say "No, I can't come to work." And *everybody* did it!
Well, we got action fast because nobody went to work.

Army Veteran: I was one of the organizers of the Area Taxpayers
Association. There were two of them [taxpayers associations]. They
had this one of ours, and then they had another one. They were a bit
more radical. They were more vocal, let's put it that way. They
actually put a few members on the school board. We got one, and they
got two or three of them on.

Navy Veteran: I did run for the union position at work. The only thing
that was open, that I could have had possibly a chance at, was as
secretary of the local. So I tried that, and lost. I'll try it again this year.
But the thing is, my running slate was trying to get this new president
in, which we did anyway. I didn't win but my support did help him to
get the new presidency.

As a group, the servicemen were characterized by a greater degree
of participation in political activities than their nonservice cohorts.
Twelve of the veterans, as compared to seven of the nonveterans, had
engaged in some form of unconventional political behavior (that is,
other than registering and voting). On an individual basis, moreover,
the average veteran had involved himself in a wider range of "power"
activities than his nonveteran counterpart: only two of the nonveterans, as opposed to seven of the veterans, had engaged in more than a
single type of political action (for example, writing to an official in public
office *and* taking part in a strike).

Perceptions of Applied Power

When asked to identify the organizations they felt wielded the
greatest amount of power nationally, the two groups differed dramati-

cally. The servicemen generally viewed the situation as one of concentrated economic power, whereas the nonservicemen either held no opinion on the subject or else tended to believe that such power was dispersed.

Comments made by nonveterans:

No, I can't really say that there's anything dominating; no one group dominating the other.

Well, no one has power to the point that I feel threatened.

I never thought about it, but I imagine there's no group with too much power.

Comments made by veterans:

Ex-Army Specialist: Big business, like oil, they just control the country, that's all there is to it. Big business just seems to really control you. They do what they want to do, that's what it comes down to.

Ex-Marine Sergeant: There are some industrial monopolies that I think should be disbanded. I just think it's against the so-called free enterprise system. The equality just isn't there.

Ex-Navy Petty Officer: Oil companies have entirely too much power, both political and monetarily. There were scandals of oil companies in this area; oil distributors that put a strangle-hold on the people. Politically they were backed up by elected officials. To me, whether it be national or whether it be local, it's the same thing. They're strangling us at the present time. And I feel that they have too much power. They deal with the consumer but yet they're screwing the consumer. Also, the public utilities. It's a monopoly! Where else can I go for electricity?

Ex-Army Specialist: The big companies. Why do I say that? Money! How are you going to compete? When the oil companies upped the prices, who stopped them? When the insurance companies upped their prices, or do what they want to do, who stops them? And I could throw in another one too, steel. There's no question about it. As far as I am concerned, the big money controls it and it's as simple as that.

Ex-Navy Petty Officer: I think most of your big industries. When I say "big," I'm talking about multibillion dollar. Anything that's a monopoly, in that category, I think are too big. Look at this oil and energy crisis in the last couple of years. They're telling you that there's a fuel shortage and to conserve fuel, and then when you start to conserve fuel they put the prices up on you because they say they're not making enough money! Now, when they get the prices up to where they want them and they're making enough money, now there's plenty of fuel: "Go ahead and use all you want." Now they *encourage* you to travel. So they're insulting my intelligence when they tell me there's no fuel, as far as I'm concerned. I don't like the way it was thrown at us. You know, one day you had all the gasoline you wanted for 30 cents a gallon. Then the next day there wasn't any! Then when it got to 60 cents a gallon, you got all you wanted again. Hey, it doesn't take a ton of bricks to hit me, man! I'm crazy but I'm not stupid!

Reactions to the Antiwar Movement

Unlike the selective transformations wrought by military service, the Vietnam War broadly enveloped *all* members of American society. How then did these contemporaries—servicemen and nonservicemen alike—react to that war, and to the opposition movement it spawned? Of the veterans interviewed, 12 sympathized with the antiwar movement, two expressed disapproval, and one remained undecided. Among the nonveterans, ten approved of the movement, two disapproved, and three were undecided. Not only were the veterans and nonveterans similar in their reactions, but the war was still largely regarded as being a complex and enigmatic issue by these men. Even so, some of the former military participants had become more sensitized to the ideological and propagandistic aspects of the war than those who had not served in the military.

> Navy Veteran: The war was unjust. We had no business being there. We really didn't know *why* we were there. You know, they come out with these altruistic things of "fighting for democracy." What it boils down to is sometimes we're fed a lot of bullshit. And pardon my expression, but that's the way I feel.

> Marine Veteran: I was in the service at the time. But I thought it [the movement] had its good points. There was the question of whether it was really a war and what it was worth and what it was for. Whether it was really "a fight for democracy" or "to stop the tyranny of communism." It was a tremendous amount of waste, economically and in human lives.

> Navy Veteran: You're brainwashed when you go into the military. They tell you "We're there to stop communism," and "We're there to do a lot of good things." The people of Vietnam I liked. They were good people. I once made the statement "I hate the damn gooks." But

you don't hate them; you take your oppression out on them. That's what it amounts to. But they really were good people. They were the same as us. They were just trying to make a living, that's all. I don't think it was a just war. I think it was a big business war and made a lot of people rich. I don't think it was right in that respect. I think we lost face over there; I think our country lost face.

An important qualitative element further differentiated the two groups. Six of the former servicemen, but only one nonserviceman, had experienced a fundamental change in their earlier views toward the war.

Army Veteran: At first I was resentful of those who were in the movement, who were against the war. But the more I came to an understanding of what was going on, and to what real little purpose we were actually needed in that war, then I became very strongly opposed to the war.

Air Force Veteran: Being involved in it [the war] myself, when I went *in* the service I was very much against it [the movement]. Then, when I started to see actually what *was* going on in the war, I kind of—I'm not going to say I was fully sympathetic with them—I kind of started to see some of their views. Maybe they did have something, maybe some of their beliefs were valid. Once I got involved in it, I could see.

Army Veteran: At the time, I was in the service. So I thought that they [the movement] were a group of people who really didn't know what was going on. That was *then*. *Now* I feel it was probably a good movement, a good demonstration of the opinion of the people at the time.

Army Veteran: I went in the Army in 1966 and at the time I felt I was for it [the war], that they were doing the right thing. But *now*, no way! I had friends that were killed in the war, close friends. Yeah, I was for it; I thought it was the right thing—at the time. Now, things are over with and I can see where it was wrong.

Nonveteran: In the 1960s, I think everybody was gung-ho on the U.S. and they wanted to fight for their country and to stop the communists. That was a big thing then. And then you find out in 1970 that the only reason that they were in Vietnam was for the oil offshore and personal gains for different companies. They weren't really concerned about those Vietnamese people.

This latter set of observations corresponds with the evidence obtained in a previous study of Vietnam-era veterans. According to Strayer and Ellenhorn (1975, pp. 89–90):

> Attitudes toward U.S. involvement in the war . . . reflect a major reversal compared to reported pre-induction attitudes. Whereas initially the percentage distribution was 67 percent for, 30 percent undecided, 2.5 percent against, the "current attitude" distribution was 15 percent for, 10 percent undecided, and 75 percent against.

Strayer and Ellenhorn (p. 88) also report that "while most Blacks and Mexican-Americans were either for or undecided about the war prior to their involvement in it, after completion of a tour of duty both groups were unanimously against it."

Impressions of the American Political System

In this study, the respondents were asked to express their views on the American political system. Seven of the nonveterans maintained a favorable or positive outlook.

> Nonveteran: Everybody complains about things in our country. But they say that if you visit these other countries and see how a lot of these people are living, you'd always come back here. We do have the best society. A lot of people complain about our country, but I guess basically from what I've heard, a majority of people say it's the best to live in.

Whereas almost half of the nonveterans generally supported their nation's political structure or political leadership, all 15 of the veterans held distinctly critical or negative views toward it.

> Marine Veteran: There seems to be so many issues that are cloaked in secrecy. Like the average citizen isn't told what's happening. Right now it does seem like a very complex, secretive, exclusive system. The issue of lobbyists is one that's always bothering me, too. The favoritism that it brings about seems completely unfair.

> Navy Veteran: I think basically government and politics are not that complicated. I think it's the people who *run* it who make it seem like it's complicated.

> Navy Veteran: Well, it's like this. People that *have* power, I feel that they just take it for granted that everybody's going to follow them. And being used to working that way, they do it. But people are taking more notice of it now. The FBI, they're cutting down on their investigations into crime and everything, and they're going more into politics. So politicians are going to have to take more notice of what

they're doing, think about what they're doing more, rather than just doing it and saying "Well, this is what we did, people!"

Army Veteran: I think the people who run government are the big companies. The politicians execute it, but I think a lot of that execution is influenced by the big companies. I think the big corporations really run the government, run the country.

In some instances, the remarks were focused upon a specific element of the political process rather than upon the more general features of the system itself. Four of the respondents, for example, questioned the political indoctrinating function performed by the mass media.

Nonveteran: I think first of all, the knowledge that we get about what is happening in our government comes through the media. And I just feel that we're only told what they want to tell us. For example, Watergate. Some of it was publicized—for the public. What else they deleted we'll never know. So I feel that I know very little about politics. It's *not* that it cannot be understood. When it's through my ignorance, then I don't know. But like I say, you can only know about what they'll *allow* you to know, and they just keep the rest from you.

Navy Veteran: Even when you have an election, basically the people don't elect the president. It boils down to what the electoral college says. And in California in the 1972 presidential election, CBS broadcasted Nixon as a landslide victor before the polls even opened in California! What's the point in it? The majority at this present time doesn't have the voice that I'd like to see them have. They haven't gotten it together. They haven't stood up and said "No."

Moreover, a majority of the veterans perceived a direct relationship between their military service and modification of their political outlooks.

Army Veteran: I would have to say that my political views were probably initiated in the service. Not by the government, but by those who were in there with me at the time. Like guys you were bunking with, that type of thing. They used to have fabulous discussions about government, about religion, about anything. And there were some tremendously intelligent people there. And here I went through twelve years of school and didn't realize that I didn't pay attention to what the hell was going on! But here, these guys who I was out on the rifle range with, these guys were talking about all this stuff. And it was interesting. It was just like the first time that I'd ever heard it.

And that was kind of like the birth of my political views. And then when [Bobby] Kennedy was shot, that made me even more aware of what was going on. And then the Vietnam War beyond that. There was no question that that had a lot to do with my political views. And from then on it was just kind of magnified. It just kept getting bigger and bigger.

SUMMARY

The phenomenon of politicization cannot be regarded as an absolute. There is little likelihood of a complete transformation of those "Deer Hunters" who have left their permanent community for a brief span of time. (Despite the military's potential human impact, it is limited in duration and therefore in its influence.) In relation to their nonmilitary peers, the veterans in this study indeed appear as more highly developed political beings. Contrary to the claims of some social scientists, the ex-serviceman was not found to be apathetic *or* apolitical. Often they did admit to feelings of powerlessness over circumstances beyond their immediate control or sphere of activity (for example, events occurring at the national level). Yet in other ways they revealed themselves to be acutely perceptive of political matters—though choosing *not* to become enmeshed in traditional or partisan forms of political behavior (for example, registering, voting, and so on). Rather, they preferred to exercise their limited individual powers within smaller scale and more intimate organizations such as the union local or the fraternal-type association. This may, in part, constitute a reaction to the subordinate and relatively powerless position that the "Deer Hunters" once occupied within the military hierarchy. However, this may also reflect a realistic appraisal of the available means to influence their fates and their immediate environment. Although the data do not allow me to speak more confidently about the specific causes of this phenomenon, the fact that the veterans in this study were more politicized and more critical toward this society's political system or leadership than the nonveterans indicates that military service seems to have had a powerful politicizing influence on this generation of young men.

REFERENCES

Benedek, Therese. 1946. *Insight and Personality Adjustment: A Study of the Psychological Effects of War.* New York, Ronald Press.

Benedict, Ruth. 1938. "Continuities and Discontinuities in Cultural Conditioning." *Psychiatry* 1 (May): 161–67.

Biderman, Albert. 1964. *March to Calumny*. New York: Macmillan.

Brewin, Robert. 1975. "TV's Newest Villain: The Vietnam Veteran." *TV Guide*. July 19, pp. 4–8.

DeFleur, Melvin. 1964. "Occupational Roles as Portrayed on Television." *Public Opinion Quarterly* 28 (Spring): 57–74.

Havighurst, Robert et al. 1951. *The American Veteran Back Home: A Study of Veterans Readjustment*. New York: Longmans Green.

Helmer, John. 1974. *Bringing the War Home: The American Soldier in Vietnam and After*. New York: The Free Press.

Huntington, Samuel. 1957. *The Soldier and the State*. Cambridge, Mass.: Harvard University Press.

Janowitz, Morris. 1960. *The Professional Soldier*. Glencoe, Ill.: The Free Press.

Kastenmeier, Robert. 1974. *Congressional Record*. Extension of Remarks. July 9, p. E4545.

Lane, Robert. 1962. *Political Ideology*. New York: The Free Press.

Little, Roger. 1965. "Buddy Relations and Combat Role Performance." In *The New Military*, ed. M. Janowitz. New York: Russell Sage.

Mills, C. Wright. 1959. *The Sociological Imagination*. New York: Oxford University Press.

Moskos, Charles. 1975. "The American Combat Soldier in Vietnam." *Journal of Social Issues* 31 (Fall): 25–37.

———. 1970. *The American Enlisted Man*. New York: Russell Sage Foundation.

Pilisuk, Marc. 1975. "The Legacy of the Vietnam Veteran." *Journal of Social Issues* 31 (Fall): 3–12.

Shils, Edward. 1950. "Primary Groups in the American Army." In *Continuities in Social Research*, ed. R. Merton and P. Lazarsfeld. New York: The Free Press.

Stouffer, Samuel et al. 1949. *The American Soldier: Combat and Its Aftermath*. Vols. I and II. Princeton, N.J.: Princeton University Press.

Strayer, Richard, and Lewis Ellenhorn. 1975. "Vietnam Veterans: A Study Exploring Adjustment Patterns and Attitudes." *Journal of Social Issues* 31 (Fall): 81–93.

U.S. Bureau of Labor Statistics. 1974. *Handbook of Labor Statistics: 1974*. Washington, D.C.: U.S. Government Printing Office.

Vidich, Arthur, and Maurice Stein. 1960. "The Dissolved Identity in Military Life." In *Identify and Anxiety*, ed. M. Stein et al. Glencoe, Ill.: The Free Press.

SECTION III

GOVERNMENT POLICIES AND THE VETERAN

UNPAID DEBTS TO UNSUNG HEROES: AN INTRODUCTION TO SECTION III

Charles R. Figley

This final section of seven chapters serves both as a summary and as a final testimony to the struggles of Vietnam veterans since the war. These chapters discuss institutional responses to Vietnam veterans individually and as a group. Chapter 12 by Dixon Wecter places the social movement of military veterans within historic perspective by detailing our new nation's less-than-appreciative treatment of Revolutionary War veterans. The same kind of suspicion and contempt encountered by America's first veterans was noted earlier in Waller's discussion of the world war veterans' experiences (in Chapter 2) and is discussed in this section in terms of the Vietnam veterans' treatment as losers (Paul Camacho's Chapter 13), their reputation for drug use and abuse (M. Duncan Stanton's Chapter 14), their unmet social-emotional needs (Ford Kuramoto's Chapter 15), their unrecognized psychosocial problems (Ronald Bitzer's Chapter 16), and their lack of consumer protection both within the Veterans Administration and in their promised rights to job preference in Dean Phillips' chapters 17 and 18, respectively.

This section is about activism and it is also about success: conquests over drug addiction and emotional, biochemical, and physical handicaps resulting from Vietnam; veterans' confrontations with insensitive mental health programs and VA policies; and, finally, reassertion of their rights to judicial review and veterans' preference.

Through careful analysis of numerous historical documents, Dixon Wecter provides a sobering account of the postservice adjustment problems of America's first veterans, those who fought in the Revolutionary War. He tells us about the general lack of concern among the citizens of the new republic of the United States for those who fought the revolution: more were concerned about the potential violence and shiftlessness of the recently returned combatants than about the veterans' personal welfare. For example, few Continental soldiers were paid in full; instead, they had to settle for promissory notes which often went unpaid. The returning veterans for the most part were farmers and times were hard in the immediate postwar years but gradually improved as the economy recovered. With the recovery, however, came a growing resentment toward veterans and their incessant demands for back pay and the bonuses and pensions they claimed they were promised during the war. Not until 1818 did Congress act on pensions for the needy veterans, $8 a month, and ten years later all who served were granted full pay for life. Yet prior to that time the young nation bitterly debated the "rights" of veterans in general. "Whatever smacked of soldiering, in a professional sense, reached the pitch of prejudice," notes Wecter.

In Chapter 13, Paul Camacho explicates the socioemotional by-products of losing in war. The "good" war in Vietnam changed to the "bad" war when winning shifted to losing. He observes that blame for the bad war was eventually shifted from the Congress to the military and, finally and inevitably, to the veteran. Camacho suggests that faced with compromising their favored veteran status, the traditional veterans' organizations generally rejected the Vietnam veterans, viewing them as tainted by the beating they took in Vietnam and by their bad reputation that was emerging in the media. Because of this and other negative images, most Vietnam veterans rarely acknowledged their veteran status. Camacho also notes the damage often done by well-meaning social scientists and mental health specialists who tend to overstate the problems. Perhaps the most insightful observation embodied in Camacho's discussion was the infighting that occurred during and following the war, most often to the detriment of the Vietnam veteran, among three powerful factions: the veterans' lobby in Congress, the Veterans Administration, and the Department of Health, Education and Welfare.

Chapter 14 by M. Duncan Stanton provides an interesting case study of government policies focused on Vietnam veteran problems, in this case drug use during and following military service. Drawing upon various findings of his own and others' research, Stanton notes a steady increase in marijuana use in Vietnam from 1966 to 1970 with an average use rate of between 20 to 25 percent, primarily due to its growing use among American youth at home. Stanton estimates, however, that only 9 to 10 percent of the lower grade enlisted men (that is, noncareer military personnel) became habitual users in Vietnam. It was not until the late 1960s that the military began to seriously confront the problem with drug screening and treatment programs. In terms of heroin, Stanton reports that use was due to high availability in Vietnam, unlike marijuana, which was affected by increasing stateside use.

Chapter 15 by Ford Kuramoto, former administrator and Vietnam veteran specialist within the National Institute of Mental Health, illustrates what Wecter and Camacho outlined in their chapters: recently released war veterans in general and Vietnam veterans in particular are rarely able to mobilize national support for their needs and problems. As the war came to a halt in the early 1970s, the country had grown tired of the entire Vietnam venture, including the needs and special problems of those who fought there. Kuramoto accurately questions the motives of establishment-oriented federal departments as they seemingly "cooperated" to assist the newly released Vietnam veterans in coping with the war and the backwash of the "war against the war." It is ironic that the national outreach programs that would have set up rap-group type counseling programs across the country seven years ago were killed by federal complacency and have only recently been embraced by the Veterans Administration. Part of the reason for this final success, as historians may later confrim, was the VA's new leadership, who wanted such programs more than any other agency and were willing to pay the political dues to get them.

Meanwhile, as newly appointed forces change the attitude of the VA among top administration, the endless wheels of the huge VA system continue even now to behave as they always have with a minimum of sensitivity to the special problems of a few. Ron Bitzer and others since the war have been fighting the VA at local and regional levels for VA recognition of the problems and rights of Vietnam veterans who are emotionally disabled due to their war experiences. Bitzer's Chapter 16, a revised version of his testimony before the Senate Veterans' Affairs Committee, lays out the major supporting evidence and rationale for combat-related stress reactions that have yet to be addressed by the Veterans Administration, the U.S. Congress, and the entire mental health profession. It is noteworthy, however, that efforts have succeeded in liberalizing the VA's Board of Veterans Appeals' position on recognizing combat-related stress disorders.

In his carefully researched chapter, attorney Dean K. Phillips argues that lack of court review of final VA benefit decisions are not serving the best interests of veterans and their beneficiaries. As Phillips notes, the VA processes 10 million claims a year that contain appealable issues. Of those claims that are denied, approximately 60–70,000 are appealed—half of which are settled at the regional office level. Those cases that are not settled there (e.g., 36,655 in fiscal year 1978) are reviewed by the Board of Veterans Appeals in Washington, D.C. Among the cases considered by the BVA a large majority, 85%, are denied and no appeal to any court is permitted by law, although similar benefit cases in other agencies (e.g., Social Security) are subject to court review.

Since 1974, Phillips has been a catalyst in a movement to convince Congress to enact legislation that would grant veterans the right to judicial review of unfavorable VA benefit decisions. The U.S. Senate ultimately voted favorably on such proposed legislation by unanimous consent on September 17, 1979. While a similar bill was initially being reviewed by the Senate Veterans Affairs Committee in June 1977, its primary sponsor, Senator Gary Hart, D.—Colorado, credited Phillips with first calling the judicial review issue to his attention and expressed concern that veterans' benefits were considered 'gratuities' and could be denied, reduced, or terminated without an opportunity for review by the courts. Mr. Phillips . . . indicated that because judicial review of Veterans' Administration decisions was precluded by law, veterans had been relegated . . . to the status of second class citizens."

In March 1977 Phillips became the Special Assistant to VA General Counsel Guy McMichael, and participated in the reformulation of the VA position on judicial review. On October 10, 1977 for the first time in history the VA testified that it no longer opposed having its benefit decisions being subjected to judicial review and in fact favored such review in specified circumstances.

In the final chapter, Phillips zeros in on another controversial topic, veterans' preference. In December 1978 Phillips, correctly predicted the results of the landmark June 1979 Supreme Court decision which held 7 to 2 that veterans preference was constitutional.

The key issue in the case was whether legislators intended to discriminate against women when enacting veterans' preference statutes. Women's groups claimed that since less than 2% of America's veterans are women, veterans' preference—particularly "absolute" formulas—discriminate against women as a class.

Phillips argues that veterans' preference is intended to apply to wartime veterans—a considerable precentage of whom served on active duty against their will because unlike women, they were subjected to the draft. In five court cases during the Vietnam war men made unsuccessful attempts to convince Judges that women's exemption from the draft denied men equal protection of the law.

Phillips alleges that women in general were not interested in serving in the military during wartime. He raises the points that women were subject to different standards and the percent of women in the armed forces between 1948–1967 was limited by statute to 2%. He answers by reporting that the percent of women in the military during that 19 year period averaged less than 1.2%. He notes the 2% quota was lifted by Congress in 1967 and women did not reach 2% of the Armed Forces till 1973—after U.S. ground forces were pulled out of Vietnam.

Phillips also observes that the Department of Defense reported that during the Vietnam war (1964–1973), no women's organization filed lawsuits in any of the 94 federal courts claiming that more stringent standards for women attempting to enter the military denied them equal employment opportunity.

Phillips concludes that the draft is the most sexist institution in our culture since it determines who will be drafted and killed or maimed on the basis of sex—60% of U.S. Army casualties in 1969–70 were draftees. He also concludes that because of devices such as the student draft deferment which poor Americans were less prone to utilize, minority Americans suffered a disproportionately higher percentage of casualties in Vietnam.

Phillips concludes his chapter by stating that bills which would once again require that only men register for the draft were reported favorably by the House & Senate armed services committees in May and June 1979. He observed that no women's organizations (from either an equal responsibility or equal employment opportunity standpoint) protested the fact that these bills would once again exempt women from registration for the draft.

12

WHEN JOHNNY COMES MARCHING HOME: VETERANS' "BENEFITS" IN HISTORIC PERSPECTIVE

DIXON WECTER

To be soldiers and conquerors is one thing; to excell in the arts of peace is another. So said the *Independent Chronicle* of Boston, after disbandment. First among the arts of peace was earning one's bread and butter. The Continental soldier returned to a land of open spaces and new skies, offering matchless benefits to farmer and hunter along the far frontier, but in other ways he was no child of fortune.

The longer he had served, paradoxically enough, the poorer he found himself at discharge. Late volunteers gained bounties that had been steadily boosted by local and state authorities as the war progressed; they now came home flush. This inequality added to the external friction between old-timer and rookie. Moreover, the average veteran, needing cash upon return home and having only a wallet full of promissory notes from his state and nation, haplessly fell among speculators. In the last days of the army, in the spring of 1783, jobbers had gone among the camps busily buying up soldiers' certificates, at a fraction of their face value, "for Hard Cash." Doctor Ramsay in South

Carolina, among others, lamented that "the war-worn soldier" was driven immediately to sell his wages for a pittance. "A private soldier having a demand of ten pounds against the state," remarked the *Massachusetts Sentinel*, "would be as contented in receiving two pounds from the state, as he would be in receiving the like sum from a dealer in government securities." Yet Massachusetts soldiers' notes, it reported, "have all been bought up and lodged in the hands of a few great men," to the loss of both the veteran and government. The speculator—first in soldiers' certificates, a little later in veterans' bounty lands—was the harpy of this generation, dogging the soldier's steps and approaching him in the hour of sorest need.

For times were hard, between 1783 and 1787. A nation mainly of farmers was of course cushioned against absolute destitution; no cities were filled with idle men beating the pavement. But conditions were bad enough to set teeth on edge. "Almost every person complains of the insecurity of property, and a want of confidence, as well in individuals as in the state, at a time when, by the termination of a successful war, complaints on this head ought not to exist," remarked the Salem *Gazette*, August 14, 1783, in words that fit the post-war mood of other times as well. The money-raising and debt-paying impotence of the Confederation bred distrust in business circles. Conversion of privateering to peaceable commerce—in the face of new tariff walls, now that America was neither England's colony nor France's protégé—was hard going. The towns lacked machinery to bear the load of economic self-sufficiency. These causes of the depression were less commonly aired than the charge that the British had started it. English fripperies had flooded a nation long starved of its luxuries, and drained off all the gold—so said one Continental veteran in a speech at Petersburg, Virginia, in 1786, echoing the universal plaint.

In seeking a job, the veteran apparently met no serious opposition from the women who had been doing a man's work. On the eve of the Revolution and during it, New England women particularly enjoyed more vocational freedom—as blacksmiths, tallow-chandlers, soapmakers, tanners, coach-builders—than afterward. The return of the soldier helped to oust them from such fields. Women struck their flag in prompt surrender, as happened again after Appomattox and the Armistice.

To shed light on the veteran's search for daily bread there are no labor bureau statistics and not much press comment. In those days it was taken as an individual rather than a sociological problem. David Ramsay, pioneer historian of the war, simply says from his observation that farmers, mechanics, merchants, and tradesmen, as of 1775, returned eight years later to their tasks; that "privates generally betook themselves to labor, and crowned the merit of being good soldiers by becoming good citizens." In the army, farmers and farmhands had heavily outnumbered any other group—with a fair sprinkling of crafts-men (as in a cross-section of the Pennsylvania Line studied by Carl Van Doren) like weavers, shoemakers, carpenters, saddlers, blacksmiths, millers, tailors, barbers, potters, coopers, ropemakers, tinkers, watch-makers.

For skilled artisans the demand was brisk. Among the easiest habits broken are those of wartime thrift. Scarcity of shoes—which had caused laborers to trudge barefoot up to the village outskirts with shoes in hand, or housewives to hide an old pair in some hedge or wall by the road before they shod themselves for town shopping—now called for the tanner and cobbler as soon as they were freed. A growing popula-tion, rationed of its comforts for eight years, clamored for goods and services. Discharged soldiers able to buy new civilian clothes added to the demand upon loom and shuttle. And—whatever may have been the rivalry in Boston and New York and Philadelphia between British gewgaws and homespun—account books of village merchants show that they, at least, stocked their shelves mainly with the output of local weavers.

A few industries, notably the whale fisheries and the West India trade of New England, had been wrecked by the war. Newport, for instance, was almost a ghost town, because her distilleries were closed down and her spermaceti works idle (since the wartime lesson of using tallow candles instead of sperm oil remained as a post-war preference).

But to balance such losses, new enterprises bearing some connec-tion with the war were sprouting. Powder mills could be converted into paper mills, to meet a passion for newspaper reading bred by the Revolution. As early as 1776, Congress itself had received a petition from several papermakers to release one Nathan Sellers from the army, so he could return "to make and prepare moulds, washers, and utensils for carrying on the paper manufactory." By 1789, the thirty-seven newspapers of 1776 had grown to more than one hundred; witness La Rochefoucauld's remark in the early years of peace that "from the landlord down to the housemaid they read two newspapers a day." The making of woolen cloth and of iron tools, discouraged by a jealous mother country, began to boom during the war and kept on growing— the weaving industry helped immensely by Oliver Evan's wartime invention of a card-making machine for combing raw wool and cotton. New stagecoach routes, with the wayside smithies and taverns they called for (many a tavern named for Washington or Wayne or Lafayette by the veteran who ran it), meant more opportunities for livelihood, as did plans for networks of canals. For the jobless soldier of '83, even though he might be mired in a slough of present despond, the industrial horizon looked brighter.

Even more vital was the outlook for farming. At the war's outbreak, only two to three percent of all Americans lived in the five towns with upward of eight thousand population—so that the soil was the real base of fat or lean times. Early in the Revolution from 1776 to 1780, the farmer had grown richer. Under inflation, and the sharp demand from armies and towns, prices rocketed. The tradesman, who had to buy all he ate and wore, gloomily watched the farmer meet all his bills with printing-press money. Creditors flying from debtors importunate to pay them became a standing joke of the day.

About 1781 the farmer's luck worsened. Prices fell, with the cumulative overproduction from the farm that always rolls up after the war peak is past. High taxes came in as state governments tried to finance themselves on a pay-as-you-go basis. Remembrance of flush times made the new yoke of penury harder to bear, especially if a man had been absent in uniform and so missed the only agricultural boom in memory. A group of threadbare farmer soldiers in Massachusetts and New Hampshire, deeply sunk in debt and depression, as will be seen, finally tried the solution by violence in 1786. Elsewhere, by that date, conditions had begun to improve again. From the fast-growing state of Pennsylvania in 1786, Benjamin Franklin reported that farmers were standing well upon their feet, while "our working people are all employed and get high wages." In the South, Washington had returned to a Mount Vernon seedy and debt-ridden, while General Moultrie rode home to North Hampton Plantation to find "nothing alive but buzzards." But within three years these and other plantations had begun to recover from absentee ownership. Societies for the promotion of agriculture sprang up; innovations like the cradle and cast-iron plow eased farm drudgery; many veterans like Washington himself grew keenly interested in new fruits and grains, crop rotation, and stock-breeding. Introduction of green-seed cotton proved to be the salvation of many a post-war farmer in the South.

To the veteran as agriculturist, then, the outlook was variable: somewhat dark at the war's close, but soon lightening everywhere save over New England's stony acres.

How personally did the soldier fare in a civilian world, notably among his neighbors and employers? As always, under the spell of victory nothing was too good for the soldier, yet soon he came to be blamed for disaffection and crime, decay of manners and morals, and for the taxes that provided his bonus or pension. Civilian attitudes blew hot and cold, in a post-war milieu where emotions reached the boiling point more quickly than in other times. The way of the soldier in a civilian world is a mixture of misunderstandings on both sides—soldierly impatience, civil fickleness, and murky economic problems that are the fault of neither. One question always remains: Is any cash reward commensurate with the service rendered, namely, facing death for one's country? Then, if an obligation is admitted, how shall the nation help the soldier gain a new toe-hold in society? The existence of some sort of debt is always felt. Yet the public, like any debtor whose debt is both large and vague, cannot escape a kind of embarrassment, of being ill at ease before the creditor—as well as impatient at any gesture that looks like dunning.

Some Revolutionary veterans felt perhaps too crassly that somebody owed them a living. They relied upon their families or friends for support, or wandered from town to town telling stories of their campaigns and passing the hat, or tinkering half-heartedly at odd jobs when nothing easier turned up. (In Europe, in this century, the chief perquisite of crippled soldiers was license to beg on the king's highway.) From time to time a war record or sufferings served to elicit good will. One who spent "a long and tedious captivity . . . begs leave to inform his friends in particular, and the public at large, that he has entered into the Vendue and private commission business" in Boston. In a Quaker City newspaper, one William Patterson announced that "the respects of an old soldier wait upon the public and his friends, to run him at the next election as CORONER for the city and county of Philadelphia." Thus the soldier in politics makes a modest opening bid.

Clearly, most sympathy belonged to the disabled. As early as August 25, 1776, Congress had promised half-pay to such, as long as illness or injury lasted. Loss of limb entitled the soldier to half-pay for life. But the Federal Treasury was bare, and the not unimportant detail of payment was tossed over to the states. Many local differences arose in practice, until in May, 1785, Congress decreed that all commissioned officers get half-pay during disability, and non-coms and privates five dollars a month. No artificial limbs were furnished at public cost, as in the Civil War; and vocational education, in the sense of 1919, was undreamed of. Men hopelessly wounded were expected to become the charge of their families. Public conscience did not like to see a disabled soldier starve, and rendered beggary fairly lucrative; but to remake the man, in body or mind, lay beyond the horizons of responsibility.

For veterans in distress, by reason of later illness or poverty or old age, Congress did nothing for many a year. No bloc of the rank and file existed in politics. Not till March, 1818 were needy officers and men granted a minimum eight dollars per month—seventeen years after all enlistment rolls had been destroyed in a War Office fire. Claims were pretty freely allowed, on testimony of witnesses. And, as the number of veterans dwindled, Federal generosity burgeoned. In 1828, all Continentals who had served to the war's end were pensioned to the full amount of their pay, whether standing in need of help or not. As always, this was the soldier's reward for living long. John Quincy Adams dryly observed, under date of April 7, 1834, that Revolutionary veterans were "immortal . . . they multiply with the lapse of time . . . and this day there was a petition from the son of a deceased pensioner praying that the pension might be continued to him." Later, all men who had worn the uniform for six months got pensions. Then came a sequence of widows' acts—with the last relict of a Continental veteran, Esther Damon, of Vermont, dying in 1906, aged ninety-two, one hundred and twenty-three years after the war. In his 1913 Report the Commissioner of Pensions estimated the total pension cost of the Revolution at seventy million dollars, incomparably the least expensive of our major wars.

A grant of the bonus type—half-pay for life, which Congress in 1780 had promised officers, to induce them to remain for the duration—caused bitter post-war debate. It was foreseen that taxing privates, and the widows and children of those who had fallen in the war, to support officers the rest of their lives would stir opposition. Governor Livingston, of New Jersey, proposed instead a cash sum "to enable them to enter into business, or become serviceable to the community"; others feared that life pensions would breed a class of drones "resorting to places of luxury and splendor." But Washington, with his aristocratic bias, was soon converted to the plan. In March, 1783, alarmed by the saber-rattling of the Newburgh Conspiracy, Congress voted the officers more immediate relief, by commuting half-pay for life to a lump sum of five years' full pay in the form of six percent certificates. Presently, in the summer of disbandment, opposition swept the land like a tornado. New England was its vortex. Civilians were tired to death of taxes. "If in the midst of a drowsy harangue, the word *taxes* should be mentioned," wrote an observer of the Massachusetts legislature, "the sound electrifies them in an instant, like sleeping geese." Opposition to half-pay while masking itself as sympathy for the private soldier, seems often to have come most loudly from those best able to pay taxes. War debts—including the redemption of Congress's pledge to the officers—did not strike many men of property as binding. Newspapers in the summer of 1783 are filled with sarcastic letters about officers and "the five years full pay for services they never expect to perform." Town meetings branded the scheme as greedy and nefarious. "We are become not only the objects of abuse in the publick prints and called the Harpies & Locusts of the Country," wrote a young Connecticut officer from West Point in August, "but are even so obnoxious as to be Mobbed." From the same garrison a fortnight later, Jedidiah Huntington wrote home that many Connecticut officers, alarmed by the threats of stay-at-homes and angered by such ingratitude, have begun to think about never going home, but settling on the frontier.

Some voices were raised on the other side. "I have lived long enough to know that money is the main thing," ironically wrote "A true Massachusettensian" in the Salem *Gazette* of July 10, 1783, "am highly pleased with the pious design . . . of withholding the half-pay unwarily promised to our officers in the days of our trouble." And he recalled the fable of the cat drowning in the brewer's vat who cajoled the rats into pulling her out, then turned upon them with fine contempt for "promise made in drink." One "Honorius" in the *Connecticut Courant* of September 9 remarked that the ardor of '76 now seemed like "a madness" to those townsmen whose glib resolutions the soldier had made good with blood.

So raged the debate. In the end, the promise of Congress was not flatly repudiated, but its benefit pruned by economic circumstances. The officers, receiving their six percent certificates, stood in little danger of becoming a moneyed aristocracy eddying about in "places of luxury and splendor." With the Treasury bankrupt, these certificates began quickly to depreciate. Within two or three years, the majority of the officers seem to have sold them, at rates as low as twelve and a half cents on the dollar. Few were able to hold on to their certificates until 1790, when the public debt was funded under the new Constitution and all government securities began to look up. This rewarded not the original but the current holders of certificates—in general, the bankers and speculators—for a brand of patriotism no more heroic than a willingness to bet on their country's solvency.

Meanwhile, in the South, complaints arose from the planter gentry that "everyone who bore arms, esteemed himself upon a footing with his neighbor." Snobs feared that class lines had been weakened by the democracy of the service.

Distrust of the military, in the first years of peace, took other shapes. Alexander Graydon, a frank-spoken Pennsylvania soldier in the war, recalled how the conservatives in his state showed "extreme jealousy . . . against those who had been in the army . . . (never) was the worshop of Mammon more widely spread, more sordid and disgusting. Those who had fought the battles of the country, at least in the humbler grades, had as yet earned nothing but poverty and contempt; while their wiser fellow citizens who had attended to their interests, were the men of mark and consideration." He also remembered, as a feature of the times, how prosperous stay-at-homes began to pick up military titles. Joining the militia, they would clap on a belt and sword, and scamper about a day or two in the company of a militia general. Majorities and colonelcies were thick as June blackberries. "And thus the real soldier was superseded, even in the career of glory." By a kind of Gresham's Law, the tin soldier drove the genuine article into hiding. Later, the same thing could be observed in certain aspects of the G.A.R. and American Legion.

Wise Americans hoped with Washington in 1785 that they might live to see war, "this plague of mankind, banished from off the earth." Doctor Franklin dreamed of an alliance between nations of the world to promote peace. Madison and his friends in *The Federalist* called attention to the profit motive as a breeder of wars. But none of these leaders thought remotely of repudiating the war they had won, or building a fool's paradise on peace at any price. Fearlessness for the right, they knew, was better than fearfulness of peace. Old John Sullivan, hard-bitten Indian fighter, appealing to his White Mountain neighbors not to neglect their militia, nailed the issue. He said he was "one of the number that experienced too great a share of fatigues in the war, to wish ever to see America involved in another; but to conclude that an event will not take place because we are averse to it, betrays a weakness that will not admit of an excuse."

Yet to the wishful-minded, danger seemed far away. The mass of the people were sure they had won a war to end wars. Anti-military spirit and sheer apathy could meet beneath a cloak of pacifistic isolation. The portfolio of Secretary of War was abolished, and the army, in the spring of 1784, whittled almost to the vanishing point—down to eighty privates and their officers, for guarding stores at West Point and Fort Pitt. Whatever smacked of soldiering, in a professional sense, reached the pitch of prejudice. Congress, eight months after the final peace treaty, called standing armies "dangerous to the liberties of a free people." Distrust of the soldier himself—fostered in civilian minds by the Newburgh Conspiracy, the latter-day mutinies and desertions, the stir over half-pay and the added taxes it called for—suited the popular mood of disarmament. Already, with folk memories of Lexington and Concord, an American conviction was budding that the old squirrel gun over the fireplace was good and sufficient answer to all enemies of the United States. From experience with green recruits, General Washington knew better, but in the recoil of the times his advice was overborne.

In April, 1786, a Boston citizen reported that Fort Hill was going to ruin: the gates fallen in and hinges sold for scrap iron, the embrasures crumbling, the platforms burnt as firewood by the poor Negro families thereabouts. The late recruits supposed to be on guard were nowhere to be found. "Our patriotick army were kept out of their pay, in doing their duty," added the writer," and these men are paid in the neglect of theirs." This same spring it was proposed wholly to dissolve the Boston militia. The agitation got a rise out of one satirist, in the Boston *Gazette*. Let us do away with all soldiery, he said, and hope if we are ever attacked that we can hire some mercenaries. "Publick Spirit is a dangerous thing: only recollect the confusion it made in 1774 and 1775 . . . I would therefore advise that the militia laws be abolished and repealed, that our firearms be carried to some safe place in the country, and our swords secured, lest we should cut our fingers."

Alarmists discovered a prime bogey in the Cincinnati. This officers' fraternity, formed a month before disbandment in 1783, was taken as the entering wedge of military despotism. Judge Aedanus Burke of Charleston, a former militia captain, tried to smoke out their dark designs in a much-read pamphlet. Chief grievances were the proposal to make membership in the Order hereditary and its potential influence in politics. Washington's advice, to mollify public opinion on these scores, was adopted by the first national reunion of the Cincinnati in May, 1784. Meanwhile, in the elections of that spring, a Boston candidate for state senator sensed prejudice so strong that he came down to the polls on the eve of voting and solemnly announced his resignation from the Order. Its blue ribbon had plainly become an invidious mark of caste, like the Sam Browne belt after the last war. For a long time the public watched this group of officers with narrow suspicion—fearing that they couldn't keep the Cincinnati down on the farm, after they'd gained the habit of power.

Another veterans' group, Saint Tammany, though purely local, was a makeweight against these aristocrats. Clubs honoring the legendary Indian sachem had started in Philadelphia before the war. They flourished in certain regiments of the Continental Line. On May Day, 1778, for instance, after the grim winter at Valley Forge, soldiers paraded with drum and fife around a Maypole, blossoms stuck in their tricorn hats, led by a sergeant in paint and feathers personating Saint Tammany. The meaning of these rites—seemingly a quaint blend of patriotism and phallicism—has never been elucidated. But several years after the Revolution, in New York City in 1789, an ex-soldier in the furniture business, William Mooney, revived the Tammany Society. Mooney later burnt his fingers by malfeasance in public office, and as founder did the Society no credit. Its real genius was John Pintard, a civic-minded liberal who wrote to a friend in 1790 that Tammany's "democratic principles will serve in some measure to correct the aristocracy of the city."

It was in fact the poor man's Cincinnati, recruited mainly from privates and non-coms, the artisans and mechanics and small shopkeepers of peace. It helped satisfy a hankering for uniform and regalia, drill and mummery, which demobilized armies often leave with their rank and file; its effect certainly proved more innocent than that of later nightshirts and brown shirts. Some politicians and other joiners belonged to both Cincinnati and Tammany, but to many the latter seemed a democractic runner-up. Its aims were social and benevolent, looking after the poor soldier and his widow and orphan. Like all veterans' clubs it was intensely patriotic. It urged the keeping of Revolutionary holidays, sympathized with the French Revolution, and in the nineties when war with England threatened, it mustered its members to work on the fortifications at Governor's Island. In espousing one hundred percent Americanism, Tammany in its youth so discriminated against the Irish Catholics—who later boarded and captured it—that its historian calls it a forerunner of the Know-Nothing Party.

Why did no national veterans' organization take shape? The Cincinnati had its successors in future hereditary officer's clubs like the Military Order of the Loyal Legion in 1865 or the Naval and Military Order of the Spanish-American War in 1899; but no all-inclusive body of Revolutionary veterans like the G.A.R. and the American Legion ever appeared. The reasons are probably simple. The number of privates and non-coms who saw unbroken service in the war from start to finish was comparatively small. Thanks to short-term and haphazard recruiting for the Continental Army, as well as to the aristocratic tone of the service in those days, officers of staff and line supplied the real backbone of continuity; through eight years they got to know each other far better than did average enlisted men. A private volunteering several times, possibly serving with different companies, built less comradeship with his messmates than did the bunkies of 1861–65 or the buddies of 1917–19. Furthermore, the war was waged in a scattered, regional way, by regiments drawn from states not yet fused into a union. Among those who fought in the Northern or Southern Department, on coast or frontier, the store of common memories was apt to be meager. Finally, certain caste marks, much stronger then than later, played their part. Officers preferred to be alone, did not think of widening their magic circle. To the rank and file, national and state reunions such as the Cincinnati enjoyed, in those days of difficult travel were luxuries that did not go with workbench, forge, and hoe. The great American excursion rate was still unknown.

13

FROM WAR HERO TO CRIMINAL: THE NEGATIVE PRIVILEGE OF THE VIETNAM VETERAN

PAUL CAMACHO

The individual depends on his environment in countless situations for response. In connection with the war, the veteran, specifically the young enlisted man returning from Vietnam, was expecting a particular response from the Home, a mutual positive reaction to the warrior ethos. Yet as Schuetz has pointed out (see Chapter 6, this volume), both the Homecomer and the Home have changed to such an extent that each has difficulty in recognizing the other. If his theories about the marginality of the World War II veteran were accurate then, their validity for the Vietnam veteran is equally justified.

Clearly, World War I was the "big one"—the total global conflict by which every American was affected. It was the last total war in an esentially nonnuclear world; the entire country was psychologically committed. With its conclusion the veteran returned to a resounding welcome, the ticker-tape parade. Change had occurred, yet in comparison to the 1960s it was minimal. America was still very warmly oriented to the rest of the world, although this was soon to change with the Cold War.

VIETNAM AND THE RELUCTANT WARRIORS

In contrast to this, Indochina was a totally different war: the Home was not psychologically committed, and, indeed, the military was frustrated, unable to attain a victory in a no-win guerrilla war. The soldier who fought the war also differed substantially from his predecessor in terms of exposure to the modern environment, greater educational opportunities, and generally greater worldliness. The national attitude during Vietnam contradicted the spirit that prevailed after Pearl Harbor.

But historically there has always been a general reluctance among Americans to participate in military adventures. Americans can be considered reluctant warriors in that it has usually taken some shocking catalytic event to galvanize the American public to support a national military response. Also, the decline in popularity of any war corresponded directly with the length of involvement and the casualty figures (Davis 1974 p. 98). In World War II of course the catalytic element was certainly there, and the fervor for unconditional surrender of the enemy was carefully nurtured through media manipulation, "designed to vilify the enemy while stressing the righteousness of the American cause" (Davis 1974, p. 99).

In Vietnam, however, a hateable ideological enemy was hard to define. Furthermore, after the Tet Offensive of 1968, the war effort began to deteriorate rapidly and Vietnam became a "Bad War."* American society, finding itself mired in a soured and difficult-to-justify war, began to engage in scapegoating tactics; who would bear the guilt for the unjust war? The peace dissidents had naturally attacked the administration for some time, and after Tet, support from the legislative branch began to wane. Consequently, the Congress absolved itself in the repeal of the Tonkin Gulf Resolution and the administration, by a number of means, primarily various kinds of media events,† shifted responsibility for the war to the military establishment, which was a socially acceptable target. However, the military was not about to accept responsibility; thus, a round of department-agency-institution buck-passing occurred, flowing naturally to the lower command levels. And rock bottom was of course the enlisted man, the grunt, now labeled veteran.

---

*In a general thesis the concepts of "Good War" and Bad War" became normative explanations for partially explaining many events that occurred in Vietnam. In short, during the "Good War" the war was still basically popular and troop morale was high, 1964–68. The "Bad War" is post Tet, 1968–73, when the homefront and warfront were in shambles.

†For example, after My Lai was called to the nation's attention, there was the covert operations battle. The Army ended up holding the bag in 1971 for engaging in surveillance on civilians ("persons of interest," *Life*, March 26, 1971), although as now is well known, other more dangerous cryptic agencies were heavily involved. For the most part,

THE VETERAN RETURNS

The Scapegoat

The Home society has and continues to malign the new veteran in an effort to exorcise collective guilt over the Vietnam debacle. Essentially, this is attempted by scapegoating and blaming the new veteran. "Brave and noble Warrior in World War II, the American soldier is seen as a villain after Vietnam (Peck 1974, p. 178). Yet the ramifications of such attempts are serious; they effect not only the new veteran but also the old veteran and the nation as well. The responsibility for "losing the war," once pinned on the military in general, was quickly shifted to the enlisted level; for being a poor soldier who among other things "killed women, children, and babies too," and took evil drugs, how could America possibly win the war? The military declared itself "cleansed"* when it administratively discharged the noncareer enlisted soldiers, who consequently carried the stigma of "pathological deviant" with them. The "deceased" ex-soldier is now a member of the veteran aggregate, an achieved prestige status group from which he cannot escape. This is reciprocal—that is, the veteran collective is held responsible for its scoundrels; it can deny him membership and his benefits, but he is still of them and them of him. The veteran aggregate, then, becomes infected and discreditable; the prestige symbol (being a veteran) then cannot only be contrasted but also rapidly converted to a stigma symbol (Goffman 1963, p. 43).

Again, a sign of destatusing is that the group undergoing the purge is not allowed to have a scoundrel among its kind (Sagarin 1971, p. 5). Discrimination and stigma then become a negative collective experience for veterans as a status group. From the other side of the spectrum, the older veterans definitely still enjoy a positive privilege; yet their access

---

during all this time civilian corporations managed and still manage to avoid most lines of fire, that is, corporations that were the big civilian contractors in South Vietnam, who made equipment that often was faulty—new trucks blowing rods after only 900–3000 miles of use, N-16 rifles that malfunctioned, generators that didn't, faulty ammunition, and so on.

*It is interesting that when things began to deteriorate in Vietnam, the military countered administration smears with the argument that it was their own (the administration's) fault, for forcing Moynihan and McNamara Project 100,000 "Fizz Kids" on them; they increased the delinquency rate (drug use, insubordination, and so on) in the military (see Trewhit 1971, p. 269 and Starr 1973, p. 186).

Also, in reference to My Lai, a senior ranking officer interviewed about the incident indicated that somehow Calley slipped through the OCS screen; he should never have been an officer. This implies that a real officer couldn't have done it, that only enlisted men would be capable of such acts (see *Newsweek* 1971a, p. 29).

to power, which former positive prestige enabled them to grasp, is gradually ebbing away. Given that the veterans of World War II are advancing in their age, they are becoming part of "the elderly," an "other minority" (Barron 1971). Thus the veterans' lobby as an institution is gradually weakening on one end and is stigmatized/disorganized at the other.

Despite the common ground as veterans, the new veterans are as yet a negatively privileged status group currently engaged in attempting to enhance their social status, mobility, and life chances. Yet there are those stigmatizing obstacles the Home society has erected in its attempt to exonerate itself by blaming the victims—that is, by the stigmatization or destatusing of the veteran.

For a time, the most far-reaching, negatively slanted image of the veteran was to be found in the nighttime weekly television police/detective serials. Some veterans refer to this portrayal as the "Kojak syndrome"; or, in other words, if there is a bizarre crime, check out all recently discharged Vietnam veterans. I tentatively assert that numerically there appears to have been at least one episode per month on some crime series or the like over the television seasons 1974–76 (Brewin 1975). The following *TV Guide* (1975) advertisement is typical:

> 5 6 8 9   CARIBE   CRIME
> Drama
>
> A psychotic Vietnam veteran is terrorizing
> hostages in a remote island hotel . . .

Certainly, the established veterans' organizations are aware of this. Walter Greaney, former National Commander of the Disabled American Veterans (DAV), made comment in the monthly *DAV* magazine, referring to propaganda prevalent during the war as undermining the self esteem of the soldier, and "now a similar campaign is being waged against the veteran" (Greaney 1975, p. 8).

Even the printed media illustrate this trend. On June 30, 1974, a *Newsweek* columnist covering a drug/crime article blandly noted that in the air smuggling business (for the most part marijuana, but other drugs as well) many of the pilots were unemployed Vietnam veterans (Newsweek 1975, p. 24). The statement presumes the reader's definition that most drug smugglers are Vietnam veterans. This begs the stereotype; it offers the proposition that an (albeit unfortunate) general pathologic state exists as a prevalent trait among veterans. Although emphasis is especially placed on ex-bush (front line) killers and rear echelon "druggies," the generalized "they" is nevertheless expressed; "they" have what Tom Wicker (1975) calls "The Vietnam Disease."

Drawing on *Penthouse* magazine and other sources, his article contained a particularly absurd claim that 500,000 Vietnam veterans have attempted suicide. It turned out that this statistic originated from, of all places, the White House Special Action Office.

The Student Misfit

As has been mentioned, some veterans, about 46.1 percent according to a National League of Cities report, appear to be utilizing the GI Bill. From the sample provided in the study, veterans constituted a large proportion of the student body—roughly 50 percent after World War II; this is contrasted with a less than 10 percent average for the same universities today (National League of Cities 1973, pp. 6, 23).

The following is not atypical of official insensitivity:

> At a community college north of Boston a young disabled veteran was to be honored with a flag presentation. Events of the day began with an administrative official ignorantly addressing the veteran, "Are you the wheelchair?" The trend was set, and the rest of the day's program followed suit.

At a larger Boston university, a totally blind veteran, well known to the administration, late for registration, was asked by a secretary in an admonishing tone of voice, "Why?, didn't you see the posters all over the campus?" Again from the Model Cities report, one veteran expressed the following: "Liberals hate us for killing and conservatives hate us for not killing enough" (p. 5).

Thus a *Newsweek* (1971b) article concerning the veteran on campus is fairly accurate. The veteran is apprehensive upon entering college. He generally keeps a low profile. "Unlike the veterans of World War II, today's veterans seem resolved to fade passively into the campus woodwork." This recalcitrance of the veteran to show himself is explained by Goffman (1963) as "controlling the information." If possible, the veteran on campus will remain low-keyed if his perceptability will allow it. The veteran can thereby manage the "tension information"; by not revealing himself as a member of a "discreditable" status group, he avoids being considered a "discredited" person. In short, he endeavors to pass.

Some professional research can also be misleading, particularly the psychological and sociological output. Such studies and articles by professionals (often well meaning) nevertheless suffer from exaggeration; they concentrate on a narrow clinical approach or operate in a context of limited information, which can amount to the same; they too end up blaming the victim. The society, in trying to assuage its guilt, stigmatizes the enlisted ex-soldiers; "they," the dirty workers, are thereby discredited as witnesses; hence, their testimony to the undesirable past of Vietnam becomes conveniently invalid (see Pollack, White, and Gold 1975, in which they label the combat group "killers").

In sum then, the new veteran has negative status compared to the socially "clean" veterans of previous wars. Had the Vietnam conflict been a "Good War" they would have more than likely been the recipient of positive prestige and benefits as the protectors of the values of the Home society. As it was, however, they fought a "Bad War" and consequently suffer various forms of stigmatization. They become the living negation of the tenets they were supposedly fighting to preserve. Subject to ridicule for fighting and insulted for not winning, they are generally regarded as just so much refuse in the hearts and minds of America.

THE VETERANS' QUASI-CASTE WELFARE SYSTEM

What Can the Vietnam Veteran Expect from the Same Government That Issued Him the Vietnam War?

As had been noted, the new veteran who has entered college has done so under difficult circumstances that can account for his reluctance to be identified. That some of the veterans in college could be identified was a response to two federal programs developed under HEW auspices, VETP and VCOI.* This HEW concern with the new veterans that began in June 1973 represents a direct threat to the major bureaucratic boundary systems as they were then constituted. Therefore, somewhat later, around June 1974, after suffering from a considerable amount of bad publicity and feeling its proprieties attacked by HEW interest in the new veteran, the VA countered VCOI with a strikingly similar and seemingly competing "Vet Reps on Campus Program." During the ensuing months, carefully worded HEW and VA letters circulating among program coordinators and less-subtle articles in the American Legion's monthly magazine (Matthews 1973) as well as in its *Legislative Bulletin* (1974) lend credence to the notion that there exists more than a little bureaucratic infighting over "control" of the new veteran.

Yet the question of control irrefutably goes beyond the new

---

*VETP: Veteran Educational Training Program, a hastily developed remedial program originally funded under OEO's Head Start. VCOI: Veteran Cost of Instruction; also known as Veteran Cost of Instruction Program, a more inclusive program with its own funding from the Office of Education.

veteran. The VA and officials of the traditional veterans' lobby realized that they were being assaulted from both ends; that is, they were being criticized for their indifferent and callous treatment of the new veteran. At the same time, there were growing calls for the dismantling of the VA hospital system with reorganization under a National Health Insurance Plan, for example, under HEW. To say the least, the veterans' lobby is hostile toward any program of national health insurance such as advocated by the Ralph Nader report or the VA. Legislation, which threatens the VA system, consequently effects the veterans' lobby and therefore upsets the status quo of the nation's third largest bureaucracy. Indeed, James M. Wagonseller, national commander of the American Legion, on an official visit to Massachusetts, vowed to keep the VA hospital-medical care system for veterans only. In an address entitled "Every Veteran Has a Stake in System," Wagonseller (1975, p. 1) stated:

> This matter involves veterans of all ages from the oldest World War I veteran to the youngest Vietnam Era veteran . . . every veteran has a stake in the maintenance of this great system . . . if it slips away from us, the veteran . . .[might find] that it is no longer available to him— except perhaps by waiting in a long line behind people who have not rendered any special service to America as the veteran has.

And the VA/veteran lobby system is not under fire by Nader alone. A Twentieth Century Task Force study on policies toward veterans "calls for integration of the nation's veterans' programs into the general social welfare system" (*Reveille* May 1977, p. 5). Obviously, what the Legion and other established veterans' organizations fear is the very real possibility of being reduced to a nonlobby, or, having achieved positive prestige, which in the past provided avenues to levers of power, being converted to a negative form whereby they will be ascribed to "other minority" status. In this case they would be another marginal collective in what Michael Harrington would refer to as the antisocialist welfare category. Thus as Goffman (1963, p. 45) notes, the "sign," in this case acquiring veteran status, can become vestigial, while the "informational function . . . remains constant or increases in importance." Veteran prestige, in and of itself, is declining; yet the transfer of control of the veterans' programs to HEW authority as opposed to a separate Veterans Administration means the veteran is even more vulnerable, being susceptible to the judgment of a "nonnative," and perhaps even "unwise" administrator. Dependent on an indifferent HEW bureaucracy, they would have considerably less access to levers of power and correspondingly less influence in the national political scene.

It appears then that the Vietnam veterans, despite their stigma and negative privilege, not only present a dilemma to the traditional veteran status groups for being "scoundrels" but also represent a point of contention among the big three bureaucracies (Defense, HEW, VA) as well. By way of the warrior ethos, the veteran aggregate is interwoven in the fabric of the nation. Yet all veterans are products of the Department of Defense and a charge of the Veterans Administration. The Department of Health, Education and Welfare then can be perceived as an interloper, a rival agency that threatens an old coalition— Defense, the VA, and the traditional veterans' lobby—by courting the new veteran with its VCOI program.

THE VIETNAM VETERAN AS TERTIUS

It is interesting to view the phenomenon from the standpoint of triadic models as developed by George Simmel (Wolf 1964) and refined by Theodore Caplow (Cuzzort 1969). As a status group, the traditional veterans' organizations were and still are quite at home with the VA; but the new veterans have felt rejected by this organization. Thus Vietnam veterans represent Simmel's "tertius," being wooed by the "carrot" of innovative HEW programs, however poorly run and pushed by the "stick" of resentment they feel toward the VA. Again, this is understandable, given the VA's inept handling of the new veterans' problems.*

Below this surface lie even more fundamental reasons that can perhaps explain the sensitive relations between the veteran and the VA. Generally speaking, many veterans link the VA with the traditional veterans' lobby as cofunctionaries maintaining a web of group affiliations with Defense and the massive defense machinery. Herein lies the dilemma: the older veteran was sold on anti'ism', and its defense correlary, the military-industrial complex. I maintain that the new veteran is anti-war, does not and will not support massive defense spending.

Thus the veterans, and in this framework HEW as well, represent an anti-defense expediture force. In short if granted their inheritance,

---

*Much criticism was leveled at the VA during the fall and winter 1973–74. The agency was accused of being insensitive to the veterans' problems even by traditional organizations such as the VFW, which was critical of medical reorganization (Massachusetts VFW, *News*, November 1973). Another area attacked was their inefficiency in distributing the veterans' educational benefit checks and reluctance to award these benefits to those with "grey area" discharges (bad conduct and undesirable), regardless of the fact that many of these were administrative "cop-outs" on the part of efficiency-report-conscious military officers. This topic is well covered by numerous newspaper articles to be found in the New York *Times*, *Washington Post*, and so on.

control of the veteran's lobby, and consequently access to the upper echelons of the VA, the new veteran would represent a stumbling block, even if only at the middle levels of power to the military and industrial elite who have perennially enjoyed a warm reception of national veterans' conventions. Thus the VA/veterans' lobby could represent tertius, playing the more powerful bureaucracies off against each other. This, of course, necessitates that the veterans, and particularly the Vietnam veterans, *must* achieve closure, *become* "veteran conscious." As Simmel notes, the third element must know, " . . . how to put the forces combined against him into action against one another." (Wolf 1964, p. 162)

Yet the new veterans must be wary of seemingly greener pastures advocated by HEW. One of the difficulties of course is that they would be one element in a larger nonveteran population. Also veterans may then be forced to deal with more than one agency. The difficulties with university cooperation in the administration of HEW's VCOI program is an example of the double-barrelled bureaucracy, the Scylla–Charybdis, through which the veteran must navigate. Hence, the opposite side of the coin is revealed. If the service functions to the veteran, now performed by an innovatively deficient Veterans' Administration, were absorbed by HEW, as the American Legion cautions against, then a powerful element in the veterans' camp is lost—namely, their own agency. This could only be interpreted as a crucial blow to the new veterans' access to even the middle levers of power.

Max Weber (Gerth and Mills 1972) felt the coming of bureaucracy would stimulate the social environment because it would be necessarily less parochial, relying on expertise of the individual rather than familial connections to acquire a position in the bureaucracy. Yet he was perceptive in that he realized that stagnation would be a product of overbureaucratization. In this country, especially since World War II, we now have reached a point where there exists a surfeit of expertise, where people are in many cases overqualified. In a traditional return, then, chances of employment may increasingly rest on other criteria such as family or business connections.

Those who offer different perspectives (or as McGarvey [1973, p. 149] would agree, intelligence that does not please) concerning how the system "ought" to function will be a threat to the status quo. Subsequently, those in power will seek opportunities to ignore or disenfranchise these people. The new veterans, being more antiwar and opposed to massive defense spending than veterans of other wars, by their very existence, appear as a threat to the inefficient yet extremely profitable military-industrial, subsidy-run, cost-overrun complex (Melman 1974, pp. 56–57). Thus it appears that one very plausible solution, for those whose interest lies in continuing the maintenance of such a system, is to disenfranchise the new veteran. Nullifying the power of the waning aging veterans' lobby now remedies the problem of having to deal with a hostile and presumably more consolidated and youthful lobby in the future.

Thus we arrive at a point where Max Weber's notion of negative privilege and Peter Blau's concept of quasi-caste merge and may be related to the veteran situation. In his article Blau (1974, p. 632) indicates that one of the dangers of the consolidation of social parameters, resources, and power is the resultant social distinction that "fortifies subgroup solidarities and inhibits the intergroup relations that are essential for macrosocial integration." As a negatively privileged heterogeneous collective, the new veteran suffers from status inequality in much the same way as do racial/ethnic (black, Hispanic) groups and other minorities such as the elderly. Specifically, they are victims of great status differentiation and are restricted in their mobility through their lack of intergroup contacts and intragroup fractionalism. Veterans then become related to these and other negatively privileged groups in that they occupy similar powerless positions. Their poverty, for example, is one salient parameter that works to restrict mobility and intensify competition at these lower levels of the stratification ladder.

As veteran solidarity wanes, subgroup homogeneity along old racial/ethnic lines is fortified; and horizontal competition, hence friction, among the poor is increased. The fact that veterans are antiwar and possibly estranged from the political system is irrelevant if they become another discreditable and powerless minority, members of a quasi caste.

Of course, it is recognized that a great deal more research must be done in this area, but one can close here with a few comments. To what extent this trend—destatusing of the veteran—is related to the increase in the minority population within the armed services is unknown. However, any increase of minority representation would necessarily be passed on to the veteran population. So here lies a possible explanation for the decline of the veterans' prestige, the latter's minority group character. Thus with an expanding welfare state, Vietnam veterans are beginning to represent a new change, a heterogeneous minority status group that qualifies with more homogeneous minorities as members of an ever-developing welfare quasi caste.

REFERENCES

American Legion. 1974. *Legislative Bulletin*. May 15.

Barron, Milton L. 1971. "The Aged as a Quasi-Minority Group." In *The Other Minorities*, ed. E. Sagarin. Waltham, Mass.: Ginn.

Blau, Peter. 1974. "Parameters of Social Structure." *American Sociological Review* 39, no. 5 (October).

Brewin, R. 1975." TV's Newest Villain: The Vietnam Veteran." *TV Guide*, July 26, pp. 4–8.

Cuzzort, Ray P. 1969. "How to Lose at Games: The Coalition Theories of Theodore Caplow." In *Humanity and Modern Sociological Thought*. New York: Holt, Rinehart and Winston.

Davis, Vernon. 1974. "Levee en Masse, C'est Fini: The Deterioration of Popular Willingness to Serve." In *New Civil-Military Relations*, ed. J. P. Lovel and P. S. Kronenberg. New Brunswick, N.J.: Transaction Books.

Gerth, Hans, and C. Wright Mills. 1972. *From Max Weber*. New York: Oxford University Press.

Goffman, Erving. 1963. *Stigma*. Englewood Cliffs, N.J.: Prentice-Hall.

Greaney, Walter. 1975. "Commander's Comments: Outlook for 1975." *DAV Magazine*, January.

Matthews, Joe. 1973. "The Nader Report on Vietnam Veterans—A Review." *Legion* (American Legion Magazine), June.

McGarvey, P. T. 1973. *C.I.A.: The Myth and the Madness*. Baltimore, Md.: Penguin Books.

Melman, Seymour. 1974. *The Permanent War Economy*. New York: Simon and Schuster.

National League of Cities–U.S. Conference of Mayors. 1973. Final Report: *Findings and Recommendations*, Special Veterans' Opportunity Committee, Veterans' Educational and Training Service, September 13.

Newsweek. 1975. "Drugs: Sky High." June 30.

Newsweek. 1971a. "The Calley Verdict: Who Else Is Guilty?" April 12.

Newsweek. 1971b. "A Long Way from Vietnam." October 4.

Peck, Martin S. 1974. "The Role of the Military in American Society vis-a-vis Drug Abuse: Scapegoat, National Laboratory and Potential Change Agent." In *New Civil-Military Relations*, ed. J. P. Lovel and P. S. Kronenberg. New Brunswick, N.J.: Transaction Books.

Pollack, John; D. White; and F. Gold. 1975. "When Soldiers Return: Combat and Political Alienation among White Vietnam Veterans." In *New Directions in Political Socialization*, ed. D. Schwartz and S. K. Schwartz. New York: The Free Press.

Reveille. 1977. A VETS Bulletin/National League of Cities. May.

Sagarin, Edward. 1971. "From the Ethnic Minorities to the Other Minorities." In *The Other Minorities*, ed. E. Sagarin. Waltham, Mass.: Ginn.

Starr, P. 1973. *The Discarded Army*. New York: Charterhouse.

Trewhit, H. L. 1971. *McNamara: His Ordeal in the Pentagon*. New York: Harper & Row.

TV Guide. 1975. May 12.

Wagonseller, John A. 1975. Massachusetts *Legionaire* 3 (April).

Wicker, Tom. 1975. "The Vietnam Disease." New York *Times*, May 27.

Wolf, Kurt H., ed. 1964. *The Sociology of George Simmel*. New York: Macmillan.

14

THE HOOKED SERVICEMAN: DRUG USE IN AND AFTER VIETNAM

M. DUNCAN STANTON

Illegal drug abuse by military personnel in Vietnam has been a cause célebre for at least the past 11 years. The subject has been surrounded by considerable rhetoric, conjecture, and emotion issuing from people of differing political and philosophical persuasions. This chapter is an attempt to briefly summarize and put in perspective some of the major findings, issues, and results of the Vietnam drug controversy. Of the more than one dozen research surveys on Vietnam drug use that have been undertaken, coverage will primarily be given to those that are both methodologically most sound and that provide findings that are most generalizable. Clinical papers and anecdotal accounts will generally not be cited and more emphasis will be given to data for personnel in the Army, which was the seat of the problem and within which more research was performed. In short, highlights will be presented and an attempt will be made to draw meaning from the whole Vietnam drug experience.

THE MARIJUANA YEARS

In the mid- and late 1960s reports started to drift back to the

United States that servicemen in Vietnam were using marijuana. Since the majority of these reports originated from individuals who either did not have the status or the credibility to engender public confidence, most of them were afforded little attention. Nor was public caution in this area unwarranted, since it was indeed true that people who used drugs more heavily tended to overestimate the incidence of use in Vietnam, and there was a high correlation between an individual's usage levels and his estimations of others' use (Stanton 1972). By the fall of 1970, however, congressional subcommittees were startling the nation with newly uncovered reports that a significant and increasing number of our soldiers in Vietnam were using marijuana with some regularity, a good percentage of them wanted marijuana legalized, and at least a quarter of them intended to use it when they returned to the States. All this resulted in a massive campaign by the military in Vietnam to suppress drugs, particularly marijuana, along with the implementation of a number of in-country rehabilitation and education programs.

What, in fact, was the situation really like? Marijuana was an indigenous plant to Southeast Asia and had been around for a long time. It was easily grown and differed from its Western counterparts primarily in its potency—its effects approached those of some of the major hallucinogens. Nonetheless, despite its availability, its use by U.S. troops was not extensive in the early 1960s. It was not until later in the decade that it began to gain favor, and this appears to be in direct relation to the development of similar practices among same-age youth in the United States.

To this point, Table 14.1 is an attempt to chart the progression of several facets of Vietnam drug use across six studies that sampled at various points in time. These studies were selected primarily because they surveyed broad cross-sections of enlisted personnel stationed in Vietnam and also because they allow us to make fairly accurate estimates as to the dates their respondents entered and (more accurately) left Vietnam. An underlying assumption is that since most soldiers served a 12-month Vietnam tour, those who were leaving, for example, in mid-1968 had entered approximately one year earlier, that is, mid-1967; the study by Frenkel, Morgan, and Greden (1977) is backdated six months, as soldiers were surveyed in-country rather than at departure, and their average elapsed tour at that point was six months. As with all such studies, the data are retrospective and except for the late 1969 study by Stanton (1972) in which incoming personnel were sampled, all data are derived from samples of people either in the country or leaving together at approximately the same time. Inspection of the table reveals that from the fall of 1966 to the fall of 1970 there

TABLE 14.1: Trends among Army Enlisted Personnel in Pre-Vietnam and in-Vietnam Use of Marijuana and Heroin/Morphine[a]

(Estimated date of Vietnam entry)

	Fall 1966[b] N = 584	Mid 1967[c] N = 223	Mid 1968[c] N = 234	Late 1968[d] N = 995	Late 1969[d] N ≈ 995	Spring 1970[e] N = 1011	Fall 1970[f] N = 451	Early 1972[g] N = 1007
Marijuana								
Ever used *before* Vietnam	12	9	27	31	35	46	41	—
First used in Vietnam	19	12	—	22	—	18	28	—
Ever used *in* Vietnam	29	—	—	50	—	59	69	—
Heroin/Morphine								
Ever used *before* Vietnam	—	—	—	3	4	6	3	9
First used in Vietnam	—	—	—	0	—	17	31	5
Ever used *in* Vietnam	—	—	—	2	—	23	34[h]	14

[a] All figures are expressed in rounded percentages for each group surveyed. Dashes indicate data not available or, with respondents who were entering Vietnam, in-country use was obviously not determined. Estimated dates of entry were established retroactively, i.e., back-dated one year from out-processing from Vietnam, except for the 1972 study (Frenkel, Morgan, & Greden, 1977) which was back-dated 6 months.
[b] Roffman and Sapol (1970).
[c] Casper et al. (1968).
[d] Stanton (1972).
[e] Nelson and Panzarella (1971).
[f] Robins (1974), Robins et al. (1975).
[g] Frenkel et al. (1977).
[h] Twenty to 21 percent of the 451 respondents were considered addicted to narcotics at some time during their tour.

was a relatively steady increase in the number of Army enlisted personnel who had used marijuana prior to entering Vietnam. (The most notable exceptions are the data from mid-1967 by Casper, Janeck, and Martinelli [1968], but the methodology of this study—personal interviews by uniformed strangers as respondents were about to leave the country—was the sort that might depress admissions of drug use; this is especially true since, at that time, respondents were likely to fear that identifying themselves as drug users might delay their departure.) In sum, the increase in pre-Vietnam use from year to year, as one might expect, corresponds closely with the increases noted among civilian youth for the same period. This point has been underscored by Robbins and associates in a comparison of their Vietnam returnees with a national sample of age-comparable males surveyed by Johnston (Robins, Helzer, and Davis 1975; Johnston 1973), and in their own sample of nonveterans (Robins, Hesselbrock, Wish, and Helzer 1978).

Further inspection of Table 14.1 reveals that the percent of people who initiated marijuana use for the first time in Vietnam fluctuated somewhat over this period, but, again with the exception of Casper et al. [1968], hovered around 20 to 25 percent. In addition, while scrutiny of the third row in the table suggests a fairly constant increase overall in Vietnam drug use, closer inspection seems to indicate that this was due more to the influx of a greater number of pre-Vietnam users than to an increase in the number of people who initiated use in Vietnam. In other words, the trend for more people to initiate marijuana use in Vietnam pales in comparison with the increasing number of prior users who were entering the country.

It should be noted that Table 14.1 does not show the *extent* to which soldiers were using marijuana. Suffice it to say that from 1967 to 1971 the proportion of enlisted men who used it "heavily" (20 or more times) in Vietnam increased from 7 to 34 percent. However, the proportion of "habitual" users (200+ times) *entering* Vietnam remained at 7 to 8 percent for the years 1968 through 1970, and the proportion of habitual users *in* Vietnam also stabilized at 17 to 18 percent between 1969 and 1971 (Nelson and Panzarella 1971; Roffman and Sapol 1970). Thus, about 9 to 10 percent of the lower-grade enlisted men first *became* habitual users, that is, smoked marijuana at least every other day, during this period.

Whereas we are dealing here primarily with marijuana, it should be noted that a certain amount of amphetamine and barbiturate abuse also existed at that time. In addition, the smoking of opium joints or "O.J.s"—marijuana cigarettes dipped in opium—was not uncommon.

What was being done about this "problem"? For the most part, not a great deal in the earlier years. It was not until 1967 that the Army included a drug education component in its brief preparatory course for troops departing for overseas assignments (Holloway 1974). However, when Roffman and Sapol obtained credible survey data on drug use in the same year, their findings were pretty much ignored and, they claimed, suppressed (Anderson 1970). To be sure, the Army's Criminal Investigation Division (CID) spent a lot of time fighting drugs; in the Central Coast area where the author was stationed during late 1969, 75 percent of the CID's "major" cases were for marijuana offenses— primarily possession. From a treatment standpoint, several clinical reports appeared in the USARV *Medical Bulletin* in 1968, but it was 1969 before a few bona-fide treatment programs appeared—most notably within the Fourth Infantry Division (which even had an amnesty provision) and the Eighth Field Hospital. Ironically, by the time publicity mounted over marijuana in late 1970, the heroin epidemic had been in full swing for at least six months.

HEROES AND HEROIN

The heroin days began in early 1970 when 90 to 96 percent pure heroin became available on a countrywide basis. Although there had been some Thai "red rock" heroin available before then, it was far from widespread and of much less purity. The new heroin derived from opium poppies grown in the "golden triangle" of Thailand, Burma, and Laos, which is the source of approximately 70 percent of the world's illicit supply of opium. This heroin was 15 to 30 times as pure as that which retails in the United States and was so cheap that a respectable "habit" could be maintained for $8 to $10 a day—a fraction of stateside rates. In addition, it was less easily detected, easier to transport, gave a better "high," and unlike marijuana, which slows down the perception of time, it was reported to speed it up. Self-administration was usually through smoking cigarettes laced with it or "snorting" it through the nostrils. Only about 18 percent of the users injected it at all, and for many, this was only an occasional practice (Robins 1974). However, the longer that men used heroin during their tour, the more likely they were to resort to injection (Robins, Helzer, and Davis 1975; Robins 1974).

Unlike marijuana, with which so many soldiers had had pre-Vietnam experience, heroin use, especially before 1971, was clearly a Vietnam phenomenon. Based on the years for which data are available, we see from Table 14.1 that pre-Vietnam heroin use was uncommon. Comparison of the last four studies corroborates other reports of the sudden upturn of heroin use between 1969 and 1971, followed by a tapering off in late 1971 and early 1972. Of particular note is the fact that a fifth of the Army enlisted men who served in Vietnam from approximately the fall of 1970 to September 1971 were addicted to narcotics at some time during their tour (Robins, Helzer, and Davis 1975; Robins 1974). This is not to say that marijuana, O.J.s, amphetamines, and barbiturates became passé with the heroin increase, but that they just didn't receive the publicity and perhaps became less controversial in the shadow of heroin. Another factor contributing to the obscurity of at least the latter two drugs was that they were used almost exclusively by men who also used narcotics, and thus they were upstaged (Robins 1974).

What were the causes of this epidemic? Zinberg (1972) claimed that the military crackdown on marijuana forced many soldiers to resort to heroin. McCoy (1972) disputes this since military leaders had been cracking down on marijuana for several years prior to the heroin influx, and Robins (1974) obtained data documenting that marijuana was easily obtainable throughout the heroin years. McCoy also downplays the importance of GI boredom, disenchantment with the war, and feelings of victimization in producing the heroin epidemic. He claims the major factor was profit—$88 million worth—for a number of powerful South Vietnamese officials. He also claims the process was expedited by the Cambodian invasion of 1970, which opened up previously unavailable smuggling routes. His case is a strong one, thoroughly researched and extensively documented; it should not be dismissed lightly. Certainly *somebody* had to be making money off all that "stuff."

ACTIONS AND REACTIONS

What steps were taken by the military in Vietnam to stem the tide of drug abuse and cope with its problems? Some of the earlier efforts undertaken during the marijuana years have already been mentioned. For a good while the military at the Pentagon level had either denied or sidestepped the drug issue, claiming that it did not exist or existed only among a few select soldiers who had been heavy users prior to military service. With mounting publicity the military still tended to protect its turf and resisted an "all is forgiven" approach that it feared might undermine discipline. Traditionally, drug offenders had been punished and/or discharged, and the military did not want the responsibility of long-term rehabilitation. This conflicted with the congressional view that rather than turning drug addicts loose on the streets, the military held the responsibility to eliminate addiction in those who developed it under military auspices. Consequently, in October 1970 the Defense Department issued a policy on drug abuse that emphasized education, preservice screening of addicts, and encouraged (but did not require) amnesty. True, the new policy was an advance, but Wyant (1971) claims it was generally viewed in Congress as merely a concession that had no uniformity and no teeth.

Whereas the Army had adopted a countrywide voluntary treatment program in Vietnam in October 1969, it was in December 1970 that an official regulation entitled "Drug Abuse Prevention and Control" was published and promulgated. (A similar policy was later embraced by the Navy and the Air Force; the Marines never did capitulate.) This new amnesty policy places responsibility on individual commanders for its implementation and allowed that soldiers could not be punished for merely admitting the use of drugs. The first six months of 1971 saw many such programs emerge and dissolve. In the author's opinion, these programs were, for the most part, ineffectual, partly because of the inexperience of the people designated to carry them out. There was also a good deal of distrust in them since confidentiality—a keystone of such endeavors (Stanton 1973)—was not always maintained with the necessary consistency. Holloway (1974) and Zinberg (1972) have outlined some of the shortcomings of these programs, while their major contribution, aside from the assistance they may have rendered some drug users who requested it, was toward the decriminalization of drug use.

From the public's view, spring of 1971 was a time of realization. In April Congressmen Morgan F. Murphy, Jr., and Robert H. Steele of the House Foreign Affairs Committee returned from Vietnam and proclaimed that 10 to 15 percent (that is, 30,000 to 45,000) of the troops in Vietnam were addicted to heroin. Soon three congressional committees were investigating drug use in the military (whereas none were investigating civilian use). People were learning that more soldiers were being evacuated from Vietnam for drug addiction than for war wounds, and that 16,000 servicemen had been punitively or administratively discharged in the two previous years for drug abuse; 11,000 of these were ineligible for VA treatment. In June, President Nixon declared his "war against drug abuse" and within a few days what the soldiers facetiously termed "Operation Golden Flow" commenced at the departure locations of Long Binh, Cam Ranh Bay, and Da Nang. Soon nine drug rehabilitation centers were established. Golden Flow utilized the FRAT (Free Radical Assay Technique) to screen for opiate use through urinalysis. Soldiers with "dirty" urines were diverted into a quarantine area at out-processing centers where physical examinations, drug history, and other clinical observations were obtained (Baker 1972). This usually resulted in at least a week's delay of the individual's departure date. Many drug users had ceased drug use five or more days before leaving the country and were not picked up in the screen so that 5.5 percent eventually came out drug positive. In mid-autumn the Army began conducting unannounced urine tests in randomly selected military units; approximately 5 percent of personnel screened in this manner were opiate positive, but the variability was great among units, ranging from 1 to 20 percent. By November, departure screenings were at 3 percent positive and down to 1.5 percent by May 1972 (Peck 1973). The Army felt that this screening procedure, combined with its other drug programs, had served to effectively reverse a heroin epidemic, although it was granted that a rate of even 1.5 percent was not to be taken lightly; the Army's assertion is confirmed by the Frenkel et al. data (1977) in that only 5 percent of the soldiers reported first use of heroin in Vietnam, use before Vietnam had risen to 9 percent, and the number of reported users *in* Vietnam had dropped to 14 percent by early to mid-1972. The screening program has been challenged by a number of critics as an invasion of privacy, although it was somewhat surprising that 90 percent of Robin's (1974) respondents approved of the departure screenings and 74 percent approved of the surprise sweeps made within the various units; 96 percent were also against legalizing narcotics or reducing penalties for their use (Robins, Helzer, Hesselbruck and Wish 1978).

When a drug user returns from Vietnam, what then? Let us take a look at Army efforts to deal with this problem. Since mid-1971, the Army has initiated approximately 35 Drug and Alcohol Programs in stateside installations. In 1972 the Army set guidelines for its Alcohol and Drug Abuse Programs that were oriented toward both prevention and rehabilitation. The latter, of course, was of greater importance to the returning Vietnam drug user. These guidelines specified that the drug user must have had eight consecutive weeks of negative urine tests and rehabilitative efforts were extended to all drug abusers for a period from 30 to 60 days. Those who responded well would be continued in a long-term rehabilitation program that was integrated with their military duties, while those who did not would be referred to the Veterans Administration for rehabilitation in a civilian setting; they would also receive honorable discharges. The Army's goal was to return soldiers to full effective duty or provide continuity of care for those to be separated. An important part of the philosophy was that, while medical and psychological elements were important, drug abuse was viewed primarily as a *social* problem to be dealt with in the unit rather than in the hospital or stockade.

AFTER DISCHARGE

What do we know about drug use and its effects on the Vietnam veteran after his discharge from military service? The discussion here will deal with drug-related issues rather than overall post-Vietnam adjustment, and most attention will be directed toward veterans who actually served in Vietnam as opposed to those in the VA's more inclusive category of Vietnam-era veterans.

The most extensive study of the drug experiences of Vietnam returnees has been done by Lee Robins and associates at Washington University in St. Louis in which veterans were first interviewed eight to 12 months after their departure from Vietnam (Robins, Helzer, and Davis 1975; Robins 1974) and then again at a point approximately three years after their Vietnam tour (Robins and Helzer 1975; Robins, Helzer, Hesselbrock, and Wish 1978; Robins, Hesselbrock, Wish, and Helzer 1978). Some of the findings were: (1) As many pre-Vietnam heavy narcotic users ceased narcotics use in the first year after Vietnam as did heavy narcotic users who started in Vietnam; (2) the number who used narcotics in the first year after returning was nearly identical to the number who reported using narcotics (mostly codeine) before Vietnam, but the shift for post-Vietnam use was toward "harder" narcotics, for example, codeine before, heroin after; (3) of those who injected heroin for the first time in Vietnam, half never used narcotics again after Vietnam and only 16 percent became readdicted; (4) two-thirds of the "narcotic virgins" (no use before Vietnam, addiction in Vietnam) had not used narcotics during the first year after their return; (5) whereas half of all narcotic users *in* Vietnam became addicted, only 12 percent of users became addicted during the post-Vietnam period; (6) over 90 percent of the men who were addicted in Vietnam did not become addicted during the subsequent three years; (7) many of the 10 percent of Vietnam addicts who became readdicted during the follow-up period did so only for brief periods; (8) half of the Vietnam addicts used heroin at some point during the three-year follow-up period, but not to the extent of becoming readdicted; and (9) overall, Vietnam experience led to increased drug use (compared to nonveterans) over the three years, but this difference was not as great as had been publicly feared.

A number of findings have emerged from other investigations of returnees who were addicted in Vietnam. In general, these veterans seem to have a more favorable prognosis (Robins 1974; Nace and Meyers 1974), less MMPI (Minnesota Multiphasic Personality Inventory) pathology (Hampton and Vogel 1973), and lower arrest rates (Mintz and O'Brien 1979) than comparable nonveteran addicts. They also tend to attribute their drug use to their military service more than do veterans who did not serve in Vietnam, and a majority of them used drugs particularly as a relief from the fear and tensions of war (Mintz and O'Brien 1979). Whether they returned to urban or rural settings may also be important, as Nace, O'Brien, Mintz, Ream and Meyers (1978) found in a 28 month follow-up of heavy narcotics users in Vietnam, that 76% had not become readdicted; these veterans lived in a large metropolitan area and their abstinence rate is somewhat lower than the 90% reported by Robins and associates (above) for a broader cross-section of veterans addicted in Vietnam.

One of the most unfortunate and occasionally tragic effects of the Vietnam drug situation was that some men were refused employment simply because they had served in Vietnam, that is, employers considered this *prima facie* evidence of drug addiction. Further, those who were awarded discharges under other-than-honorable conditions because of their drug involvement often found it impossible to get jobs; they were also denied veterans' benefits and VA medical treatment. Although the Department of Defense reversed itself on this in 1971 and allowed these individuals to apply for review of their discharges, this process is not a particularly swift one and damage had already been done in some cases.

What about treatment? In 1970 and early 1971 the Department of Defense had left it up to the individual as to whether he wished to undergo VA treatment for his drug addiction. This did not seem to work, as practically none of the servicemen who were either recently or about to be discharged cared to take advantage of VA facilities. When the war on drugs commenced, the VA was put under considerable political pressure to mount a massive effort to deal with the drug problems of servicemen approaching or completing discharge. Approximately 70 to 75 programs were established across the country, and initially many of them had few if any "patients." In the last half of 1971 and through early 1972, the VA decreed that any form of drug abuse was to be considered a medical emergency. This meant that no VA hospital could refuse hospitalization to a veteran with a drug problem whether or not the hospital itself had a bona-fide "drug program." By mid-1975 there were 53 VA Drug Dependence Treatment Programs in existence, most of which included such modes as the therapeutic community; Vietnam returnees composed about 43 percent of the 8,500 to 9,000 veterans enrolled at that time. On a nationwide basis about one-half of the patients were on methadone maintenance, although the percentage was higher for programs located in large cities. More recently, however, Nace et al. (1978) have data indicating that a significant percentage of veterans are in need of treatment for alcohol or depression problems, but have not sought treatment.

DISCUSSION AND CONCLUSIONS

What conclusions can we draw as to the meaning and consequences of the Vietnam drug experience? As mentioned earlier, two major contributing factors were the relaxation of taboos against drug abuse in the United States plus the availability of illicit drugs at low cost in Vietnam itself. The availability argument begs the question in some ways, however, since these substances would not have been used, no matter how available, unless soldiers felt a need for them. What we had was a form of massive self-medication utilizing substances that, in addition, provided thrills and were amenable to a kind of small-group communion experience. Certainly factors such as curiosity, rebellion, escape, and antifatigue were also important, along with deterioration in morale/discipline concomitant with mounting disenchantment with the war. However, whereas these drugs were used as coping devices (Bey and Zecchinelli 1970), it should be remembered that another drug, alcohol, has a long history of use as a combat-zone coping device. In theaters of war one encounters a certain subtle encouragement to indulge in hedonistic practices and to drink heavily, particularly in the rear areas away from the actual combat situation—which is where most illicit drug use also occurred in Vietnam. Where the Vietnam troops went "wrong" was to supplement or supplant the medication normally prescribed by society and the military by daring to try drugs other than spirituous. It is pretty much a value judgment whether marijuana and heroin are "worse" than alcohol, and the fact that many men may have actually been helped in their attempts to cope with a tremendously stressful situation through the use of the latter two drugs is often overlooked (Stanton 1972; Bey and Zecchinelli 1970; Colbach and Parrish 1970). Thus, in the context of Vietnam, it seems fair to say that in many cases today's drug abuser is yesterday's alcoholic.

The question as to whether drug use affected performance of military duties in Vietnam is one not easily answered. After devoting considerable thought to this issue and speaking to numerous mental health professionals who had served in Vietnam, Colbach and Parrish (1970) concluded that marijuana had not seriously affected the military mission and that there should have been no sense of urgency about eliminating it. Concerning heroin, my own conclusion, drawn from the numerous reports on the subject plus similar discussions over the past eight to nine years with interested and experienced parties, is that Colbach and Parrish's statement holds for this drug, too, especially as it pertains to job performance; except for individuals who felt it helped them perform better under combat conditions, it was used primarily in rear areas. To further elaborate, a study by Ingraham (1974) seems pertinent. From extensive interviews of heroin-addicted Vietnam returnees, he concluded that their performance was not seriously affected, they did not see themselves as "junkies" or "addicts," combat stress was not a major factor for most in contributing to use, they did not consider themselves members of the counterculture, and almost all of them were able to maintain their heroin habits from their army pay without recourse to theft.

Clearly, the Vietnam drug situation became a political football. It was seen as another reason why we should not have been in Vietnam. Scapegoating of the military was fanned by the press and abetted by antiwar forces on the political left and by those on the right who expressed concern for the morale and strength of the armed forces. The military also served as a focal point for scapegoating over the issue of drugs in the larger society (Peck 1973). The Vietnam situation made people face some stark realities about drug use and aroused emotion to the point that a good deal of repressive drug legislation was passed. However, as Rohrbaugh, Eads, and Press (1974) have stated, it appears that the perceived public health menace embodied in the returning serviceman "addict" may, in some respects, have been overexaggerated.

On the other hand, it is possible to discern some positive effects of this ill-wind, especially in the field of drug abuse treatment and research. The military drug abuse treatment model, established at the behest of the president's Special Action Office for Drug Abuse Prevention, became a testing ground for drug programs in the nation as a whole, partly because suitable treatment methods had not been developed up to that time. Although it may have been to a great extent inaugurated in response to political pressure, the Defense Department's move to alter discharge policy for drug use, combined with its recommendations for treatment for identified users, did serve to decriminalize drug use. The Vietnam experience dispelled many myths and misconceptions about, for example, heroin addiction, as it was found that physiological addiction was neither as persistant nor as untreatable as had previously been believed (Robins and Helzer 1975; Robins, Helzer, Hesselbrock, and Wish 1978; Robins, Hesselbrock, Wish, and Helzer 1978). For example, not all the soldiers who were taking up to 4,000 or 5,000 milligrams of heroin per day for a month or more showed severe withdrawal, thus refuting the position commonly held up to that time that 240 milligrams was the nonwithdrawal maximum (Ream 1974). Consequently, a case was made for the importance of the environment in addition and also for the importance of nonphysiological factors (for example, economic, family) in the maintenance of addiction. In fact, a common reason for becoming "clean" before exit from Vietnam was to avoid the stigma, humiliation and hassle from family and friends of returning home a "junkie" (McGlothlin, 1975; Stanton,

1977). Such findings helped to reduce cynicism and instill hope for treatment success in a field which had been choking for years on 90% failure rates.

The long-term negative effects of Vietnam drug abuse are not so well documented. Certainly those who were refused jobs because of actual or fancied Vietnam drug habits suffered harm. Although treatment has been provided for veterans who use drugs heavily, the danger that those who were mistreated subsequent to discharge and have thus become estranged, alienated, second-class citizens, may be a very real one. To the author's knowledge, clear determinations have not been made as to the relative contribution of Vietnam drug use versus other aspects of the war in generating negative aftereffects.

REFERENCES

Anderson, J. 1970. "GI Drug Abuse Hushed Up." Washington *Post*, August 9.

Baker, S. L. 1972. "U.S. Army Heroin Abuse Identification Program in Vietnam: Implications for a Methadone Program." *American Journal of Public Health* 62: 857-60.

Bey, D. R., and V. A. Zecchinelli. 1970. "Marijuana as a Coping Device in Vietnam." *USARV Medical Bulletin* (USARV Pamphlet 40) 22: 21-28.

Casper, E.; J. Janecek; and H. Martinelli. 1968. "Marijuana in Vietnam." *USARV Medical Bulletin* (USARV Pamphlet 40) 11: 60-72.

Colbach, E., and M. D. Parrish. 1970. "Army Mental Health Activities in Vietnam: 1965-1970." *Bulletin of the Menninger Clinic* 34: 333-43.

Frenkel, S. I.; D. W. Morgan; and J. F. Greden. 1977. "Heroin Use Among Soldiers in the United States and Vietnam: A Comparison in Retrospect." *International Journal of the Addictions* 12: 143-54.

Hampton, P. T., and D. B. Vogel. 1973. "Personality Characteristics of Servicemen Returned from Vietnam Identified as Heroin Abusers." *American Journal of Psychiatry* 130: 1031-32.

Holloway, H. C. 1974. "Epidemiology of Heroin Dependency among Soldiers in Vietnam." *Military Medicine* 139: 108-13.

Ingraham, L. H. 1974. "The Nam and the World: A Description of Heroin Use by U.S. Army Enlisted Men Serving in the Republic of South Vietnam." *Psychiatry* 37: 114-28.

Johnston, L. 1973. *Drugs and American Youth.* Ann Arbor: Institute for Social Research, University of Michigan.

McCoy, A. W. 1972. *The Politics of Heroin in Southeast Asia.* New York: Harper & Row.

Mintz, J. and C. P. O'Brien. 1979. "The Impact of Vietnam Service on Heroin Addicted Veterans." *American Journal of Drug and Alcohol Abuse* 6: 39-52.

Nace, E. P., and A. L. Meyers. 1974. "The Prognosis for Addicted Vietnam Returnees: A Comparison with Civilian Addicts." *Comprehensive Psychiatry* 15: 49-56.

Nelson, K. E., and J. Panzarella. 1971. *Preliminary Findings—Prevalence of Drug Use,*

Enlisted Vietnam Returnees Processing for ETS Separation, Oakland Overseas Processing Center. Report for Department of the Army (Department of Neuropsychiatry, Letterman General Hospital, Presidio, San Francisco), March.

Peck, M. S. 1973. "The Role of the Military in American Society Vis-a-vis Drug Abuse: Scapegoat, National Laboratory and Potential Change Agent." In *The New Civil-Military Relations: Agonies of Adjustment to Post Vietnam Realities*, ed. by J. P. Lovel and P. Kronenberg. New Brunswick, N.J.: Transaction Books.

Ream, N. W. 1974. "Lessons from Vietnam: An Overview of Research." Paper presented at the North American Congress on Alcohol and Drug Problems, San Francisco, December.

Robins, L. N. 1974. *The Vietnam Drug User Returns*. Special Action Office Monograph, Series A, no. 2. Washington, D.C.: U.S. Government Printing Office, 1974.

Robins, L. N., and J. E. Helzer, 1975. "Drug Abuse among Vietnam Veterans— Three Years Later." *Medical World News*, October 27, pp. 44-49.

Robins, L. N.; J. E. Helzer; and D. H. Davis. 1975. "Narcotic Use in Southeast Asia and Afterward." *Archives of General Psychiatry* 32: 955-61.

Robins, L. N.; J. E. Helzer; M. Hesselbrock; and E. Wish. 1978. "Vietnam Veterans Three Years after Vietnam: How Our Study Changed Our View of Heroin." In *Yearbook of Substance Abuse*, ed. L. Brill and C. Winick. New York: Human Sciences Press.

Robins, L. N.; M. Hesselbrock; E. Wish; and J. E. Helzer. 1978. "Polydrug and Alcohol Use by Veterans and Nonveterans." In *A Multicultural View of Drug Abuse: The Selected Proceedings of the National Drug Abuse Conference—1977*, ed. D. Smith, S. Anderson, M. Buxton, T. Chung, N. Gottlieb, and W. Harvey. Cambridge, Mass.: Schenkman.

Roffman, R. A. and E. Sapol. 1970. "Marijuana in Vietnam: A Survey among Army Enlisted Men in the Two Southern Corps." *International Journal of the Addictions* 5: 1-42.

Rohrbaugh, M.; G. Eads; and S. Press. 1974. "Effects of the Vietnam Experience on Subsequent Drug Use among Servicemen." *International Journal of the Addictions* 9: 25-40.

Stanton, M. D. 1977. "Family Treatment of the Drug Addicted Veteran." In *Changing Families in a Changing Military System*, ed. E. J. Hunter. San Diego, California: Naval Health Research Center.

———. 1973. "The Soldier." In *Outsiders USA*, ed. D. Spiegel and P. Keith-Spiegel. San Francisco: Rinehart.

———. 1972. "Drug Use in Vietnam." *Archives of General Psychiatry* 26: 270-86.

Wyant, W. K. 1971. "Coming Home with a Habit. *The Nation*, July 5.

Zinberg, N. E. 1972a. "Heroin Use in Vietnam and the United States." *Archives of General Psychiatry* 26: 486-88.

———. 1972b. Rehabilitation of Heroin Users in Vietnam." *Contemporary Drug Problems*: 263-94.

15

FEDERAL MENTAL HEALTH PROGRAMS FOR THE VIETNAM VETERAN

FORD H. KURAMOTO

The U.S. government has a long history of providing assistance to those who have fought in the service of their country. The U.S. military uniformed services have been served by the U.S. Public Health Service since 1798 and by the Veterans Administration since 1930.* The federal government under the Carter administration provided an amnesty program to draft evaders as well as a major jobs program for Vietnam veterans. These current events raise a variety of issues regarding the role of the federal government in meeting the mental health needs of Vietnam-era veterans.

The purpose of this chapter is to briefly discuss selected federal programs and activities that deal with the mental health needs of Vietnam veterans. The factors and forces that led to certain kinds of federal programs were often political in nature and were important considerations both during and after the Vietnam War.

The attitudes of some Vietnam veterans toward federal mental health programs may not be very positive, and the Veterans Administration has been the target of criticism by veterans' groups. Regardless

---

*A further historic note is that the organization that later became the National Institute of Mental Health was established in 1946.

of the attitudes, the federal government programs will continue to have a major impact on the lives of veterans because of the magnitude of the programs. It should be noted, however, that this chapter is an attempt to describe selected federal programs relevant to the topic, regardless of their merit. It is not an attempt to justify or present arguments to prove that the programs are necessarily meritorious. Much of the discussion will identify some of the complex political forces (and others) that influence federal programming for veterans. It is hoped that this description of the political/bureaucratic dynamics will help clarify the issue of institutional responsiveness and the direction future Vietnam veteran advocacy and planning efforts should take.

GOVERNMENT-SUPPORTED VIETNAM-ERA VETERANS' PROGRAMS

There are a number of federal programs designed to serve a wide variety of veterans' needs, The Veterans Administration being the agency most often thought of in this context. VA hospitals treat great numbers of young and old veterans for a wide range of physical and mental disabilities. The various veterans' financial benefits provide disability payments, and the VA housing benefits help veterans buy homes. In addition, millions of Americans have received GI Bill assistance through the VA educational benefits program.[1]

In 1977 the Carter administration called for a $1.5 billion Jobs Program for Vietnam Veterans. The Department of Labor (DOL) has recognized that jobs for mostly young Vietnam veterans are a high priority and that much needs to be done to reduce the relatively high jobless rate among these citizens.[2] Comprehensive Employment and Training Act (CETA) has been providing a special focus on the job training needs of Vietnam veterans, albeit with limited success to date.[3] Although not often considered a "veteran's" benefit, per se, the U.S. Civil Service Commission (as well as other civilian programs) provides certain hiring advantages for veterans in the form of "veterans' preference points" in the job application process.[4]

The Carter amnesty program, which is a revised version of the Ford administration's pardon program, could also be considered a kind of major program to help meet certain political and social needs of the Vietnam War draft evaders. President Carter indicated that he wanted to heal the wounds of a divisive war, but his amnesty program was controversial and it received mixed reactions from the Vietnam-era veteran "communities" in several countries.[5]

NIMH PROGRAMS RELEVANT TO VIETNAM VETERANS

The National Institute of Mental Health (NIMH), has provided mental health services to veterans, young and old, through the Community Mental Health Center (CMHC) grant system.* In addition, the NIMH Hospital Staff Development and Hospital Improvement Programs have helped upgrade the care provided in the state hospitals, which undoubtedly served some veterans over the years. While most veterans are served in VA hospitals, many Vietnam veterans have also been served in CMHCs. According to recent NIMH estimates, over 100,000 Vietnam veterans have been provided treatment through federally funded CMHCs during 1974. Most of these veterans were probably in the ages between 25 and 45.[6]

In addition, NIMH has funded a major research project entitled "A Study of Veterans: Impact of the Vietnam War" (Grant No. MH–26832–0181) sponsored by the Center for Policy Research in New York City.[7] This research project, which is now being conducted (through 1980), will interview a sample of Vietnam-era veterans and nonveterans as well as the "exiles" in Europe and Canada. The purpose of these interviews is to determine why some young men decided to serve in the Vietnam War and why some did not. An attempt will also be made to identify the mental health implications of the Vietnam War experience on those who did serve.

Another research project was conducted collaboratively with the Department of Defense (DOD), the VA, and the NIMH. This project dealt with the problems of drug abuse among returning Vietnam veterans.[8] This collaborative study found that Vietnam veterans had significant problems with drug abuse and that the war experience led many of these veterans into a civilian life that involved the use and abuse of drugs. A second collaborative study involved DOD, VA, and NIMH to improve mental health care provided to Vietnam veterans in St. Louis, Missouri.[9]

Finally, the NIMH staff has provided substantial amounts of technical assistance and consultation to several Vietnam-era veterans' service programs throughout the United States. In addition, NIMH has developed an annotated bibliography on the subject of Vietnam-era veterans. This bibliography deals with the psychological aspects of the social adjustment of these veterans and related topics.[10]

---

*The Community Mental Health Center program was established in 1963 by PL 84–164. The current authorizing legislation is PL 94–63. There are over 550 operational CMHCs.

The Institutes of the Alcoholism, Drug Abuse and Mental Health Administration (ADAMHA), U.S. Public Health Service, have also provided significant substance abuse services to Vietnam-era veterans. For example, in 1974 the National Institute on Alcoholism and Alcohol Abuse (NIAAA) serviced an estimated 70,000 Vietnam-era veterans. During the same reported period, the National Institute on Drug Abuse (NIDA) served a substantial number of Vietnam-era veterans.[11]

VA PROGRAMS RELEVANT TO VIETNAM VETERANS AND THE SCHOTTLAND REPORT

The VA has also developed a number of specialized mental health programs to reach out to Vietnam-era veterans. There were, at one time, special projects in VA hospitals in Los Angeles, Palo Alto, Seattle, and Albuquerque. In some cases, bilingual outreach teams, staffed by Vietnam veterans, searched for fellow veterans to help them deal with some of their mental health, education, employment, and other problems. These outreach efforts were very important in creating an accessible linkage between the VA institution and young veterans in the community. The Schottland report is one of a few documents that attempts a comprehensive evaluative study of the VA mental health system.

A major document that touches on many Vietnam veterans issues, this report was made to the U.S. Senate Committee on Veterans' Affairs and the Subcommittee on Health and Hospitals. It was developed in draft form by Dr. Charles Schottland, a consultant to the U.S. Senate Committee on Veterans' Affairs in 1973.[12] The extensive report is based on a series of site visits and interviews that attempted to evaluate the status of VA mental health programs (for all veterans). The report indicates, for example, that $2 billion annually is expended by the VA to provide medical care, usually in VA institutions. There are over 170 VA health care "stations" where some type of mental health services are provided. The VA has over 30 psychiatric hospitals, and operates over 115 general hospitals with psychiatric programs. A total of approximately $12 billion annually is spent for all types of VA benefit programs.

Over 160,000 VA employees are involved in health care services. The VA medical care delivery system of over 170 hospitals with more than 95,000 beds capacity is equivalent to one out of eight of all hospital beds in the United States. The VA maintains a contractual relationship with over 200 outpatient clinics, 65 nursing home units, 40 day treatment centers, 16 dormitories, 3 blind rehabilitation centers, 26 different specialized medical services, 16 day hospitals for psychiatric patients, and 75 mental hygiene clinics.

The psychiatric and mental health programs involve at least 100 VA hospitals that have affiliations with over 85 medical schools, 52 dental schools, 304 nursing schools, 75 schools of social work, and 95 graduate departments of psychology. This psychiatric and mental health portion of the vast VA medical service accounts for over 50 percent of the total VA medical program.

According to Schottland's report, there are a number of major changes that are taking place in the VA health system relevant to this study. First, there has been a continuous decrease in in-patient services and a corresponding increase in out-patient services throughout the system. Second, there is a decrease in the mental hospital populations. Of those patients remaining, many have schizophrenic diagnoses; they are older, and more of these patients have alcoholism problems. Third, there is an increase in community mental health facilities, a shift from institutional care to community care. Fourth, there is an increasing interest in mental health services on the part of nonmental health agencies that work with veterans. Fifth, there is an increasing involvement of various mental health (and mental health-related disciplines) in an interdisciplinary approach to care. Sixth, there has been a great deal of advancement in the quality and use of "psychoactive drugs" by the VA since the mid-1950s.

The VA has generally had a good reputation for providing quality mental health services to the extent that their restricted program permits. However, Schottland outlines a number of issues that his research indicated were important to consider. He listed nearly 30 comments and recommendations about how the quality of the VA mental health system might be improved, including the following:

More linkages and collaboration among VA hospitals and other community resources are needed. This includes NIMH-supported CMHCs
   and other out-patient facilities. It is noted that Vietnam veterans may
   find VA services much more accessible if they are in the community.
VA ought to provide for the family therapy modality or make resources
   available, since many mental health problems cannot be adequately
   dealt with when only the veteran himself (or herself) is involved.
There needs to be a change in the Medicare/Medicaid benefit packages
   so that VA hospitals may be reimbursed for some of their services.
The VA hospitals and federally-funded CMHCs ought to establish close
   collaborative relationships in their local areas.
Most veterans with nonservice-connected disabilities ought to be
   eligible for the full range of VA benefits. Very often, Vietnam

veterans do not receive appropriate benefits because establishing service-connected eligibility for mental health problems is difficult to clearly determine.

The Vietnam veterans are a special category of veteran, requiring special attention and programs of higher relevance.

The aging veteran also needs special services focused on care for the chronic patient, deinstitutionalization, and special alcoholism programs.

FEDERAL AGENCY DYNAMICS REGARDING MENTAL HEALTH PROGRAMS FOR VIETNAM-ERA VETERANS: A CASE STUDY

In order to illustrate some of the complex factors and forces that sometimes shape federal agency policy concerning Vietnam-era veterans in the area of mental health, a brief study will presented. It will use an actual case of federal agency response to the needs of Vietnam-era veterans. The case will be called the "National Self-help Project" for the purposes of presentation.

The story begins in early 1973 when a major conference was held to examine the special needs and concerns of Vietnam-era veterans. The conference was convened by a national church organization and funded by a private foundation. A broad cross-section of those interested in Vietnam-era veterans' issues participated, including Vietnam-era veterans, church representatives, scholars, the VA, and NIMH. As a result of the conference, the National Self-help Project for Vietnam-era veterans was initiated.

There were at that time a number of various store-front type self-help projects for Vietnam-era veterans, but this particular self-help project was to have a national scope, which was to help tap a variety of public and private funding sources. The purpose of the project was to help develop a network of Vietnam-era veterans' service projects that would operate out of private service centers. The centers would employ Vietnam-era veterans as peer counselors, but would also involve various trained service staff and public agency representatives. The National Self-help Project was promoted by a steering committee that was formed as a result of the 1973 conference.

This steering committee made a variety of federal agency contacts subsequent to the conference, including ACTION, the Department of Labor, the VA and NIMH. Initially, the hope was to acquire funding for a series of service projects in ten cities around the United States. The proposal by the National Self-help Project hoped to capture funding from ACTION, VA, NIMH, and others.

At one point in 1973, ACTION made a verbal commitment to

provide a portion of the funding with the expectation that other agencies would "match" ACTION's support. The VA had indicated that it would strongly consider funding the project, and NIMH indicated that it was interested but was not prepared to make a commitment one way or the other at that time. Later it turned out that ACTION was not able to follow through with its verbal commitment, the VA was not able to identify and provide funds, and NIMH indicated that it would be able to help only by asking the federally funded CMHCs to cooperate with the ACTION- and VA-funded components. In short, the National Self-help Project simply did not get funded, even though there were certain indications that agencies were willing to do so.

It should be stated that during this period (in 1973 and 1974), there was a great deal of media reporting on how the Nixon administration politicized federal agencies. There were those who thought that ACTION and the VA had a large number of former "CREEP" (Committee to Re-elect the President) members operating in those bureaucracies. This politicization of federal agencies tended to create problems for the National Self-help Project in part because of the Nixon administration's sensitivities about the progress of the Vietnam War and its support of the Thieu regime in Saigon. The Nixon administration was loathe to make the Vietnam War appear any more complex and difficult than it was for Americans back home. Therefore, ACTION and the VA were very confused and conflicted about domestic policies to which they should be responsive with respect to Vietnam-era veterans.

At one point ACTION was interested in supporting the National Self-help Project because of certain suggestions from the Nixon Domestic Council about ameliorating the problems of the Vietnam-era veteran population. On the other hand, the VA was less anxious to confront the issue of special needs of Vietnam-era veterans (such as the so-called post-Vietnam syndrome) because of pressures to behave as though these veterans were not different than all the others. The VA Central Office mental health staff in Washington, D.C., advocated programs to reach out and help meet the special needs of Vietnam-era veterans; but the administrator of the VA at that time was in considerable political trouble (and later resigned). He was therefore unwilling to make any real decisions that might be controversial, including launching any visible Vietnam-era veterans' projects in light of difficulties that American forces were having in Vietnam at that time. Note, too, that the Nixon administration and the VA administrator perceived some Vietnam-era veterans as part of an antiwar movement—"hippie," "yippie" types of youth. They were political adversaries from the Nixonion view-point.

In the end (after much vacillation), the Veterans Administration took the concept developed by the National Self-help Project proposal—

that is, to develop a network of outreach centers—and decided to launch a similar program without substantial involvement by the National Self-help Project. In short, the National Self-help Project was "ripped off" and undercut. During most of that time period, the VA Central Office mental health staff were very supportive of the National Self-help Project, but they were unable to prevent the undercutting of the project by the VA. The political undercurrents of that day were treacherous.

Meanwhile, the NIMH and the VA had been collaborating in a number of ways for some time. For example, a NIMH-supported CMHC in Philadelphia had a contract with the nearby VA hospital to provide community support services for deinstitutionalized VA patients in Philadelphia. Several examples of this type existed around the country, although the Philadelphia collaboration is the most notable. Thus, when the VA launched its own version of the National Self-help Project with two pilot outreach centers (in Wichita, Kansas, and San Francisco) NIMH was fully prepared to assist. Initially the idea was to form a network of agencies, including the VA, NIMH, and local Vietnam-era veterans' self-help groups. In short, the projects never achieved the initial goal of involving the three groups in developing a collaborative network in San Francisco and Wichita. As it turned out, the VA did establish an outreach center using Vietnam-era veterans as employees in these two cities, but no real collaboration was developed with NIMH-funded CMHCs (although CMHCs were willing) and/or local Vietnam-era veterans' grass-roots, self-helf organizations. The VA tended to prefer running its own program, controlling it in a manner similar to other VA projects.

As mentioned earlier, NIMH funded a major Vietnam-era veterans' research project. While NIMH was unable to support the National Self-help Project, it was able to fund this research project. NIMH was hesitant to fund a service project for Vietnam-era veterans because it was believed that the VA was the appropriate, responsible agency to provide the necessary services. It was concerned, in part, about inter-agency "turf" sensitivities, that is NIMH did not wish to get into an area or domain that was considered to be that of the VA. In addition, NIMH felt it had more than enough to do in trying to assure the survival of its CMHC Program, which was under heavy pressures from the Nixon administration.

THE PRESENT STATUS OF VA AND NIMH ACTIVITIES, AND PROSPECTS FOR THE FUTURE

At present, the VA is supporting a handful of outreach and special projects focused on the mental health needs of Vietnam-era veterans. The NIMH is supporting a research project and is making some efforts to more effectively identify the utilization of federally-funded CMHC services by Vietnam-era veterans. An initial research project to study the psychological adjustment of these veterans was recently expanded by the VA to study a much larger population. The Congress and the VA hope that the study will help improve VA services to this population.

After much national neglect, President Carter's amnesty program has drawn attention to the needs of Vietnam-era veterans. Americans must again confront the painful issue of the Vietnam War, the fall of Saigon in 1976, the influx of approximately 200,000 Indochinese refugees, and the President's controversial amnesty program in light of the normalization of relations with the People's Republic of China.

Obviously, the legacy of the Vietnam War sometimes creates unsettling reactions from Americans wanting to forget. The normalization of U.S. relations with Communist China reinforces the political irony surrounding the U.S. involvement in Vietnam. There are also a number of examples of how the needs and concerns of Vietnam-era veterans with respect to mental health still exist. For example, there was a violent incident involving a Vietnam veteran in Washington, D.C., who had been wounded in Vietnam and had an outstanding military record. In this case, the Vietnam veteran had trouble readjusting to society and inexplicably took some people hostage. In another case, a Vietnam veteran shot at the police while experiencing a "traumatic war neurosis." In an unusual move the local prosecutor dropped the charges on the basis that the man was not responsible for his actions. There are, of course, other examples.[13]

It appears to this observer that the Carter administration will not use the Nixonian tactics of manipulating the federal bureaucracy. This does not mean, however, that the needs of Vietnam-era veterans do not need to be advocated at the highest levels of government. The Carter administration has obviously indicated an interest in paying attention to the needs of Vietnam-era veterans through a jobs program for veterans and the declaration of amnesty. However, President Carter's recent actions do not deal directly with a large number of mental health-related issues for these veterans, including the need for more relevant service programs and other supportive services to help maintain family and financial stability.

Since Vietnam-era veterans often feel powerless, it is ironic to consider that veterans of previous wars have wielded substantial influence on the federal bureaucracy and politicians. The bulk of this political influence tends to be in the hands of veterans who are members of traditional veterans' organizations from wars previous to the Vietnam War. In contrast, Vietnam-era veterans and their 1960s generation tended to be the subject of government investigations and have remained on the periphery of legitimate political representation and influence.

It is this writer's observation that Vietnam-era veterans will have to creatively develop a "new activism" in order to generate an impact on the legitimate political process. Obviously, Vietnam-era veterans have a right to responsive representation from all levels of government. But these veterans as a group may need to find some political way of actively pressing for their own needs more effectively. It is unfortunate that many Vietnam-era veterans recognize that they have a range of special needs but for a variety of reasons do not wish to overtly acknowledge their needs as veterans. They would rather forget and leave the Vietnam War in the past. Many of these veterans wish simply to put the war and all of its implications behind and not really deal with them. Thus, many Vietnam-era veterans who might be able to support an active political thrust are not willing to come forward as Vietnam-era veterans' program supporters.

NOTES

1. Pat Reilly, "Meeting the Emotional Needs of Vietnam Era Veterans," an unpublished staff paper of the Seattle Veteran's Action Center, 1973, pp. 1–2; and Michael Satchele, "Our Hidden War Casualties," Washington *Star News*, July 22, 1973, p. A–1.

2. Austin Scott, "U.S. Seeks Jobs for 200,000 Viet Vets," Washington *Post*, January 28, 1977, p. A–1.

3. Office of Human Development, Department of Health, Education and Welfare, *Health and CETA*, March 1976, p. 32.

4. Alcohol, Drug Abuse, and Mental Health Administration, HEW, "Affirmative Action Plan for Employment of Handicapped Individuals and Disabled Veterans," September 1976.

5. Sharon Conway, "Families of Vietnam War Victims Divided on Pardon Issue," Washington *Post*, January 17, 1977, p. C–1.

6. Memorandum from Walter B. Coleman, OPC, ADAMHA, "Veterans Treated in ADAMHA Funded Programs," August 2, 1976.

7. Kadushin, Charles, and Loufer, Robert, "A Study of Veterans: Impact of the Vietnam War," unpublished Grant Application by Center for Policy Research, New York, June 1975.

8. Lee N. Robins, "A Follow-up of Vietnam Drug Users," Special Action Office for Drug Abuse Prevention, Executive Office of the President, Series A, No. 1, April 1973.

9. Reimbursable Agreement Between the Veterans Administration and National Institute of Mental Health (RA-MH-72-6), January 27, 1972.

10. Muriel Reich, "The Vietnam Era Veteran: A Bibliography," NIMH, November 1973. Another related NIMH publication is National Clearinghouse for Mental Health

Information, *Veterans With Mental Disorders, 1968–1970*. NIMH Mental Health Statistics, Series A, No. 12, 1970.

11. Personal Communication, November 18, 1976.

12. Charles I. Schottland, "Notes for Report to the U.S. Senate Committee on Veterans' Affairs and Subcommittee on Health and Hospitals," U.S. Senate Committee on Veterans' Affairs 1973.

13. William Greider, "The Old, Unhealed Wounds of Vietnam" Washington *Post*, January 23, 1977, p. A–1; Mary Ann Kuhn, "A Love-Hungry Christmas Thief's Luck Ran Out," Washington *Star*, December 19, 1975, p. A–1; and "War Casualty: Verdict for a Troubled Vet," *Time*, February 19, 1979, p. 23.

16

CAUGHT IN THE MIDDLE: MENTALLY DISABLED VETERANS AND THE VETERANS ADMINISTRATION

RONALD BITZER

If the plight of the Vietnam veteran were not a tragedy it would be a black comedy. In testimony before Congress I have documented numerous cases of Veterans Administration discrimination against veterans—particularly Vietnam veterans—whose mental disability originated in or was aggravated by military service. This chapter will attempt to explicate the "tragedy" by focusing on several major facets of the plight of mentally disabled veterans. The first aspect of the problem is the military itself.

MILITARY DISCHARGE PROCEDURES

The administrative discharge system became an important tool used by military officals in the Vietnam conflict to rid the military of personnel deemed unsupportive of the mission and to keep the lid on dissent.

Two types of administrative discharges—Undesirable (now called Discharge under Other-than-Honorable Conditions) and General—provided the means to release individuals with mental health problems from the military. Military regulations allow a determination of unsuitability to lead to a General discharge; a determination of unfitness to an Undesirable discharge. Both determinations present peculiar problems for subsequent claims to the Veterans Administration for a disability rating.

A general discharge is given for inability to perform satisfactorily without fault to the individual. One of the seven reasons for a General discharge was "personality disorder."[1] During the Vietnam era the Army employed solely this reason to issue General discharges more than other branches of the military.[2]

Recently the Army has been forced to amend its discharge regulations so that a diagnosis of a character and behavior disorder *alone* cannot result in a General discharge.[3] Also, a psychiatric examination is necessary to support the diagnosis of a personality disorder. Even if it does not lead to a general discharge, once diagnosis of a personality disorder is made, often after one hasty interview with a psychiatrist,[4] the veteran with a claim for VA service-connected mental disability has detrimental evidence in his military file for that claim.

An Undesirable discharge (Discharge under Other-than-Honorable Conditions) is given for misconduct that signifies blame on the part of the veteran. It is important to note that three of the eight reasons supporting an undesirable discharge are frequent involvement of a discreditable nature with civil or military authorities, drug abuse, and an established pattern of shirking.[5] A mentally ill person could demonstrate any or all of these behaviors and thereby qualify him/herself for an Undesirable discharge.

In 1971 a VA psychiatrist wrote about this pattern of Undesirable discharges from Vietnam:

> Several factors contribute to the lack of early recognition of psychiatric casualties in Vietnam. Some men complaining of emotional symptoms are simply sent back to the field by command or by medical officers. More often, emotional conflict manifests itself in "acting out" or unacceptable behavior that leads to disciplinary measures. There is an extensive use of administrative discharges, many under other than honorable conditions (i.e., Undesirable discharges), expeditiously to get rid of "bad apples." Such individuals are often diagnosed as having so-called "character disorders."[6]

The Undesirable discharge constitutes a serious barrier to a veteran seeking eligibility for any VA entitlement, including disability compensation.[7] Reports show that bad discharged veterans who can apply for a VA determination on eligibility for benefits have less than one chance in ten for a favorable decision.[8]

Other avenues of relief exist for the mentally disabled bad discharged veteran. The military Discharge Review Board is more likely to upgrade his discharge than the VA is to allow benefits with the less-than-honorable discharge. The Board for the Correction of Military Records has the power to award a medical discharge for service-incurred disability, but the Center for Veterans' Rights has just begun to explore this avenue.

MILITARY PSYCHIATRY

The Vietnam era resulted in additional problems for the psychiatric service of the military. It is apparent that the military psychiatrist is primarily an agent of the military and only secondarily an agent of the patient.[9] "The primary objective of the Army psychiatric program is the reduction of non-effective military performance due to psychological causes."[10]

The ability of military psychiatrists to predict effective performance by mental health patients at a military hospital has been questioned in a study that involved 124 hospitalized psychiatric military personnel at Walter Reed Army Hospital. It reported: First, although 23 percent of the experimental group of 73 patients had an admitting diagnosis of schizophrenia or functional psychosis and about 3 percent had an admitting diagnosis of character and behavior disorder, all but four had a discharge diagnosis of character and behavior disorder.[11]

Second, the psychiatrists' accuracy in selecting those patients who would fail as soldiers was only .40. "This study has shown that the staff psychiatrist was not able to predict the future behavior of the individual patients. . . . In the normal operation of mental hygiene facilities in the Army, the psychiatrist is often asked to make such predictions or recommendations after contact with a soldier for as little as half an hour or perhaps a few hours."[12]

Psychiatry in the military is also deemphasized in disciplinary matters that may be manifestations of a mental health problem. A Department of Defense publication for military psychiatrists, for example, states: "Conditions [or psychiatric illness] in mild to moderate form do not prevent the individual from 'recognizing the difference between right and wrong' or from 'adhering to the right.' Hence, they do not absolve the individual from criminal accountability."[13]

The extreme circumstances extending recognition of a mental health condition to a disciplinary situation are described in the manual:

Individuals with severe anxiety reactions in combat circumstances may experience greater than average difficulty in avoiding offenses against the military code. . . . These include the true panics. . . . The most common expression of true panic on the battlefield is the panic run, in which, usually during a shelling, the individual deserts cover and dashes about impulsively, as often toward the enemy as away, exposing himself to flying shell fragments.[14]

The manual goes on to state that military lawyers do not become involved in many of these cases because the victims of true panics are usually either killed or wounded on the battlefield.

VIETNAM AND MENTAL HEALTH PROBLEMS

Combat places stress on institutions as well as individuals, and the Vietnam conflict was no exception. To decrease this stress on itself the government has sought to downplay the incidence of psychiatric problems among Vietnam combat veterans during active duty and in the immediate period after their return from Vietnam and separation from the military.[15] In fact, one could conclude that concern about the safety of society rather than the mental health needs of Vietnam veterans fostered government studies of combat-related psychiatric problems. For example, one study states: "It appears, however, that most young men will not behave violently on their return from Vietnam."[16]

In reporting to Senator Cranston on October 13, 1969, the Chief Medical Director of the Veterans Administration noted that "the number of psychiatric casualties appears to be smaller than what was incurred in previous conflicts. There are a number of explanations for this: the one-year rotation, provision of treatment facilities as close to the combat areas as possible and the intermittent nature of the combat situation."[17]

Testimony given at the Winter Soldier Investigations of Vietnam Veterans Against the War in 1971. Robert Lifton, a psychiatrist who later wrote *Home from the War*, stated:

There's a lot of effort on the part of various people, many of them in the government, to prove things statistically about Vietnam. They've been doing that ever since the war began. The statistics now—and of course they always turn out to be false—but one of the statistics now is that all this talk about disturbances or dehumanization of disturbance in Vietnam GIs doesn't apply because they have statistics that the psychiatric cases have diminished as compared with the Korean or World War II. I want to expose that statistic for what it is. In other words, it doesn't really tell us anything. . . . Most of the harmful behavior that occurs in Vietnam is due to the malignant environment we create there, an environment of murder. For instance, the men who killed others at My Lai, let's say, had no discernable or diagnosable psychiatric disease. They were, I would say, in an advanced state of numbing and brutalization and under enormous pressures. The kind of thing that could happen to any one of us, were we put under similar training and that kind of situation.

But they don't have any nameable psychiatric impairment; they'll never be diagnosed. The same is true for many who have various forms of drug addiction. As you know, many people with drug addiction don't come into medical facilities even in this country and don't fit into any statistics. So when one begins to examine the extraordinary impairment and destructiveness of the Vietnam War on all levels of American society, one shouldn't be led by these narrow statistics about psychiatric cases.[18]

In his poem "Emotions," Al Hubbard, one of the original organizers of Vietnam Veterans Against the War, gives the following insight into a combatant's way of coping with the war:

> Sacrificing a portion of your consciousness
> so as not to have to deal with the
> guilt of being there, and
> forming mental blocks
> so as not to have to deal with the
> guilt of having been there.[19]

Psychiatric treatment facilities were described by a Vietnam veteran and psychiatrist, David Galacia:

The psychiatric office (it had a real fancy name—Chief of Department of Psychiatry and Neurology) was fine except there was no other psychiatrist and there was no neurologist. So I was it. I had a social worker and two techs. And I had to fight like hell when they went home to get some more techs to replace them.

The area, the type of degradation I felt this particular service of medicine was held in, was incredible. Here I sat with my office in the back of the Special Services library. That wasn't bad enough. We continued under this. But my inpatient service was an open ward and I'd just like to describe the ward very briefly to you.

There was a huge ward that was subdivided. . . . Down the sides from the nursing station, because it seemed the best thing to do, the psychiatric patients were housed. This would include anyone from a psychopath to a neurotic to a psychotic. And the kicker to this was that in the middle was the intensive care unit for cardiac patients who were on monitors. . . .

I had a paranoid patient walking around there one night, I was told, after I left the ward, talking about how people were drawing knives on him, etc., etc. You know, if you are in a state of paranoia, and you're walking around seeing people that are having all their blood taken out of them, and you go for a further walk and you see people on cardiac monitors, it's pretty bad.

I could not send a seriously ill alcoholic or a seriously ill drug addict out of country. In essence, I found myself in a real quagmire. I had no effective means of really treating him and no effective means of sending him on where he could get better treatment. So he ended up going back to his unit.

Insofar as getting people in the hospital for heroin addiction and opiate addiction, the best we could offer was to hospitalize them and sort of work them off their habit with thorazine, because at that time when I was there, methadone was not available to me. I asked for it and I never did get it. This is a much more effective means of taking someone off of heroin or opiates than thorazine.[20]

The epidemic drug use by U.S. soldiers in Vietnam constitutes an important factor in the mental health of the young men and women who were exposed to potent opiate and marijuana drugs. The precise relationship between drug use and psychiatric problems, however, is not clear. VA psychiatrists wrote in 1971: "The alleged high incidence of drug use in Vietnam has been a matter of considerable concern with serious yet-to-be-answered questions about its relationship both to incidents of 'excessive' violence and to psychiatric sequelae of service in Vietnam."[21] Two of the ten published surveys of drug use among U.S. soldiers in Vietnam, however, did note a higher incidence of marijuana use among psychiatric patients than among other patients and enlisted personnel. In mid-1968, 52.1 percent of the psychiatric patients reported that they had used marijuana; 41.6 percent reported use beginning in Vietnam.[22] In the same year 56 percent of the psychiatric patients in the Fourth Infantry Division said they had used marijuana in Vietnam compared to 35 percent of the surgical patients.[23]

Evidence does exist that marijuana use can foster the development of a prolonged psychosis:

It is commonplace for psychiatric personnel working in Vietnam to be confronted with a psychosis, marked especially by paranoid ideation, loosening of associations, time disorientation, and recent memory loss, associated with a history of marijuana smoking.

Although usually of a few days duration, occasionally the symptoms do not remit after one to two weeks of hospitalization, phenothiazine treatment and supportive psychotherapy. Such persistence of symptoms is most often seen in individuals who are personality disorders and who have been smoking large amounts of the drug.[24]

Certainly the widespread use of drugs, whether marijuana, opiates, or alcohol, related to the need for release from the tensions of Vietnam duty. For some soldiers light marijuana use may have served as self-therapy to avoid becoming neurotic about the circumstances of their existence. The drug that is one person's crutch in moderate use may be another person's poison in excessive use.

In this respect the bizarre nature of war, including the Vietnam conflict, should be remembered. As Galacia has observed, "When you get there [Vietnam] you arrive with your ethics, your values. After a while you get the impression that the standard operating procedure for the day is anything goes there. If you're involved in an atrocity, other people have done it too, and you have something in common. Three days after you're there you're part of it or in for a year of bedlam."[25]

The ability of U.S. soldiers to adjust to these circumstances was seriously compromised by a deliberate Department of Defense policy beginning in 1965 to accept persons of lower mental standards into the wartime military. This policy, called Project 100,000 in view of the goal of including 100,000 people with Armed Forces Qualification Test (AFQT) scores between 10 and 30 (Category IV) additionally each year, resulted in a Vietnam-era military comprised of 25 percent Category IV personnel.[26] Studies by the military and former officials of the Clemency Program have documented that Project 100,000 personnel were more likely to be assigned to the combat arms and more likely to develop disciplinary problems and to receive less-than-fully-honorable discharges.[27] No study has documented what has happened to the survivors of the Project 100,000 after release from the military. There is a definite need to study this problem further.

The peacetime military has moved toward accepting far fewer of the Category IV applicants and the military has given the following reason for rejecting applicants of a low mental aptitude: "It is a reasonable assumption that individuals with lower intellectual capacity have greater difficulty in adjustment than persons of average intelligence and thus more frequently become psychiatric problems or disciplinary offenders."[28]

MENTALLY DISABLED VIETNAM VETERANS IN VA HOSPITALS

Statistics for Vietnam-era veterans in VA psychiatric hospitals and on the disability compensation rolls for a psychiatric disorder show disparities that may support my contention of routine denials of psychiatric disability compensation claims.

Psychiatric treatment has been the number-one reason Vietnam-era veterans have been hospitalized. In fiscal year 1971, for example,

33.4 percent of all Vietnam-era veterans in VA hospitals were discharged after psychiatric treatment.[29] An annual census of patients remaining in VA hospitals on October 1, 1975, showed that 63.6 percent of all Vietnam-era patients were hospitalized for psychiatric or psychotic reasons.[30]

Although the military did refer more psychiatric illnesses to the VA than any other problem (60 percent of all referrals by the Armed Forces Medical Regulating Office between 1965 and 1976),[31] it is important to note that Vietnam veterans often seek treatment from non-VA facilities for mental health problems. The recently published study, "Health Care for the American Veteran," reported that "Younger veterans are more likely to use non-VA facilities for episodes of psychiatric care."[32] Furthermore, "The 1970 census found that slightly more than half of the veterans hospitalized for psychiatric problems are in state, city, county or private hospitals."[33]

The magnitude of psychiatric problems for veterans as evidenced by hospitalization in just VA facilities is not reflected in the statistics of military disability separation and VA disability compensation.

Psychiatric disorders accounted for approximately 14 percent of all disability separations for Army personnel in Vietnam from 1965 to 1969.[34] This figure has also been employed by the government to deemphasize the relative seriousness of psychiatric casualties in Vietnam, since one-third of all disability separations in World War II pertained to psychiatric disorders.[35]

Discharge from the military for medical reasons is the result of military procedures that benefit officers more than enlisted personnel and higher ranking officers more than lower ranking officers,[36] so that disability separations may not reflect the amount of mental problems in the Vietnam-era military. The failure of the military to process a mentally disabled veteran with a medical discharge does not preclude the veteran's application to the VA for disability compensation, provided that the VA must not first determine eligibility with an Undesirable discharge.

V.A. disability compensation statistics show that:

Vietnam-era veterans with mental disabilities are more likely to be seriously disabled. Almost one-third of the mentally disabled Vietnam-era veterans are rated 100 percent disabled; they constitute almost one-half of all totally disabled, service-connected Vietnam-era veterans.

Many of the mentally disabled veterans are seriously disabled but are receiving much less monetary support than the 100 percent disabled veteran. More than one-third of the veterans have disability ratings of 50 to 90 percent. A 70 percent disabled veteran may not be able to find employment with his mental disability, yet his disability compensation check is only 43 percent as large as the veteran with a 100 percent disability rating.

Only 7.8 percent of the almost 500,000 Vietnam-era veterans considered disabled by the VA have a mental disability. Both the absolute number and percentages of Vietnam-era veterans in VA hospitals for psychiatric treatment exceed comparative figures for mentally disabled veterans on VA compensation rolls.

Rate of Psychiatric Disabilities 7.8 percent	Rate of VA Psychiatric Hospitalization 35–60 percent
Number Rated Mentally Disabled 36,453	Number Treated for Mental Illness in Fiscal Year 1975 40–60,000*

This comparison of figures does not prove that the VA could award disability compensation to many more mentally disabled veterans than it does now. Factors other than a service-connected disability may explain psychiatric hospitalization after discharge from the military. Nevertheless, they do shed some light on a closer examination of VA procedures for determining both the service connection and rate of mental disabilities.

Problems in psychiatric treatment of veterans, not necessarily Vietnam veterans, have been studied with respect to the Veterans Administration. They include the following topics: reluctance of the Vietnam veteran to seek assistance from the VA; the trend toward the diagnosis of personality disorders in VA hospitals; and the significance of the one-year presumptive period for service-connected disability compensation.

RELUCTANCE OF THE VIETNAM VET TO DEAL WITH THE VA

The U.S. Senate's Veterans' Affairs Committee has received testimony on the attitudes of the Vietnam vet toward the VA. Jan Scruggs has reported that "Fifty-two percent of veterans who felt that Vietnam had 'caused psychological problems' held a negative attitude toward seeking help for these problems through VA services."[37]

All Vietnam-era veterans have failed to obtain VA disability compensation at a comparable rate to World War II veterans. A former administrator of the Veterans Administration reported in 1977: "In

---

*These figures are only an estimate; they do not consider veterans in non-VA psychiatric hospitals, which may double the actual VA figure.

1951 [six years following the end of World War II] 10.8 percent of the total World War II veteran population was in receipt of compensation; and in 1976, 5.7 percent of the total Vietnam-era population was in receipt of compensation."[38]

Explanations for the lower disability rate for Vietnam-era veterans include the unwillingness of young persons to seek confirmation that they are disabled, the failure of veterans today to apply to the VA or to appeal an unfavorable decision with the assistance of a service organization, and possible disparities in the crippling effects of the two wars. Certainly the fact that many Vietnam-era veterans seek psychiatric treatment in non-VA facilities does not encourage further dealings with the Veterans Administration.[39] In California, for example, younger veterans in need of mental health treatment often avoid VA psychiatric hospitals because of their reputation for extensive use of drugs.[40] This problem was identified by the comptroller general in an April 1975 report to Congress, "Controls on Use of Psychotherapeutic Drugs and Improved Psychiatrist Staffing Are Needed in Veterans Administration Hospitals." On September 22, 1977, the VA administrator concurred with the following recommendation of the National Academy of Sciences report: "The demonstrated practices of overprescribing and incorrect prescribing of drugs in the treatment of psychotic patients and the inappropriate utilization of antipsychotic drugs for psychoneurotic patients require urgent correction through education and quality-assurance reviews."[41]

DIAGNOSES OF PERSONALITY DISORDERS BY THE VA

A comparative study of psychiatric patients in a VA hospital from three different wars indicates a trend toward more diagnoses of personality disorders, a trend that is not completely supported by testing data. The authors note, "While the incidence of schizophrenia appears to be relatively constant, the proportion of patients receiving a primary diagnosis of personality disorder has increased markedly from less than seven percent in the World War II era to 36 percent today."[42]

Data from MMPI (Minnesota Multiphasic Personality Inventory) supported the trend toward more symptoms of personality disorders and fewer symptoms of neurosis. The increase in character disorder codes, however (from 8.6 in World War II veterans to 16.6 percent in Vietnam veterans), does not support the sixfold increase in diagnoses of personality disorders. It is interesting to note, moreover, that the authors pointed to a change in maladjustment among veterans whereby Vietnam veterans were more likely to "act out" their behavior than to internalize anxiety to neurotic symptoms. This "acting out" could have led to a bad discharge for misconduct for those individuals who were still in the military. As has been described above, both the diagnosis of a personality disorder and the bad discharge undermine the claim for a mental disability claim from the Veterans Administration.[43]

THE ONE-YEAR PRESUMPTIVE PERIOD

The VA will consider evidence for a service-connected mental disability that is at least 10 percent disabling if it is dated within one year after discharge from the military.[44] This requirement for mental disabilities was not always so strict. World War I veterans, for example, could be rated service-connected for a neuropsychiatric disability that manifested itself to at least a 10 percent degree before January 1, 1925.[45]

World War I policy was later deemed to be too costly for the government.

> Before the entrance of the United States into World War II, it was decided to try to prevent the high rate of discharge of personnel for neuropsychiatric defects and disabilities. The experience of World War I showed that over 97,000 men were admitted to hospitals for neuropsychiatric disorders from 1 April 1917 to 31 December 1919. This situation had resulted in considerable cost to the government, since these men became beneficiaries of the Veterans Administration.[46]

Traditional veterans organizations chafed under the one-year limitation for evidence in mental disability claims from their experience in counseling many disabled veterans from World War II. Their lobbying to expand the presumptive period to two or three years after discharge failed in the early 1950s. Congress decided that mentally disabled veterans could be rated for VA treatment purposes only if the disability could be documented more than one but less than two years after discharge.

The response of AMVETS to this new law was that for the first time in U.S. history the government was denying compensation for disabilities that the government recognized as service-connected.[47] The representative of American Veterans of World War II (AMVETS) Rufus Wilson, testified before a House Committee on this problem:

> We have had many, many experiences with veterans who have had mental breakdowns and developed a psychosis 3,4, and even 5 years

after service as a direct result of their period of active duty in the Armed Forces.

We have been firmly convinced for a long period of time that this mental breakdown was caused directly by the transition from a civilian to a military life during a time of war and then a subsequent transition back to the original way of living. There are many perfectly normal people within the U.S. who do not have the mental capacity or the emotional make-up to allow them to make such a drastic change without serious mental disturbances.[48]

The VA lobbied against the position of the veterans' organizations. In a report to the Senate Labor and Public Welfare Committee, the VA stated: "If circumstances of service so conflict with the mental make-up of an individual so to cause a psychosis, that psychosis would have become existent at that time and not many months or years after service."[49]

The statement of the American Legion representative is helpful in documenting the ways the VA denied claims from mentally disabled veterans. Dr. Hyman Shapiro stated:

In most cases the development of a psychosis is so slow and insidious that it can be present to a disabling degree for months or years before the condition is recognized.

A great deal has been said this morning about the present law providing the VA with authority to service-connect a psychosis of more than one year where the psychosis was not so diagnosed within the year. I will state that the very, very small percentage—an infinitesimal number of them, in my experience—have had such service-connection. And we have case after case that has been turned down.

All too frequently affidavits of those close relatives, of those closest to the afflicted person, and in the best position to testify, are given scant consideration, usually on the grounds that these relatives have a personal interest in the outcome of the claim for compensation.

Who is there to state with certainty that the condition did not have its roots in the individual's war service? . . . The war rips him out of his environment and places him in a rigid situation, and very often in a situation that is intolerable to the individual.[50]

Clearly the one-year presumptive period for evidence of a mental illness is a problem for Vietnam veterans as well as for World War II veterans. A lobbying group for Vietnam veterans, Vietnam Veterans Against the War, had identified the one-year presumptive period as a problem and sought to expand the period to two years. A description of legislative proposals by VVAW explained bill H.R. 4530, "affectionately known as the VVAW bill, to amend section 312 of Title 38 of the United

States Code, by providing a two-year presumptive period of service connection for psychosis which developed within two years from the date of separation from active service."[51]

In terms of lobbying in Washington it was unlikely that VVAW would have achieved what the American Legion and AMVETS failed to obtain after World War II. While VVAW was demanding from Congress that it "enact immediately legislation providing the necessary funding for structuring and implementation of drug rehabilitation and psychotherapy programs for returning veterans of the Indochina War," it was also demanding "the immediate, unilateral, unconditional withdrawal of all United States Armed Forces and Central Intelligence Agency personnel from the countries of Vietnam, Cambodia, Laos and Thailand."[52] Because of the controversial demands and actions of VVAW, it became subverted by government infiltration and could not become a more effective national lobbying group for Vietnam veterans in Washington.[53]

CONCLUSION

According to studies and government reports, the Vietnam veteran does not have a greater potential for violence than veterans who did not serve in Vietnam and his readjustment problems do not warrant a clinical disagnosis of "post-Vietnam syndrome."[54] While these conclusions may inhibit Congress from considering the mental health problems of Vietnam veterans, it should be noted that these problems do not necessarily disappear with the expiration of the one-year presumptive period in VA claims.

One study has shown that

combat experience increases the probability of the presence of emotional illness many years after combat. . . . The combat stress situation does seem to foster certain concepts in patients about the resulting reaction. These concepts appear to influence patients' adjustments to their disabilities, and very definitely impose severe limitations on their acceptance of psychiatric treatment. Hopefully, proper early management of combat precipitated emotional illness can forestall this development. If not, these patients present an almost insurmountable therapeutic problem 15 to 20 years later.[55]

A recently published study by a national group headquartered at Purdue University reported that 25 percent of the Vietnam veterans have difficulty sleeping because of nightmares, many relating to their military experience.[56]

In view of the disparity between the mental health problems of Vietnam-era veterans and the restrictive policies of the Veterans Administration, I recommend further study directed to changes that would affect the most seriously ill individuals.

First, the military should consider introduction of MMPI testing for all personnel who show emotional or disciplinary problems. Such testing would provide the data to support any diagnosis of a personality disorder. Second, the Veterans Administration should consider broadening the evidence of a mental disability within one year after discharge to include statements of family and friends that are later supported by professional diagnoses of mental illness. Third, the government should sponsor a study of the readjustment of Project 100,000 veterans to civilian life in particular, and the long-term adjustments of Vietnam combatants in general.*

NOTES

1. Department of Defense Directive 1332.14.

2. Department of Defense, *Task Force on the Administration of Military Justice*, Vol. IV, p. 151. In fiscal year 1971, 72 percent of the Army's general discharges were for character and behavior disorders; Navy's general discharges, 13.9 percent; Marine Corps, 26.6 percent; and Air Force, 37 percent.

3. *Lipsman* v. *Secretary*, No. 76-1175 U.S. District Court for the District of Columbia.

4. Casmier Wichlacz, Franklin Del Jones, and Stephen Stayer, "Psychiatric Predictions and Recommendations: A Longitudinal Study of Character and Behavior Disorder Patients," *Military Medicine*, February 1972, p. 58.

5. Department of Defense Directive 1331.12.

6. George Soloman, "Psychiatric Casualties of the Vietnam Conflict," *Modern Medicine*, Spring 1971.

7. William Tiffany and William Allerton. "Army Psychiatry in the Mid-60s," *American Journal of Psychiatry*, January 7, 1967, p. 819.

8. William Smith, an attorney in Los Angeles, has received a VA report on favorable decisions in claims with undesirable and bad conduct discharges that shows a 4.7 percent success rate in the 1974–76 period. The Nader study reported a 7 percent success rate. See Paul Starr, *The Discarded Army* (New York: Charterhouse, 1973), p. 177.

9. Thomas Szasz, *Law, Library and Psychiatry* (New York: Collier Books, 1975), p. 30.

10. Albert Glass, Kenneth Artiss, James Gibbs and Vincent Sweeney, "The Current State of Army Psychiatry," *American Journal of Psychiatry*, February 1961.

11. Wichlacz, Del Jones, and Stayer, op cit., p. 55.

12. Ibid., p. 58.

13. Departments of the Air Force, Army and Navy, "Psychiatry in Military Law," June 24, 1968, p. 3–9.

Editors' note: Efforts by members of the Consortium on Veterans Studies resulted in the VA's Board of Veterans Appeals preparing a specific memorandum on posttraumatic disorders (see Appendix to this chapter). This recent memorandum from the chairman of the board will partly correct some of the problems raised by Bitzer in this chapter.

14. Ibid.

15. Jonathan Borus, "Incidence of Maladjustment in Vietnam Returnees," *Archives of General Psychiatry*, April 1974; Robert Strange and Dudley Brown, "Home from the War: A Study of Psychiatric Problems in Vietnam Returnees," *American Journal of Psychiatry*, October 1970; Robert Strange, "Psychiatric Perspectives of the Vietnam Veteran," *Military Medicine*, February 1974; Charles Stenger, "Perspectives on the Post-Vietnam Syndrome," Veterans Administration, July 1974.

16. Strange, "Psychiatric Perspectives," op. cit., p. 97.

17. "Oversight of Medical Care of Veterans Wounded in Vietnam," Subcommittee on Veterans Affairs, Committee on Land and Public Welfare, 1969 and 1970, Part one, p. 5.

18. Robert Lifton, "Vietnam Veterans Against the War," Social Action Files, State Historical Society, Madison, Wisconsin.

19. *ibid*.

20. David Galacia, in *ibid*.

21. George Soloman, Vincent Zarcone, Robert Toerg, Neil Scott, and Ralph Maurer, "Three Psychiatric Casualties from Vietnam," *Archives of General Psychiatry*, December 1971.

22. E. Casper et al., "Marijuana in Vietnam," *United States Army Republic of Vietnam Medical Bulletin*, September–October 1968, pp. 60–72. Survey at American Division and Cam Ranh Bay, mid-1968, 46 psychiatric patients, 46 dispensary patients, 234 enlisted men entering Vietnam through Cam Ranh Bay and 233 leaving. Ever used marijuana: psychiatric, 52.1 percent; dispensary, 32.6 percent; incoming, 27.7 percent; outgoing, 20.6 percent. Percentage of users who began in Vietnam: psychiatric, 41.6 percent; dispensary, 20.0 percent; incoming, 4.6 percent; outgoing, 58.6 percent.

23. "Marijuana Use in Vietnam: A Preliminary Report," *United States Army Republic of Vietnam Medical Bulletin*, September-October 1968, pp. 58–59. The 1968 questionnaire was administered to 100 surgical patients and 50 psychiatric patients.

24. Raymond Crowe, "Marijuana Associated Psychosis in Vietnam," *Military Medicine*, July 1970.

25. New York *Times*, February 7, 1971.

26. Office of the Assistant Secretary of Defense, Manpower and Reserve Affairs, "Project 100,000." December 1969, p. x. William Strauss, a former official of the Clemency Program, reported that the Clemency Board also saw Category V individuals in about 0.5 percent of the cases. These individuals had mental test scores so low that they should have never been allowed in the military. The Center for Veteran's Rights has also counseled Category V veterans of Vietnam who were inducted from Los Angeles.

27. Ibid., pp. 5, 29; *Task Force*, op. cit., Vol. IV, p. 160. Strauss also reported that Category IV personnel had 2.5 times the court-martial rate and one-third of all the less-than-honorable discharges.

28. Glass et al., op. cit., p. 682.

29. Veterans Administration, "Data on Vietnam-era Veterans," June 1971, p. 18.

30. Veterans Administration, "Data on Vietnam-era Veterans," October 1976, p. 30.

31. Ibid., p. 33.

32. National Research Council, National Academy of Sciences, "Study of Health Care for American Veterans" (Washington, D.C.: U.S. Government Printing Office, June 7, 1977), p. 172.

33. Ibid., p. 170.

34. "Oversight of Medical Care," op. cit., p. 104.

35. Ibid., p. 18.

36. The Special Subcommittee on Retired-Pay Provisions of the House Armed Services Committee reported in 1972 that 18.3 percent of the retired military personnel

were retired for disability effective June 30, 1971. The percentages of officers retired for disability varied with their rank as follows:

	Percent		
Rank	1971	1970	1969
0–10	47.6	44.0	42.7
0–9	42.0	41.3	39.7
0–8	33.2	32.0	32.3
0–7	25.9	26.4	26.7
0–6	16.4	16.4	16.6
0–5	11.9	10.8	10.6
W–4	11.1	10.8	10.6

(from House Armed Services Committee report no. 92–80, 92d Cong. 2d sess. 1972, p. 17660).

37. Jan Scruggs and Berman, "The Vietnam Veteran: A Preliminary Analysis of Psychosocial Consequences," p. 6 (unpublished study for University of Maryland).

38. Richard Roudebush in a letter to Center for Veteran's Rights, February 11, 1977.

39. National Research Council, op. cit., p. 172.

40. Interviews with patients at Brentwood VA Hospital and Vietnam veterans in "Still at War," by the S.A.W. Film Collective, 1974 (undistributed film).

41. National Research Council, op. cit., pp. 283–84. Veterans Administration news release, September 22, 1977.

42. Gordon Braatz, Gayle Lumry and M. Suzanne Wright, "The Young Veteran as a Psychiatric Patient in Three Eras of Conflict," Military Medicine, May 1971, pp. 455–56.

43. See note 8.

44. 38 USC 312.

45. World War Veterans Act of 1924.

46. Department of the Army, "Marginal Man and Military Service: A Review," December 1965, p. 69.

47. Subcommittee on Veterans Affairs, "Hearings on Bills Seeking to Extend the Presumptive Period for Disease of Psychosis, H.R. 5891 and 5892," January 16, 1952, p. 755.

48. Ibid., pp. 755–56.

49. Ibid., p. 755.

50. Ibid., pp. 744–47.

51. "VVAW Legislative Proposals and Endorsements," Vietnam Veterans Against the War, op. cit.

52. "Open Letter to Congress of the United States—Demand for Public Hearings on Redress of Grievances of Veterans of the Indochina War." in Ibid.

53. A June 7, 1977, letter from Director Clarence M. Kelley of the Federal Bureau of Investigation to Ron Bitzer indicates that the FBI will release at least 12,000 pages from its files on VVAW.

54. Charles Stenger, "Perspectives on the Post-Vietnam Syndrome." U.A., July, 1974. He did note (p. 5): "There is more evidence that the current tendency toward character and behavior disorders noted by Bourne in his studies of combat veterans reflect a cultural tolerance of acting out behaviors. If so this may both mask and delay the occurrence of other psychiatric diagnostic conditions, as psychosis, in those Vietnam veterans who experienced and were adversely affected by their traumatic combat and reentry experiences."

55. Demmie Mayfield and Donald Fowler, "Combat Plus Twenty Years: The Effect of Previous Combat Experiences on Psychiatric Patients," *Military Medicine*, October 1969, pp. 1353–54.

56. C. R. Figley, *Stress Disorders Among Vietnam Veterans* (New York: Brunner/Mazel, 1978).

APPENDIX TO CHAPTER 16

Office of the Chairman
Board of Veterans Appeals
Washington, D.C. 20420

August 18, 1978

MEMORANDUM
NO. 01-78-12

SUBJECT: POSTTRAUMATIC DISORDER

1. GENERAL

Following is a discussion of the subject Posttraumatic Disorders which should be inserted as paragraph 9 of Chairman's Numbered Memorandum No. 01-76-2, dated June 29, 1976, Instructions in Selected Medical Specialties.

2. NEW PARAGRAPH NUMBER 9 OF CHAIRMAN'S NUMBERED MEMORANDUM 01-76-2

[9. POSTTRAUMATIC DISORDERS

a. *Classification Term—Posttraumatic Disorder.* Rather than the use of the term "post Vietnam syndrome" it is preferable to classify this disability as "posttraumatic disorder" since it affects not only Vietnam veterans but also veterans of other wars including survivors of concentration camps, prisoners of wars, and victims of any extraordinarily stressful event.

b. *Criteria.* Not all neuroses are posttraumatic. The following criteria are most important when reviewing claims folders to determine the presence of a postraumatic disorder and any etiology it may have to the service experience:

(1) There must be a recognizable stress-producing incident

which would be expected to evoke a significant symptom of stress in almost all individuals. Examples would include combat, internment as POW, witnessing the killing of buddies and civilians, and surviving an airplane crash or natural disaster. Whether the traumatic incident was sufficient to cause the subsequent symptoms is a matter which must rest with the judgment of the Board Member.

(2) Symptoms of maladjustment must arise within a few days or months following the traumatic incident. A period of more than 1 year following a stressful situation wherein there is no abnormal emotional symptomatology would certainly dismiss the possibility of a post traumatic disorder.

(NOTE: In reviewing some of the literature describing long-term effects of concentration camp victims, combat veterans, survivors of natural disasters, the literature is consistent in demonstrating some sort of recognizable emotional maladjustment shortly after the incident. Even in those factual situations establishing a rather long period of normal behavior followed by a psychiatric disorder there had been an initial indication of emotional instability at a time proximate to the traumatic event.)

(3) Certain criteria are necessary to establish the diagnosis and are common among the population exposed to a significant traumatic event. Examples include:

(a) Reexperience of the traumatic event.

1. Recurrent and disturbing recollections of the event.

2. Recurrent dreams of the event. Or,

3. Suddenly acting or feeling as if the traumatic event were occurring.

(b) Significant withdrawal from the environment beginning after the traumatic event.

1. Markedly diminished interest in one or more significant activities.

2. Feelings of detachment from others. Or,

3. Marked constriction of expression of feelings.

(c) Some of the following may be present.

(NOTE: These are not usually found prior to the traumatic event.):

> 1. Hyperalertness or exaggerated startle response.
>
> 2. Initial, middle, or terminal sleep disturbance.
>
> 3. Guilt about surviving when others have not, or about behavior required to achieve survival.
>
> 4. Memory impairment or trouble concentrating.
>
> 5. Avoidance of activities that arouse recollection of the traumatic event.
>
> 6. Intensification of symptoms by exposure to events that symbolize or resemble the traumatic event.

c. *Post Service Psychiatric Disorders*. It is clear that psychiatric disorders following active military duty are not necessarily etiologically related to that military duty.]

SYDNEY J. SHUMAN
Chairman

Distribution: E F G N
Research Center (01C1) 2 copies
Chief Attorney, AIRS (01C1)

17

SUBJECTING THE VETERANS ADMINISTRATION TO COURT REVIEW

DEAN K. PHILLIPS

During the past half-century, the country has seen the development of what many consider to be a fourth branch of government—administrative agencies. Among these agencies is the Veterans Administration, which encompasses 225,000 employees stationed at 57 regional offices and 172 medical centers across the United States. The VA's fiscal year (FY) 1980 budget approaches $22 billion, approximately $14 billion of which is dispensed directly to veterans, their dependents, and survivors under various veterans' benefit programs mandated by Congress, such as compensation, pension, and educational assistance.

This chapter is dedicated to Mary Sinders and Donald Zeglin with appreciation to the faculty and staff of the University of Denver College of Law.

Editors' Note: For years the Congress has granted the Veterans Administration virtual immunity from court review. This immunity extended to all questions of law or fact in benefits cases upon which the VA and individual veteran claimants might disagree. Since 1974 Phillips has been a catalyst in the movement to convince Congress to enact legislation that would permit VA clients, just like clients of the Social Security system, to take the VA to court to settle a claim (e.g., the Board of Veterans Appeals turns down 30,000+ cases a year which can not be appealed anywhere). As special assistant to the VA General Counsel (1977–1979), Phillips was active in the reformulation of the VA's

Except for congressional oversight, the administration of veterans' benefit programs by the VA takes place under a closed system. The agency promulgates its own regulations, adjudicates individual claims in accordance with these regulations, and renders final factual and legal determinations in individual cases. Under 38 U.S.C. 211(a), neither interpretation of regulations nor the findings of fact are subject to judicial review.

REGULATIONS

Because of exceptions in the Administrative Procedure Act (APA) [5 U.S.C. 553(a) (2)], the VA is exempt from the "notice and comment" requirements in its rule-making procedures in benefit programs. Accordingly, when Congress enacts legislation providing for specific benefit programs for veterans to be administered by the VA, that agency is not required by statute to print proposed regulations in the *Federal Register*. Thus, the agency is not required to provide the general public with notice and the opportunity to comment on the manner in which the VA plans to implement benefit programs mandated by Congress. In April 1972 the VA promulgated a regulation (38 C.F.R. 1.12) whereby it announced its intention to voluntarily comply with the "notice and comment" provisions of the APA. In more recent years the VA has printed proposed regulations in the *Federal Register*. However, the VA did not begin cross-indexing final regulations with interim regulations often previously printed in the form of "circulars" in the *Federal Register* until February 1979. Prior to that time, individuals had, at best, a difficult time attempting to track final regulations with proposed and interim regulations that they are intended to supersede. Additionally, a considerable amount of VA policy-implementing material—generally in the form of internal "circulars," manuals, and program guides—is not easily accessible to the general public and is generally not printed in the *Federal Register*.

Because regulations, by their nature, often may take as long as two or more years to become final and printed in the Code of Federal

---

position on this issue. In October, 1977 for the first time in history the VA informed Congress that it no longer opposed judicial review and in fact favored it in certain circumstances. In 1979 three of the largest American veterans organizations (Veterans of Foreign Wars, Disabled American Veterans, and the American Veterans (AMVETS) went on record supporting judicial review of benefits cases in the VA. Accordingly the Senate on September 17, 1979 voted by unanimous consent to enact S-330 which would subject final VA benefit decisions to court review. At this writing the House of Representatives has taken no action on this matter.

Regulations (CFR), the VA often utilizes "circulars" as an interim measure through which to implement policy changes often mandated by statute. In some instances, these regulations and circulars may appear to be inconsistent with and more restrictive than the actual language of the statute they are designed to implement.

As a general proposition [see *Abbott Laboratories* v. *Gardner*, 387 U.S. 136 (1967) and Chapter 7 of the APA], an individual who feels dissatisfied by the final decision of an administrative agency can take that agency to federal district court *unless* Congress has provided that such decisions are not judicially reviewable. Under 38 U.S.C. 211(a), VA decisions "on any questions of *law or fact*" with respect to VA benefit programs are final and not subject to judicial review. A literal reading of section 211(a) indicates that the VA's interpretations of statutes and resulting regulations, circulars, and manuals are not reviewable by the courts. Questions of fact that may arise during the adjudication of individual claims are also not subject to judicial reviews.

CLAIMS FOR VA BENEFITS

The 57 VA regional offices receive about 10 million claims for benefits yearly that contain potentially appealable issues. If an initial claim for benefits is denied, the veteran (or survivor or dependent) is notified in writing of the general reason for denial and provided with information on how to initiate an appeal, obtain respresentation, and obtain a hearing. The veteran is afforded the right to a hearing at any stage of the adjudicative process. An appeal of an initial denial is obtained by filing a "Notice-of-Disagreement" (NOD) within one year of receiving the initial denial. A total of 60,000–70,000 NODs are filed yearly at the various regional offices. Generally, within 90 days of the receipt of a NOD, the VA will furnish the claimant a "Statement of the Case" that will set forth in writing a decision, summary of the evidence, and applicable laws and regulations.

The veteran can also request a hearing at that stage of his appeal. About half of the 64,841 claims that resulted in "Statements of the Case" in FY 1978 were settled at the regional office level—10,208 of which were granted at that stage in the adjudication process. Upon the mailing of the "Statement of the Case" by the VA, the veteran has 60 days within which to file a "Substantive Appeal." In FY 1978, 36,655 such appeals were filed with all the regional offices. At this point, the veteran can file additional evidence and request a hearing at either the regional office by VA employees who act as agents for the Board of Veterans Appeals (BVA); the BVA in Washington, D.C.; or a traveling section of the BVA that visits the regional offices on a periodic basis. In FY 1978 there were about 1,400 hearings before the BVA in which there were personal appearances by claimants or their representatives.

All hearings at the regional office and BVA levels are nonadversary in nature and the subpoenaing and cross-examination of witnesses is not permitted. Through the provisions of 38 C.F.R. 3.102, any reasonable doubt in a case will be construed in favor of the veteran. There is representation in about 80 percent of the cases reviewed by the BVA. Veterans are often represented by members of veterans' service organizations who do so at no cost to the veterans. While veterans can be represented by attorneys, an attorney is limited by statute [38 U.S.C. 3404(c)] from charging more than $10 for his services, although he can seek reimbursement for office expenses under 38 C.F.R. 14.650. Consequently, only 2 percent of the 35,000 claimants with cases heard by BVA yearly are represented by attorneys.

The BVA is comprised of 16 three-member panels stationed in the Washington, D.C., area. Fifteen panels are comprised of two attorneys and one physician. The remaining panel consists of three attorneys to review legal issues. BVA members are appointed by the VA administrator with the approval of the president of the United States.

In FY 1978 the BVA reversed 12.5 percent of the cases it reviewed in favor of the claimant and remanded another 13.4 percent to regional offices for further development—about 28 percent of which were ultimately reversed.

Once the BVA has rendered a final decision in a particular case—whether it turns on a question of law or fact—under 38 U.S.C. 211(a) the decision is not reviewable in court. If the claimant is able to later submit new and material evidence, the BVA will reopen the claims [38 U.S.C. 4004(b)].

Modifications in VA procedures in 1960 provided that the "Statement of the Case" must indicate pertinent information in writing, the BVA will remain independent and no longer review proposed VA policy in an advisory capacity, and the BVA has the authority to secure at no cost to the veteran an independent medical opinion from a non-VA physician that often results in decisions favorable to the veteran. However, under 38 U.S.C. 4004(c) the BVA is *bound* in its decisions by VA regulations, instructions of the administrator, and precedent opinions of the VA general counsel.

QUESTIONS OF LAW NOT REVIEWABLE—AN EXAMPLE

In December 1974 Congress overrode President Ford's veto of

what was to become PL 93–508 (The Vietnam Era Veterans' Readjustment Act of 1974). Section 202 of this law amended 38 U.S.C. 1661 to permit veterans an additional nine-month eligibility time for educational benefits toward an undergraduate degree. Thus, many veterans who were previously eligible for a maximum of 36 months' GI Bill benefits could now have a total of 45 months of educational benefits. Section 202 added the following language: "Plus an additional number of months, not exceeding 9, as may be utilized in pursuit of a program of education leading to a standard undergraduate college degree. . . ."

VA officials in Washington, D.C., in issuing DVB Circular 20–74–113 Appendix D, appeared to restrict the eligibility of veterans who applied for the additional nine months of eligibility beyond the language of the statute itself. The VA required that veterans be limited to the use of this additional nine months for only undergraduate degree credit that is consistent with the statute. However, under the above circular, the VA further stated that in order to be eligible for the extra nine months, "the veteran . . . must have been enrolled in a standard undergraduate college or first professional degree program at an institution of higher learning *at the time that original entitlement was exhausted.*"

Nothing on the face of the statute adds this further restriction on eligibility for the nine-month extension. However, based on the circular, the VA regional offices across the United States were directed to reject perhaps thousands of potential veterans' applications for the nine-month additional eligibility that the terms of the statute appeared to grant them.

In December 1974 a Vietnam veteran represented by this writer applied for the extra nine months of eligibility P.L. 93–508 on its face provided him. He had previously exhausted his full 36 months of educational entitlement in a master mechanic and instrument repairman training program from 1967 to 1971. The veteran was an excellent student who had scored in the upper 2 percent in a Standard IQ test. However, in order to qualify for consideration for promotion, he needed a college degree. Since he was separated from active duty in 1965, his eligibility for education benefits would expire in June 1976. Understandably, the student felt it was imperative that he begin college classes as soon as possible.

He began classes in January 1975 and in March 1975 received notice from his VA regional office that his claim for education benefits was denied because "your entitlement was exhausted when you pursued your apprenticeship training. The 9 months extension is not permitted unless you are enrolled in an undergraduate program at the time your entitlement was exhausted."

He was advised of his right to appeal the decision, right to representation, and right to a hearing. Accordingly, he filed a "Notice of Disagreement" on March 19, 1975, requesting a hearing and alleging that the VA "circular" paraphrased in his denial letter was more restrictive than the law itself. The veteran was aware that President Ford had vetoed what was to become P.L. 93–508 and was concerned that the VA may have been encouraged by the Office of Management and Budget to construe the provisions of that law very narrowly.

On April 23, 1975, the veteran received the "Statement of the Case" from the VA regional office, which once again denied his claim for benefits and under the subheading "pertinent laws and regulations" cited as authority "VA Circular 20–74–13, Appendix D." This was the wrong circular in that it dealt with "energy conservation," but the veteran had no way of knowing that since the circular was not attached to this document or the initial denial. Since the circular had not been printed in the *Federal Register*, neither the veteran nor the general public had ready access to it.

Since the BVA in Washington, D.C., was the next step in the appellate process, the veteran apparently filled out a "Substantive Appeal." However, since the BVA is bound by VA regulations, the veteran had no chance of reversal. Nearly six months later, in October 1975, the veteran received a denial from the BVA that concluded that it had been intended by Congress that the veteran could receive the extra nine months of entitlement only if he had been enrolled in a standard college degree program when he had exhausted his original 36 months of entitlement.

If he had switched from his instrument repairman course to a standard college degree program the month before he exhausted his original entitlement, he would have apparently been subsequently eligible for the nine extra months of educational assistance under P.L. 93–508.

The final agency decision contained no reference, general or specific, to congressional hearings or reports. This was a case in which there were no disputed facts and the threshold issue was clearly a question of law—whether a VA regulation (circular) was more restrictive than the statute it was intended to implement.

The VA adjudication and appeals process undergone by the veteran took nearly ten months and he never received the hearing he had requested in writing. During that period his eligibility delimiting date expired since the law required that he must complete all his educational programs by June 1976.

In October 1976 Congress passed P.L. 94–502, which clearly

permitted the utilization of nine extra months of educational assistance regardless of whether the first 36 months of eligibility were utilized in the pursuit of a standard undergraduate degree. However, the veteran described above considered his case moot since his eligibility expired earlier that year.

A careful review of the legislative history of the entire nine-month extension matter as provided for in P.L. 93–508 leads this writer to speculate that if the case had gotten to court, the veteran may have had no better than an even chance of winning. However, because of the language of 38 U.S.C. 211(a), the BVA decision was final and a questionable VA regulation was unchallengeable in court. A favorable court decision in his case would have undoubtedly affected the eligibility of many veterans. It would appear that the proper forum for the consideration of the intent of Congress with respect to a questionable regulation would be the federal courts—particularly since the final VA appellate body (Board of Veterans Appeals) cannot overrule VA regulations, administrator's instructions, or VA general counsel's precedent opinions.

However, because federal district courts are courts of limited jurisdiction, individuals bringing suit against federal agencies cannot expect such courts to rule on the merits of particular cases until a key issue has first been decided—whether that court has the authority (jurisdiction) to hear the case in the first place. When a question of law or fact involving a VA benefit decision has been challenged in federal court, Justice Department attorneys representing the VA almost without exception inform the court that it has no jurisdiction to hear the case since under 38 U.S.C. 211(a) VA benefit decisions are not judicially reviewable. Consequently, most courts have refused to hear the merits of complaints veterans have filed with respect to VA benefit decisions.

A LEGISLATIVE AND JUDICIAL HISTORY OF THE "NO REVIEW" CLAUSE

In passing the Tucker Act in 1887 [now codified in 28 U.S.C. 1346(d)], Congress clearly intended to prevent the federal courts from reviewing claims for pension. In 1924 the decisions of the administrators of the Veterans Bureau and the War Risk Insurance Bureau— which preceded the VA—were held by the Supreme Court to be "final and conclusive and not subject to judicial review . . . unless the decision is wholly unsupported by the evidence or is wholly dependent upon a question of law . . . or clearly arbitrary or capricious" [*Silberschein* v. *United States*, 266 U.S. 221 (1924)]. Five years later the Supreme Court upheld a 1926 finality statute passed by Congress with respect to the World War I adjusted compensation program—*Williams* v. *United States*, 278 U.S. 255 (1929).

The Economy Act of 1933 resulted in a finality clause (Public Law No. 2, 73d Cong., Section 5) similar in language to the current 38 U.S.C. 211(a).

> All decisions rendered by the Administrator of Veterans Affairs under the provisions of this title, or the regulation issued pursuant thereto, shall be final and conclusive on all questions of law and fact, and no other official or court of the United States shall have jurisdiction to review by mandamus or otherwise any such decision.

In *Lynch* v. *United States*, 292 U.S. 571 (1934), the Supreme Court interpreted the intent of the above finality clause as absolutely precluding the courts from reviewing VA benefit decisions in pension and compensation cases. The court cited *Frisbie* v. *United States*, 157 U.S. 160 (1895), which held that there was no vested legal or property right to a pension that was a privilege or gratuity.

In August 1940, Congress enacted an even stronger finality clause that was upheld in *Van Horne* v. *Hines*, 122 F.2d 207 (D.C. Cir. 1941), *cert. denied*, 314 U.S. 689, *reh. denied*, 314 U.S. 717 (1942). The court held that there were no vested rights in "gratuitous" VA benefits and that accordingly Congress precluded from court review VA final decisions involving these benefits.

However, the language of the 1940 enactment applied the finality clause to questions of law or fact concerning "A *claim* for benefits . . ." rather than all *decisions* of the administrator. Subsequent challenges were received favorably by the District of Columbia Circuit Court of Appeals, which construed the finality provisions of section 211(a) narrowly. Those opinions that commenced with *Wellman* v. *Whittier*, 259 F.2d 163 (D.C. Cir. 1958), and culminated in *Tracy* v. *Gleason*, 379 F.2d 469 (D.C. Cir. 1967), held that the term "claim" related only to an *initial claim* for veterans' benefits and, therefore, the finality statute did not preclude decisions to discontinue benefits. The *Tracy* opinion became the basis for approximately 450 actions in nature of mandamus by Philippine widows whose benefits had been terminated under a Veterans Administration rule presuming remarriage in the existence of certain circumstances. Judgments against the VA were entered in a number of those cases, one such ground was that the VA rule was inconsistent with congressional intent in statute sections defining the term "widow" and setting forth terms of benefits entitlement.

When called to the attention of Congress, the decisions of the

Court of Appeals and the District Court of the District of Columbia resulted in the following 1970 amendments to 38 U.S.C. 211(a) (P.L. 91–376):

> ... the decisions of the Administrator on any question of law or fact under any law administered by the Veterans Administration providing benefits for veterans and their dependents or survivors shall be final and conclusive and no other official or any court of the United States shall have power or jurisdiction to review any such decision by an action in the nature of mandamus or otherwise.

While final VA decisions in veterans' benefit cases remained immune from judicial review at least in part because they were viewed as privileges or gratuities, recipients of other benefit programs were entitled to judicial review of final negative decisions of their claims. Nearly 90 million Americans covered by the Social Security Disability program are permitted judicial review of negative agency decisions. This judicial review has been available since 1956. Under the scope of review set forth in 42 U.S.C. 405(g), about 10,000 such cases a year are heard by the federal courts. During 1978; nearly 50 percent of the adverse agency decisions heard by federal courts were ultimately reversed in favor of the social security disability claimants.

In a landmark 1970 due process case, the Supreme Court held that welfare payments were not privileges or gratuities but property to which a recipient had a legitimate expectation to continued payment [*Goldberg* v. *Kelly*, 397 U.S. 254 (1970)]. The court ruled that before welfare payments could be reduced or terminated, a recipient had the right to prior notice and the opportunity for a pretermination hearing during which the recipient was entitled to confront adverse witnesses and present his own evidence. The right to judicial review is also extended to individuals under the Unemployment Compensation, Black Lung, Railroad Retirement; Social Security Disability, and Supplemental Security Income programs.

However, the 1970 amendments to 38 U.S.C. 211(a) effectively killed the access to the courts provided by the line of cases spawned by *Wellman*. This position was articulated in *DeRoudulfa* v. *United States*, 461 F.2d 1240 (D.C. Cir. 1972), *cert. denied*, 409 U.S. 949 (1972). The court reasoned:

> The constitutional adjudications find common ground in the thesis, as expressed by the First Circuit, that "veterans" benefits are gratuitous and established no vested rights in the recipients . . . [citing *Milliken* v. *Gleason*, 332 F.2d 122, 123 (1st Cir. 1964) *cert. denied*, 379 U.S. 1002

(1965); and the origin of that proposition in *Lynch* v. *United States*, 292 U.S. 571 (1934), and other Supreme Court decisions] and despite possible indication that the thesis may be waning, [with reference to *Goldberg* v. *Kelly*, 397 U.S. 254 (1970)] we are obliged to accept it unless and until it is disapproved.

JOHNSON V. ROBISON: CONSTITUTIONAL QUESTIONS OF LEGISLATION REVIEWABLE

A landmark decision with respect to the finality provision subsequent to the 1970 amendments was *Johnson* v. *Robison*, 415 U.S. 361 (1974). In that case, the Supreme Court held that section 211(a) does not bar judicial review of constitutional questions involving veterans' benefits *legislation*:

> Plainly, no explicit provision of § 211(a) bars judicial consideration of appellee's constitutional claims. The section provides that "the *decisions* of the Administrator on any question of law or fact *under* any law administered by the Veterans' Administration providing benefits for veterans . . . shall be final and conclusive and no . . . court of the United States shall have power or jurisdiction to review any such decision. . . ."
>
> The prohibitions would appear to be aimed at review only of those decisions of law or fact that arise in the *administration* by the Veterans Administration of a *statute* providing the benefits for veterans. A decision of law or fact "under" a statute is made by the Administrator in the interpretation or application of a particular provision of the statute to a particular set of facts. Appellee's constitutional challenge is not to any such decision of the *Administrator*, but rather to a decision of Congress to create a statutory class entitled to benefits that does not include I-O conscientious objectors who performed alternative civilian service.

In an unreported case, *Wallace* v. *The Administrator of Veterans Affairs*, No. 14499 (D. Conn., filed December 23, 1974), the VA unsuccessfully argued that the court had no jurisdiction to hear a case involving the reduction of a veterans' disability compensation without a prior hearing. The court held that rather than reviewing a decision of the VA administrator, it was establishing whether his due process rights to notice and a pretermination hearing were met by the VA. Accordingly, the court ordered an examination by a court-appointed physician and dismissed the action after the examining physician confirmed the VA evaluation. However, as the result of this case, the VA strengthened its due process requirements involving notice, hearing, and appellate rights of veterans receiving disability compensation (38 C.F.R. 3.103).

PLATO V. ROUDEBUSH: CONSTITUTIONAL QUESTIONS OF VA PROCEDURES REVIEWABLE

In *Plato* v. *Roudebush*, 397 F. Supp. 2195 (D. Md. 1975), the federal district court in Maryland extended the *Robison* doctrine to include VA procedures when it held that section 211(a) did not exempt VA procedural policies from constitutional review by the courts.

In *Plato*, the VA terminated a widow's pension payments without first granting her notice and the opportunity for a pretermination hearing. The court held that constitutional interpretation is not committed to agency discretion but is a judicial function and ruled that the VA should have granted the claimant notice and the opportunity for a hearing consistent with the *Goldberg* doctrine.

As a result of the *Plato* decision, the VA modified its procedures by providing for notice and the opportunity for a hearing before terminating or reducing benefit payments in the areas of pension, dependency and indemnity compensation, and death compensation (DVB Manual, M 21-1, paragraph 14.36).

The Department of Justice declined the VA's request for an appeal to clarify the *Plato* ruling that expanded court jurisdiction of the *Robison* doctrine from constitutional questions involving legislation to questions of VA procedure. With one exception that involved an initial claim for benefits rather than the termination or reduction of an existing award [*Anderson* v. *Veterans Administration*, 559 F.2d 935 (1977)], the holding in *Plato* appears to be indicative of the general trend of the case law.

In another unreported case [*Waterman* v. *Roudebush*, No. 4-77-70 (D. Minn., December 15, 1977)], the senior judge of the Minnesota Federal District Court ruled that the absence of notice and right to a hearing before the VA terminated education benefits was a denial of due process rights guaranteed by the Fifth Amendment. The court ordered the VA regional office to provide notice and the right to a pretermination "interview" before terminating education benefits in cases in which veterans were making "unsatisfactory progress" under the criteria of PL 94-502. The Justice Department ultimately decided against pursuing its appeal before the 8th Circuit Court of Appeals. However, the VA did not subsequently modify its procedures with respect to the termination of education benefits by the 56 other VA regional offices outside the jurisdiction of the Minnesota Federal District Court.

THE WAYNE STATE CASE: 6TH CIRCUIT
RULES VA REGULATIONS REVIEWABLE

A more recent challenge to section 211(a) was rendered by the Court of Appeals in *Wayne State University* v. *Cleland*, 590 F.2d 627 (6th Cir. 1978). This class-action suit was brought by Wayne State University and two of its veteran students who challenged the validity of certain VA regulations. The regulations in question require veterans to be enrolled in a course of study that scheduled at least 12 "standard classroom sessions" per week in order to qualify for full-time educational assistance benefits. The district court found the regulations invalid as promulgated without statutory authority [440 F. Supp. 811 (1977)].

The Justice Department appealed the lower court's decision arguing that section 211(a) precluded judicial review of the validity of Veterans Administration regulations and, in the alternative, that the administrator had sufficient authority under 38 U.S.C. Sec. 210 to promulgate the regulations at issue.

The circuit court agreed with the district court's finding that section 211(a) does not preclude challenges to the administrator's authority to promulgate regulations. The court found that the reasoning of the Supreme Court in *Robison* was equally appropriate in *Wayne State*:

> Suits challenging the authority to promulgate regulations will not involve the federal courts in the day to day operations of the VA. Neither will our construction of § 211(a) spawn suits requesting federal courts to second guess the Administrator on the merits of particular claims for benefits or termination of such benefits. Suits challenging statutory authority of the Administrator will not involve the courts in the complex and technical niceties of VA policies, but rather will seek a determination where the regulations have been promulgated pursuant to a congressional grant of authority.

The court also noted that an interpretation to the effect that 211(a) bars judicial review of VA regulations would require finding a congressional intent to insulate the limits of the VA administrator's authority. The court then concluded that such a construction is not supported by the legislative history of section 211(a) and would raise serious doubts about the statute's constitutionality.

The court further stated that its review of the cases interpreting section 211(a) further demonstrated its inapplicability to challenges to the administrator's authority to promulgate regulations. Citing a number of cases, the court stated:

> The cases where section 211(a) has barred judicial review have all involved suits challenging the Administrator's decisions concerning individual claims for benefits or terminations of existing benefits. No decision of the Supreme Court or this court has construed section 211(a) to bar judicial review of the Administrator's authority to promulgate regulations.

After agreeing with the district court that federal jurisdiction for the suit existed, the circuit court applied the three-prong test articulated by the Supreme Court in *Citizens to Preserve Overton Park Inc.* v. *Volpe*, 467 F. Supp. 508 (1979) to determine validity of the regulations in question. Accordingly, the court found that the VA regulation complied with each part of *Overton Park* standard and that the district court erred in finding the regulation void. However, after noting that the district court's conclusion was based on statutory grounds that did not reach the plaintiff's constitutional challenges to the implementing statute and the regulations promulgated thereunder, the circuit court remanded the case to the district court for a determination of those constitutional issues.

In *Evergreen State College* v. *Cleland*, No. C 78-87M (W.D. Wash, March 21, 1979), the court found challenged VA education regulations valid but held that they applied more narrowly than the VA contended. The court reasoned that the VA lacked the express authority to interpret "semester hours" as requiring standard class sessions and thus reducing educational benefits to veteran students to a part-time rate. Accordingly, the VA was ordered to pay full-time residence training benefits to veterans attending the plaintiff community colleges based on school certification criteria rather than those provided for in the VA Regulations and Circular 20-77-16. On December 3, 1979 the Justice Department filed an appeal with the 9th Circuit Court of Appeals.

In *Merged Area X (Education)* v. *Cleland*, No. C 78-46 (N.D. Iowa 1978), [appeal filed, No. 78-1757 (8th Cir., October 16, 1978)] the district court held that it had jurisdiction to hear the case and ruled that the VA had no statutory authority to promulgate and implement certain VA education regulations and Circular 20-77-16. The case was appealed to the 8th Circuit. On August 1, 1979 that court upheld the lower court ruling that the legal question involving the VA regulation was subject to judicial review despite the language of section 211(a). The court reversed the lower court in holding that the VA had not exceeded its statutory authority in promulgating the regulations in question.

Because courts in general have only recently granted jurisdiction in cases challenging legislation, procedures, and regulations in VA matters, there is no substantial body of case law in the field of veterans' benefits. Furthermore, several of the 11 circuit courts of appeals are experiencing a considerable backlog. For example, at this writing the 9th Circuit Court of Appeals has yet to decide on an appeal filed with it more than three years ago involving a federal district court decision ordering the Los Angeles VA regional office to give student veterans 30 days prior notice to any suspension, reduction, or termination of education benefits [*Devine* v. *Miller*, No. CV76-0592—IH (C.D. Cal., August 11, 1976, appeal entered, No. 77-1430 (9th Cir., October 1976)].

For these reasons the VA, in effect, sometimes administers benefit programs in accordance with the terms of court orders that vary from jurisdiction to jurisdiction.

RECENT LEGISLATIVE EFFORTS TO SUBJECT VA BENEFITS DECISION TO JUDICIAL REVIEW

In 1977 Senator Gary Hart (D. Colorado) introduced Senate bill 364, which would have required that the VA modify its hearing and adjudication procedures to comply with the provisions of Title 5, Chapter 5 (APA), that final VA benefit decisions be subjected to judicial review as set forth in title 5, Chapter 7 (AP), and that the $10 restriction on attorney's fees be modified. During 1977 the Senate Committee on Veterans' Affairs conducted five hearings at which many organizations and individuals commented on S. 364. For the first time since the issue had come to public attention in the 1950s, the Veterans Administration and the Justice Department testified that they no longer opposed the concept of final VA benefit decisions being subjected to judicial review. In fact, the VA position as presented by VA General Guy H. McMichael III on October 10, 1977 favored judicial review of constitutional questions of legislation, regulations, and procedures. Mr. McMichael stated that the VA deferred to Congress on the issue of whether factual questions in individual cases should also be subject to court review.

Criticisms of S. 364 included the fear that compelling the presence and cross-examination of witnesses as required by Chapter 5 of the APA would destroy current informal VA hearing procedures. There was also concern that the scope of judicial review as set forth in section 706 of the APA could result in courts doing *de novo* reviews and substituting their judgments for those of the agency rather than limiting their review to weighing the evidence in the administrative record.

Senator Hart agreed to withdraw his bill after Senator Alan Cranston, chairman of the Senate Committee on Veterans' Affairs, assured him that his staff would assist in the redrafting of a bill tailored to meet many of the criticisms of S. 364 and that such a measure would be voted upon in the Senate by May 1979. During 1978 the staff of the Senate Committee on Veterans' Affairs developed a 25-page bill that was introduced by Senators Hart and Cranston on February 1, 1979— S. 330. The framers of S. 330 attempted to address many of the previous criticisms of S. 364 by incorporating proposed changes within title 38 U.S.C. rather than totally subjecting the VA to all the provisions in Chapters 5 and 7 of title 5 (APA). Additionally, the subpoenaing and cross-examination of witnesses and *de novo* review were not permitted in S. 330. The Senate Committee heard testimony on S. 330 on February 22 and March 22, 1979.

At the same time, the Department of Health, Education and Welfare, with the approval of the administration, was encouraging legislation (H.R. 2854, section 401) that would dramatically reduce the scope of judicial review provided in Social Security disability cases for more than two decades. The HEW bill would have permitted court review of questions of law—statutes, regulations, and procedures—but would have no longer permitted court review of questions of fact that are currently reviewable under the "substantial evidence" standard, 42 U.S.C. 405(g). On March 20, 1979, a House subcommittee voted 7 to 2 to reject the administration's proposed language.

While that proposed narrowing of the scope of judicial review was rejected, it may be indicative of a trend. On December 15, 1978, a Plenary Session of the Administrative Conference of the United States failed to vote favorably on a Conference subcommittee recommendation that questions of law and fact in final benefit decisions be subject to judicial review. On March 9–10, 1978, the Judicial Conference of the United States reaffirmed an earlier resolution in which that body deferred to Congress the question of whether final VA benefit decisions should be subject to court review. However, the Conference indicated that if Congress did decide in favor of judicial review of such cases, a special court of veterans' appeals rather than federal court review would be more advisable.

A 1977 study done for the Center for Administrative Justice ("Study of the Social Security Administration Hearing System," October 1977, Jerry L. Mashaw Project Director), is often quoted by those who are not convinced the case has been made for judicial review of questions of fact at issue in final VA benefit decisions (transcript of the

December 15, 1978, Plenary Session of the Administrative Conference of the United States pages 32–34—remarks by Kenneth Culp Davis). While the authors of the Mashaw Study examine the question whether judicial review of questions of fact in disability cases is desirable, they contend that "few would seriously question the necessity for judicial review on questions of law, particularly constitutional law" (p. 274).

While the House Committee on Veterans' Affairs in 1960–62 was instrumental in the establishment of several provisions that strengthened due process protections in VA regional office and BVA hearings, that body has expressed little interest in considering the issue of judicial review in the immediate future.

It is the opinion of this writer that if the scope of review in proposed legislation were primarily *limited to questions of law*, (that is, constitutional questions and questions of statutory construction) and any review of questions of fact either be narrowed considerably or precluded, the possibility for more serious support by major veterans' organizations and favorable action by the House Committee on Veterans' Affairs would be considerably enhanced. VA regulations and circulars define the eligibility of veterans for many benefits provided by Congress. A modification in a VA regulation if forced by a court order could affect literally thousands of veterans. The embryonic state of development of veterans' case law appears to indicate that the courts may ultimately determine that questions of law in veterans' benefit cases are judicially reviewable as was concluded at the Circuit Court of Appeals level in *Wayne State* and *Merged Area*. However, it remains to be seen how the other nine circuits (and possibly the Supreme Court) may rule on this question. Until this time, 94 various federal district courts will generally be bound by the decisions of their respective circuit court.

A brief review of case law indicates that circuit court decisions involving questions of law—such as the overturning of regulations and procedures—favorably affect the eligibility of thousands of claimants in other benefit programs. For example, *Vitek* v. *Finch*, 438 F.2d 1157 (4th Cir. 1971), the Court of Appeals reversed a district court decision and held that the opinion of a claimant's treating physician is entitled to great weight as it reflects an expert judgment based upon a continuing observation of patients's condition over a prolonged period of time.

In *Bozwich* v. *Mathews*, 558 F.2d, 475 (8th Cir. 1977), the Court of Appeals held that a Social Security ruling that presumed a claimant was not entitled to Black Lung benefits was unreasonable because it conflicted with the clear legislative purpose of the statute and shifted to the miner the burden of producing evidence to show some greater disability than would otherwise be required by the statute. In a similar ruling, *Hubbard* v. *Califano*, 598 F.2d 623 (1979) the 4th Circuit Court vacated a

Social Security ruling that there is an inference that total disability does not exist unless X-ray or ventilatory tests establish disability. Instead, the court held that a variety of tests can be utilized rather than just those two to determine extent of disability, for example, blood gas studies, electrocardiograms, physical performance tests, medical history, and affidavits of spouses.

In *Liberty Alliance of the Blind* v. *Califano*, 568 F.2d 333 (3rd Cir. 1977), the Court of Appeals remanded a lower court ruling in holding that HEW had improperly interpreted and applied the Social Security Amendments of 1972 in determining the amount of Supplemental Security Income benefits for blind persons.

CONCLUSION

Subsequent to the March 22, 1979 hearings, Chairman Cranston directed his staff to narrow the proposed scope of review of questions of fact in S. 330. Accordingly, the language providing for the "substantial evidence" scope of review of fact determinations was replaced by the "arbitrary and capricious" standard. On May 3, 1979, the Senate Committee on Veterans' Affairs voted favorably by a margin of 9 to 1 to report S. 330 as amended. This was the first time a congressional committee voted favorably on proposed legislation specifically designed to subject final VA benefit decisions to judicial review.

Immediately prior to that vote, Senator Strom Thurmond (R. South Carolina) proposed an amendment that would have limited the scope of review to questions of law. While this amendment was defeated 6 to 4, it may be indicative of the language of a measure that might be considered by the House Committee on Veterans' Affairs. When questioned on the record, V.A. General Counsel McMichael favored the Thurmond amendment. Proponents of judicial review consider the action on May 3, 1979, as very favorable in that the issue was no longer whether there should be judicial review of final VA benefit decisions but rather what the scope of that review should be. On September 17, 1979, the Senate enacted S. 330 by unanimous consent. At this writing the House Committee on Veterans Affairs has taken no action on this matter.

The proper forum for the final interpretation of the intent of Congress with respect to questionable regulations is the federal courts. This is particularly necessary in the case of the VA since, by statute, its final appellate body (BVA) is required to defer to VA regulations, administrator's instructions, and general counsel's precedent opinions.

18

THE CASE FOR VETERANS' PREFERENCE

DEAN K. PHILLIPS

The National Organization for Women oppose(s) any state, federal, county, or municipal employment law or program giving special preference to veterans.

The above resolution, which indiscriminately opposes *all* veterans' preference laws, was adopted by the National Organization for Women (NOW) at their 4th Annual Convention in September 1971. At that time, American soldiers were still dying on the battlefields of Indochina. This resolution was printed in the 1973 NOW publication "Revolution: Tomorrow is NOW." A proposed modification drafted in consultation with this author by the individual who chaired NOW's committee on Women in the Military was ignored at the 9th Annual NOW Convention in 1976. This proposal would have supported Veterans preference for disabled veterans and more limited preference for non-disabled veterans. A legislative aid from NOW's Washington, D.C. office advised this author that the ". . . 1971 NOW veterans preference resolution has not been rescinded or modified and still represents NOW's official

This chapter is for Don MacMillan, Len Gilmer, and Dennis Rhoades. With special appreciation to Ed Lukey, Tom Kiley, and Guy McMichael. It is not the official Veterans Administration position, nor does it reflect VA opinion.

position." A proposed change similar to that submitted in 1976 was (at the request of the Federally Employed Women) resubmitted and again ignored at the October 1979 NOW Annual Convention and December board meeting.

During the past three generations, the United States has become involved in World War II, Korea, and Vietnam. Those who served on active duty during these three armed conflicts at the very least experienced a disruption in life style, generally from two to four years at very low pay,[1] and at worst were disabled or killed. In fact, 523,000 American military personnel died and more than 2.7 million were disabled during that period. Due to several factors, the casualties of these wars were suffered almost exclusively by men. One major factor was that while the military often had to draw its infantry, armor, and artillery soldiers from draftees, women have been completely exempt from the draft. Two other apparent factors include statutes, regulations, and policies limiting the percentage of women comprising the armed forces and more restrictive enlistment standards for women. Consequently, more than 98 percent of America's 30 million veterans are men. Any examination of the validity of veterans' preference in civil service employment and how it has or has not discriminated against women should be considered within this framework.

Until 1972 the number of Military Occupation Specialities (MOS) available to women has been highly restricted and women have been subject to higher standards for enlistment. For example, men have been required to meet only those standards established for the particular MOS for which they enlist, sometimes not requiring a high school degree. On the other hand, women must have either earned a high school degree or passed a comparable equivalency examination.

However, in order to determine whether the extreme language of the aforementioned 1971 NOW resolution can be justified, a review of efforts of American women to enter the military (particularly during time of war) must be considered. During World War II, when the United States had an available manpower pool about half as large as that during Vietnam, 16.5 million Americans served on active duty—350,000 of whom were women. The role of women was exclusively limited to noncombat jobs, although those women stationed in Europe lived in the same conditions as noncombatant men and suffered the same casualty rates as noncombatant men (0.5 percent). Following World War II, the number of women on active duty dropped from 266,000 (2.2 percent of 12.1 million personnel) in 1945 to 14,000 or 1 percent of the 1.4 million total strength in 1948.[2]

In 1948 Congress passed legislation that precluded women from comprising more than 2 percent of total active duty strength. This statute remained on the books until 1967 when it was repealed by PL 90–130.

When the Korean War broke out, very few women attempted to enlist in the armed forces. A 1977 Department of Defense Background Study reports:

> With the advent of the Korean war, an unsuccessful effort was made to recruit some 100,000 women to meet the rapidly expanding manpower requirements. Young women just were not interested in serving, perhaps because of the unpopularity of that war at the time. Between 1948 and 1969, even including nurses, the percentage of women in the military never exceeded 1.5 percent and averaged 1.2 percent of the total active strength.[3]

At the time of the escalation of the Vietnam War in 1964 the percentage of women on active duty was less than 1 percent of the total military strength. It would appear that again women generally were not interested in entering the military. Despite the fact that Congress lifted the 2 percent statutory bar in 1967, women did not reach 2 percent of total active duty strength until mid-1973,[4] six years later. American ground troops had been pulled out of Vietnam in March of that year. Undoubtedly, the low percentage of women in the military during Vietnam might be in part attributed to the unpopularity of the war and enlistment standards that were more strict for women. Another factor was that prior to 1972 only 35 percent of all enlisted MOSs were opened to women. That year a Pentagon decision resulted in over 80 percent of MOSs opening to women by 1976.

Currently, major restrictions on the recruitment of and duties assigned to women in the U.S. military establishment are not explicitly incorporated in federal law. According to the conclusions of a 1977 Brookings Institution study, it is the current policies established by the individual military services themselves that limit opportunities for women.[5] A reading of the July 22 and September 1, 1977, hearings before a subcommittee of the Joint Economic Committee of the U.S. Congress indicates that despite the fact that most MOSs are now opened to women, females comprise only 6.6 percent of active duty personnel, and long-range armed forces plans call for the percentage of women serving on active duty to be about 10 percent of our total strength.[6] The Department of Defense reports active duty women were 19,000 in 1964; 25,000 in 1968; 117,000 in 1978; and the goal for FY 1984 is 208,000.[7] The Brookings study refers to surveys indicating that, in general, neither female nor male members of the armed forces appear to oppose the concept of assigning women to combat units or aboard naval combat vessels. However, the report concludes that "many of the women who endorse a combat role for women do not appear to want such a role for themselves."[8] Nevertheless, women have correctly concluded that their preclusion from assignment to combat vessels under 10 U.S.C. 6015 had adversely affected their chances for career advancement and in 1978 a class-action suit in which the American Civil Liberties Union represented female Navy personnel was successful in overturning the statute that had limited assignment of women to hospital ships and transports [*Owens* v. *Brown*, 455 F. Supp. 291 (1978)].

Regardless of the various factors that resulted in very few women serving on active duty during the Vietnam War, the fact remains that the brunt of the "blood and guts" years of the Vietnam era was borne by men. During the decade that has become known as the Vietnam era, the manpower pool was double that of World War II when nearly 25 million young men were of draft age. Over 9.3 million ultimately served on active duty and 3.1 million in Vietnam.

An extensive and well-researched study done in conjunction with Ralph Nader's Center for the Study of Responsive Law concluded that the soldiers who fought in Vietnam were hardly drawn at random from the general population.[9] Student draft deferments grew by 900 percent between 1951 and 1966[10] and were primarily utilized by middle class youths who had the money and life style conducive to college. Hence, much of the fighting in Vietnam was done by the working class and urban poor who were less able to utilize that legal dodge.

In 1965 many youths were enlisting in the military service as a means of upward social mobility that they could not find in civilian life,[11] only to find themselves carrying a rifle. By 1965 one soldier of every six killed in Vietnam was a draftee. However, as the scope of the war became more prolonged and manpower needs increased, Americans became aware of the fact that enlistment in the infantry, armor, or artillery increased the odds of being wounded or killed. Consequently, increasingly fewer men enlisting in the armed forces requested combat arms MOSs. Since the armed forces had to rely on the draft to meet manpower needs in the combat arms, draftees began to shoulder an ever-increasing load of the fighting. By 1966 one of every five Americans killed was a draftee. In 1967 and 1968 more than one of every three American soldiers who died was a draftee. By 1969 and 1970 draftees suffered more than 40 percent of total U.S. casualties in Vietnam and 60 percent of U.S. Army combat deaths. Draftees comprised 54 percent of those wounded in 1969.[12] By 1970 less than 5 percent of individuals enlisting requested that they be trained for infantry, armor, or artillery.[13] That year 57 percent of Army casualties were draftees.[14] Enlistees who had not requested any specific MOS or duty station, and had been sent to Vietnam in combat arms slots, comprised 30 percent of the 1970 casualties. Thus nearly 90 percent of U.S. casualties that year were suffered by individuals who had not requested combat arms training or Vietnam duty. The casualty rate for draftees is illustrated in Tables 18.1 and 18.2.

Because of advances in medical techniques and the courage of helicopter medivac pilots and crews, Vietnam veterans survived crippling wounds that would have been fatal due to shock or loss of blood in previous wars. Thus, the percentage of Vietnam soldiers suffering amputation or disabling injury to their legs or feet was 300 percent higher than in World War II and 70 percent higher than in Korea.[15]

Casualty rates were disproportionately higher for blacks who enlisted for combat arms MOSs earlier in the war and for their younger

TABLE 18.1: Army Draftee Casualties as a Percentage of Total Army Enlisted Casualties, 1965–70

	Killed in Action	Wounded
1965	28	24
1966	34	35
1967	57	58
1968	58	57
1969	62	54
1970	57	57

Source: "Extension of the Draft and Bills Related to the Voluntary Force Concept and Authorization of Strength Levels," Hearings before the Committee on Armed Services, House of Representatives, 92d Cong., 1st sess., February 23-25, March 1-5, 9-11, 1971.

TABLE 18.2: Army Draftees Killed in Action as a Percentage of Total Army Enlisted Killed in Action for Selected Occupational Groupings, 1965–70

	Infantry	Armor	Artillery	Medical	Helicopter Crews
1965	29.0	30.0	27.3	45.0	9.1
1966	34.6	30.6	35.9	44.1	28.8
1967	60.6	49.5	50.4	52.9	36.8
1968	63.5	49.6	59.5	50.4	21.0
1969	68.8	50.0	59.5	50.8	18.6
1970 1st half	69.4	42.1	55.4	54.2	23.7
Cumulative	60.1	49.5	55.1	50.4	22.6

Source: "Extension of the Draft and Bills Related to the Voluntary Force Concept and Authorization of Strength Levels," Hearings before the Committee on Armed Services, House of Representatives, 92d Cong., 1st sess., February 23-25, March 1-5, 9-11, 1971.

brothers who were later drafted while many of their predominantly white counterparts were safe in college under the mantle of the student draft deferment. Blacks comprised less than 5 percent of college enrollments in 1965.[16] Department of Defense reports indicate that between January 1961 and April 1975, 57,505 American soldiers died in Vietnam.[17] While blacks averaged about 9.3 percent of total active duty personnel in 1965–70,[18] they suffered 7,241 or 12.6 percent of the deaths—35.5 percent in excess of their percentage of the U.S. armed forces and 30 percent in excess of their presence in Indochina. (During the Vietnam fighting, blacks comprised 10 percent of U.S. armed forces in Southeast Asia.) Disproportionately high casualty rates for Spanish-surnamed soldiers have also been reported.[19]

The unusually high casualty rates for minorities during Vietnam in part can be attributed to Project 100,000, which the Department of Defense implemented in October 1966. Under this program, more than 300,000 men whose intelligence induction tests scores were between the tenth and thirtieth percentiles were no longer determined ineligible for induction. Thirty-seven percent of these Project 100,000 men were sent to the infantry units in Vietnam. During the first years of the program, 225,000 men were admitted into the military under the modified mental standards, but only 7.5 percent of them received remedial education. Reportedly, more than 41 percent[20] of this group were black; more than 40 percent of the Project 100,000 men were given combat-related assignments in infantry, armor, or artillery; and half of the Army and Marine contingent went to Vietnam. By the time they were an average of 18 months into their period of service, the Project 100,000 men had been decimated—10 percent were either killed, wounded, or received less-than-honorable discharges.[21] For political reasons, the 1 million-member force comprised of the Reserves and National Guard was not called to active duty to serve in Vietnam. The activation of 3 percent of that force occurred in 1968, but those individuals were mainly support troops. Understandably, there were long waiting lists to enter the Guard and Reserve units—at the end of 1968, the waiting list for the Army National Guard exceeded 100,000. Only 1 percent of the National Guard Reserve soldiers were blacks.[22]

Despite the fact that the agony of Vietnam was suffered almost entirely by men, and a disproportionate percentage of minority men, treatises on sex discrimination often ignore perhaps *the most blatantly sexist policy* in our nation's history: the limitation of the drafting of those who will die and be crippled in combat exclusively to the male sex. A case in point is a lengthy sex discrimination law school text released in 1975.[23] The text quotes a woman whose complaint ignored the plight of Project 100,000 soldiers:

Military service benefits, especially for the young with limited education or training, accompany the responsibility. Since October 1966, some 246,000 young men who did not meet the normal mental or physical requirements, have been given opportunities for training and correcting physical problems, while such opportunities are not open to their sisters.[24]

The editors give only the briefest attention to the hardship suffered by those who served in combat in World War II, Korea, and Vietnam or the loss of time suffered by those who served in noncombat roles during those wars, much less the gruesome plight of Project 100,000 soldiers. Ironically, upon their release from active duty, very few veterans find that their military training has prepared them to assume many civilian jobs. A 1969 Bureau of the Budget Report, limited to those veterans who secured employment, found that only 12 percent had used skills or training gained in the military.[25] A 1973 Veterans Administration study reported that less than half of the veterans surveyed received any technical or academic training while on active duty. Of those veterans who had received training, only 29.6 percent indicated that their training was helpful in obtaining a civilian job. Individuals who entered the military with less than a high school degree (for example, Project 100,000 people) fared even worse: "About half as many of the veterans with 1 to 11 years of schooling received technical or vocational training in the service as those who had a high level of education attainment.[26]

A blatant misunderstanding of Project 100,000 was demonstrated in a January 1979 civil action filed against ten federal agencies by Sears, Roebuck and Company. Sears apparently attempted to prevent the federal government from enforcing affirmative-action statutes and regulations. Sears claimed that the government created a disproportionately white male management segment of the population, in part, through its military institutions—the subjection of only males to the draft and the limitation on the percentage of women permitted in the armed forces. Sears alleged that training and education in the military and subsequently under the GI Bill has been exclusively utilized by males. Incredibly, Sears cited Project 100,000 as an example of the army turning "into the nation's largest school."[27] This suit was dismissed May 15, 1979, for failure on the part of Sears "to present a justiciable case or controversy."

During the Vietnam era, men argued unsuccessfully before federal courts that Congress' exemption of women from the draft denied men the "equal protection" guaranteed them under the Constitution. In all five cases the men were ultimately unsuccessful as the courts ruled that the subjection of only males to the draft was rationally related to a legitimate power of government—to raise and support armies under Article I, section 8 of the Constitution.[28]

THE VETERANS' PREFERENCE ACT OF 1944

In June 1944, the month allied paratroopers and infantry soldiers made the Normandy landings at tremendous human cost, the 78th Congress passed PL 359: The Veterans' Preference Act of 1944. In addition to breaking new ground for veterans, this law codified the various statutory, regulatory, and executive-order provisions that had already been in existence.

Among its several sections, the act provided for an addition of five points to the civil service test scores of nondisabled war veterans. Ten points were added to the passing test scores of disabled veterans, and compensably disabled veterans were then placed at the head of the civil service register. Ten points were also granted to widows and wives of severely disabled veterans. Although the points could not be used for promotions, they could be used more than once. This procedure applied to government jobs other than some positions in the excepted service where no examinations are given (for example, scientists) or the positions of guards, elevator operators, and custodians where veterans were granted absolute preference. In addition, the "rule of three" provided that if a veteran were among the top three applicants for a particular job with a government agency, in order to bypass the veteran and select a nonveteran, the agency was required to receive written permission from the Civil Service Commission. Veterans were also granted certain job retention rights over nonveterans with similiar status and performance records in the event of a reduction in force. Additionally, due process rights in cases of disciplinary action, such as dismissal or suspension from civil service jobs, were granted veterans, widows, and wives of severely disabled veterans. After some debate, what was to become PL 359 passed the House and ultimately the Senate with only one negative vote. A reading of the statute and the legislative history that includes the Hearings, House, and Senate Reports,[29] and a review of excerpts from the *Congressional Record* during the period immediately prior to the passage of the act, indicate that although readjustment appeared to be a major concern of Congress, it was clearly the intent of Congress to place no restriction on the number of times an eligible individual could utilize veterans' preference. Nor did Congress set a date after which a veteran could no longer exercise veterans' preference. However, for the positions of guards, elevator operators, messengers, and custodians, the preference was to extend for the duration of the war and for a period of five years following the conclusion of the war. Congress had the authority to permit this particular preference to continue, and it is still implemented at this writing.

The hearings indicate that the proposed legislation was nearly universally embraced. However, the National Civil Service Reform League and the League of Women Voters urged that points not be added to the test score of an eligible veteran, widow, or wife of a severely disabled veteran unless the score was a passing one.[30] N. P. Alifas, president of District 44, International Association of Machinists, introduced a statement that urged the bill not be passed. While he did not claim the veterans' preference law might adversely affect women as a class, Alifas warned of "having the population divided into two rival camps for the next couple of generations." He further warned that the proposed legislation "go[es] so far in giving preference to ex-servicemen and women . . . that American citizens without military service may as well seek other employment if now in the [civil] service and refrain from making application for government positions in the future."[31] After some effort Alifas was able to persuade the chairman of the Senate Committee on Civil Service to include his written testimony on the record.

While Congress ended five-point preference for post-World War II veterans, it later granted five-point preference to those nondisabled veterans who served on active duty during the Korean War. Ten-point preference was retained for veterans disabled even during peacetime and that policy exists to this day. Individuals entering the military between 1955 and 1966 were not eligible for five-point preference. However, five points were granted nondisabled veterans (PL 89-554, September 6, 1966) upon the expansion of the Vietnam War. In September 1967 Congress provided the five-point preference retroactively for nondisabled veterans who served during the years 1955-67 [PL 90-83(6)(B)]. The granting of this five-point preference to those entering active duty was not terminated until the passage of PL 94-502 in October 1976. Hence, Congress responded to the Vietnam War by extending five-point eligibility to individuals who served during the nearly 22-year span between 1955 and 1976. Thus, far more than the 9.3 million who served during the Vietnam era, including 3.1 million who served in Vietnam, were eligible for the five-point preference. Additionally, while theoretically not in the job market, nondisabled veterans who served during the Korean War and World War II remain eligible for five-point preference.

As the Vietnam War drew to a close, an increasing number of

women's organizations called either for an end to or a reduction of veterans' preference. A 1975 study by the Women's Program Committee of the Denver Federal Executive Board reviewed the effects of the Veterans' Preference Act of 1944.[32] While grossly understating the plight of draftees by observing that "those drafted into military service may have suffered disruptions in their normal life style, . . ." the study concluded that veterans' preference had an adverse effect on the employment prospects of women since less than 2 percent of America's 30 million veterans are females. Reportedly nonveteran females accounted for 53 percent of the Civil Service certifications but only 44 percent of the selections, while veteran males accounted for only 27 percent of those certified but 34 percent of those selected for Civil Service jobs. The study pointed to a 1974 Civil Service Commission report on handicapped veterans who indicated that of 199,592 veterans studied who were receiving ten-point veterans' preference, only 10 percent were coded as handicapped under the Civil Service Commission's criteria for reporting physical impairment.[33] From this, the Women's Committee study concluded that many veterans receiving ten points as being disabled were not significantly adversely affected by military service. The study pointed out that to be eligible for ten preference a veteran need only establish the present existence of a service-connected disability or be receiving compensation, disability retirement, benefits, or pension based on a public statute. The fact that such disability need not be suffered as the result of combat wounds was illustrated with the example of a veteran whose ten-point disability preference was reportedly the result of the loss of an eye while playing handball. The Denver study further reported that the average number of active duty years served by male veterans studied that received preference points was 16.7 years, thus implying that many veterans enjoying preference points were not first-term enlistees or draftees but retired career officers and noncommissioned officers.[34]

The adverse effects of veterans' preference on women in federal hiring were later cited in a comptroller general's report to the Congress in 1977 in which examples of federal civil service registers "blocked" by veterans were cited.[35] This report recommended that Congress consider limiting veterans' preference to a one-time use and/or imposing a time limit for use of veterans' preference. These recommendations were based on responses received by the General Accounting Office from numerous government agencies.

The report also revealed that the same agencies reported using "questionable procedures to obtain women who cannot be reached on the CSC (Civil Service Commission) registers." Specific examples included:

Writing job descriptions to fit the qualifications of particular (nonveteran female) applicants.

Listing jobs with CSC as "intermittent" employment to discourage veteran applicants.

Requesting and returning certificates unused until veterans who are blocking the register have been hired by another agency or for other reasons are no longer blocking the register.[36]

On October 4, 1977, Alan K. Campbell, chairman of the U.S. Civil Service Commission, testified before the House Subcommittee on Civil Service and stated that veterans' preference had seriously impaired the employment prospects of women in the 2.8 million-member federal civil service.[37] He reported that veterans comprise 25 percent of the national labor force but hold down about 50 percent of the federal jobs.

On May 22, 1978, during hearings before the House Committee on Post Office and Civil Service, Chairman Campbell reported that barely half of veterans hired by the federal government in 1977 were Vietnam-era veterans:

> Finally, in relation to the specifics of the impact of veterans' preference, not only on women but on veterans competing with veterans, 45 percent of the veteran hires last year were veterans who served before Vietnam. That means that the Vietnam veteran today is competing with the pre-Vietnam veteran for jobs, and obviously at a disadvantage because of the greater experience the older veteran has.[38]

No information was presented by Campbell to indicate how many of the pre-Vietnam veterans hired had served between 1955 and 1964.

In the years following the passage of PL 359, nearly all 50 states and many local governments have adopted veterans' preference policies that vary widely in scope from "absolute" preference as in Massachusetts and New Jersey to minimal five- or ten-point "one time" use preference in Colorado. Often the preference is similar to federal preference that could be placed roughly in the middle of a degree-of-preference continuum. When challenged in the federal district and circuit courts and the U.S. Supreme Court, all of these statutes have ultimately been upheld as constitutional.

It might appear that the Civil Rights Act of 1964 would provide an effective vehicle for establishing a *prima facie* case of discrimination against women through the use of statistics. This would then shift the burden to the defendant (government) to justify its practice of extending preference to veterans—particularly in those jurisdictions where such preference is absolute. However, in enacting Section 712 of the Civil Rights Act of 1964 [42 U.S.C., Section 2000(e), et seq.], Congress specifically exempted veterans' preference from attack under the act: "Nothing contained in this subchapter shall be construed to repeal or modify any federal, state, territorial, or local law creating special rights or preferences for veterans."

As a result, the Civil Rights Act has generally not been an avenue of approach for those who would challenge veterans' preference. Two more recent exceptions may or may not indicate a new trend. One exception resulted when a nonveteran female attorney successfully utilized Title VII of the Civil Rights Act in alleging sex discrimination with respect to the Veterans Administration's longstanding policy of submitting only names of veterans for appointment to membership of the Board of Veterans Appeals, *Krenzer v. Ford*, 429 F. Supp. 499 (1977). The court held that the policy of total exclusion of nonveterans was not created by statute and, therefore, the court did not permit the exemption under section 712 when it ruled in favor of the plaintiff. The VA did not request that this decision be appealed.

Another exception occurred February 5, 1979, when the federal judge for the Northern District of Illinois held that the Chicago Regional Office of the Veterans Administration and the U.S. Civil Service Commission had violated the rights of women and black Veterans Administration employees under Title VII of the Civil Rights Act.[39] Claims adjudicators had been hired from a special Civil Service list comprised mainly of white Vietnam-era veterans with college degrees. The court held that the federal government had gone beyond any legal authority it had been granted by Congress—despite the exemption in section 712 of the act. The Solicitor General denied the VA request that this case be appealed.

THE MASSACHUSETTS CASE

The Massachusetts statute was the subject of a landmark June 5, 1979, decision rendered by the U.S. Supreme Court, 442 U.S. 256 (1979). The constitutionality of that statute was upheld by a vote of 7 to 2. The statute provides that all disabled and nondisabled veterans with passing test scores must be ranked ahead of nonveterans even if the nonveteran scored higher on the competitive examination. This is far more absolute than the five- and ten-point federal preference statute. On March 29, 1976, this case first gained national attention as *Anthony v. Massachusetts*, 415 F. Supp. 485 (1976) when a three-federal-judge panel voted 2 to 1 to declare that the "absolute" Massachusetts preference was unconstitutional in that it denied women equal protection of the law as guaranteed by the Fourteenth Amendment.

While the lower court acknowledged that the Massachusetts statute "was not enacted for the purpose of disqualifying women from receiving civil service appointments, . . ."[40] it held that the current formula was too severe and recommended a "point system" similar to that utilized by the federal government as acceptable alternative.[41]

Because of the constitutional question involved, the Massachusetts attorney general appealed the district court decision directly to the U.S. Supreme Court. On October 11, 1977, the U.S. Supreme Court, by a vote of 6 to 3, vacated the lower court order and remanded the case back to that court with specific instructions (46 U.S. Law Week 3237–38). These instructions directed the lower court to apply the Washington v. Davis, 426 U.S. 229 (1976) doctrine, which held that in order to prove a claim of invidious discrimination under the equal protection argument, a plaintiff must prove that there was an actual intent to discriminate on the part of the legislature when it enacted a statute that resulted in an adverse impact upon a particular class.

Since in its March 1976 decision the lower court had conceded that the Massachusetts legislature had not intended to discriminate against women when it passed its veterans' preference statute, it appeared that upon remand the lower court would apply Washington v. Davis in a manner that upheld the constitutionality of the veterans' preference statute.

However, on May 3, 1978, in its application of the Washington v. Davis doctrine, the lower court ruled 2 to 1 that the Massachusetts legislature intended to discriminate in passing an absolute veterans' preference statute. The two member majority justified this conclusion by claiming that since 98 percent of veterans are male and only 2 percent are female, the legislature "intended" to injure the employment interests of women in passing an "absolute" veterans' preference law [Feeney v. Massachusetts, 451 F. Supp. 143 (1978)].

In June 1978 the attorney general of Massachusetts appealed this latest decision and in October 1978 the U.S. Supreme Court agreed to hear the case. After seeking input from the general counsels of numerous government agencies,* the Solicitor General of the United States filed a 42-page amicus brief with the U.S. Supreme Court in December

---

*Editors' note: As the special assistant to the VA general counsel, Mr. Phillips was actively involved in the preparation of a November 1978 memorandum in which the VA encouraged the Solicitor General of the U.S. to file a brief urging the U.S. Supreme Court to uphold the constitutionality of the Massachusetts veterans' preference statute. While

1978. This brief defended the general concept of veterans' preference and requested that the U.S. Supreme Court uphold the constitutionality of the "absolute" Massachusetts veterans' preference statute, observing that

> in many respects, military gender distinctions operate to the disadvantage of men, not in their favor. Conscription extends only to men, and only men are sent into combat. Thus, all women in the military have entered the service voluntarily, while many men have not. We recognize, of course, that seemingly preferential treatment is not always benign, and that women as well as men may suffer because of gender distinctions in the military. Nonetheless, in significant respects, men have plainly been disadvantaged by the gender distinctions established by the military. The district court's assumption that the veterans' preference perpetuates a form of discrimination against women is therefore not altogether accurate.

The Solicitor General further contended that the lower court's distinction between "purpose and intent" was illusory and that it could not properly conclude the Massachusetts preference statute's adverse effect on women was intended by the legislature. (In its prior decision the lower court conceded that the legislature intended to benefit veterans rather than to injure women.) The Solicitor General later permitted four separate government agencies each represented by a female general counsel (Equal Employment Opportunity Commission, Department of Labor, Department of Defense, and Office of Personnel Management) to file a subsequent amicus brief in February 1979. The brief, while taking no position on the validity of the Massachusetts statute, attempted to draw a distinction between the "absolute" preference formula of Massachusetts and the more moderate federal formula. Oral arguments were heard February 26, 1979 (47 *U.S. Law Week*, 3579-80).

It is ironic that the mantle of the equal protection clause of the Constitution that had been denied those men who tried to prove in court that the draft was sexist during the Vietnam War was now being utilized by nonveteran women who claim that some forms of veterans' preference deny them equal protection of the laws. Because sex, unlike race, has been held not to be a "suspect" classification by the Supreme Court, men attempting to avoid the draft utilizing the aforementioned equal protection argument were able to convince the courts to apply

the VA memorandum was not supportive of lifelong "absolute" preference for nondisabled veterans as a policy issue, it warned that the striking down of such a statute from a constitutional standpoint would ultimately render less absolute forms of preference vulnerable to future constitutional challenge.

only the "rational basis" test in their cases. Thus the government had to prove only that the drafting of exclusively men was reasonably related to the accomplishment of a legitimate power of government—raising and maintaining the armed forces. Under the "strict scrutiny" test, which the courts apply if the plaintiff claims denial of equal protection by government action on the basis of race (a suspect classification), the government is held to a considerably tougher standard: It must prove that its classification must be necessary to promote a compelling government interest. Since the Massachusetts veterans' preference statute recently at issue is neutral on its face (and because sex has not yet been held to be a suspect classification),[42] it is not surprising that in applying *Washington* v. *Davis* the U.S. Supreme Court found the Massachusetts statute did not deny women equal protection of the law.

Combat veterans in particular were angered at the rather cavalier reference to the draft laws made by the lower court in *Feeney*: "women have always been ineligible for the draft."[43] Rather than concluding that women have always been *ineligible* for the draft, that court would have been more accurate in stating that women have never been *subjected to* the draft. This is particularly so in light of the high casualty rates of draftees in Vietnam. The lower court also stated that "from 1948 until 1967, women were prohibited from making up more than 2 percent of the total personnel in the armed forces."[44] That court ignored the fact that after the 2 percent statutory bar was lifted in 1967, women in 1968, 1969, 1970, 1971, and 1972 still failed to comprise even 2 percent of the armed forces, while many of their male counterparts were faced with a most onerous task in Indochina. NOW and nine other organizations filed a 27-page amicus brief with the U.S. Supreme Court addressing *Feeney* and claiming that "women's participation in the military had been severely limited throughout American history." However, the fact remains that most women did not seek enlistment in the military during the Korean and Vietnam Wars and, hence, belated cries of denial of equal protection, particularly from NOW, have a hollow ring. In fact, a June 1, 1979, letter from the director of Freedom of Information and Security Review of the Department of Defense reported that *from 1964 to 1971 women filed no lawsuits in any of the 94 federal district courts claiming that restrictive statutes, regulations, or policies injured their employment opportunities by making it more difficult for them to enlist in the military. During the entire Vietnam War (1964–73)* no such suits were filed against the Departments of the Army or Navy and only two such suits were filed against the Department of the Air Force during the later stages of the war (1971 and 1972) and women's organizations did not participate as plaintiffs in either suit.

A review of previous court decisions with respect to challenges to veterans' preference statutes gave a rather clear indication that the Supreme Court would uphold the constitutionality of the Massachusetts statute.[45] Future efforts to modify veterans' preference statutes will probably be limited exclusively to legislative action.

ADMINISTRATION EFFORTS TO MODIFY THE FEDERAL LAW

With the exception of eliminating life-long preference for veterans retiring with the equivalent rank of major or above (PL 95–454, section 307) the administration effort to modify veterans' preference during the 95th Congress was unsuccessful. Under that proposal, as originally presented in March 1978, nondisabled Vietnam-era veterans would have been limited to a one-time use of the preference, which would have to have been utilized within ten years after separation from active duty. That would have immediately eliminated the eligibility of about one-half of those who served during the Vietnam era and two-thirds of those who actually served in Indochina. Major veterans' organizations argued that this would violate an implied contract the government made with those who served on active duty during time of war. While they did not think this reasoning could apply to those veterans seeking federal employment who served on active duty from January 1955 to September 1966 and were "grandfathered" in under the Vietnam-era amendments to the Veterans Preference Act of 1944, many Vietnam-era veterans knew that World War II and Korean War veterans had been provided the opportunity to use preference points more than once with no time limit. For that reason some thought it unfair that Vietnam-era veterans should be limited to a one-time use that must be exhausted within ten years after separation. In June 1978 the time limit was changed to 15 years by the House Committee on Post Office and Civil Service. On September 11, 1978, the House of Representatives rejected the administration proposal to modify veterans' preference by a vote of 222 to 149. The House then voted 281 to 88 to retain veterans' preference in federal civil service in its current form. It would appear that an effort to modify veterans' preference prospectively in the event of another war rather than retrospectively may fare more successfully in the Congress.

It appears unlikely that any substantial modification of the Veterans Preference Act of 1944, as amended, will be enacted by the 96th Congress. In May 1978, Campbell reported that barely half of the veterans hired in federal service in 1977 were Vietnam–era veterans. By implying that Korean War and World War II veterans comprised nearly half the veterans hired that year, he justified the administration modification efforts as in the best interests of Vietnam-era veterans. However, subsequent to the defeat of that measure, Campbell reported different conclusions in May 1979: "We found that Vietnam Era Veterans accounted for 71 percent of all the veterans hired [in federal government] in fiscal 1978. In calendar year 1976 that rate was 68 percent."[46]

While there have been some more recent efforts on the part of the Department of Defense to expand the role of women in the military, the fact remains that DOD's goal calls for women to comprise no more than 10–11 percent of military personnel by FY 1984. Effective October 1, 1979 the policy was modified so that the disparity in Army enlistment standards has been considerably narrowed. (The attrition rate for women, though still higher than for men has dropped significantly since a 1975 directive which no longer permitted automatic discharge upon pregnancy.) Effective Oct. 1, 1979, the Army enlistment standards were modified so that they are virtually the same for men and women. The impetus for the liberalization of this policy was at least in part a court challenge by the American Civil Liberties Union.[47]

DÉJA VU: REGISTRATION FOR THE DRAFT

At the same time the assertion that veterans' preference denies women equal protection was under review by the U.S. Supreme Court, the House Armed Services Committee reported favorably 30 to 4 in May, 1979, on proposed legislation (HR 4040 sections 812–815) that if enacted as written would have required that *only men* register for the draft. While this provision was later killed by a House vote of 252–163, a similar measure (S. 109) was reported favorably 12 to 5 by the Senate Committee on Armed Services on June 19, 1979. If enacted, as written S. 109 also would have required that only males register for the draft. At this writing S. 109 has not yet faced a full Senate vote. Although there was public notice of the House and Senate Armed Service Committee hearings on this matter, a review of the witness lists, Committee Reports, and Hearing transcripts indicates that no womens' organizations offered oral or written testimony before these commit- tees claiming that women should be "eligible for the draft" from either an equal employment opportunity or equal responsibility point of view.[48] It is the opinion of this writer that if this proposed legislation is enacted and men are subject to the draft, numerous lawsuits will be filed by them claiming that the subjection once again of only men to draft registration denies them equal protection of the law. In a case decided subsequent to the Vietnam War, the U.S. Supreme Court established a three-tiered test redefining the standard for violations of the equal protection clause in sex discrimination cases.[49] Accordingly, in the opinion of this writer, it is now an open question whether men would be successful if they filed suits challenging the constitutionality of any future legislation that continues to exempt women from draft laws. If such suits are filed and prove successful, the issue of whether the Equal Rights Amendment would require women to face any future draft laws would then be a root question.

NOTES

1. Soldiers at pay grade E-3 received the following monthly salaries (which include combat pay) while in combat zones: 1944, $76; 1952, $144.37; and 1968, $193.70. *Military Compensation Background Papers: Compensation Elements and Related Manpower Cost Items Their Purpose and Legislative Background*, Department of Defense, Third Quadrennial Review of Military Compensation, Office of the Secretary of Defense, August 1976.

2. Office of the Assistant Secretary of Defense (Manpower, Reserve Affairs, and Logistics), *Use of Women in the Military—Background Study*, May 1977.

3. Ibid.

4. Ibid, Table I.

5. Martin Binkin, and Shirley J. Bach, *Women in the Military*. (Washington, D.C.: Brookings Institution, 1977).

6. "The Role of Women in the Military," Hearings before the Subcommittee on Priorities and Economy in Government of the Joint Economic Committee, 95th Cong., 1st sess., July 22 and September 1, 1977.

7. *America's Volunteers*, A Report on the All-Volunteer Armed Forces, Office of the Assistant Secretary of Defense (Manpower, Reserve Affairs, and Logistics), Washington, D.C., December 31, 1978, p. 70.

8. *Women in the Military*, op. cit., p. 52, footnote 38

9. Paul Starr, *The Discarded Army: Veterans After Vietnam*. (New York: Charterhouse, 1973).

10. Lawrence M. Baskir and William A. Strauss, *Chance and Circumstance: The Draft, the War, and the Vietnam Generation* (New York: Knopf, 1978), p. 22.

11. A. S. Albro, *Civilian Substitution—Studies Prepared for the President's Commission on All-Volunteer Armed Force*, Study No. Five, November 1970.

12. "Extension of the Draft and Bills Related to the Voluntary Force Concept and Authorization of Strength Levels," Hearings before the Committee on Armed Services, House of Representatives, 92d Cong., 1st sess., February 23–25, March 1–5, 9–11, 1971.

13. "Defense Report/Draftees Shoulder Burden of Fighting and Dying in Vietnam," *National Journal*, August 15, 1970.

14. 1971 Hearings before the Committee on Armed Services, op. cit. p. 172.

15. *The Discarded Army*, op. cit., p. 54.

16. 113 Cong. Rec. 10000 (1967) (remarks of Congressman Hawkins).

17. Department of Defense, *U.S. Casualties in Southeast Asia by Grade and Military Service*, unpublished, December 31, 1978.

18. U.S. Bureau of the Census, *Statistical Abstracts of the United States 1977*, 98th ed., p. 368, Table 587.

19. Dr. Ralph Guzman, *Mexican American Casualties in Vietnam. The Congressional Record*, Vol. 115, October 8, 1968, pp. 29292–93.

20. *Chance and Circumstance*, op. cit., p. 129

21. Office of the Assistant Secretary of Defense (Manpower and Reserve Affairs), *Project One Hundred Thousand: Characteristics and Performance of 'New Standards' Men*, December 1969.

22. *Chance and Circumstance*, op. cit., p. 49

23. Barbara Allen Babcock et al., *Sex Discrimination and the Law-Causes and Remedies*, (Boston: Little, Brown, 1975).

24. Ibid, p. 177.

25. Bureau of the Budget, *A Survey of Socially and Economically Disadvantaged Veterans*, November 1969.

26. Veterans Administration, Office of Controller, *Readjustment Profile for Recently Separated Vietnam Veterans*, conducted by the Department of Veterans Benefits, June 1973.

27. *Sears, Roebuck and Company* v. *Attorney General of the United States et al.*, Civil Action 79-0244 filed January 24, 1979, dismissed May 15, 1979, in the U.S. District Court for the District of Columbia, p. 18.

28. *United States* v. *St. Clair*, 291 F. Supp. 122 (1968); *Suskin* v. *Nixon*, 304 F. Supp. 71 (1969); *United States* v. *Cook*, 311 F. Supp 618 (1970); *United States* v. *Dorris*, 319 F. Supp. 1306 (1970); and *United States* v. *Reiser*, 394 F. Supp. 1060 (1975), *rev'd* 532 F. 2d 673 (9th Cir. 1976).

29. "Preference in Employment of Honorably Discharged Veterans where Federal Funds are Disbursed," Hearings Before the Committee on Civil Service, U.S. Senate on S. 1762 and H.R. 4115, May 19 and 23, 1944; "Extension of Preference to Veterans who Desire to Compete for Positions in the Federal Service," Report No. 1289 to accompany H.R. 4115 by the House of Representatives, March 27, 1944; "Extension of the Draft and Bills Related to the Voluntary Force Concept and Authorization of Strength Levels," Hearings before the Committee on Armed Services, House of Representatives, 92d Cong., 1st sess., February 23–25, March 1–5, 9–11, 1971.

30. "Preference in Employment of Honorably Discharged Veterans," op. cit. pp. 34 and 68.

31. Ibid, p. 63–64.

32. Federal Women's Program Committee, Denver Federal Executive Board, *Veterans' Preference Act Study—A Review of the Discriminatory Aspects of the Veterans' Preference Act of 1944, as amended*, Spring 1975.

33. Ibid, pp. 6–7.

34. Ibid, pp. 17–18.

35. Comptroller General of the United States, *Conflicting Congressional Policies: Veterans Preference and Apportionment* v. *Equal Employment Opportunity*, Report to Congress, September 29, 1977.

36. Ibid, p. 20.

37. "Hearings before the Subcommittee on Civil Service," Committee on Post Office and Civil Service, House of Representatives, October 4–5, 1977.

38. "Hearings before the Committee on Post Office and Civil Service House of Representatives, 95th Cong., 2d sess. on H.R. 11280 March 14, 21; April 4, 5, 6, 11, 12, 28; May 8, 12, 15, 22, and 23, 1978. "Civil Service Reform" Serial No. 95–65 at page 785.

39. *Jeanette Thompson et al.* v. *Administrator of Veterans Affairs et al.*, U.S. District Court, Northern District of Illinois 74-C-3719.

40. *Anthony* v. *Massachusetts* at 495.

41. Ibid, at 496.

42. In two cases a plurality of the U.S. Supreme Court justices did rule that sex was a suspect classification: *Frontiero* v. *Richardson*, 411 U.S. 677 (1973) and *Schlessinger* v. *Ballard*,

498 U.S. 419 (1975). In the former case, the court held unconstitutional a government policy denying certain benefits to the dependents of female armed forces personnel readily available to male personnel. In the latter case the majority opinion upheld a Department of the Navy statute mandating the separation from active duty of the male plaintiff for twice failing to be promoted within a nine-year period while similarly situated female officers had 13 years in which to secure promotion before mandatory separation. The court found that restrictions upon sea duty for women had provided them with fewer promotional opportunities.

43. *Anthony* v. *Massachusetts* at 490.

44. Ibid, at 489.

45. Subsequent to *Washington* v. *Davis*, three equal-protection challenges to veterans' preference legislation have been unsuccessful: *Branch* v. *DuBois*, 418 F. Supp. 1128 (1976); *Bannerman* v. *Dept. of Youth Authority*, 436 F. Supp 1273 (1977); *Ballou* v. *State, Department of Civil Service*, 372 A.2d 333 (App. Div. 1977), *aff'd*, 75 N.J. 365, 382 A.2d 1118 (1978).

Prior to *Washington* v. *Davis*, equal-protection attacks on the federal Veterans' Preference law were unsuccessful: *White* v. *Gates*, 253 F.2d 868, *cert. denied*, 356 U.S. 973 (1958); and *Colemere* v. *Hampton*, N.C. 72-72 (D. Utah, October 11, 1973).

Additionally, the federal act has been enforced by the U.S. Supreme Court without any suggestion of possible constitutional infirmity. *Hilton* v. *Sullivan*, 334 U.S. 323 (1948).

Constitutional attacks on state veterans' preference statutes have likewise been unsuccessful: *Koelfgen* v. *Jackson*, 355 F. Supp. 243 (1972), *aff'd mem.* 410 U.S. 976 (1973); *Feinerman* v. *Jones*, 356 F. Supp. 252 (1973); *Rios* v. *Dillman*, 499 F. 2d 329 (5th Cir. 1974).

46. Statement of Alan K. Campbell, director, Office of Personnel Management, before the Committee on Veterans' Affairs, U.S. Senate at Oversight Hearings with Regard to Veterans' Employment Programs and Policies, May 23, 1979, at page 8.

47. *Breaman* v. *Brown*, Civil Action 79-0512 filed February 15, 1979, in the U.S. District Court for the District of Columbia.

48. While not concerning themselves with disadvantages men as a class have been subjected to because of this nation's draft laws, several women's organizations have (particularly since the end of the Vietnam War) gone on record requesting the expansion of employment opportunities for women in the military. See testimony before the Military Personnel Subcommittee of the House Armed Services Committee, November 16, 1979 by the ACLU's Women's Rights Project, the Federally Employed Women, and the Women's Equity Action League. Also see "The Role of Women in the Military" Hearings before the Subcommittee on Priorities and Economy in Government of the Senate Economic Committee, 95th Congress, 1st Session, July 22 and September 1, 1977.

49. *Craig* v. *Boren*, 429 U.S. 190 (1976).

A POSTSCRIPT: WELCOMING
HOME THE STRANGERS

Charles R. Figley

When the Consortium on Veteran Studies was organized in the early months of 1975, the socioemotional climate of the country was very different than it is today, particularly with reference to the Vietnam veteran. At that time, 7 million men and women recently released from military service, most with honorable discharges representing honorable service to their country, were viewed by many as suspect, tainted, dangerous, undisciplined, inferior.

Back in the early 1970s the federal government, including the Congress, reflected the public antipathy and barely acknowledged the needs and problems of Vietnam veterans. Programs designed to help the Vietnam veteran were masterfully conceived but ineffectively administered at the highest levels of government, with various bureaucracies and personalities bickering over which one had jurisdiction while the large and aging veterans' organizations led the fight in Congress to back *their* Veterans Administration regardless of the consequences to the Vietnam veteran. In the mid-1970s the mental health professions barely recognized the plight of the emotionally disabled Vietnam veteran. Hawkish psychiatrists maintained that the *Diagnostic and Statistical Manual*, the psychiatrists' dictionary of mental disorders, did not recognize combat fatigue or any other stress disorder originating from a catastrophic event. Perhaps with some overreaction, "dovish" psychiatrists and other practitioners believed that emotional disorders among returning veterans could reach epidemic proportions. The post-Vietnam syndrome became a frightening buzz word among clinicians and journalists but, in fact, was a thinly veiled position of opposition to the war: stop the war or more young killers will be released to terrorize the population. Since those days there have been dramatic and precedent-setting changes that have depoliticized the debate over the mental health of Vietnam veterans. Powerful and prestigious bodies have deliberated the issues and have concluded that as a group the Vietnam combat veteran is neither a walking time bomb nor an invincible robot; that a vast majority of the survivors of the war are leading productive lives and are more emotionally stable than the general population. However, the catastrophic stress of combat leaves its marks on the psyche that require both time and confrontation to erase; and a small but significant minority of *combat* veterans are suffering from the frightening and debilitating aftershock of Vietnam and should be helped. They are getting that help now.

Back in 1975 when the Consortium was born, it had been six years since Max Cleland, a triple amputee Vietnam veteran from Georgia, testified to Congress that Vietnam veterans' spirits need mending as well as their bodies, that programs must be developed to help Vietnam veterans—especially the combat veterans—readjust to being civilians and to get on with their lives. In 1975 the Veterans Administration grudgingly admitted problems but failed to launch comprehensive research programs to investigate how these new vets were adjusting. The only research supported was done within the walls of VA buildings; VA researchers studied only those veterans who never showed up long enough to tell them what was on their minds, and then only cursorily. Although the VA trained more social workers, psychiatrists, psychologists, and psychiatric nurses than any other health system, few trainees were trained in the special needs of Vietnam veterans or any other special problems of the military service veteran. The VA employees themselves were often ignorant of the effects of the war; those who did suspect a combat-related problem rarely offered such diagnosis, fearing rejection or ridicule by their colleagues. Almost everyone in leadership positions refused to acknowledge combat-related stress disorders. However, the number of believers has grown considerably over the last several years. At this writing the VA is in the process of launching a national outreach program, independent of the mainstream VA system, which will be directed by Donald Crawford, a Vietnam veteran himself, and staffed throughout the nation in cities by other Vietnam veterans. The program was the result of intense lobbying on the part of several loosely organized factions held together by the Vietnam Veterans Council with its close association with the 18-member Vietnam Veterans Caucus coordinated by Michigan Representative David Bonior.

The same caucus guided passage of a national Vietnam Veterans Week, May 28–June 3, 1979, which included the special White House ceremony in which the president passionately welcomed home the forgotten warriors. The mood of the country was changing rapidly in favor of the Vietnam veterans.

This changing attitude is particularly prevalent across the nation's college campuses, with the memories of antiwar activism and burning ROTC buildings fresh on everyone's minds. Today's collegian was still in grade school during the Kent State disaster and is hardly aware of the negative images of those men who did America's dirty work that was shown on nightly newscasts. The campuses are quiet today. Today lectures, workshops, and seminars are springing up on campuses everywhere to discuss the war years and discover that the same ones condemned for fighting in Vietnam were the ones newscasts showed returning home to egg throwing and name-calling, as many had received when they had left a year earlier. The tragedy is that many who fought the war, beginning with the Vietnam Veterans Against the War, ended up condemning the warrior as well. Their loss is much greater than those who only opposed the war. Vietnam veterans are being invited to speak on college campuses in addition to the historians, sociologists, and political scientists. The vets will be back to tell their story because most of us are ready to listen now. It is within this context, the climate of tolerance and compassion, that Vietnam veterans can truly be understood and valued as human beings and Americans trying to do what they believed at one time to be right in a cause that turned out to be wrong. This is a clear sign that America is finally welcoming home the Vietnam veteran.

Only recently have the news and entertainment media begun to seriously face the plight of the Vietnam veteran, not only as a drug-crazed psycho, but as a victim. Portrayals of the sick vet in films like *Dog Day Afternoon* and TV cop shows like *Hawaii Five-O* and *Kojak* have been replaced by enlightened and well-researched programs on the experiences of the Vietnam veteran with enough detail to recognize and treat the problems and praise the strengths, yet quite entertaining even for the TV crowd at the corner bar. This was achieved on January 12, 1979, when "Vets," an episode in the popular *Lou Grant Show*, was aired to millions of homes across the country and in Canada. In a single hour more people were told more about Vietnam veterans since the war than any other source. It is not coincidental that since the showing, Vietnam combat veterans are showing up at mental health centers, VA hospitals, and outpatient clinics in numbers never reached in any other time, including the war years. This is good. It is the beginning of the end of the Vietnam nightmare.

This new enlightenment and its accompanying healing effect was not only due to the *Lou Grant Show*, however. The two Academy Award-winning movies this year were *The Deer Hunter* and *Coming Home*. Their titles imply their thesis: the former, the conquerer, a Hemingwaian warrior, the latter a guy next door. One had to give up much, to lose the use of his legs, yet was capable of feeling so much of life and wishing to do something about his feelings. The other is about friendship, endurance, pride, revenge, honor of one who refuses to feel the pain of Vietnam in both his body and soul. In the end, both protagonists in both films survive to go on, it appears, with full and productive lives. The characters they played touched a nerve in all but a few Vietnam combat veterans. They had arrived home. Indeed, they fell just short of a folk-hero status when their group is portrayed by Hollywood's leading stars: Jon Voight's Luke Martin in *Coming Home* and Robert DeNiro's Michael in *The Deer Hunter*. They were real people, just like the vast majority of Vietnam veterans, and we liked them whether they supported the war or not; whether they were proud of what they did or not; whether they can block the feelings or not.

Perhaps the most important, if not the most symbolic, sign of the Vietnam vets' return was the White House ceremony on a mid-week afternoon, Wednesday, May 30, 1979, during the first and only Vietnam Veterans Week. Assembled in the East Room were over 200 Vietnam veterans and their guests, whether they were for or against the president's moderate record of support for Vietnam veterans. In the front row sat several men in wheelchairs, including Ron Kovic, author of the highly acclaimed *Born on the Fourth of July*, Larry Roffee, director of the maverick Paralyzed Veterans of America, and Robert Muller, frequent administration critic and recently designated leader of the Vietnam Veterans of America. Facing them on the stage was Max Cleland, administrator of Veterans Affairs. All four lost the use of their legs as soldiers in Vietnam. All waited for President Carter to look them in the eyes and say, "Happy Vietnam Veterans Week," and present a postage stamp minted in their honor. The president must have realized the irony of it all, a postage stamp and a pat on the back for losing your legs, for when he entered the room and leaped onto the stage to hug Cleland (as he did when he swore him into office in 1976) he swerved around to address his audience, his eyes lowered to the front row of men in wheelchairs. Everyone in the room knew he was moved by what he sensed at that moment. In a slightly quivering voice, President Carter brushed aside a staff-prepared speech and said welcome home in his own way: "The nation has not done enough to respect, to honor, to recognize, and reward the special heroism [of the Vietnam veteran] . . ." He said that many viewed these vets as "unfortunate reminders of the war that was different" and to offer one's life under these conditions "requires an extra measure of patriotism and of sacrifice." After asking permission from author and Vietnam veteran Phillip Caputo to quote from his book, *A Rumor of War*, Carter paraphrased Caputo's painfully graphic description of fighting in Vietnam ending with: "We love you for what you were and what you stood for and we love you for what you are and what you stand for." It was an emotional speech, surprising even the most hardened of White House press. As Fred Barnes from the Washington *Star* wrote the next day, "President Carter, in one of the most emotional appearances of his 28-month presidency, has appealed for public respect for veterans of the Vietnam war." He noted that

"Carter seemed to be sincerely moved by the presence of so many veterans, some of them in wheelchairs . . . [and] his eyes glistened with tears . . . [and] his voice broke at least once, and it appeared that he was barely able to speak at times. Sweat spread over his face after a few minutes, and in the end, the address generated considerably more applause than most of his speeches do these days." The Washington *Post*'s Myra McPherson made similar observations. The stranger felt more at home.

The mood of the country is very different now; programs are going forward, others will follow. The work of mobilizing scholars and practitioners to correct images and problems of Vietnam veterans gave birth to the Consortium and as these images and problems are being faced and fixed the Consortium will cease, turning over its achievements, lessons, and assets to structures that have far more challenging and far-reaching goals. For the Vietnam veterans who have struggled, worked hard, and achieved since the war, as well as those who are still struggling, for them, finally, it is good to be home, with or without a welcome.

INDEX

ABOUT THE EDITORS AND CONTRIBUTORS

*†CHARLES R. FIGLEY, PH.D.

Dr. Figley served in Vietnam with the Third Marine Amphibious Force (1965–1966). He is founder and director of the Consortium on Veteran Studies; consultant to numerous mental health research and treatment agencies including the Naval Health Research Center, Center for POW Studies, Veterans Administration, National Institute of Mental Health and the President's Commission on Mental Health; and author of numerous scientific works focusing on traumatic stress reactions, including his latest volume, *Stress Disorders among Vietnam Veterans: Theory, Research and Treatment* (1978). Presently Dr. Figley is an associate professor and director, Family Research Institute, Purdue University (West Lafayette, Indiana).

*SEYMOUR LEVENTMAN, PH.D.

Dr. Leventman became interested in Vietnam veterans as a specialist in race and ethnic studies. He has written several scientific papers focusing on veterans within the context of racial identity, victimology, and classic sociological theory. He has presented papers on veterans issues at conferences of both the American Sociological Association and American Psychological Association. Presently Dr. Leventman is an associate professor of sociology at Boston College.

*RONALD M. BITZER, M.A.

Mr. Bitzer has worked for many years as an activist for patient and prisoner rights, serving as a member of the Inmate Committee for Higher Education at Soledad Prison, and as co-founder of Swords to Plowshares, a veterans' rights organization in San Francisco. Presently Mr. Bitzer is director of the Center for Veteran's Rights in Los Angeles and is co-editor of *Discharge Upgrading Newsletter* (Veterans Education Project of Washington, D.C.).

*†PAUL R. CAMACHO, M.A.

Mr. Camacho, who served in Vietnam as an infantry sergeant with

---

*Member of the Consortium on Veteran Studies
†Vietnam veteran

the Second Battalion, Ninth Marine Division (1968–1969) and was wounded in action, has been active in veterans' rights activities in the Boston area. He has presented numerous scientific papers at various national professional meetings including the American Sociological Association, and has served as a fellow of the Inter-University Seminar on Armed Forces and Society. Presently Mr. Camacho is a doctoral student in Sociology at Boston College.

FRANK FREIDEL, PH.D.

Dr. Freidel is among the world's most respected historians. He has written 16 historical monographs, including *Splendid Little War* (1958) and *Dissent in Three American Wars* (1970), which directly relates to the Vietnam veterans' experience. Dr. Freidel is currently Charles Warren professor of American History at Harvard University.

*LOCH K. JOHNSON, PH.D.

Dr. Johnson spent several years studying the Vietnam veteran, especially those disabled by the war. He has served as special assistant to Senator Frank Church (D-Idaho) on foreign policy, staff director for the Subcommittee on Oversight of the House of Representative's Committee on Intelligence, and former American Political Science Association Congressional fellow. Dr. Johnson is currently associate professor of political science at the University of Georgia.

ANDREW I. KOHEN, PH.D.

While associate director of the National Longitudinal Surveys of Work Experience Project (Center for Human Resource Research) at Ohio State University, Dr. Kohen conducted socioeconomic research on a large sample of veterans. He also delivered a paper on job changing behavior at the Office of Naval Research and Smithsonian Institution's conference, "First Term Enlisted Attrition." Dr. Kohen is currently an associate professor of economics, specializing in human resource economics, at James Madison University (Virginia).

*†FORD H. KURAMOTO, D.S.W.

From 1966–1969 Dr. Kuramoto was a clinical social worker in the U.S. Army. Later, as executive assistant to the Director, Division of Mental Health Service Programs with the National Institute of Mental Health, Dr. Kuramoto served as a consultant to various groups, agencies, and individuals interested in veteran-related research and services. Currently Dr. Kuramoto is a member of the faculty in the Department of Psychiatry and Behavior Sciences, School of Medicine,

University of California at Los Angeles and full-time director of the Los Angeles Day Treatment Center.

*†FRED MILANO, PH.D.

Following his service as an Air Force officer (1963–1968), Dr. Milano completed his doctoral dissertation entitled "The Generational Divide," upon which his chapter in this volume is based. Currently Dr. Milano is an assistant professor of sociology at the Appalachian State University (North Carolina).

*CHARLES C. MOSKOS, JR., PH.D.

An internationally respected scholar in military sociology, Dr. Moskos conducted personal field research in Vietnam in 1965 and in 1967 which involved extended stays with several combat units. This research resulted in his classic work, *The American Enlisted Man* (1970). His most recent book is *Peace Soldiers: The Sociology of a United Nations Military Force* (1978). Dr. Moskos is professor of sociology at Northwestern University.

*DEAN K. PHILLIPS, M.A., J.D.

A decorated former U.S. Army Paratrooper, Mr. Phillips served with the 101st Airborne Division. He later served as Vice Chairman of the Colorado Board of Veterans Affairs where he drafted successful state legislation granting tax credits for blind and paraplegic veterans, waiver of tuition at state schools, and liberalizing the state's Veteran's Reemployment Rights Laws. He was also active in lawsuits against several federal government agencies concerning the implementation of veteran's programs. Considered an expert in the areas of judicial review of the Veterans Administration and veteran's preference and employment issues, Mr. Phillips presently serves as a Special Assistant to the Administrator of Veterans Affairs in Washington, D.C.

ALFRED SCHUETZ, PH.D. (1899–1959)

Among Professor Schuetz's seminal works is *Phenomenology of the Social World* (1930). "The Homecoming," his chapter in the present volume, was first published in the *American Journal of Sociology* toward the end of World War II. Prior to his death Dr. Schuetz was Professor Emeritus of Sociology, New School for Social Research (New York City).

PATRICIA M. SHIELDS, PH.D.

Dr. Shields completed her doctoral dissertation research on the determinants of the enlistment and the draft during the Vietnam era and reported her findings at the meetings of the American Statistical Association, the Southwest Social Science Association, the Southern Economic Association, and the Southwest Federation of Administrative Disciplines, as well as in the chapter in this volume (Chapter 9 with Andrew Kohen). Dr. Shields is currently an assistant professor of public administration, Department of Political Science at Southwest Texas State University.

*CLARK C. SMITH, PH.D.

Dr. Smith organized and currently directs the Vietnam Veteran's Oral History Project. He served as editor of *The Ally* (1968–1972), which had a circulation during the Vietnam War of over 100,000 active duty GIs and Vietnam veterans. Dr. Smith's chapter is among the first publications to emerge from his oral history project; forthcoming are *Brothers: An Oral Narrative of the Black Experience in Vietnam* and *The Short-Timers: Soldiering in Vietnam, 1965–1972*. Currently, Dr. Smith is a professor in the Department of Rhetoric, University of California at Berkeley.

*WILLIAM T. SOUTHERLY, M.S.

Mr. Southerly has worked as research scholar with the Consortium on Veteran Studies since 1976. He participated in the American Psychological Association's research symposium, "Residue of War: The Vietnam Veteran in Mainstream America" in 1977. He has completed a masters thesis focusing on the antecedents of unemployment among Vietnam veterans. Mr. Southerly is currently a doctoral candidate and research associate at the Family Research Institute, Purdue University.

*†M. DUNCAN STANTON, PH.D.

Dr. Stanton served as a clinical psychologist and Army captain with the 98th Medical Detachment in Vietnam. While in the Army he was involved in several research projects resulting in many publications focusing on Vietnam veterans' adjustment including drug abuse and race relations. Since 1974 he has directed a highly successful clinical treatment and research program for drug-addicted veterans and their families. Among his recent work is a chapter (with Charles Figley) focusing on family therapy with Vietnam veterans, in *Stress Disorders Among Vietnam Veterans: Theory, Research, and Treatment* (1978). Dr. Stanton, in addition to directing the Addicts and Families Program of Philadelphia Child Guidance Clinic, is also an associate professor of psychology in the Department of Psychiatry, University of Pennsylvania School of Medicine, as well as Director of Family Therapy, Philadelphia VA Hospital Drug Dependence Treatment Center.

WILLARD WALLER, PH.D. (1899–1945)

Although not a veteran himself, Professor Waller was a passionate and compassionate spokesman for the armed forces fighting in and returning from World War II. A highly respected family sociology scholar, Dr. Waller wrote two important books in the veteran studies field: *War and the Family* (1940) and *The Veteran Returns* (1944), part of which is in Chapter 2 of the present volume. Dr. Waller died while traveling to make a speech on the post-war adjustment problems of returning war veterans. He was professor of sociology at Columbia University at the time of his death.

DIXON WECTER, PH.D. (1906–1950)

Dr. Wecter, among the world's most respected historians, wrote two important and seminal works in the veteran studies field: *Heroes in American History* (1941) and *When Johnny Comes Marching Home* (1944), part of which in included in Chapter 12 of this volume. He was a Rhodes scholar, a professor of history at Oxford University (England) and professor of history at the University of California (Berkeley).

*NORMA J. WIKLER, PH.D.

Dr. Wikler's doctoral dissertation in sociology, from which her chapter in this volume is taken, focuses on returning combat veterans of Vietnam. Her latest book (with Marilyn Fabe) is the highly successful *Up Against the Clock* (Random House, Inc., 1979). Currently Dr. Wikler is an associate professor of sociology at the University of California at Santa Cruz.

*JOHN P. WILSON, PH.D.

Dr. Wilson is founder and director of the Forgotten Warrior Project, funded by the Disabled American Veterans to investigate the post-military adjustments of Vietnam veterans. As a result of his research, the DAV, under Dr. Wilson's guidance, established a multi-million-dollar outreach program in over 60 cities across the nation to provide, among other things, psycho-social readjustment counseling. He won the Consortium on Veteran Studies' Research Award in recognition of this work. Currently Dr. Wilson is visiting associate professor of Psychology at Michigan State University.